This is an intensive one-year introductory course in Japane
those who wish to work at a slower pace. Students who fini
have a firm grasp of how the language works and enough k
writing system to tackle everyday written material with no more than a dictionary. Particular attention is paid to questions of grammar which foreign learners often find difficult, so Book one can also serve as a reference grammar. *An Introduction to Modern Japanese* uses both spoken and written forms from the outset. There are word lists for each lesson, and a comprehensive vocabulary for the whole course. Book two provides exercises to accompany the fifty-two lessons in Book one.

An Introduction to Modern Japanese

Book 1: Grammar Lessons

An Introduction to Modern Japanese

Book 1: Grammar Lessons

RICHARD BOWRING
Professor of Modern Japanese Studies
University of Cambridge

and

HARUKO URYŪ LAURIE
Senior Language Teaching Officer
University of Cambridge

CAMBRIDGE
UNIVERSITY PRESS

PUBLISHED BY THE PRESS SYNDICATE OF THE UNIVERSITY OF CAMBRIDGE
The Pitt Building, Trumpington Street, Cambridge, United Kingdom

CAMBRIDGE UNIVERSITY PRESS
The Edinburgh Building, Cambridge CB2 2RU, UK
40 West 20th Street, New York NY 10011–4211, USA
477 Williamstown Road, Port Melbourne, VIC 3207, Australia
Ruiz de Alarcón 13, 28014 Madrid, Spain
Dock House, The Waterfront, Cape Town 8001, South Africa

http://www.cambridge.org

First published 1992
Reprinted with corrections 1993, 1994, 1995, with further corrections 2002
First paperback edition 2004

A catalogue record for this book is available from the British Library

Library of Congress cataloguing in publication data
Bowring, Richard John, 1947-
An Introduction to Modern Japanese / Richard Bowring and Haruko Uryū Laurie
p. cm.
Includes index.
Contents: bk. 1. Grammar Lessons
ISBN 0 521 43839 X (bk. 1) hardback
1. Japanese language – Textbooks for foreign speakers – English. 2. Japanese language – Grammar. I. Laurie, Haruko Uryū. II. Title.
PL539.5.E5B68 1992
495.6′82421 – dc20 92-12777 CIP

ISBN 0 521 43839 X hardback
ISBN 0 521 54887 X paperback

Transferred to digital printing 2002

Contents

Preface

This textbook grew as a response to a specific need. Although a number of introductions to Japanese were and are readily available, none of them happened to fit the particular situation we found ourselves in, which demanded that students be able to tackle a short story written in Japanese within six months of starting the language, and that they should be in a position to at least attempt newspaper articles within a year. It was found that the commonest approach to language teaching today, which rightly stresses oral skills and communicative competence based on situational drills in a social context, demanded far more time than was available and, for good reasons, tended to ignore the written form of the language, especially in the early stages. So it was that we were forced to create something very different. Although the results will not be to everyone's taste, it is hoped that many students of the language will find it useful. What we can say with certainty is that it has proved to be effective in practice.

Recent years have seen a startling increase in the number of publications designed to introduce the language to an ever-expanding market. They can be broadly divided into those that operate exclusively in romanised Japanese, and those that do not. Foremost among the first group is undoubtedly Eleanor H. Jorden's new book *Japanese: The Spoken Language* (Yale University Press, 1987–). The care and scholarship that has gone into its preparation is such that it fully deserves to outsell her earlier textbook, *Beginning Japanese* (Yale University Press, 1962–3), which itself went through no less than thirty reprints. It is a model of its kind; but Jorden's premise has always been that the written and spoken forms of the language must be quarantined off from each other, and that a good knowledge of the spoken is an absolute prerequisite before the rigours of the written form can be attempted. It is perhaps a measure of the difficulty of the writing system that such a step should be thought necessary, for no serious teacher of Sanskrit or Arabic would ever consider it desirable, if it were indeed considered possible. By and large, students who learn with this method certainly have good oral skills, but it takes a long time before they really come to grips with the written form. As it was our duty to cater for the student who was willing and able to move fast, and who had to come to grips with the written form of the language as soon as possible, such a course was of little help.

For many students the writing system itself is one of the major fascinations of Japanese, and despite the formidable obstacles it presents in the early stages, it seems perverse to throw away such an important motivational factor at the outset. It is also our experience that early familiarisation with the script helps prevent the habit of visualising Japanese in its romanised form. The guiding principle of this textbook, therefore, is almost the exact reverse of Jorden's: namely, that despite the undoubted difficulties of the script, reading and speaking are mutually reinforcing activities that should and can be presented together.

There are, inevitably, a number of problems associated with this approach. First, the complexity of the Japanese writing system means that the student of the language is faced with not only an alien grammatical structure and an alien lexicon, but also a large number of characters to be memorised. It must be admitted that Jorden's answer is kinder; given that we aim to provide a comprehensive introduction to both spoken *and* written Japanese, this textbook is certainly not for the faint-hearted. The greatest drawback is that the student may be slowed down too much by the burden of characters and begin to feel frustrated by a lack of general progress.

Second, there is the fact that we have reverted to some extent to a more traditional grammar-based approach, for which we make no apology. The primary purpose of book 1 is indeed to introduce the basic elements of Japanese grammar and to monitor grammar, basic vocabulary, and characters, so that all three are introduced in a coordinated manner. It is undoubtedly the presence of the characters that has provided us with the greatest problem: not only are some of the commonest words written with complicated characters, but the visual logic of the characters themselves is by its very nature unconnected to matters of grammar. The compromise that has been reached is that the introduction of various readings of specific characters has been strictly controlled, so that a certain amount of repetitive learning is automatically built into the course.

Third, an inevitable result of such a grammar-based approach is that the student usually gains a strong foundation for understanding the structure of sentences at the initial expense of oral skill and fluency. Partly this is a natural result of not having enough time and of not living within a Japanese speaking environment. The exercises provided in book 2 may help to some extent, although they are not rote drills; they have been designed to make the student think, rather than simply repeat certain patterns.

The conscious decision to use romanisation as little as possible brings with it another decision that will be immediately apparent to someone used to the 'Jorden' approach. Matters of pronunciation, intonation and pitch accent, although they have not been entirely disregarded, are treated in far less detail. Although certain aspects of this course do lend themselves to self-study, it is generally assumed that the textbook will be taught by a native speaker of the language, and that correct pitch accent cannot really be learned from a series of diacritical marks. Accent is therefore not marked in the romanised keys, which are in any case hidden away on purpose at the back of each lesson so as to try and force the student to concentrate on the Japanese script. Any deeper discussion of the morphophonemic structure will not be found either, because the very nature of the Japanese syllabary precludes such analysis.

One advantage of being able to concentrate on the grammar, however, is that certain tricky problems such as *wa* versus *ga* and *-eba* versus *-tara*, which are often finessed, have been met head-on and treated in considerable detail in the belief that they are 'problems' precisely because they represent facets of the Japanese language that mark its real difference from our own, and that the earlier an awareness of the differences inherent in each linguistic system is signalled, the better for the student. As an academic subject, the teaching of Japanese as a foreign language is still in its infancy, and to anyone coming from learning a European language the lack of ready-made satisfactory grammatical rules is surprising. This does *not* mean that Japanese is either vague or intrinsically less ordered that a European language. It does mean that until quite recently no particular need has been felt to delve very deeply into those aspects of the language that often trouble those of us approaching the language from the outside. Mistakes made by learners are sometimes explained away as being a matter of 'nuance' where in actual fact they involve fundamental misconceptions. It is freely admitted that an uncomfortably large number of these problem areas still remain unclear, but it is to be hoped that the many long hours of discussion and disagreement as to exactly why 'X is acceptable when Y is not' have resulted in a certain degree of helpful clarification. A textbook is not the place to experiment too much with new grammatical analyses, but there are still so many fuzzy areas left in Japanese grammar and usage that some new suggestions and approaches were considered essential.

Book 1 is the heart of the course; it comes with a detailed contents list and a grammar index. Book 2 contains exercises, word lists for each lesson and comprehensive vocabularies. The course is designed for classroom teaching by a native speaker. Students should try and work through the Introduction and learn *hiragana* before attempting the course proper. The lessons take the form of an initial text, usually but not always a conversation, followed by detailed grammatical notes. The conversations have been designed to be as natural as possible, within the constraints imposed by the order in which the grammar is introduced, and they are worth memorising before the next lesson is tackled.

Each lesson has been designed to build on its predecessor, so the temptation to jump ahead should be resisted. To repeat, the exercises in book 2 are not simply pattern practices, but are at times quite complicated. Time spent on them will be repaid. As far as learning characters is concerned, we recommend either F. Sakade, ed., *A Guide to Reading and Writing Japanese* (Tōkyō: Tuttle, rev. edn, 1961) or W. Hadamitzky and M. Spahn, *A Guide to Writing Kanji and Kana*, 2 vols. (Tōkyō: Tuttle, 1991).

Many people have helped with this textbook over some six years of work and more drafts than either of us care to remember. Most of all, the authors wish to thank Mr Okazaki Tomomi, who was lector in Japanese at Cambridge during three years of its gestation. He devoted many hours to the production of exercises and examples in the penultimate draft, although he was not able to participate in the final product and so should not be held responsible for any of its oddities or shortcomings. We also wish to thank our students, past and present, for their patience and for their awkward questions, some of which they may now find answered within these pages.

For those interested in technical details, camera-ready copy was produced by the authors using Microsoft Word 4 and Sweet Jam, with laser output from an NTX-J printer.

Introduction

1 THE LANGUAGE

1.1 Genetic affiliation

It might seem to the casual observer that Japanese is closely related to Chinese, but nothing could be further from the truth. Admittedly Japanese 'looks' similar to Chinese and has absorbed a large number of Chinese words over the centuries, but these loanwords are merely a sign of cultural contact, not of genetic affiliation. Indeed, it would be difficult to think of two languages more dissimilar: Chinese being originally monosyllabic (now largely disyllabic), tonal, and isolating, with a subject–verb–object (SVO) order; Japanese being polysyllabic, atonal, and agglutinative, with a subject–object–verb (SOV) order. It was precisely this vast gulf between the two languages that caused so many problems when the Japanese tried to adapt the Chinese script to their own ends in the eighth and ninth centuries.

The whole question of where the language comes from is a highly charged subject in Japan, for the idea that Japanese is in some way unique, *sui generis* and without parallel, is a potent and indeed comfortable myth in times of self-doubt. A great many books and articles dealing with the origins and peculiarities of the language are produced for the general reading public, and they sell extremely well. The roots of the language are indeed uncertain. Some scholars, perhaps the majority, argue that it is related to Korean and to the Altaic group of languages that is found throughout central Asia as far west as Turkey. Similarities in the way verbs are formed point to a common origin. Certainly if one were to restrict oneself to syntax alone, Japanese and Korean are so similar as to appear obvious sister languages. The problem lies with the vocabulary, where it has proved extremely difficult to identify words with a common root that could not at the same time simply be loanwords from Korean into Japanese.

The relative scarcity of sets of words that are clearly connected with each other is something that plagues Altaic linguistics in general and renders the kind of safe comparative work common within the Indo-European group highly problematic. Neither does it help that the phonological characteristics of Japanese and Korean are quite distinct: Korean allows consonant clusters and has a distinction between aspirates and non-aspirates that never seems to have existed in Japanese. And if it remains difficult to clarify this relationship, any hope of being able to reach further back is a forlorn one indeed. The major obstacle is the so-called time-depth: if Japanese and Korean in fact diverged from one another in the past, it may well have occurred as long as 5,000 years ago. This in itself makes reconstruction of a possible language tree extremely difficult, although it remains tempting. It should be mentioned here, perhaps, that Ainu, which is restricted to the northern islands of Japan and which is now almost extinct, has no obvious relationship to Japanese and is treated as yet another isolate.

If the syntax still makes one look north or north-west to the Asian continent, certain aspects of the vocabulary and the phonology (in particular the fact that Japanese has open syllables and allows simple word reduplication for plurals and other uses, such as onomatopoeia) draw one south, either to the Austronesian group, or even as far afield as south India. Fairly good sound correspondences have in fact been identified here, particularly in the area of agricultural vocabulary. All that can be said at present, however, is that there is a growing consensus that Japanese may well be a hybrid, a mixture between Altaic in the grammar and syntax and perhaps Austronesian in the lexicon. It is probable that the mixture is complex: verbs from the south, for instance, adopting inflections from the north. Whatever the truth of the matter, we know that even today the language is unusually hospitable to foreign loanwords, which can be absorbed into the structure of the language with surprising ease.

1.2 General comments

Japanese is an SOV language, and the rule that the verb must appear in sentence-final position is strictly observed, except for occasional inversion for purposes of emphasis. The modifier always precedes what is being modified. A general and quite useful distinction can be made between *variable* words, which inflect in one form or another, and *invariable* words, which never change their shape (table 1).

As one might expect, much of the grammar is concerned with the variable forms, in particular the verbal inflections, which are rich in aspectual and modal distinctions and which can reach a considerable length, especially in the older forms of the language.

Table 1 Basic distinctions

Variable	*Invariable*
true verbs, in form root + stem + suffix(es)	nouns, including interrogatives etc.
descriptive verbs, equivalent to English 'adjectives'	particles, interjections, conjunctives
the copula, marking the 'is' of equivalence: a = b	adverbs etc.

Verbs change by adding a series of suffixes and endings for tense, aspect and mood, but they are not marked for either person or number. It is all the more surprising then that the subject of a Japanese sentence, particularly in the spoken language, is omitted whenever possible. The reasons for this relative uninterest in marking person lies not so much with the grammar as with a cultural preference for oblique statements. Context is usually enough to tell listeners what they need to know, and a major role is played by the highly developed system of respect language. It is perhaps this aspect of the language that causes the learner so many problems, because, although clues are always present, it sometimes demands a detailed knowledge of Japanese society and custom to interpret them correctly. The respect language marks nouns where necessary, but the system is most highly developed in the verbs, every one of which is, or can be, marked either 'humble' or 'respectful' depending on the status of the subject. In the commoner verbs, this can involve not just a special inflection but a completely different form altogether.

Sentences are also marked either 'plain' or 'polite' with reference to one's interlocutor. Indeed it is true to say that no spoken Japanese sentence is without a marker or series of markers relating the speaker of the sentence to the addressee. The constant presence of this so-called pragmatic aspect of language in the lexicon and grammar is one of the distinguishing characteristics of the language. Ways have been found to circumvent this in written styles, where it can be an unnecessary intrusion, although it is still the case that the narrative voice in Japanese fiction is usually more insistent than it is, say, in English; and the suppression or neutralisation of this element was one of the major concerns of modern writers when they tried to create a new literary language out of the colloquial in the early years of the twentieth century.

What this means, of course, is that speakers of Japanese, be they native or foreign, must be constantly aware of social distinctions and appropriate ways of saying things. Not that this makes it unique, but in Japanese such concerns are overtly expressed in the choice of words and verb endings. To this extent Japanese is highly formalistic and ritualised, with such phrases as 'would you deign to?' and 'could I not perhaps have the favour of your doing?' being common and indeed *de rigueur* in the most ordinary of situations.

The Japanese lexicon is large, not only because of its antiquity but also because of its propensity for borrowing, first from Chinese, later from Portuguese and Dutch, and more recently from English. The majority of these loanwords have been nouns, mainly because Japanese nouns are invariable, remaining unchanged for case, gender and even number: this makes their absorption a relatively simple matter in terms of structure. Words of Chinese origin account for over 50 per cent of modern Japanese vocabulary, although words of English origin are now extremely common in all walks of life, especially advertising. Whenever a word is borrowed it is of course altered so that it will fit the fairly inflexible phonemic structure of Japanese. This has been true throughout history. The complex consonantal clusters and tonal variations that are typical of Chinese have all been ironed out, so contributing to an embarrassing increase in the number of homophones; and the 'difficult' sounds of western European languages have likewise been naturalised to the extent that they are not readily intelligible to the foreigner who might speak the language in question. So one comes across words such as:

volume	→	*boryūmu*	milk	→	*miruku*
Arbeit	→	*arubaito*	Cambridge	→	*kenburijji*
restaurant	→	*resutoran*	coffee	→	*kōhī*

What is perhaps a little more disconcerting is the habit of extreme abbreviation:

word processor	→	*wādo purosessā*	→	*wāpuro*
supermarket	→	*sūpā māketto*	→	*sūpā*
strike	→	*sutoraiki*	→	*suto*
basic salary raise ('base up')	→	*bēsu appu*	→	*bea*

2 THE WRITING SYSTEM

2.1 A mixed system

In many ways it was by an unfortunate quirk of history that Chinese was the first written language the Japanese were to encounter; an already difficult script had to be transformed and adapted into something even more complicated. It is no exaggeration to say that the Japanese use the most complex writing system in the world today. One might assume that this represented an intolerable burden, but such is not the case. It has led to a stylistic richness hardly dreamt of in the West and has certainly not held back the cultural or scientific development of the nation.

Modern Japanese is written with a combination of four different systems: romanisation, the two syllabaries, known as *hiragana* and *katakana*, and Chinese characters, known as *kanji*. All four can sometimes be found together in the same sentence, although the frequency of use of any particular system will depend on the subject and the style. A rough distribution of these systems is as follows:

Romanisation	Trade marks, acronyms, page numbers (Arabic and Roman), advertisements
Hiragana	Grammatical elements: particles, inflections, suffixes etc.
Katakana	Loanwords, other than of Chinese origin, 'italics'
Kanji	Chinese loanwords, Japanese nouns and verbal roots

2. 2 Romanisation

Unlike the situation in Chinese, where different systems of romanisation abound, there are only two systems of romanising Japanese in common use today. The differences are quickly learned. Table 2 shows the traditional arrangement of syllables for basic, voiced and palatalised sets. In the table a few cases have alternates listed in brackets. The main system shown here is the so-called Hepburn system, after the American missionary James Curtis Hepburn (1815–1911), who devised it for his *Japanese–English Glossary*, first published in 1867. This is in common use mainly because it allows speakers of English to produce a reasonable approximation to the Japanese sound with very little effort. The alternative system is known as the 'kunreishiki' or 'cabinet instruction system', devised, as the name suggests, by the Japanese government. Both systems have their defenders, and it is fortunate that the differences are in fact slight and hardly create an impediment to study or recognition.

Table 2 Traditional arrangement of syllables

Basic										
a	ka	sa	ta	na	ha	ma	ya	ra	wa	n
i	ki	shi (si)	chi (ti)	ni	hi	mi		ri		
u	ku	su	tsu (tu)	nu	fu (hu)	mu	yu	ru		
e	ke	se	te	ne	he	me		re		
o	ko	so	to	no	ho	mo	yo	ro	[wo]	
Voiced										
	ga	za	da		ba, pa					
	gi	ji (zi)	ji (zi)		bi, pi					
	gu	zu	zu		bu, pu					
	ge	ze	de		be, pe					
	go	zo	do		bo, po					
Palatalised										
	kya	sha (sya)	cha (tya)		bya, pya					
	kyu	shu (syu)	chu (tyu)		byu, pyu					
	kyo	sho (syo)	cho (tyo)		byo, pyo					
	gya	ja (zya)		nya	hya	mya		rya		
	gyu	ju (zyu)		nyu	hyu	myu		ryu		
	gyo	jo (zyo)		nyo	hyo	myo		ryo		

NB: The syllable *wo* in this table is distinguished from *o* in *hiragana* and *katakana* but not normally in romanised form. There are also double consonants, *kk, ss, tt, pp,* for instance, and long vowels (written in this textbook *ā, ī, ū, ē, ō*) which are roughly twice the length of the normal short vowels.

2. 3 *The syllabaries*

These syllabaries are known by the generic term *kana*. They were developed in the eighth and ninth centuries by simplifying those Chinese characters that were being used purely for their sound value rather than for their meaning.

Table 3 *Hiragana*

Basic										
あ	か	さ	た	な	は	ま	や	ら	わ	ん
い	き	し	ち	に	ひ	み		り		
う	く	す	つ	ぬ	ふ	む	ゆ	る		
え	け	せ	て	ね	へ	め		れ		
お	こ	そ	と	の	ほ	も	よ	ろ	を	
Voiced										
	が	ざ	だ		ば、ぱ					
	ぎ	じ	ぢ		び、ぴ					
	ぐ	ず	づ		ぶ、ぷ					
	げ	ぜ	で		べ、ぺ					
	ご	ぞ	ど		ぼ、ぽ					
Palatalised										
	きゃ	しゃ	ちゃ		びゃ、ぴゃ					
	きゅ	しゅ	ちゅ		びゅ、ぴゅ					
	きょ	しょ	ちょ		びょ、ぴょ					
	ぎゃ	じゃ		にゃ	ひゃ	みゃ		りゃ		
	ぎゅ	じゅ		にゅ	ひゅ	みゅ		りゅ		
	ぎょ	じょ		にょ	ひょ	みょ		りょ		

Voicing is produced by adding a diacritical mark to the top right hand corner of the *kana*: *ka* か → *ga* が for example. Palatalisation is shown by adding a small *ya* ゃ, *yu* ゅ, or *yo* ょ to the *kana*: *ki* き → *kya* きゃ. Double consonants are shown by a small *tsu* っ, which precedes the sign in question: *tte* って. For the correct stroke order see the end of this introduction.

Table 4 *Katakana*

Basic

ア	カ	サ	タ	ナ	ハ	マ	ヤ	ラ	ワ	ン
イ	キ	シ	チ	ニ	ヒ	ミ		リ		
ウ	ク	ス	ツ	ヌ	フ	ム	ユ	ル		
エ	ケ	セ	テ	ネ	ヘ	メ		レ		
オ	コ	ソ	ト	ノ	ホ	モ	ヨ	ロ	ヲ	

Voiced

ガ	ザ	ダ	バ、パ
ギ	ジ	ヂ	ビ、ピ
グ	ズ	ヅ	ブ、プ
ゲ	ゼ	デ	ベ、ペ
ゴ	ゾ	ド	ボ、ポ

Palatalised

キャ	シャ	チャ		ビャ、ピャ		
キュ	シュ	チュ		ビュ、ピュ		
キョ	ショ	チョ		ビョ、ピョ		
ギャ	ジャ		ニャ	ヒャ	ミャ	リャ
ギュ	ジュ		ニュ	ヒュ	ミュ	リュ
ギョ	ジョ		ニョ	ヒョ	ミョ	リョ

As with *hiragana,* voicing is produced by adding a diacritical mark to the top right hand corner of the *kana*: *ka* カ→ *ga* ガ for example. Palatalisation is shown by adding a small *ya* ヤ, *yu* ユ, or *yo* ヨ to the *kana*: *ki* キ → *kyu* キュ. Double consonants are shown by a small ツ, which precedes the sign in question: *tte* ッテ.

The simplification took two forms. *Hiragana* (table 3) emerged from the cursive form of the character taken to an extreme: 安→あ, 宇→う; it was used for the writing of personal communications, poetry, and was the main medium for the court women who dominated the writing of fiction in the late tenth and eleventh centuries. *Katakana* (table 4), on the other hand, developed from the habit of taking part for whole: 阿→ア, 呂→ロ, and first emerged in official documents and in the writing of Buddhist priests. The psychological effect of choosing to write in one rather than the other syllabary differs, of course, through history; today *katakana* is largely reserved for loanwords or to make a word stand out, much as we use italics. Any deviation from the norm can in fact be quite disturbing to read. A whole passage where the grammatical elements are expressed in *katakana* is likely to be of pre-Pacific War provenance and will now have a somewhat martial flavour.

Note that the *kana* syllabaries, although phonographic, are not alphabets, which represent an analysis of syllables in terms of their constituent consonants and vowels. Syllabaries are not designed to represent single consonants. There is a *kana* sign for *ka*, for instance, but it is simply not possible to write down the consonant *k* in isolation. Since Japanese syllables are by and large 'open', being either single vowels or consonant plus vowel, this does not cause any practical problems, but it has had considerable impact on the traditional analysis of the language. It should also be remembered that although either *hiragana* or *katakana* on its own would theoretically be adequate for transcribing the language, certain cultural and linguistic factors, such as the very high incidence of homophones, have conspired to make Chinese characters indispensable.

2.4 *Kanji*

One of the commoner misconceptions is that Chinese characters are in fact ideographs: signs that represent ideas. This is somewhat misleading, as it can give the impression that thought can be directly written down without the medium of language and that Chinese writing is somehow more 'direct' than a phonetic system. In fact characters are more accurately described as constituting a morphemic script, in that each character represents a morpheme, namely the minimal meaningful unit in a language. In Chinese this may mean a whole word or just part of a word. The important thing is that the character represents a linguistic unit rather than a disembodied idea.

Chinese characters are used to write the large number of Chinese words that have been borrowed over the centuries; the vast majority of such words have been nouns. As we have seen, nouns in Japanese are uninflected and never alter their shape and so the process of borrowing on this particular level has been fairly straightforward (table 5).

Table 5 Words borrowed from Chinese

Character	*Reading*	*Constituent parts*	*Meaning*
大学	*dai-gaku*	great-learning	university
電話	*den-wa*	lightning (hence electricity)-speak	telephone
人口	*jin-kō*	people-mouth(s)	population
東京	*Tō-kyō*	east-capital	Tōkyō

Note how these words, which mean the same thing in both Chinese and Japanese, are made up of two characters, hence each character here can be said to be standing for a morpheme: part of a word rather than a whole word. The Japanese did not stop here, however; they took the further step of using Chinese characters to write native Japanese nouns, reading them as Japanese (table 6):

Table 6 Using *kanji* to write Japanese words

Character	*Japanese word*	*Meaning*
人	*hito*	person, man
口	*kuchi*	mouth

So far, so good. Now it will be seen that the characters 人 and 口 can be read in two different ways: *hito* and *kuchi* when they occur on their own and are representing a native Japanese word, and *jin* and *kō* when they are representing a Chinese loanword. *Hito* is what the character 'means' in Japanese, just as we would say that 人 means 'person' or 'man' in English. But the character 人 already had a Chinese pronunciation, the modern Japanese equivalent of which is *jin*. (It is because the sound *jin* is only a Japanese approximation rather than the original Chinese sound that this is called the Sino-Japanese reading of the character). We have, therefore, the interesting situation, where one character has two or more readings (table 7):

Table 7 Different readings for one *kanji*

人	*JIN* (Sino-Japanese reading or *on-yomi*) *hito* (Japanese reading/meaning or *kun-yomi*)

As a very general rule, if the character is part of a compound then it should be pronounced with the *on-yomi*; if it appears in isolation it is pronounced in its *kun-yomi*. Beware, however, because exceptions to this rule are frequent, especially where names are concerned.

So much for nouns, which are simple in that they do not inflect. The real problem occurs when we encounter verbs in Japanese, which are highly inflected. The Chinese script is not able to deal with inflections of this or any other sort and so the *hiragana* syllabary must be brought into play to write down those parts of the verb that change. Happily, Japanese verbs inflect at the end rather than in the middle or at the beginning. The various forms of the verb 'speak', for example, will be represented as in table 8, with the Chinese character standing for the uninflected root of the verb and *hiragana* being used to write down the different inflected endings:

Table 8 Inflections of the verb 'speak'

話す	*hana-su*	speaks
話した	*hana-shita*	spoke
話したい	*hana-shitai*	wants to speak
話さなかった	*hana-sanakatta*	did not speak

Table 9 shows a typical dictionary entry for the character 話, which is used for both a noun and the root of a verb.

Table 9 Sample dictionary entry

話	*WA* (as in 電話 *denwa* 'telephone') *hana-su* , speak *hanashi*, a talk, a speech

The difficulties, as well as the fascinations, of the script should now be apparent. There are some 2,000 *kanji* in common use today: this is the minimum number required in order to be able to read a newspaper, and the minimum that all students in compulsory education must be taught. Novels, journals and specialist magazines are not restricted in this way, however, so it is probably fair to say that the average educated Japanese can in fact passively recognise some 3,000–4,000 characters. There may, of course, be times when a character or set of characters is recognised and understood but the reading either not known or forgotten. If the publishing house considers a word to be particularly obscure, they can insert the reading (usually in the *hiragana* syllabary) alongside the characters in small type to indicate the correct pronunciation: it is then termed *furigana*. It is this phenomenon that prompted the scholar and diplomat Sir George Sansom to write: 'One hesitates for an epithet to describe a system of writing which is so complex that it needs the aid of another system to explain it.' Remembering how unfamiliar *kanji* are written can also be a problem. The unusually high rate of literacy in Japan is partly attributable to the fact that basic literacy is defined as the ability to read the syllabaries and a limited number of characters only.

The burden that retention of Chinese characters represents can, however, be overemphasised. Most children manage to learn them and it has been discovered, for example, that dyslexia of the type that is triggered by the vagaries of English spelling is not prevalent in Japan. In any case, such is the powerful cultural significance of characters in Japan, and such is the vital role that they play in the task of discriminating between the many homophones in the modern language, that it now seems highly unlikely that they can ever be discarded.

2.5 Construction of characters

Characters are either single entities or made up of two or more elements: the most important of these elements are the radical and the determinant. Conventionally, for the purpose of classification, all characters are assigned to one of 214 radicals and one locates them in the dictionary by identifying the radical and then counting the extra strokes. 話, for instance, would be located under the left-hand element 言 ('word') + six extra strokes. You will soon find yourself learning the main radicals and being able to find a character in a dictionary as fast as you can locate an English word in an English dictionary. Some radicals are a rough guide to general meaning:

言	word/speech	木	tree/wood	手	hand/doing

The character 話 is clearly divisible left/right with 言 as the radical, whereas 電 'lightning' is clearly divisible top/bottom and the radical is on the top: 雨, meaning 'rain'. It is important to observe the correct stroke order because this will help you recognise characters written by hand. General rules are:

1 Left before right

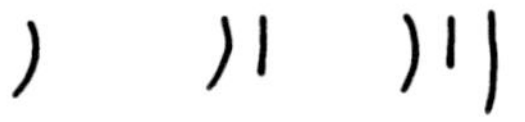

2 Top before bottom

3 Horizontal before vertical 一 十 except inside characters

4 With a clearly symmetrical shape, centre first, then left, then right

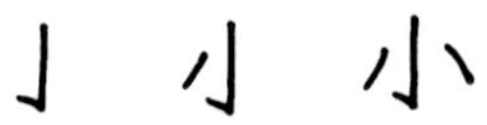

5 Vertical line protruding beyond horizontals written last

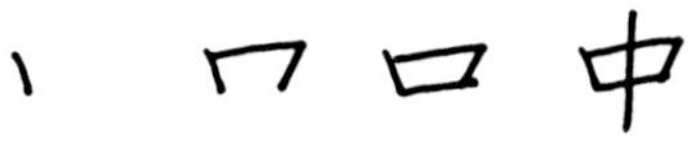

6 Horizontal line protruding beyond verticals written last

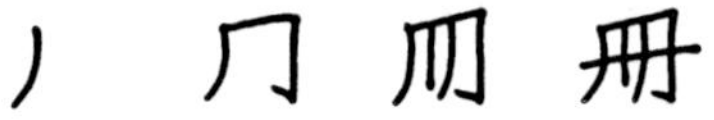

7 Right-to-left diagonal before left-to-right diagonal

8 Note the hooks ㇇ and ㇆

9 Three sided top enclosure written first

10 Top-left enclosure written first

11 Bottom-left enclosure usually written first

but if enclosed part seems to be larger, then enclosure is written last

12 Full enclosure finished bottom last

3 PRONUNCIATION

3.1 Introduction

Refer again to the table of romanised syllables (table 2). The best way to learn pronunciation is of course to copy a native speaker. You will not be given a full phonetic description at this point. Japanese is not that difficult to pronounce for native speakers of English, but there are a few sounds that need special care and attention.

(a) There are only five vowels, which are pronounced shorter and sharper than English vowels and with minimal lip activity. Long vowels must be given double time with no break. This is very important; a failure to distinguish clearly between long and short vowels is a typical mistake that could even get you into trouble. Note that a *u* in final position may be so short that it disappears: as in the very common *desu* and *masu*.

(b) The consonants are by and large as in English except that *k, g, t, d, b, p,* are all *un*aspirated. Note this because the English equivalents are quite strongly aspirated, especially at the beginning of words. You may find this difficult to achieve at first. One way to practice this is to expel most of your breath and then try to pronounce the words.

(c) Double consonants are produced by tensing the consonant, 'catching it' and holding on to it for an instant.

(d) *g* may become nasalised when it occurs inside a word or phrase. This nasalisation is a marked feature of Tōkyō speech and is often a matter of individual preference.

(e) *h* becomes *f* before the vowel *u*: *fu* is technically known as a labial fricative, a puff through half-closed lips. The teeth are only marginally involved and you must take care *not* to let the top teeth touch the inside of the lower lip.

(f) *r* is neither English *r* nor *l*. It is produced by resting the tongue very lightly on the alveolar ridge (just behind the upper teeth) and then rapidly releasing this contact. With slightly more tension, setting the tip of the tongue against the upper teeth, this sound actually approaches an English *d*.

(g) the syllabic *n*, such as occurs at the end of the word *Nihon*, is a long nasal sound which usually remains unreleased. The sound comes not directly through the nose but from the back of the mouth, and it is 'unreleased' in the sense that the tongue should not touch the roof of the mouth. Before *p*, *b*, or *m*, as in the word *shinbun*, it takes on the colour of an *m*. Failure to give it full weight is another typical mistake.

3.2 *The concept of 'beats'*

[While reading this section refer back to table 3.]
For the purposes of pronunciation, it is useful to think of each word being made up of one or more 'beats'. Generally every *kana* or graph is given the same amount of time; thus a four-*kana* word such as だいがく *da-i-ga-ku* is pronounced with four beats. The following points should be given particular attention:

(a) Syllabic *n* ん counts for a full beat, so the word ほん *hon* consists of two beats and the word ほんもの *honmono* consists of four.

(b) Note that palatalisations such as きゃ *kya*, しゃ *sha*, and ぎゃ *gya*, are treated as full *single* beats, not double. It is therefore important to distinguish as soon as possible between palatalisation and a true や *ya* sound. See table 10.

Table 10 Distinguishing palatalisation

Palatalised	*True*
きゃ・く *kyaku* 'guest'	き・や・く *kiyaku* 'agreement'
しょ・く *shoku* 'job'	し・よ・く *shiyoku* 'selfish desire'

(c) Double consonants, marked with a small っ preceding the consonant in question, are worth two full beats. See table 11.

Table 11 Distinguishing single and double consonants

Single	*Double*
さ・か *saka* 'slope'	さ・っ・か *sakka* 'writer'
も・と *moto* 'origin'	も・っ・と *motto* 'more'

(d) You should also take particular care to distinguish between short and long vowels. The distinction is absolutely crucial and yet rather difficult for English speakers to grasp. The general rules of orthography are in table 12.

Table 12 Distinguishing between long and short vowels

Short	*Long*
お・ば・さ・ん *oba-san* 'aunt'	お・ば・あ・さ・ん *obā-san* 'grandmother'
お・じ・さ・ん *oji-san* 'uncle'	お・じ・い・さ・ん *ojī-san* 'grandfather'

(e) Note that there are irregularities between sound and spelling in the two cases of long *ē* and long *ō*. Except for the word for 'yes' ええ *ē*, the long vowel *ē* is written with the *kana* for *ei*, and for this reason you will often find it romanised as such. By and large the long vowel *ō* is written *ou*, although you will not find this normally mirrored in romanisation (table 13).

Table 13 Long and short vowels: writing

Short	*Long*
て・き *teki* 'enemy'	て・い・き *tēki* 'fixed period'
せ・か・い *sekai* 'world'	せ・い・か・い *sēkai* 'correct answer'
く・ろ *kuro* 'black'	く・ろ・う *kurō* 'hardship'
こ・り *kori* 'stiffness'	こ・う・り *kōri* 'wicker basket'

3.3 The pitch accent

Accent in Japanese is based on entirely different principles to accent in English. English uses stress with a combination of light-medium-heavy patterns. A 'pitch accent' on the other hand requires a high-low pitch for each word. As an English speaker you will consciously have to avoid putting stress on any one syllable at the expense of the other. You will also, unless you have an extremely sharp ear for this kind of thing, find it difficult at first to pick up these changes in pitch. On occasion they may seem so slight as to be non-existent, but they are usually present and are rather important. There are times when it will actually make a difference in meaning. It is also one of the ways in which dialectal differences are manifest, and no matter how fluent you eventually become, lazy pitch awareness will betray you on the phone. You should make an effort from the very beginning to listen to how Japanese is pronounced by your native language teacher: the first step is to recognise the pitch changes and to know what to listen for.

Unfortunately there are no simple rules by which accent can be predicted. Rules do exist but they are fairly complicated. The best policy for the beginner is to try and learn the basic accent of each word as it comes along. Most of the larger Japanese–English dictionaries do mark accent and it is worth paying attention to this at an early stage. One rule which may help, and which is certainly worth remembering, is that the first beat of a word is always on a different pitch from the second one, at least as far as the standard Tōkyō accent is concerned. Study table 14 to get a general idea of how pitch accent operates:

Table 14 Pitch accent (1)

は・な・や *hanaya* 'flower shop'	さ・く・ら *sakura* 'cherry'	あ・お・い *aoi* 'blue'
と・う・きょ・う *Tōkyō* 'Tōkyō'	な・が・さ・き *Nagasaki* 'Nagasaki'	う・み *umi* 'sea'
きょ・う・と *Kyōto* 'Kyōto'	ま・く・ら *makura* 'pillow'	が・っ・こ・う *gakkō* 'school'

When single words are combined into longer phrases adjustments must sometimes be made to the basic pattern. Again, there are no simple rules but you should be aware that this will happen and be on the look-out for it. By and large the effect of spoken Japanese is one of constant undulation as each pitch accent on the word level flows into the next.

Occasionally, as we noted above, pitch can actually make a difference to the meaning of the word. Table 15 has some examples. Not too much should be made of this phenomenon, however. Although a wrong pitch may occasion the odd stare and even produce momentary incomprehension, Japanese is not a tonal language like Chinese, where pitch is always vital. If you still find the concept of pitch difficult to grasp, remember there are twenty ways of saying 'yes' in English, some of which mean 'no'.

Table 15 Pitch accent (2)

さ・け *sake* 'salmon'	さ・け *sake* 'sake'
に・ほ・ん *Nihon* 'Japan'	に・ほ・ん *nihon* 'two bottles'
じゅ・う・びょ・う *jūbyō* 'serious illness'	じゅ・う・びょ・う *jūbyō* 'ten seconds'

3.4 *The phonetics of loanwords*

Loanwords, other than from Chinese, are all expressed in *katakana*. Refer back to to table 4. The rules for writing are the same as for *hiragana* except for long vowels, where all that is needed is a dash after the relevant graph. See the example in table 16.

Table 16 Long vowels written in *katakana*

ア・ー・ト *āto* 'art'	ク・イ・ー・ン *kuīn* 'queen'	ジュ・ー・ス *jyūsu* 'juice'

Loanwords are fully naturalised into the Japanese sound system and as a result you will find that they are unusually difficult to recognise. This may at times be awkward because Japanese are often puzzled when you do not recognise a word that is 'obviously' foreign. These words are used quite widely in modern Japanese and you will have to become adept at picking them out. Because of the need to accommodate certain sounds not normally found in the native sound system, some unusual *katakana* combinations are used. These are listed in table 17. Notice that, as with palatalisation, the second element is reduced in size in order to show that the combination is to be seen as worth only one beat.

Table 17 *Katakana* employed for loanwords

	ツァ (tsa)		ファ(fa)		ヴァ (va)
	ティ (ti)	ディ (di)	フィ(fi)	ウィ (wi)	ヴィ (vi)
	トゥ (tu)	ドゥ (du)			ヴ (vu)
	テュ (tyu)	デュ(dyu)			
シェ(she)	ツェ (tse)		フェ(fe)	ウェ (we)	ヴェ (ve)
ジェ(je)	チェ (che)				
	ツォ (tso)		フォ(fo)	ウォ (wo)	ヴォ (vo)

Because Japanese syllables are open, foreign words that contain the consonant + vowel pattern are easily naturalised. Table 18 shows a few common examples that will cause you no problems.

Table 18 Consonant + vowel loanwords

ピ・ア・ノ *piano* 'piano'	カ・メ・ラ *kamera* 'camera'	パ・ノ・ラ・マ *panorama* 'panorama'

The majority of foreign words do not fit into this simple pattern, however, and you will encounter what may appear to you to be some fairly strange concoctions. Table 19 contains a representative sample. Many foreign words were and still are being adopted into Japanese. Most of them are from English, but this often gives you only the smallest of advantages. Not only is the pronunciation altered out of all recognition, but the meaning may be either more or less specific. We end this section with an example of four words, all of foreign origin, that have unusually specific meanings.

(a) カード *kādo* is from the English and is used for an index or catalogue card.

(b) カルテ *karute* is from the German 'Karte' and is only used for a patient's record in hospital.

(c) カルタ *karuta* is from the Portuguese 'carta' and refers to Japanese playing cards. This word has become so domesticated that it is often written in *kanji*: 歌留多.

(d) トランプ *toranpu* is from the English 'trumps' and is used to refer to modern Western playing cards.

Table 19 Further loanword examples

ポ・テ・ト *poteto* 'potato'	ゲ・ー・ム *gēmu* 'game'	ナ・イ・フ *naifu* 'knife'
ミ・ル・ク *miruku* 'milk'	サ・ラ・ダ *sarada* 'salad'	テ・ン・ト *tento* 'tent'
ル・イ・ス *Ruisu* Lewis	ル・ノ・ワ・ー・ル *Runowāru* Renoir	ロ・ン・ド・ン *Rondon* London
ベ・ニ・ス *Benisu* Venice	ベ・ト・ナ・ム *Betonamu* Vietnam	ベ・ル・ギ・ー *Berugī* Belgium
ス・ミ・ス *Sumisu* Smith	サ・ッ・チャ・ー *Satchā* Thatcher	チ・ケ・ッ・ト *chiketto* 'ticket'
チ・ッ・プ *chippu* 'tip'	ラ・ジ・オ *rajio* 'radio'	ディ・ス・コ *disuko* 'disco'
ロ・ケ・ッ・ト *roketto* 'rocket'	バ・ケ・ツ *baketsu* 'bucket'	ポ・ケ・ッ・ト *poketto* 'pocket'

4 DIALECTS

Dialect variation within Japan is as rich as in most European countries, many dialects being almost mutually unintelligible. As elsewhere, the standard speech adopted for official, nationwide communication has always emanated from the centre of political and cultural power. From earliest times to the eighteenth century, this has been Kyōto, but from around the end of the eighteenth century the centre finally shifted to Edo (Tōkyō), where it has remained ever since. Educated Tōkyō speech is now the standard for television and radio, although regional accents often show through. Considerable social stigma is attached to those local accents from the north and the far south, the degree of opprobrium being in direct relation to the degree of comprehensibility by outsiders.

Dialect groups can be analysed along two rather different lines, depending on whether one is searching for differences in vocabulary and inflection on the one hand or pitch accent on the other. Differences in vocabulary and verb inflections show a clear East-West split running north from just west of Nagoya. Differences in pitch accent show a somewhat more complicated doughnut situation with the accents in the Kyōto and Ōsaka area differing from the group of accents in both eastern and far western Japan, which have clear similarities.

5 WRITING STYLES

Partly because there are many levels at which classical Chinese can be absorbed into the system, and partly because of the continued divergence between the spoken and written language, Japanese has a very rich stylistic history. The use of Chinese can range from writing in classical Chinese proper, through a heavily sinified version of Japanese, down to today's styles. 'Sino-Japanese 1' in table 20 refers to those styles that make an attempt to 'look' Chinese although the underlying structure and method of reading reveal their Japanese origins. 'Sino-Japanese 2' refers to those styles that are essentially Japanese but contain a large number of loanwords and a few constructions influenced by Chinese, so making them distinct from the 'purer' forms used in Japanese poetry, for example.

Major breaks in style occur, of course, in the Heian period, with the invention of the *kana* syllabaries, and at the beginning of the Meiji period, when the modern styles began to emerge. All writings listed in table 20 both under Sino-Japanese 2 and 'Pure' Japanese that pre-date *c.* 1908 are now known as 'classical Japanese', a language distinct enough to have to be learned at school. Note how recently this shift has occurred. Even so, a considerable gap remains between spoken and written varieties of the language. A recent survey showed that, on average, words of Chinese origin comprised only 24 per cent of a typical conversation; for the written newspaper language the figure jumped to a remarkable 77 per cent.

6 FURTHER READING

The compilation and marketing of dictionaries is, like much else in Japan, a growth industry. As you proceed, you will find yourself having recourse to a veritable army of them: the following is just an introductory discussion.

Table 20 Differences in written styles

Period	*Classical Chinese*	*Sino-Japanese 1*	*Sino-Japanese 2*	*'Pure' Japanese*
Nara 710–94	Official documents, Chinese poetry, Buddhist writings	Male diaries and letters		Japanese poetry
Heian 794–1185	Official histories, Chinese poetry (declining)	Official documents, male diaries	Tale collections	Emergence of *kana*, female writings, Japanese poetry
Medieval 1185–*c.*1600	Chinese poetry, Official documents in foreign relations	Male letters, official documents, historical events	Military romances, tales, popular religious writings, Nō texts	Japanese poetry
Tokugawa *c.*1600–1868	Chinese poetry (revival), philosophical and historical prose	Male letters, official documents	Samurai romances, other 'serious fiction'	Fiction, *haikai* poetry, playscripts
Post-restoration 1868–*c.*1908	Male diaries, some prose	Official documents, some prose	Modern newspaper styles, fiction, poetry and playscripts	
*c.*1908–1945		Male diaries	Modern newspaper styles, fiction, poetry and playscripts	
Post-war–			All modern written styles	

At the outset all you will need is either F. Sakade, ed., *A Guide to Reading and Writing Japanese* (Tōkyō: Tuttle, rev. edn, 1961) or W. Hadamitzky and M. Spahn, *A Guide to Writing Kanji and Kana*, 2 vols. (Tōkyō: Tuttle, 1991), both workbooks. P. G. O'Neill, *Essential Kanji* (Tōkyō: Weatherhill, 1973) or W. Hadamitzky, *Kanji and Kana* (Tōkyō: Tuttle, 1981) are also useful: although they are not really dictionaries, they tell you how to write the characters and give the main readings and meanings. A. N. Nelson's *Japanese–English Character Dictionary* (Tōkyō: Tuttle, 2nd rev. edn, 1974) will soon become an indispensable companion, allowing you to move from character to reading to English equivalent with relative ease. Another more recent dictionary is M. Spahn and W. Hadamitzky, *Japanese Character Dictionary* (Tōkyō: Nichigai Associates, 1989), which has the added advantage that one can look up words on the basis of the second character in a compound, not just the first. From either of these dictionaries, it is not difficult to wean yourself on to a Japanese–Japanese character dictionary, the best one-volume one being Ogawa Tamaki's *Shinjigen* (Tōkyō: Kadokawa Shoten, 1968). Always remember, however, that as you proceed it is wise to learn compounds rather than single characters. Avoid dictionaries that advertise a 'new approach' to character analysis, because you will end up having to learn two systems instead of one. You can, of course, also look up words on their phonetic basis. There are many small dictionaries of this type, but you should get into the habit of referring to Masuda Kō's *Kenkyūsha's New Japanese–English Dictionary* (Tōkyō: Kenkyūsha, 4th rev. edn, 1974) wherever possible. The most important one-volume Japanese–Japanese dictionary of this type is Shinmura Izuru's *Kōjien* (Tōkyō: Iwanami Shoten, 4th rev. edn, 1991),which takes you from *kana* to *kanji* to meaning.

A general discussion of the language and its cultural setting can be found in R. A. Miller, *The Japanese Language* (Chicago University Press, 1967), and the more recent M. Shibatani, *The Languages of Japan* (Cambridge University Press, 1990). If you have any further questions about grammar go to S. Makino and M. Tsutsui, *A Dictionary of Basic Japanese Grammar* (Tōkyō: The Japan Times, 1986) or the highly technical 1198-page S. Martin, *A Reference Grammar of Japanese* (New Haven: Yale University Press, 1975). The honorific system is well described in P. G. O'Neill's programmed course *Respect Language in Modern Japanese* (London: Luzacs, 1966); details of how the modern writing system evolved can be found in G. B. Sansom, *An Historical Grammar of Japanese* (Oxford University Press, 1928, repr. 1968), pp.1–68, and the best way to compare Chinese, Japanese and Korean writing is to read the relevant lucid chapters in G. Sampson, *Writing Systems* (London: Hutchinson, 1985). For more information on matters of pronunciation the best reference is T. J. Vance, *An Introduction to Japanese Phonology* (Albany: State University of New York, 1987). When the going gets really rough turn to Jack Seward, *Japanese in Action* (Tōkyō: Weatherhill, 1968) for some light relief. There is a good chapter on 'How to sound better in Japanese than you really are.'

7 Kana Practice

7.1 Hiragana

あ	a	一 ナ あ あ	
い	i	い い	
う	u	ヽ う	
え	e	ヽ ラ え	
お	o	一 オ お お	

か	ka	フ カ か	
き	ki	一 ニ キ き	
く	ku	く	
け	ke	し に け	
こ	ko	フ こ	

さ	sa	一 ち さ	
し	shi	し	
す	su	一 す す	
せ	se	一 十 せ	
そ	so	一 乙 そ	

た	ta		
ち	chi		
つ	tsu		
て	te		
と	to		

な	na		
に	ni		
ぬ	nu		
ね	ne		
の	no		

は	ha		
ひ	hi		
ふ	fu		
へ	he		
ほ	ho		

ま ma	一 ニ ま	
み mi	み み	
む mu	一 む む	
め me	丶 め	
も mo	し も も	

や ya	つ や や	
ゆ yu	ゆ ゆ	
よ yo	一 よ	

ら ra	丶 ら	
り ri	l り	
る ru	ス る	
れ re	l れ れ	
ろ ro	ス ろ	

わ wa	｜ わ	
を [w]o	一 ち を	
ん n	ノ ん	

が	ぎ	ぐ	げ	ご
ざ	じ	ず	ぜ	ぞ
だ	ぢ	づ	で	ど
ば	び	ぶ	べ	ぼ
ぱ	ぴ	ぷ	ぺ	ぽ

きゃ	きゅ	きょ	にゃ	にゅ	にょ
ぎゃ	ぎゅ	ぎょ	ひゃ	ひゅ	ひょ
しゃ	しゅ	しょ	びゃ	びゅ	びょ
じゃ	じゅ	じょ	ぴゃ	ぴゅ	ぴょ
ちゃ	ちゅ	ちょ	みゃ	みゅ	みょ
ぢゃ	ぢゅ	ぢょ	りゃ	りゅ	りょ

7.2 Katakana

ア	a	フ ア	
イ	i	ノ イ	
ウ	u	丶 ⺍ ウ	
エ	e	一 丅 エ	
オ	o	一 才 オ	

カ	ka	フ カ	
キ	ki	一 二 キ	
ク	ku	ノ ク	
ケ	ke	ノ 𠂉 ケ	
コ	ko	フ コ	

サ	sa	一 十 サ	
シ	shi	丶 ⺀ シ	
ス	su	フ ス	
セ	se	フ セ	
ソ	so	丶 ソ	

タ	ta	ノ ク タ	
チ	chi	ノ ニ チ	
ツ	tsu	丶 丷 ツ	
テ	te	一 二 テ	
ト	to	丨 ト	

ナ	na	一 ナ	
ニ	ni	一 ニ	
ヌ	nu	フ ヌ	
ネ	ne	丶 ラ ネ ネ	
ノ	no	ノ	

ハ	ha	ノ ハ	
ヒ	hi	一 ヒ	
フ	fu	フ	
ヘ	he	ヘ	
ホ	ho	一 十 オ ホ	

マ ma	フ マ	
ミ mi	丶 ニ ミ	
ム mu	㇜ ム	
メ me	ノ メ	
モ mo	一 二 モ	

ヤ ya	フ ヤ	
ユ yu	㇆ ユ	
ヨ yo	㇆ ヲ ヨ	

ラ ra	一 ラ	
リ ri	㇑ リ	
ル ru	ノ ル	
レ re	レ	
ロ ro	㇑ ㇕ ロ	

ワ wa	⼂ ワ	
ヲ [w]o	一 ニ ヲ	
ン n	丶 ン	

ガ	ギ	グ	ゲ	ゴ
ザ	ジ	ズ	ゼ	ゾ
ダ	ヂ	ヅ	デ	ド
バ	ビ	ブ	ベ	ボ
パ	ピ	プ	ペ	ポ

キャ	キュ	キョ	ニャ	ニュ	ニョ
ギャ	ギュ	ギョ	ヒャ	ヒュ	ヒョ
シャ	シュ	ショ	ビャ	ビュ	ビョ
ジャ	ジュ	ジョ	ピャ	ピュ	ピョ
チャ	チュ	チョ	ミャ	ミュ	ミョ
ヂャ	ヂュ	ヂョ	リャ	リュ	リョ

Lesson 1

Study the following sentences:

これは本です。

それは何ですか。
これはえんぴつです。

それはペンですか。
ええ、そうです。
はい、これはペンです。

あれはノートですか。
いいえ、あれはノートではありません。本です。
いいえ、そうではありません。あれは本です。

これは何ですか。

本

ノート

ペン

えんぴつ

かぎ

ふで

めがね

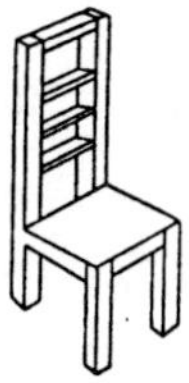

いす

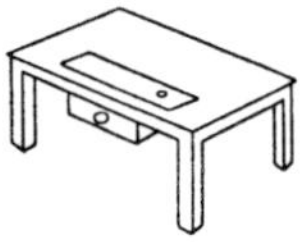
つくえ

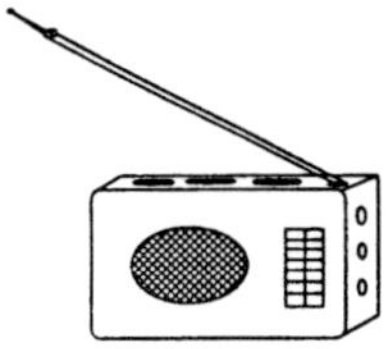
ラジオ

テレビ

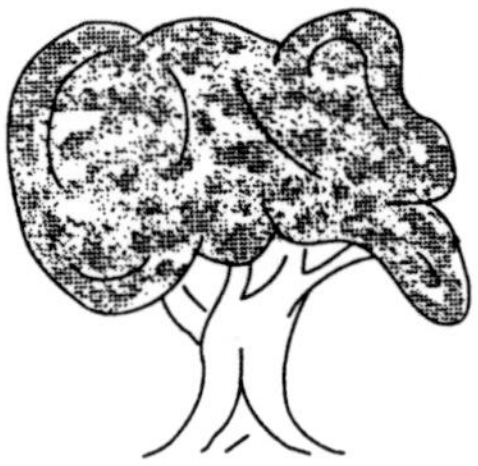
木

花

かさ

山

川

Comment

The first set of utterances you will learn are simple statements which either describe a series of objects or ask what they are. For this you will need to know words for 'this' and 'that', a few nouns, the topic marker, and the word for 'is'. Remember that the word-order of a typical Japanese sentence is subject-object-verb. Try to act out the sentences as you say them. The style here is in the normal polite form. Note that here, in the very first lesson, three different writing systems are already in use.

kanji	本	*hon*
katakana	ペン	*pen*
hiragana	つくえ	*tsukue*

You are being introduced to the written language more or less 'as it is' from the very beginning. It will look daunting to you at first but you will get used to it quite quickly. You should not attempt to begin, however, without having first ensured that you can read *hiragana* at the very least with ease.

1.1 'This thing' and 'that thing'

> これは本です。
> それはえんぴつです。

これ is a demonstrative noun meaning 'this thing here'. Japanese nouns are extremely simple compared to nouns in most European languages: they are uninflected for either gender or number and they retain their form wherever they occur in the sentence. This is *one* area where Japanese will cause you no trouble. これ forms a set of three such words together with それ 'that thing there' and あれ 'that thing over there'. The distinction between these is felt to be strong in Japanese and you should try to use them correctly from the very beginning. One usually responds with これ to a question containing それ, and with それ to a question containing これ. あれ is employed when two people involved in a conversation are equally distant from the object.

1.2 The particle は

は is a particle which, like all such particles in Japanese, follows the word to which it refers and is pronounced together with that word. Note that it is written irregularly with は, the *kana* for *ha*, although it is pronounced *wa*. It has a number of uses:

(a) it marks the topic or theme of the sentence
(b) it implies a contrast

In most of the sentences in this lesson it is operating as a topic or theme marker, subduing the word to which it is attached and shifting attention elsewhere. You will see later how the concept of topic/theme differs from that of subject. Here, the important thing to notice is that the word governed by は, namely これ, is already within the world of discourse. The word is marked off as a topic, and what follows is a statement, which can be either a question, a remark, or some new information about the topic.

1.3 The copula

です is the copula, a type of word which will probably be new to you. Although it is usually translated as 'is', it has certain unique properties, which distinguish it from the Japanese verb proper. It cannot, for example, stand on its own; and so it is best to think of it as a separate category. It has nothing to do with 'existence' and its basic meaning is that of equivalence: A = B, A 'is' B. This is very important to grasp at this early stage, because the English verb 'to be' is used for both existence and equivalence. In Japanese you must keep these two concepts clearly distinguished. Note that the noun that precedes the copula does not need a particle. Note also that the final *u* in です is usually reduced to a whisper: *des*~~*u*~~.

1.4 Asking a question

> それは何ですか。
> これはえんぴつです。

何（なん）is an interrogative noun meaning 'what?' か is a sentence-final particle indicating that a question is being asked. It is normally pronounced with a slight rise in pitch. The word order here is: *noun - topic marker - noun - copula*. To make a sentence into an interrogative, one either replaces the noun before the copula with the interrogative noun 何, adding か at the end, as in the first example, or one simply adds か as in あれはノートですか 'Is that a notebook?' No change in word order is needed. Note that the pattern of statement and response is far more regular in the Japanese than in the English.

これは何ですか。
What is this? (*lit.* As for this thing here, what is (it)?)

それは本です。
That is a book. (*lit.* As for that thing there, book is.)

1.5 'Yes'

それはペンですか。	はい、これはペンです。
	ええ、そうです。

はい means 'yes' but its use is fairly limited in daily conversation. Expect to hear the more colloquial ええ more often, particularly from women. Although one usually translates はい/ええ as 'yes', it is important to recognise that in actual usage the meaning is closer to 'I understand' or 'I am following you'. It is often used on the telephone as a kind of interjection, the main function of which is to reassure the other party that you are still on the line and listening. You must not therefore always interpret はい/ええ as an affirmative statement: the possibilities for misunderstanding are infinite. When responding to a question with more than just はい/ええ, one can either repeat the question minus the question marker か, or one can substitute the word そう, meaning 'correct' or 'so'.

1.6 'No'

あれはノートですか。
いいえ、あれはノートではありません。
いいえ、そうではありません。

いいえ means 'no'. For a negative response the copula です now has to be cast into its negative form, ではありません, which you will often find being contracted to じゃありません. Keep in mind, however, that じゃ is only used in spoken Japanese and that では is obligatory when writing. You will have noticed that the negative form of the copula involves another は. は is being used here not as a topic marker but as a marker implying contrast, and this will be discussed in more detail later. For the time being, just learn ではありません as a unit and register the fact that は is often employed in negative sentences in this way.

Key to sentences

Romanisation	*Translation*
Kore wa hon desu.	This is a book.
Sore wa nan desu ka.	What is that?
Kore wa enpitsu desu.	This is a pencil.
Sore wa pen desu ka.	Is that a pen?
Ē, sō desu.	Yes, it is.
Hai, kore wa pen desu.	Yes, this is a pen.
Are wa nōto desu ka.	Is that a notebook?
Iie, are wa nōto de wa arimasen. Hon desu.	No, that is not a notebook. It's a book.
Iie, sō de wa arimasen. Are wa hon desu.	No, it's not. That's a book.
Kore wa nan desu ka.	What is this?

Lesson 2

Study the following sentences:

これは私の本です。

あの男の子はだれですか。
弟の友達です。

あの女の方はどなたですか。
私達の学校の先生です。

あれはだれの絵ですか。
(あれは) ピカソの (絵) です。

このかさはどなたのですか。
(そのかさは) 山川さんのです。

それは妹さんのめがねですか。
いいえ、これは妹の (めがね) ではありません、姉のです。

この車は日本のですか。
いいえ、それは日本のではありません、イギリスのです。

Comment

This lesson deals with, among other things, how to express possession of something: 'mine', 'yours' etc. It also introduces the whole question of the social context within which you will be using the language. You must always ask yourself as to the nature of your relationship with whomever you are talking, because your vocabulary will have to change accordingly. In this sense, Japanese is far more context sensitive than English. This is known as 'changing register' and learning how to do this quickly is a major hurdle in studying the language.

2.1 Noun modification with の

これは私の本です。

Look at the following phrases. They all illustrate examples of one noun being modified by another. The fundamental rule here is that *the first noun modifies the second.*

私の本	my book
日本の車	a Japanese car
木のつくえ	a wooden desk
私達の先生	our teacher
妹のめがね	my younger sister's glasses
めがねの男	the man with glasses
女の子	a girl

The particle の simply indicates a connection between the two nouns. Sometimes this relationship can be one of possession, as in 私の本, sometimes one of attribution as in 木のつくえ. The English equivalent will therefore differ according to the type of modification. Note how useful this particle is: English has to employ a large number of different constructions to achieve the same result. Occasionally, however, you may find this very usefulness gives rise to ambiguity: 男の子, for example, could be either 'man's child' or 'boy', depending on context.

When answering a question in which this pattern is involved, you may omit the second noun, again very much as in English.

あれはだれのかさですか。
Whose umbrella is that?

あれは兄のかさです。 That's my elder brother's umbrella.	or	あれは兄のです。 That's my elder brother's.

2.2 'Who' and 'whose'

あの男の子はだれですか。
弟の友達です。
あの女の方はどなたですか。
私達の学校の先生です。

Both だれ and どなた are interrogatives meaning 'who?' どなた is more polite and should be used in preference to the somewhat abrupt だれ unless you find yourself in a situation where you can dispense with such formalities. Note the following contrast:

(a) あれはだれの絵ですか。	ピカソの (絵) です。
(b) これはどなたの絵ですか。	山本先生のです。

The question in (a) is impersonal in the sense that it refers to who painted the picture, and you are not assuming that the person to whom you are speaking has any connection with the painter. You therefore use だれ. If, however, you are asking to whom the picture belongs, as in (b), it would be more natural to use どなた, because some kind of personal relationship may well be involved.

2.3 この/その/あの

このかさ　　そのかさ　　あの女の方

These words この/その/あの belong to a special category of noun that we shall call prenouns. Prenouns are identified as a separate category because they occur immediately before other nouns with no intervening particle, although in fact a word such as この is derived from the noun こ ('this') + の. These words cannot occur by themselves. We have here a set of three: この 'this', その 'that' and

あの 'that over there'. Always remember that they *cannot* stand on their own and in usage they correspond to English demonstrative adjectives. When these words occur with inanimate objects or animals their use is quite regular, but when they are used in phrases that refer to people, この方 (read かた) 'this person', その方 'that person', あの方 'that person over there', you must take more care. Let us suppose that you want to say 'This is a teacher from our school'. If the person referred to were present and standing near to you, you would say この方は私達の学校の先生です. You would definitely *not* use その方, just as in English it would be impolite to say something like 'and is she your younger sister's teacher?' if the person concerned were standing next to you and within hearing. その方 would only be used if you were saying 'Is the person you have just been discussing (or you have just mentioned) your younger sister's teacher?' あの方 is used when the person is standing some way off, or if you are referring to a mutual acquaintance, who need not necessarily be present.

It should already be clear from this explanation that constant attention must be paid to the social situation around you, if you are to speak correctly. This will be a recurrent theme of this course.

2.4 'I' and 'you'

The words 私 (read わたくし) 'I' and あなた 'you' must be used with great caution and you cannot assume that they can be used either as often or as widely as their English counterparts. Note that, although they are translated as personal pronouns in English, they are really nouns in Japanese with the literal meanings of 'private, secret' and 'that side over there'. In due course you will find that there are many more different equivalents for 'I' and 'you' in Japanese than there are in English, but paradoxically the general rule is: avoid them whenever possible. Constant use of these words is a sure sign of a clumsy foreign speaker. In the case of 'I', it is considered presumptuous to keep on referring to oneself explicitly and in most contexts matters are quite clear without mentioning 'I' at all. It is for this reason that many Japanese sentences give an initial impression of being 'subjectless'.

For the second person, 'you', the normal practice when addressing others directly is to use their family name (or given name if they are very close friends) plus the polite suffix さん: so 山川さん. In the beginning you will find yourself wanting to use あなた as often as you use 'you' in English, but you must make a special effort to resist this, because it can actually cause offence. In general, あなた is used only by women, but again only in certain circumstances. It is, for instance, the usual way a wife addresses her husband when in the home. Women also use this word commonly with close friends. Men use あなた only rarely, occasionally perhaps when addressing women who are younger than themselves. If you think of あなた as being the equivalent of 'my dear' you will at least err on the side of caution.

For the third person, 'he' 'she' or 'they', play safe at this early stage and restrict yourself to using the family name plus さん. If you do not know the person's name or have forgotten it, use the locutions mentioned in 2.3, あの方, その方 etc.

2.5 Kinship terms

妹(いもうと)さんの。

Kinship terms in Japanese are arranged in pairs on a neutral/respect basis. The following is an initial list of the most common terms. A more complete chart of kinship terms will be found in appendix I.

neutral		*respect*	*meaning*
父	(ちち)	おとうさん/おとうさま	father
母	(はは)	おかあさん/おかあさま	mother
兄	(あに)	おにいさん/おにいさま	elder brother
姉	(あね)	おねえさん/おねえさま	elder sister
弟	(おとうと)	おとうとさん	younger brother
妹	(いもうと)	いもうとさん	younger sister
祖父	(そふ)	おじいさん/おじいさま	grandfather
祖母	(そぼ)	おばあさん/おばあさま	grandmother

You must take great care to observe the social constraints on each of these words. As a general rule use the neutral set when talking to others about your own family and the respect set when referring to members of another family. In such a context 父 would therefore mean 'my father' and おとうさん/おとうさま 'your father'. There are two quite common occasions, however, when this rule does not apply.

(a) When directly addressing members who are above you in the hierarchy, which would usually mean all those members who are older than you, you should use the respect series: おとうさん, おかあさん, おにいさん, おねえさん etc.

(b) When talking about such members to other members of your own family, you should again use the respect series. But what if the family member you are referring to is younger than you are? Clearly you will not feel like showing undue respect. You solve this problem by simply using his or her given name. Note that this is the fourth time in one lesson that we have drawn your attention to the necessity of making constant decisions and choices about which word to use in which particular social context.

Key to sentences

Romanisation

Kore wa watakushi no hon desu.

Ano otoko no ko wa dare desu ka.
Otōto no tomodachi desu.

Ano onna no kata wa donata desu ka.
Watakushi-tachi no gakkō no sensei desu.

Are wa dare no e desu ka.
(Are wa) Pikaso no (e) desu.

Kono kasa wa donata no desu ka.
(Sono kasa wa) Yamakawa-san no desu.

Sore wa imōto-san no megane desu ka.
Iie, kore wa imōto no (megane) de wa arimasen; ane no desu.

Kono kuruma wa Nihon no desu ka.
Iie, sore wa Nihon no de wa arimasen; Igirisu no desu.

Translation

This is my book.

Who is that boy?
He's a friend of my younger brother.

Who is that woman?
She's a teacher at our school.

Whose painting is that?
It's a painting by Picasso.

Whose is this umbrella?
That umbrella is Mr Yamakawa's.

Are those your younger sister's glasses?
No, these are not my younger sister's glasses; they are my elder sister's.

Is this car a Japanese one?
No, that's not a Japanese one; it's an English one.

Lesson 3

At an autumn festival in Tadashi's university

山川 一	(やまかわ はじめ)	日本人	男	**56歳**
山川 正	(やまかわ ただし)	日本人	男	**28歳**
山川 実	(やまかわ みのる)	日本人	男	**21歳**
木下 明子	(きのした あきこ)	日本人	女	**22歳**
ジョン・スミス		イギリス人	男	**27歳**
マリー・ペレ		フランス人	女	**25歳**

Tadashi introduces Akiko to his father.

正	おとうさん、こちらは実のお友達の木下明子さんです。
一	ああ、そうですか。始めまして。
木下	始めまして。木下明子です。どうぞよろしくお願いします。
一	こちらこそ、よろしく。

Tadashi then introduces Akiko to John and Marie.

ジョン	正さん、今日は。
正	やあ、今日は。木下さん、こちらはジョン・スミスさんとマリー・ペレさんです。
木下	始めまして。木下明子です。どうぞよろしく。
ジョン	こちらこそどうぞよろしく。木下さんは学生さんですか。
木下	ええ。
正	木下さんは弟のお友達です。
マリー	そうですか。大学はどちらですか。
木下	京都です。マリーさんも学生さんですか。
マリー	ええ、私も学生です。
木下	ジョンさんは。
ジョン	私は医者です。

Comment

Not everyone listed here is actually present, but they will all play a major part in the conversations that follow. From now on the lessons will consist largely of such conversations. Take care to look up all the vocabulary before going on to tackle the grammar explanations that follow. The situation in which this particular conversation occurs is a fairly informal one but, even so, introductions demand certain formalities to be observed. We have here a typical exchange of introductory formulae that you will be able to use on most occasions. Learn these by heart as soon as possible. Take note of when the polite さん is used.

3.1 Names

おとうさん、こちらは実のお友達の木下明子さんです。

Family names always come first, given names next. By and large it is by their family name, *not* their given name, that people identify themselves in public. 山川 and 木下 are family names. If you were called 山川正, you would normally introduce yourself or identify yourself as 山川です or 山川正です. Given names are used only within the family or with small children. Note here how the son Tadashi addresses his father with the respectful おとうさん. The word he then uses to indicate Akiko, こちら, means 'this side/direction/person' and is polite precisely because it is a little vague. The use of the word here implies general politeness both to the father and to Akiko. He then refers to his younger brother by simply using his brother's given name, Minoru, only to swing back again immediately to refer politely to Akiko.

3.2 The polite prefix お

お友達

Not only does Tadashi give Akiko her full name and add さん, but he also calls her Minoru's お友達. This formal prefix お can be applied to a variety of nouns but by no means all, so you should not try to use it indiscriminately. Tadashi uses it here because he wishes to be polite about Akiko, particularly in her presence.

3.3 Initial greetings

> ああ、そうですか。始めまして。
> 始めまして。木下明子です。

The father shows polite interest with the equivalent of 'Ah, indeed. How do you do?' そうですか is very often used in conversation as a response to new information. Although it takes an interrogative form, ending with the particle か, it does not really signify a question; it shows polite but uncommitted interest, somewhat like the English 'really?' or 'is that so?' You will find that Japanese conversations, especially telephone conversations, demand somewhat more of these fillers than English. 始めまして means something like 'we begin our relationship' and is used when meeting someone for the first time. The grammar of the introductory formulae that follow is quite complex and will be explained at a later stage. You should therefore learn them as set phrases and use them as such. They are extremely useful. You will find that Japanese is full of set phrases that are expected to be produced almost automatically in various social situations.

Akiko responds with a further 始めまして and then introduces herself. Note that さん is missing here. *Never* use it when referring to yourself.

3.4 Further greetings

どうぞよろしくお願いします。
こちらこそ、よろしく。

どうぞよろしくお願いします literally means 'Please, I desire your favour'. It can be used together with 始めまして or in isolation, and the general effect is the equivalent of an English 'How do you do?' or 'Pleased to meet you'. The commonest reply to this will be こちらこそ、よろしく literally meaning 'It is *I* who desire your favour', and you should train yourself to use it as an automatic response on being introduced. The father could have simply echoed Akiko with a どうぞよろしく, but being an older man he prefers to leave off the 'please' at this juncture as a very slight sign of condescension. Note how the word こちら 'this side' that Tadashi previously used to refer to Akiko is now being used by Hakime to refer to *himself*. At first sight this may seem odd, but it can and does happen because the word refers primarily to a direction and is therefore highly sensitive to context. こそ is a particle which puts special emphasis on the noun it follows.

3.5 Talking to foreigners

正さん、今日は。
やあ、今日は。

John, who is about the same age as Tadashi, greets him with the correct さん ending, and then follows this immedately with the simple greeting 今日 (こんにち) は, which just means 'today' and signifies 'hello'. But John has broken the rule about family names only, and in a purely Japanese context this would be somewhat familiar. This relaxation of the rules happens quite often when foreigners are involved and it is not really John's 'fault'. As the conversation proceeds you will notice that once Akiko has been introduced, she herself breaks the rule, although she also takes care to retain the polite さん. From this you can infer that the conversation is informal and that the relationship is not a professional one. The people concerned, especially the two foreigners, are probably under thirty. The use of given names in this way represents a commonly encountered gesture in the direction of foreign norms of language and behaviour, particularly American-style informality. John has picked up on this and uses the given name. This would be unlikely to occur if the conversation were between two Japanese. Tadashi goes on to emphasise the relaxed nature of the exchange by coming out with the brusque male greeting やあ 'hey!'

3.6 Linking nouns

> 木下さん、こちらはジョン・スミスさんと
> マリー・ペレさんです。

The particle と links nouns together in simple addition. Note that と *cannot and must not* be used to link two sentences or phrases. Pay particular attention to this point, because you may well be tempted to use と in this way in the early stages by simple analogy with the English 'and'.

3.7 'And which is...?'

> 大学はどちらですか。

Note how the question 'And which is your university?' is phrased in the Japanese. 大学 is topicalised with は and this is then followed by the word どちら, a polite interrogative noun meaning 'which direction?', or 'which one?'

3.8 Inclusive も

マリーさんも学生さんですか。

The inclusive particle も highlights the noun it follows: 'Marie too' or 'John too'. Note how も, by drawing the word it follows *into* the sentence, has in a sense the opposite effect to は, which marks the topic *off* from the rest of the sentence.

3.9 'How about you?'

ジョンさんは。

In the course of a conversation in English one can often omit the verb in an interrogative sentence because it is so obvious: 'How about you?' The same thing applies in Japanese. This is achieved by breaking off at the particle は and pronouncing it with a slight rise in pitch so as to indicate that a question is being asked: ジョンさんは↗ 'And how about John?'

Key to conversation

Romanisation

Yamakawa Hajime	Nihonjin	otoko	gojūrokusai
Yamakawa Tadashi	Nihonjin	otoko	nijūhassai
Yamakawa Minoru	Nihonjin	otoko	nijūissai
Kinoshita Akiko	Nihonjin	onna	nijūnisai
Jon Sumisu	Igirisujin	otoko	nijūnanasai
Marī Pere	Furansujin	onna	nijūgosai

Tadashi	O-tōsan, kochira wa Minoru no o-tomodachi no Kinoshita Akiko san desu.
Hajime	Ā, sō desu ka. Hajimemashite.
Kinoshita	Hajimemashite. Kinoshita Akiko desu. Dōzo yoroshiku o-negai shimasu.
Hajime	Kochira koso, yoroshiku.
Jon	Tadashi san, konnichi wa.
Tadashi	Yā, konnichi wa. Kinoshita-san, kochira wa Jon Sumisu san to Marī Pere san desu.
Kinoshita	Hajimemashite. Kinoshita Akiko desu. Dōzo yoroshiku.
Jon	Kochira koso, dōzo yoroshiku. Kinoshita-san wa gakusei san desu ka.
Kinoshita	Ē.
Tadashi	Kinoshita-san wa otōto no o-tomodachi desu.
Marī	Sō desu ka. Daigaku wa dochira desu ka.
Kinoshita	Kyōto desu. Marī-san mo gakusei-san desu ka.
Marī	Ē, watakushi mo gakusei desu.
Kinoshita	Jon-san wa.
Jon	Watakushi wa isha desu.

Translation

Tadashi	Father, this is Miss Kinoshita Akiko, a friend of Minoru's.
Hajime	Ah, indeed. How do you do?
Kinoshita	How do you do? I'm Kinoshita Akiko. Delighted to meet you.
Hajime	The pleasure is mine.
John	Tadashi, hello!
Tadashi	Hey! Hello! Miss Kinoshita, this is John Smith and Marie Perret.
Kinoshita	How do you do? I'm Kinoshita Akiko. Delighted to meet you.
John	The pleasure is mine. Delighted to meet you. Are you a student?
Kinoshita	Yes.
Tadashi	Miss Kinoshita is a friend of my younger brother.
Marie	Oh really? Which university?
Kinoshita	Kyōto. Are you a student too?
Marie	Yes, I am too.
Kinoshita	What about John?
John	I'm a doctor.

Lesson 4

Conversation continued from lesson 3. Tadashi and Marie are talking and Marie wants to know who's who.

マリー	あの方はどなたですか。
正	私の先生です。
マリー	お名前は何ですか。
正	原教授です。
マリー	あちらの方は。
正	原先生の奥さまです。
マリー	どの方が正さんのおとうさまですか。
正	こちらです。どうぞ。

Tadashi then introduces Marie to his father.

正	おとうさん、マリー・ペレさんです。
一	始めまして。正の父です。
マリー	始めまして。どうぞよろしくお願いします。
一	こちらこそ。お国はどちらですか。
マリー	フランスです。
一	そうですか。フランスのどちらですか。
マリー	モンペリエです。

4.1 The prefix お again

> お名前は何ですか。
> お国はどちらですか。

We saw this use of お in 3.2. Sometimes it is almost obligatory, as in the case of the word for 'money', お金 (おかね), where お has become an integral part of the word and the formality has been neutralised, but お is often used where the formality is in fact a matter of being polite about other people and their possessions. Note here, for example, that お is placed in front of both 名前 and 国 to show politeness to the person concerned. But who *is* the person concerned? Only context will actually tell you. Nine times out of ten お名前 means 'your name', but it should be clear that in this particular context Marie is actually referring to the teacher's name and so you would have to translate it 'his name' here. She is being polite not only because a teacher is due respect in any case, but also because he is closely connected to Tadashi. In the second example later on in the conversation, Tadashi's father is clearly saying 'your country'. This use of お is in fact one way of avoiding direct reference to the second person. The corollary is, of course, that お is not normally used when referring to one's own possessions or to something closely connected to one.

4.2 'Way over there'

あちらの方は。

Another example of the kind of truncated question that we saw in 3.7. The word あちら means 'way over there' and, in what should now be becoming a familar pattern to you, it forms a set together with こちら 'over here' and そちら 'over there'. どちら you have already met. You will find it later on in this conversation when Tadashi's father asks Marie フランスのどちらですか 'where in France?'

4.3 Referring to different members of a family

原先生の奥さまです。 正の父です。

When you wish to talk about a member of someone else's family, the person you know best becomes the main reference point and the other members of the family will usually be identified in relation to that person. So in the first example here the person to whom Marie points is identified by Tadashi as his 'teacher's wife'. The word chosen for wife, by the way, 奥さま, is a polite one that should never be used about one's own wife.

Study the following Yamakawa family chart; it includes everyone we have met so far, and some others who will appear in due course.

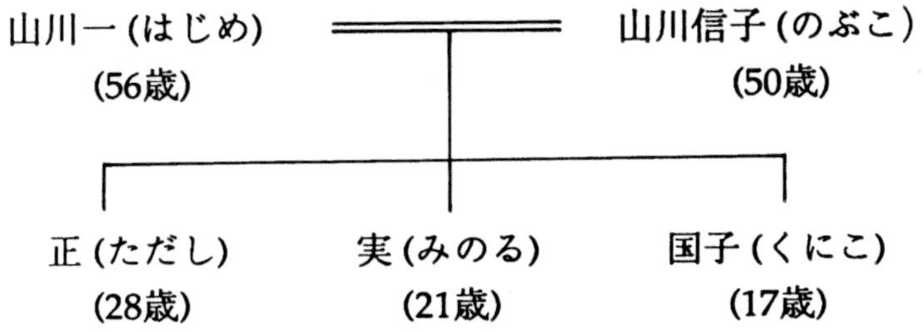

On this basis, if you are a friend or colleague of 山川 一, you will refer to

信子	as	山川さんの奥さん/おくさま
正 and/or 実	as	山川さんのむすこさん
国子	as	山川さんのおじょうさん.

However if you are a friend of 実, you will refer to

一	as	山川さんのおとうさん/おとうさま
信子	as	山川さんのおかあさん/おかあさま
正	as	山川さんのおにいさん/おにいさま
国子	as	山川さんの妹さん.

Similarly, when you introduce yourself for the first time to someone who knows one of the members of your family, you will use that particular family member as the reference point. So in the second example above, Tadashi's father introduces himself to Marie as Tadashi's father: 正の父です.

4.4 More interrogatives

どの方が正さんのおとうさまですか。

どの 'which' is the corresponding interrogative of the prenouns この/その/あの. Here it is combining with 方 (かた) to produce a polite 'which person?' Note the difference between this word, which specifically refers to choosing one out of many, and the generally polite 'who?' どなた (2.2). Marie chooses to raise the respect language a notch higher when referring to Tadashi's father with the phrase おとうさま. See the table in 2.5. For an explanation of the が here, see below.

4.5 The subject marker が

あの方はどなたですか。 versus どの方が正さんのおとうさまですか。

In this lesson a new particle が, the subject marker, is introduced. The use of は and が is probably the most difficult point in Japanese grammar, and the difference between subject and topic will be explained in detail in later chapters. At this stage, the first rule to be learned is that an interrogative noun is always followed by が when it is in the equivalent position to the English 'subject'. Conversely, if the interrogative noun appears later in the sentence, the subject will become topicalised with the particle は. In the replies to these questions the particles は and が are simply repeated in the same place.

あの方はどなたですか。	→	あの方は山川さんです。
どの方が山川さんですか。	→	あの方が山川さんです。

4.6 'Please'

こちらです。どうぞ。

どうぞ is the kind of word you use when offering things to people: 'please accept'. Here Tadashi is offering to take Marie to meet his father, and the word might be accompanied by either a little hand gesture in the direction of the father or a small nod of the head.

4.7 Numbers

You will have noticed that in lesson 3 we gave the ages of the people concerned in the conversation, but left them without comment. The important matter of how to count objects will be introduced later. Here we can take the opportunity to introduce simple numbers. To say 'fifty-six years old' in Japanese you would say the number for fifty-six, as listed below, with the word 歳 (さい), which means 'years old'. What follows is a list of basic Japanese numbers: the kind you will use for counting years, counting on your fingers, or for doing arithmetic.

units:

0	零	れい、ぜろ、まる	5	五	ご
1	一	いち	6	六	ろく
2	二	に	7	七	しち、なな
3	三	さん	8	八	はち
4	四	し、よん	9	九	きゅう、く

teens:

10	十	じゅう	15	十五	じゅうご
11	十一	じゅういち	16	十六	じゅうろく
12	十二	じゅうに	17	十七	じゅうしち/なな
13	十三	じゅうさん	18	十八	じゅうはち
14	十四	じゅうし/よん	19	十九	じゅうく/きゅう

tens:

20	二十	にじゅう	60	六十	ろくじゅう
30	三十	さんじゅう	70	七十	しち/ななじゅう
40	四十	し/よんじゅう	80	八十	はちじゅう
50	五十	ごじゅう	90	九十	きゅうじゅう

hundreds:

100	百	ひゃく	600	六百	ろっぴゃく
200	二百	にひゃく	700	七百	ななひゃく
300	三百	さんびゃく	800	八百	はっぴゃく
400	四百	よんひゃく	900	九百	きゅうひゃく
500	五百	ごひゃく			

thousands:

1,000	千	せん	6,000	六千	ろくせん
2,000	二千	にせん	7,000	七千	ななせん
3,000	三千	さんぜん	8,000	八千	はっせん
4,000	四千	よんせん	9,000	九千	きゅうせん
5,000	五千	ごせん	10,000	一万	いちまん

The readings よん for 4 and なな for 7 are borrowed from a second set of numbers which will be introduced later. よん is used in preference to し because the latter is homophonous with a word meaning 'death' and なな may also be used because しち can be misheard as いち. Note that Japanese has a separate word for 10,000. This you will find rather difficult at first because 'a hundred thousand' is expressed in Japanese as 十万 'ten ten-thousands' or 10,0000.

Key to conversation

Romanisation

Marī	Ano kata wa donata desu ka.
Tadashi	Watakushi no sensei desu.

Marī	O-namae wa nan desu ka.
Tadashi	Hara kyōju desu.
Marī	Achira no kata wa.
Tadashi	Hara sensei no okusama desu.
Marī	Dono kata ga Tadashi-san no o-tōsama desu ka.
Tadashi	Kochira desu. Dōzo.

Tadashi	O-tōsan, Marī Pere san desu.
Hajime	Hajimemashite. Tadashi no chichi desu.
Marī	Hajimemashite. Dōzo yoroshiku o-negai shimasu.
Hajime	Kochira koso. O-kuni wa dochira desu ka.
Marī	Furansu desu.
Hajime	Sō desu ka. Furansu no dochira desu ka.
Marī	Monperie desu.

Translation

Marie	Who is that person over there?
Tadashi	My teacher.
Marie	What is his name?
Tadashi	Professor Hara.
Marie	And that person over there?
Tadashi	That's Professor Hara's wife.
Marie	Which one is your father?
Tadashi	Here he is. I'll introduce you.

Tadashi	Father, this is Marie Perret.
Hajime	How do you do? I'm Tadashi's father.
Marie	How do you do? Delighted to meet you.
Hajime	The pleasure is mine. Where are you from?
Marie	France.
Hajime	Oh really? What part of France?
Marie	Montpellier.

Lesson 5

Mr Brown is on his way to a meeting at the Tōzai Bank.

歩行者　すみませんが、今 何時ですか。
ブラウン　十時十五分すぎです。
歩行者　どうもすいません。
ブラウン　いいえ。あのう、ここは大手町駅の北口ですか。
歩行者　そうですよ。
ブラウン　東西銀行はどこですか。
歩行者　ええと、東西銀行はあのビルです。
ブラウン　どうもありがとうございます。
歩行者　いいえ、どういたしまして。

Mr Brown arrives at the Tōzai Bank.

ブラウン　ブリティッシュ・エンジニアリングのブラウンです。
長谷川　始めまして、東西銀行の長谷川です。どうぞよろしく。
ブラウン　こちらこそ、どうぞよろしく。

They exchange name cards.

ブラウン　こちらが長谷川さんの銀行の電話番号ですか。
長谷川　そうです。3335-9871 、内線 402 番です。
ブラウン　ありがとうございます。
長谷川　二階の方へどうぞ。
ブラウン　どうも、失礼します。

They reach the first floor.

長谷川　どうぞ、こちらへ。
ブラウン　ミーティングは十時半からですね。
長谷川　ええそうです。十時半から十二時までです。

Comment

This conversation is designed to introduce you to time and to explore numbers a little further. It should be contrasted with the two previous conversations, in that it involves two businessmen; the style will therefore be somewhat more formal.

5.1 'Excuse me'

すみませんが

The grammar of this expression will be explained in a later lesson. Learn this as a phrase meaning 'Excuse me, but...' It is very useful as a way of catching someone's attention. The passer-by uses it in this way first. However, it reappears in the next thing he says: どうもすいません. (The terms すいません and すみません are interchangeable.) The second example means 'sorry to have troubled you'.

5.2 Time

今 何時ですか。
十時十五分すぎです。

今 (いま) is a noun meaning 'now'. Note that it should be considered as belonging to a special subset of nouns because it can occur in this adverbial role without a particle. O'clock is expressed by adding the nominal suffix 時 (じ) to the numbers that you have already learned in the previous lesson.

o'clock

一時	いちじ	七時	しちじ
二時	にじ	八時	はちじ
三時	さんじ	九時	くじ
四時	よじ	十時	じゅうじ
五時	ごじ	十一時	じゅういちじ
六時	ろくじ	十二時	じゅうにじ

Minutes are expressed by adding the suffix 分 (ふん、ぷん).

一分	いっぷん	六分	ろっぷん
二分	にふん	七分	ななふん
三分	さんぷん	八分	はちふん/はっぷん
四分	よんぷん	九分	きゅうふん
五分	ごふん	十分	じゅっぷん

As in English, there is a way to express a.m./p.m.: 午前 (ごぜん) and 午後 (ごご) respectively. 7 a.m. is 午前七時 (ごぜん しちじ), 6 p.m. would be 午後六時 (ごご ろくじ). There is no word for 'quarter', but 半 (はん) means 'half': 三時半 (さんじはん) 'half past three'. 'Noon' is expressed by the word 正午 (しょうご). すぎ is 'past' and 前 (まえ) is 'before'. As in English, すぎ can be, and often is, omitted. 'A quarter to ten' would be 十時十五分前 (じゅうじ じゅうごふん まえ) and 'twenty past eight' would be 八時二十分 (はちじ にじゅっぷん). The twenty-four hour clock is used in Japan as much as it is used in England, for timetables, etc.

5.3 Asking directions

> あのう、ここは大手町駅の北口ですか。

あのう, here, is another way of catching someone's attention, just as in English we would either say 'er' or cough. ここ is part of another set of nouns, in this case nouns that refer not to 'this thing' これ and 'that thing' それ but to place: ここ

'this place', そこ 'that place' and あそこ 'that place over there'. 'Where?' is どこ.

5.4 The particle よ

そうですよ。

There are a number of particles that come at the end of phrases or sentences and that give statements a particular rhetorical force. よ is one of them. It has the effect of exerting slight pressure and so can sound pushy if overused. It should not be used in formal situations. Here the passer-by is saying something like 'Indeed it is!' or 'Yes, that's right!'

5.5 Hesitation

ええと、

One sure-fire way to sound better in Japanese than you really are is to learn the proper hesitation sounds as soon as possible and to force yourself to use them whenever you need to hesitate. Only in this way can you 'become' Japanese in your speech. ええと is a true hesitation sound, the Japanese equivalent of 'um' or 'er'. Here the passer-by is presumably looking around, trying to get his bearings and remember where the bank is.

5.6 Saying 'thank you'

どうもありがとうございます。
どういたしまして。

The grammar of common phrases is often quite complex. Full explanation will therefore be left until later. Just learn them as they are for the present. The first phrase is the normal way of saying 'thank you'. You will also find it as どうもありがとうございました (see conversation lesson 6), どうもありがとう, ありがとう or simply どうも. The second is the traditional response: 'not at all'.

5.7 Identifying yourself

始めまして、東西銀行の長谷川です。

When you identify yourself to someone in Japan, you should get in the habit of giving more than just your name. If you work for a company you would preface your name with the name of the company to which you belong, because it is an integral part of the role that you are playing. As a student you would normally say that you were from such-and-such a country or university. When people are sought for on the public address systems at Japanese railway stations for example, it is normal for either a company name or the name of the city where they live to be added as part of the information. It is almost as if one is slightly naked without this addition. In this case Mr Hasegawa identifies himself as an employee of the Tōzai Bank and Mr Brown responds in kind.

5.8 Name cards

こちらが長谷川さんの銀行の電話番号ですか。

The exchange of name cards is a vital part of business life in Japan. It is a very good example of how the Japanese will quickly adopt and adapt a foreign custom (in this case a Victorian English one) if it suits their social structures and adds something useful. A person's name card (名刺 *meishi*) should always be handled with respect. It is normal, for instance, to accept a name card with both hands. To give a card is to initiate a relationship, be it friendly or purely business. There is also an implicit acceptance that the card may be used by the other person as proof that this relationship now exists. It is for this reason that eminent people distribute their cards with care. But a card is not merely something with a name and an address that can be filed away for future reference; the information that it holds is of immediate use. Its shape and the typeface will tell you a lot about the owner. A businessman will have a simple card, perhaps with the company's logo. It will measure exactly 55 × 90 mm, so that it can fit into a standard card holder, and the printing will probably be vertical. A professional woman's card will be considerably smaller with rounded edges, a smaller elegant typeface and the printing may well be horizontal. An artist or a politician may well have something rather more individualised, with a florid typeface and high quality paper. For the businessman, perhaps the most important piece of information is the rank of the holder, which will be written in the top right-hand portion of the card. This will tell him the other's status and rough age, and so allow him to gauge the correct level or register of language to employ.

When Mr Brown says こちらが here he is pointing to the card and to the telephone number 電話番号 that will be printed bottom left.

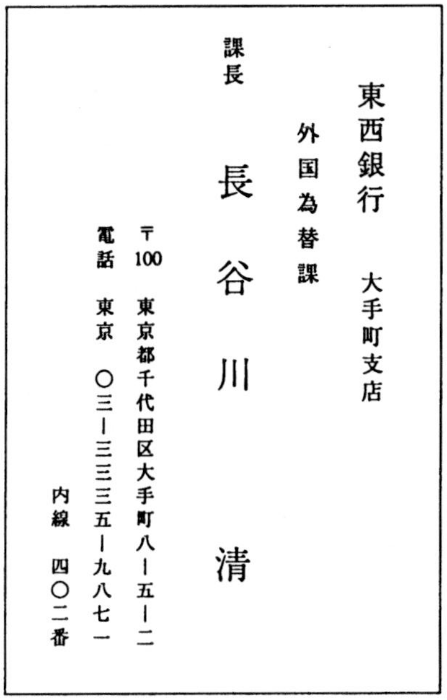

5.9 Telephone numbers

そうです。3335-9871 、内線 402 番です。

Telephone numbers are read out as a series of single numbers, just as in English we say 'three, three, five', not 'three hundred and thirty-five'. You can, if you wish, insert a の in between the number of the local exchange and the actual phone number, and if you were being a little formal, or simply trying to make yourself clear over a bad line, you might also add the word 番 (ばん): 3335-9871 will therefore be さんさんさんご (の) きゅうはちななないち (ばん). Internal extension numbers 内線 (ないせん) are as in English: 'extension 402' being 内線よんれいに.

5.10 Floors in a building

二階の方へどうぞ。

The word 二階 here is best understood as a compound noun. Japanese number floors on the American model and so there is no 'ground floor'. 二階 (にかい) will therefore have to be translated as 'first floor' in the UK. The 'second floor' will be 三階 (pronounced さんがい rather than さんかい) and the 'third floor' 四階 (pronounced よんかい, *not* しかい). Room numbers are expressed with the word 番: 二階の 254 番.

The particle へ, pronounced *e*, indicates direction 'to' or 'towards'. It occurs again in Hasegawa's next statement: どうぞ、こちらへ, 'This way please.'

5.11 Further excuses

どうも、失礼します。

Note how the words どうも and どうぞ are paired here, どうも being an almost automatic response. The grammatical details of the second part of this expression, 失礼します, will come a little later in the course. For the time being, learn it as a set phrase. It literally means 'I am going to be rude' and can be used in many situations: when disturbing someone, when finishing a telephone call or when leaving a room. Having met and exchanged cards, Mr Hasegawa now lets Mr Brown go upstairs ahead of him to his office, and Mr Brown apologises for going in front of him.

5.12 'From' and 'to'

ミーティングは十時半からですね。
ええそうです。十時半から十二時までです。

から and まで are temporal particles meaning 'from' and 'up to' or 'until' respectively.

朝から晩まで	from morning till evening
五時から六時十五分まで	from five to quarter past six
これから	from now (from this point)
それから	after that
あれから	after that

5.13 は as topic marker

> 東西銀行はどこですか。
> 東西銀行はあのビルです。
> ミーティングは十時半からですね。

Anything in a sentence can become the topic but here we investigate cases where the subject becomes the topic, i.e. where the subject marker が is replaced by は. The normal rule is that は de-emphasises the noun that it follows, mainly because that word usually refers to something which is 'old information'. By subduing what precedes it, は throws attention onto what follows. As we saw in 3.4, it is only natural that when the subject is an interrogative it can never be made into a topic with は, because an interrogative will always draw maximum attention.

どちらが木下さんのかさですか。
Which is Kinoshita's umbrella?

When the interrogative is *not* the subject, then the subject is usually transformed into the topic in order to allow the attention to shift to the interrogative, as in 東西銀行はどこですか. Note how English finds such topicalisation somewhat unnatural.

木下さんのかさはどちらですか。
lit. Kinoshita's umbrella is which one?

The same rule of emphasis versus de-emphasis applies to sentences without an interrogative.

(a) この本は山川さんのですか。
(b) この本が山川さんのですか。

As は de-emphasizes the noun it follows, (a) could be translated 'Is this book *Yamakawa's*?' が, on the contrary, draws attention to the noun it follows, hence (b) could be translated 'Is *this book* Yamakawa's?'

One more example to see how this works: if you are walking around London with a Japanese friend and you find yourself facing an imposing building, you might say:

あれはナショナル・ギャラリーです。
That's the National Gallery.

You have both just seen the building and so know to what あれ refers; it is old information. The new information you are providing is the name of the building. But now suppose that you have already been talking about the National Gallery or are on your way to the Gallery and suddenly arrive in front of it, you would then be more likely to say:

あれがナショナル・ギャラリーです。

Your mind or your conversation has been on the Gallery and the new information is therefore 'that', あれ, rather than the name.

5.14 The particle ね

ミーティングは十時半からですね。

ね is another sentence final particle that gives a statement a particular rhetorical push. It has a similar effect to the English tag phrase 'isn't it?', operating as a gesture of recognition drawing in the listener. Some people tend to overuse this particle, but it is very useful when you wish to build up a rapport.

Key to conversation

Romanisation

Hokōsha	Sumimasen ga, ima nanji desu ka.
Buraun	Jūji jūgofun sugi desu.
Hokōsha	Dōmo suimasen.
Buraun	Iie. Anō, koko wa Ōtemachi-eki no kitaguchi desu ka.
Hokōsha	Sō desu yo.
Buraun	Tōzai ginkō wa doko desu ka.
Hokōsha	Ēto, Tōzai ginkō wa ano biru desu.
Buraun	Dōmo arigatō gozaimasu.
Hokōsha	Iie, dō itashimashite.

Buraun	Buritisshu Enjiniaringu no Buraun desu.
Hasegawa	Hajimemashite, Tōzai ginkō no Hasegawa desu. Dōzo yoroshiku.
Buraun	Kochira koso, dōzo yoroshiku.

Buraun	Kochira ga Hasegawa san no ginkō no denwa bangō desu ka.
Hasegawa	Sō desu. San-san-san-go no kyū-hachi-nana-ichi, naisen yon-zero-ni ban desu.
Buraun	Arigatō gozaimasu.
Hasegawa	Nikai no hō e dōzo.
Buraun	Dōmo, shitsurei shimasu.
Hasegawa	Dōzo, kochira e.
Buraun	Mītingu wa jūjihan kara desu ne.
Hasegawa	Ē sō desu. Jūjihan kara jūniji made desu.

Translation

Pedestrian	Excuse me, do you have the time?
Brown	It's just after ten fifteen.
Pedestrian	Thank you (for your trouble).
Brown	Not at all. Ah, is this the north exit of Ōtemachi station?
Pedestrian	It is indeed.

Brown	Where is the Tōzai bank?
Pedestrian	Let me see now, the Tōzai bank is that building over there.
Brown	Thank you very much.
Pedestrian	Don't mention it.

Brown	I'm Brown from British Engineering.
Hasegawa	How do you do? Hasegawa of the Tōzai Bank. Delighted to meet you.
Brown	The pleasure is mine. Delighted to meet you.

Brown	Is this your telephone number at the bank?
Hasegawa	Yes. 3335-9871, extension 402.
Brown	Thank you very much.
Hasegawa	Please go up to the first floor.
Brown	Thank you. Do excuse me.
Hasegawa	This way please.
Brown	The meeting is from ten thirty isn't it?
Hasegawa	That's right. From ten thirty to twelve o'clock.

Lesson 6

After their meeting Mr Hasegawa accompanies Mr Brown to the door.

ブラウン	こちらの銀行には外国人もいますか。
長谷川	ええ、アメリカ人とスイス人がいます。イギリス人はこの支店にはいません。
ブラウン	そうですか。私の会社の本社にも外国人がたくさんいます。日本人も中国人もいますよ。
長谷川	そうですか。
ブラウン	すみませんが、お電話はありますか。
長谷川	ええ、もちろん。こちらへどうぞ。電話はあのつくえの上にあります。

After making a short telephone call Mr Brown returns to Mr Hasegawa.

ブラウン	どうもありがとうございました。
長谷川	どういたしまして。
ブラウン	それでは今日はこれで失礼いたします。
長谷川	失礼いたします。

6.1 True verbs

こちらの銀行には外国人もいますか。
ええ、アメリカ人とスイス人がいます。
お電話はありますか。
あのつくえの上にあります。

So far we have only met the copula です, which signified the 'is' of equivalence: A = B. Here we have our first true verbs, います and あります, both meaning the 'is' of existence. Japanese verbs come at the end of the sentence and, like the copula, do not alter for either number or person. Note the distinction between these two verbs however: います is used when the subject or topic is animate; あります must be used when the subject or the topic of this existential verb is inanimate. Plants, although 'living', count as being inanimate.

6.2 The particle に

こちらの銀行には
この支店には

The particle に denotes location in or at which something exists; it is used with both animate and inanimate subjects.

6.3 Negatives of true verbs

イギリス人はこの支店にはいません。

The whole question of how to form the negative will be dealt with in detail in lesson 15. Here we simply introduce the negative of the animate います, which is いません, and of the inanimate あります, which is ありません.

6.4 More on は

アメリカ人とスイス人がいます。
イギリス人はこの支店にはいません。

Study these two sentences carefully, because topicalisation is used in one but not the other. In the first case 'Americans and Swiss' is new information and so cannot really become a topic, at least at this point. In the second case, however, 'Englishmen' can become a topic because Mr Hasegawa knows that Mr Brown is English and so the word イギリス人 is already present as part of their discourse. It is as if Mr Hasegawa is thinking to himself 'He has presumably asked that question because he is interested in finding out whether there are any English working for my bank.'

But what is the second は doing in this sentence? You saw in lesson 1 that the second major function of は was to imply a contrast. It is this は marking contrast that is so often found in negative statements, so that although it may not be strictly incorrect to say イギリス人はこの支店にいません, it is in fact rarely said. By adding は after 支店に one can highlight what is being negated i.e. この支店, and at the same time weaken the degree of negation that the verb bears; hence the implication of this sentence is 'And as for Englishmen, there are none in this branch (but there may well be in some other branch).'

By now you may well be asking yourself: so how can one distinguish between these two roles of は: the topic and the contrast? How do we know that the first は here is topicalising? You will usually be able to tell from context, but the truth of the matter is that both roles are interconnected, because the primary role of は is to isolate. The effect of this isolation can sometimes be to produce a topic and sometimes to emphasise a contrast. Sometimes it is difficult, indeed unnecessary, to make the distinction. You will find, for instance, that in some cases a word has been topicalised precisely in order to point up a contrast. This could well be the case in the following examples:

(a) 私の大学に男の学生はいません。
(b) 私の大学には男の学生はいません。

(a) is a very simple and direct statement which negates the existence of male students in 'my university', but (b), depending on context, could well imply that although there are no male students in *my* university, there are in some *other* universities. Furthermore, は is used after 男の学生 in both sentences because they both deny only the existence of male students; obviously there are *some* students, in this case female.

6.5 Plain and polite forms

Both the copula です and true verbs like あります and います have been introduced so far in their polite forms. The kind of conversations that we have presented have demanded this level of politeness. There is also a plain form. You will be gradually introduced as to when these plain forms are appropriate; it is a matter of social context. For a start, however, study the following tables.

(a) The copula

	plain	*polite*
positive	だ	です
	である †	であります †
negative	ではない	ではありません
	じゃない ‡	じゃありません ‡

† Stilted equivalent, used only in writing or very formal occasions.

‡ じゃ is a contraction of では, much used in conversation but never in written Japanese.

(b) True verbs あります and います

	plain	*polite*
positive	ある	あります
	いる	います
negative	ない	ありません
	いない	いません

ある is known as the plain 'dictionary' or 'citation' form of the verb. Details of how these plain forms are transformed into polite equivalents will be dealt with in the next lesson, but note here that the transformation involves the ending 〜ます. More will be said about the negative form ない/いない in lesson 15.

From a grammatical point of view the plain form and the polite form of true verbs are completely interchangeable, although the switch will of course involve a change in register. The situation with the copula is not quite so simple and will be commented on further.

6.6 More on location

あのつくえの上にあります。

As you have just seen above, these existential verbs are used to create sentences that deal with place and location. The particle に can be added to other nouns to make that location more specific than simply 'at'.

Noun	+	の上 (うえ) に	on top of
	+	の下 (した) に	underneath
	+	の前 (まえ) に	in front of
	+	の後ろ (うしろ) に	behind
	+	の右 (みぎ) に	on the right of
	+	の左 (ひだり) に	on the left of
	+	の中 (なか) に	inside
	+	のとなりに	next to
	+	の向こう (むこう) に	the other side of
	+	の横 (よこ) に	on the side of
	+	の間 (あいだ) に	between

がわ 'side' can often be added to some, but not all, of these nouns to indicate even more detail: 右がわ, 左がわ, 向うがわ. Study the following question and response examples:

ピーターの前にだれがいますか。
Who is in front of Peter?

(ピーターの前に) ジュリアンがいます。
Julian is in front of Peter.

ピーターはどこにいますか。
Where is Peter?

ピーターはジュリアンの後ろにいます。
Peter is behind Julian.

このビルの中に電話はありますか。
Is there a telephone in this building?

ええ、電話は入口の右がわにあります。
Yes, there is one on the right hand side of the entrance.

Now at the risk of complicating matters, there is one difficulty that must be faced at this point, if only to avoid subsequent confusion. This lesson is your first introduction to true verbs and we have tried to stress the difference between the 'is' of equivalence (the copula です) and the 'is' of existence (the true verbs あります/います). This distinction is extremely important. The fact of the matter is, however, that both the following sets of sentences are in fact correct:

ピーターはどこにいますか。
ピーターはどこですか。

ええ、電話は入口の右がわにあります。
ええ、電話は入口の右がわです。

Why? At first sight this seems to conflate the two again. What is happening is that in certain circumstances です can be used as a substitute for another verb, as long as that underlying verb is clear from the context. Nine times out of ten this substitution occurs when the subject is topicalised with は. The sentence 東西銀行はどこですか in the conversation to lesson 5 is another example. どこにありますか would also have been correct. Observe the following:

おとうさまはどちらですか。
Where is your father?

父は今アメリカです。
Father is at present in America.

父は今アメリカにいます is another possible response here. In a sense this substitution is a natural outcome of the general desire to cut corners in colloquial speech. Another related phenomenon is the following oft-quoted example. The normal Japanese response to 'What do you want to drink?' is 私は X です. This should be understood as: 'As for myself, (my drink) is X.' Compare the situation in English when a mix-up with the drinks might lead you to say 'No, she's a gin; I'm a whisky.'

6.7 On leaving

それでは今日はこれで失礼いたします。
失礼いたします。

You will not now be surprised to hear that the grammar of these common phrases will also have to be explained in detail much later in the course. Learn them here as set phrases. それでは 'right, then', 今日は 'today', これで 'with this', and 失礼いたします, 'I am being very rude (by leaving you now)' hence 'please excuse me'.

Note that 今日は in this context is *not* read こんにちは as in 'hello' (3.4), but きょうは. This is a nice example of the complications that lie ahead for you. The pronunciation in this case has little or no connection to either the *on* or *kun* of the characters 今 *KON/KIN, ima* 'now' or 日 *NICHI, hi* 'day'. Although this may well worry and occasionally annoy you, it is not uncommon. It is really no different from writing down 'H_2O' and then deciding to pronounce it 'water'. This anomaly is known as 当て字 *ateji* ('assigned characters').

失礼いたします expresses even more respect than the phrase 失礼します that you came across in 5.11, where it meant 'excuse me'.

Key to conversation

Romanisation

Buraun	Kochira no ginkō ni wa gaikokujin mo imasu ka.
Hasegawa	Ē, Amerikajin to Suisujin ga imasu. Igirisujin wa kono shiten ni wa imasen.
Buraun	Sō desu ka. Watakushi no kaisha no honsha ni mo gaikokujin ga takusan imasu. Nihonjin mo chūgokujin mo imasu yo.

Hasegawa	Sō desu ka.
Buraun	Sumimasen ga, o-denwa wa arimasu ka.
Hasegawa	Ē, mochiron. Kochira e dōzo. Denwa wa ano tsukue no ue ni arimasu.
Buraun	Dōmo arigatō gozaimashita.
Hasegawa	Dō itashimashite.
Buraun	Sore de wa kyō wa kore de shitsurei itashimasu.
Hasegawa	Shitsurei itashimasu.

Translation

Brown	Are there foreigners working here too?
Hasegawa	Yes, there is an American and a Swiss. There aren't any British at this branch.
Brown	Really? There are many foreigners at my company's head office as well. Both Japanese and Chinese, you know.
Hasegawa	Oh really?
Brown	I wonder if there is a telephone I might use.
Hasegawa	Of course. This way please. It's on that desk over there.
Brown	Thank you very much.
Hasegawa	Not at all.
Brown	Well then, if you'll excuse me, I'll be on my way.
Hasegawa	Good-bye.

Lesson 7

Kinoshita Akiko describes her typical daily schedule.
She studies English and English literature at Kyōto University.

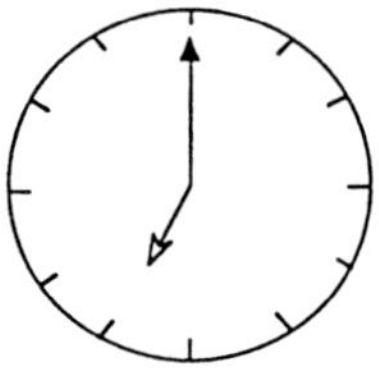

朝七時に起きます。

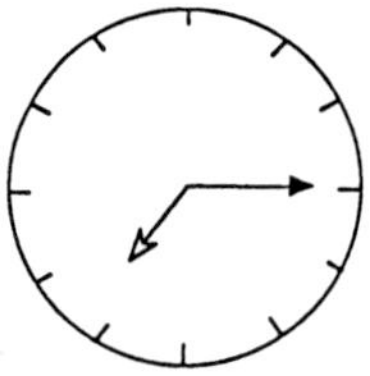

まず、ラジオでニュースを聞きます。

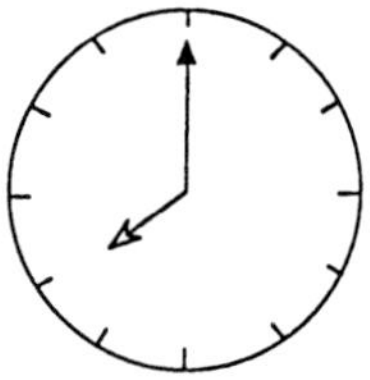

八時ごろ朝ごはんを食べます。
朝ごはんはトーストとコーヒーです。

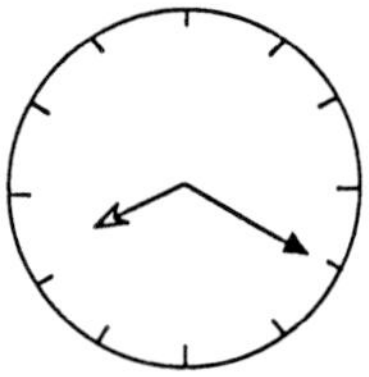

八時二十分すぎに家を出ます。
駅まで歩きます。
駅の前からバスに乗ります。
そこから大学までバスで三十分ぐらいかかります。
九時少し前に大学に着きます。

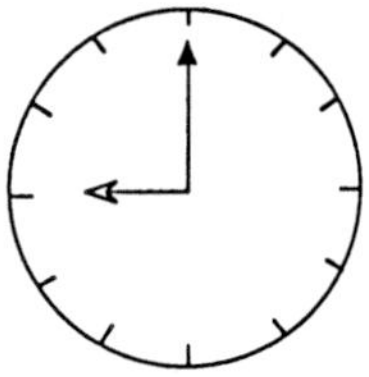

午前のクラスは九時から十二時までです。

7.1 'At seven o'clock'

朝七時に起きます。

You were introduced to the basic time terms together with words for 'from' and 'to' in lesson 5. When replying to a question about the time and saying something like 'half past eight' or 'twenty minutes to ten' you will have no need for any particle at all; but when you wish to express the concept of something happening *at* a particular time, you will need the particle に.

十二時に来ます。
I will come at noon.

五時少し前に行きます。
I will go shortly before five.

Note that the noun 朝 'morning' is used adverbially here and so does not need a particle (see 今 in 5.2). に can also be omitted when the word ごろ, meaning 'about', is used: 八時ごろ朝ごはんを食べます, but に *cannot* be omitted with the words 〜すぎ and 〜前: 八時二十分すぎに家を出ます 'I leave the house at twenty past eight'; 九時少し前に大学に着きます 'I arrive at the university a little before nine.'

7.2 More on pure verbs

朝七時に起きます。 八時ごろ朝ごはんを食べます。

You have already come across two Japanese verbs, あります and います, and in 6.5 there was passing reference to the plain form of these verbs, ある and いる.

You have also learned that Japanese verbs do not alter for person or number, nor need there be a subject overtly expressed: あります, for instance, can stand entirely on its own as a whole sentence meaning 'Yes, it is there' or some such. This lesson investigates verbs further.

Although Japanese verbs do not express either person or number, they have a variety of forms which are produced by the addition of various suffixes and endings to a series of stems. Verbs are in fact classified under three main groups, depending on how they handle these changes. The classes are always based on the plain 'citation' form, which is how you will meet Japanese verbs in dictionaries. Introduced here are the polite 〜ます form, with which you are most familar up to this point, and the conjunctive form of the verb on which it is based.

Group I

The majority of Japanese verbs in fact belong to this group. The rule that is common to all verbs in this set is that the final *-u* vowel changes to *-i* to form the conjunctive.

plain		*conj.*	*polite*		*meaning*
ある	(aru)	ari	あります	(arimasu)	exist
歩く	(aruku)	aruki	歩きます	(arukimasu)	walk
会う	(au)	ai	会います	(aimasu)	meet
行く	(iku)	iki	行きます	(ikimasu)	go
入る	(hairu)	hairi	入ります	(hairimasu)	enter
話す	(hanasu)	hanashi	話します	(hanashimasu)	talk
言う	(iu)	ii	言います	(iimasu)	say
買う	(kau)	kai	買います	(kaimasu)	buy
書く	(kaku)	kaki	書きます	(kakimasu)	write
聞く	(kiku)	kiki	聞きます	(kikimasu)	listen, ask
待つ	(matsu)	machi	待ちます	(machimasu)	wait
飲む	(nomu)	nomi	飲みます	(nomimasu)	drink
乗る	(noru)	nori	乗ります	(norimasu)	ride
使う	(tsukau)	tsukai	使います	(tsukaimasu)	use
読む	(yomu)	yomi	読みます	(yomimasu)	read

Group II

With very few exceptions, this set contains all verbs ending in either *-eru* or *-iru*. The characteristic here is that the conjunctive is formed by simply dropping the final *-ru*.

plain		*conj.*	*polite*		*meaning*
いる	(iru)	i	います	(imasu)	exist
出る	(deru)	de	出ます	(demasu)	go out
かける	(kakeru)	kake	かけます	(kakemasu)	hang
見る	(miru)	mi	見ます	(mimasu)	see
寝る	(neru)	ne	寝ます	(nemasu)	go to bed
起きる	(okiru)	oki	起きます	(okimasu)	get up
食べる	(taberu)	tabe	食べます	(tabemasu)	eat

A short list of verbs which appear to belong to this group but in fact inflect as group I verbs can be found in appendix II.

Irregular

There are only two verbs commonly listed under this heading.

plain		*conj.*	*polite*		*meaning*
来る	(kuru)	ki	来ます	(kimasu)	come
する	(suru)	shi	します	(shimasu)	do

7.3 Tense/aspect

朝七時に起きます。

The somewhat complex matter of tense and aspect will be studied later. At this point you should learn that both the plain citation form and the polite ～ます form have the basic meaning of incompletion. In due course it will be labelled the 'imperfective' for this reason. Translation will depend on context. It is used mostly for generic or habitual action which is essentially 'timeless'. So here we will have the translation 'I get up at seven thirty.' Note that this form is never used for present action. For this you must use the ～ている form which will be introduced in lesson 16. You will also find yourself sometimes translating this imperfective form with an English future: 四時まで待ちます 'I will wait until four.'

7.4 The particles で and を

まず、ラジオでニュースを聞きます。

(a) で as agent or instrumental marker

The basic meaning of で is 'by means of' or 'using'. This gives rise to the following kinds of usage:

ラジオで聞く。	hear on the radio
バスで行きます。	go by bus
電話で話す。	talk on the phone
ドイツ語で手紙を書く。	write a letter in German

(b) を as object marker

Pronounced *o* but written *wo*, を is added to the noun that is the grammatical object in the sentence.

ニュースを聞く。	hear the news
りんごを食べる。	eat an apple
本を買います。	buy a book
父を待ちます。	wait for my father
コーヒーを飲みます。	drink coffee

を can be found in another context. Look at the sentence 八時二十分すぎに家を出ます. 'I leave the house at twenty past eight.' 出る 'go out' or 'leave' is not a transitive verb and so cannot have an object in the above sense. In due course you will meet a number of verbs that use を to mark the space from which or through which motion occurs.

7.5 The particles から and まで in spacial contexts

駅まで歩きます。 駅の前からバスに乗ります。

You have already met から and まで in the context of temporal expressions. They are also used in spacial contexts. から marks motion 'from'; まで marks motion 'to' 'towards' or 'as far as'.

友達が中国から来ます。
A friend comes from China.

大学までバスで行きます。
I go to university by bus.

These particles can, of course, be linked to produce a 'from...to' pattern referring to either time or place:

ここからあそこまで
from here to there

午前六時から午後四時半まで
from 6 a.m. to 4:30 p.m.

そこから大学まではバスで三十分ぐらいです。
From there to the university takes about 30 minutes by bus.

ケンブリッジからロンドンまで車で行きます。
I (will) go from Cambridge to London by car.

7.6 More on the particle に

九時少し前に大学に着きます。

に is used as a direction marker to indicate a simple 'to' when it is unnecessary to stress 'right up to' or 'as far as': ロンドンに行きます 'go to London'. But に also occurs in a large number of what can only be called idiomatic phrases, linked to specific verbs. It is worth learning them as sets:

大学に着きます。	arrive at the university
友達に手紙を書きます。	write a letter to my friend
家に帰ります。	go home
バスに乗ります。	ride on a bus
山田さんに会います。	meet Mr Yamada
部屋に入る。	enter the room
先生に聞く。	ask the teacher

Key to sentences

Romanisation

Asa shichiji ni okimasu.

Mazu, rajio de nyūsu o kikimasu.

Hachiji goro asagohan o tabemasu.

Asagohan wa tōsuto to kōhī desu.

Hachiji nijuppun sugi ni ie o demasu.

Eki made arukimasu.

Eki no mae kara basu ni norimasu.

Soko kara daigaku made basu de sanjuppun gurai kakarimasu.

Kuji sukoshi mae ni daigaku ni tsukimasu.

Gozen no kurasu wa kuji kara jūniji made desu.

Translation

I get up at seven o'clock in the morning.

First of all, I listen to the news on the radio.

About eight o'clock I eat breakfast.

Breakfast is toast and coffee.

I leave the house at twenty past eight.

I walk to the station.

In front of the station I board the bus.

From there to the university it takes about thirty minutes.

I arrive at the university a little before nine o'clock.

The morning classes are from nine until twelve o'clock.

Lesson 8

Akiko's daily schedule continued

英語のクラスは毎日あります。
英文学の授業は木曜日にあります。
英会話のクラスは月曜日と水曜日にあります。

昼ごはんは大学の食堂で食べます。

水曜日の午後はテニスをします。
土曜日の午後はクラブ活動をします。

夕方、六時ごろ家に帰ります。

夕食は七時半からです。夜はたいていテレビを見ます。それから新聞や本を読みます。時々、友達に手紙を書きます。

十一時半ごろ寝ます。

8.1 'To have a class'

> 英語のクラスは毎日あります。
> 英文学の授業は木曜日にあります。

Take care to note the difference between the Japanese sentence here and the English translation 'I have an English class every day.' First of all, the use of topicalisation means that the Japanese is more like 'English classes: there are (classes) every day'. Secondly, by analogy with the English, you might be tempted to look for a verb meaning 'to have'. Japanese expresses it quite differently with the equivalent of 'English classes: every day are'. This is the first example of a kind of stative construction involving possession that is treated in some detail in 12.2 and that will become very familiar to you in due course. Note that with general words such as 毎日, and 朝, as you saw in 7.1, no particles are needed, but when a specific day is mentioned, like Thursday, the particle に must be used.

8.2 Days of the week

英会話のクラスは月曜日と水曜日にあります。

The days of the week are as follows. Note that the order is 'moon', 'fire', 'water', wood', 'metal', 'earth' and 'sun'.

月曜日	げつようび	Monday
火曜日	かようび	Tuesday
水曜日	すいようび	Wednesday
木曜日	もくようび	Thursday
金曜日	きんようび	Friday
土曜日	どようび	Saturday
日曜日	にちようび	Sunday

'What day of the week is it?' is 何 (なん) 曜日ですか.

曜日 is the first example you have had of a mixed set of readings, mixed in the sense that よう is the *on* 音 reading of 曜 and ひ or び is the *kun* 訓 reading of 日. This kind of compound is not uncommon.

When you romanise an expression like this you should write *nan'yōbi* rather than *nanyōbi*; the apostrophe is used to indicate that you are dealing with the two sounds *nan* + *yō*, not *na* + *nyō*.

8.3 は as topic or contrast?

英文学の授業は木曜日にあります。
水曜日の午後はテニスをします。
土曜日の午後はクラブ活動をします。

We have already seen a number of examples of the subject being topicalised by replacing the subject marker が with は. 英文学の授業は木曜日にあります can be regarded as another example of this type of sentence. However, it is also possible to interpret the は here as implying a contrast: if, for example, the speaker meant to single out the English literature classes from other classes. As we noted in 6.4, the difference is largely one that can be decided by context. If contrast were meant here, it would be signalled by a slight stress on the words 英文学の授業は. In the other two sentences, however, the words marked by は are not subjects at all. In these cases the subject, namely 'I', has been omitted. As in the first sentence, it is possible to regard the function of は here either as a topicaliser or a contrast marker, but it would be more natural to consider that in both of these cases は is implying a contrast; 水曜日の午後, for example, as opposed to other afternoons in the rest of the week.

Note the useful word する/します here meaning 'do'. It is about as ubiquitous as its English counterpart.

8.4 The particle で

昼ごはんは大学の食堂で食べます。

で marks the location at which an activity takes place:

台所でお茶を飲みます。
We drink tea in the kitchen.

駅で母を待ちます。
I will wait for my mother at the station.

フランスでピカソの絵を見ます。
We will look at Picasso's paintings in France.

Note how this usage differs from that of the に of location, which is used when existence rather than activity is involved. This can be somewhat tricky at times and will be taken up again later.

8.5 The linking particle や

それから新聞や本を読みます。

Similar to と (3.5), the particle や links nouns together, but it carries with it the extra nuance that the list is not exhaustive: りんごやみかん 'apples and oranges and so on'. If you wish to emphasise this fact, you can also use the word など, which means 'and so on' or 'etc.'

犬やねこ
dogs and cats

山や川や林
mountains, rivers and woods

ジョンやマリーなどが来ます。
John, Marie (and some others) are coming.

Note that the last や at the end of a long list is deleted, whereas the last と is optional.

マーケットで野菜やくだものを買う。
マーケットで野菜とくだもの(と)を買う。
I buy vegetables and fruit at the market.

8.6 A note on orthography

時々、友達に手紙を書きます。

When one *kanji* 漢字 is repeated in succession to form one word as here, 時時, the second 漢字 is replaced by the 'repeater' sign 々. Some common examples:

人々	ひとびと	people
山々	やまやま	mountains
日々	ひび	every day, days

Key to sentences

Romanisation

Eigo no kurasu wa mainichi arimasu.
Eibungaku no jugyō wa mokuyōbi ni arimasu.
Eikaiwa no kurasu wa getsuyōbi to suiyōbi ni arimasu.
Hirugohan wa daigaku no shokudō de tabemasu.
Suiyōbi no gogo wa tenisu o shimasu.
Doyōbi no gogo wa kurabu katsudō o shimasu.
Yūgata, rokuji goro ie ni kaerimasu.
Yūshoku wa shichijihan kara desu. Yoru wa taitei terebi o mimasu. Sore kara shinbun ya hon o yomimasu.
Tokidoki, tomodachi ni tegami o kakimasu.
Jūichijihan goro nemasu.

Translation

I have an English class every day.
The English literature lecture is on Thursday.

English conversation classes are on Monday and Wednesday.
I eat lunch in the university cafeteria.
On Wednesday afternoons I play tennis.
On Saturday afternoons I join in club activities.
In the evenings, I go home about six o'clock.
Supper is from half past seven. In the evening I usually watch television. And then I read a newspaper or a book or something.
Occasionally, I write a letter to a friend.
I go to bed about half past eleven.

Lesson 9

Tadashi gives us a description of his family. Study this Yamakawa family chart and the prose passage that follows:

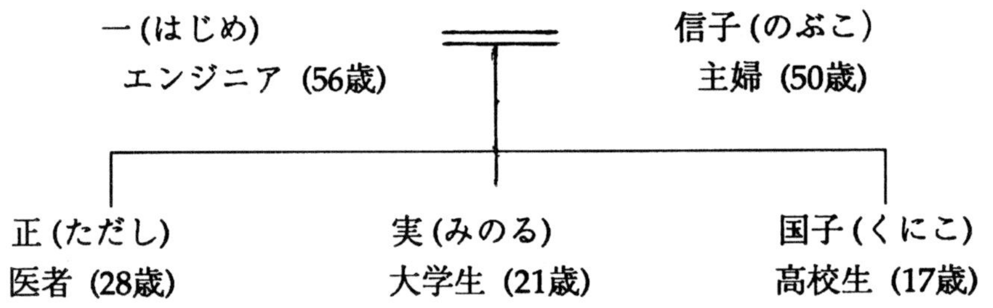

私の家族はみんなで五人です。父と母のほかに弟が一人と妹が一人います。父はエンジニアです。一年に二回仕事でイギリスに行きます。父の部屋にはコンピューターが二台もあります。弟は二十一歳です。京都大学の学生です。休みには友達と旅行に行きます。妹はまだ高校生です。毎日三時間もピアノの練習をします。私は医者です。朝から晩まで大学病院で働きます。時々夜も仕事をします。休みの日にはよく母と散歩します。

9.1 Numerical classifiers

> 私の家族はみんなで五人です。
> 一年に二回仕事でイギリスに行きます。
> 父の部屋にはコンピューターが二台もあります。

Every object in Japanese has a descriptive classifier which is used when that object is counted. It is as if one always had to say 'three head of cattle' rather than 'three cows'. There are many such classifiers in the language but fortunately some of them are shared between a number of similar objects. A short list follows:

人 (にん)	'people' (Note the exceptions ひとり 'one person' and ふたり 'two people')
歳、才 (さい)	'years old' (Note the irregular はたち for 'twenty')
本 (ほん)	long cylindrical objects, pencils, pens etc.
台 (だい)	cars, bicycles, television sets, computers etc.
個 (こ)	small things, apples, oranges, potatoes etc.
回 (かい), 度 (ど)	'times'
時間 (じかん)	'hours'
日 (にち)	'days'
週間 (しゅうかん)	'weeks'
ヶ月 (かげつ)	'months'
ヶ月間 (かげつかん)	'months'
年 (ねん)	'years'
年間 (ねんかん)	'years'
円 (えん)	'yen'
グラム	'grams'
キロ	'kilograms'
センチメートル	'centimetres'
メートル	'metres'

The question word for these is 何 (なん): 何人、何台、何時間 etc., with two exceptions: 何歳 (なんさい) 'how old' can also be expressed as いくつ and the word for 'how much' is いくら. The set of numbers used with these classifiers is, in the main, the いち、に、さん set (see 4.7) with which you should now be familiar, but the pronunciation of these combinations is not entirely straightforward, so the student is referred to appendix III for a full listing.

9.2 Using classifiers

There are two ways of combining a noun with its classifier: either りんごは三個あります, where the numeral + classifier come immediately after the noun, or 三個 (の) りんごがあります. To make the above sentences interrogative, replace 三個 with the interrogative noun meaning 'how many', namely 何個 (なんこ), and add か at the end of the sentence:

either　　りんごは何個ありますか。
or　　何個のりんごがありますか。

9.3 Idiomatic use of に to express frequency

一年に二回

Further examples:

一日に三時間	three hours a day
二ヶ月に一回	once every two months
三年に一度	once every three years

9.4 で indicating 'reason' or 'cause'

仕事でイギリスに行きます。

Study the following idiomatic phrases:

仕事で日本へ行く。
Go to Japan on business

病気で学校を休む。
Be absent from school on account of illness

9.5 Further use of も for emphasis

コンピューターが二台もあります。
毎日三時間もピアノの練習をします。

In addition to the inclusive usage, も can also be used to place strong emphasis on the word it follows, especially in conjunction with numerical classifiers.

来年はヨーロッパに三回も行きます。
I will go to Europe *three times* next year.

9.6 The particle と meaning 'with'

休みには友達と旅行に行きます。
休みの日にはよく母と散歩します。

We have already met the particle と joining nouns together (3.5). と is also used to mean 'with' when two animate nouns are involved:

私はよく弟とキャンプに行きます。
I often go camping with my younger brother.

When 'with' is elaborated as 'together with,' the Japanese phrase is いっしょに:

(私は) 母といっしょに買物をします。
I'll do the shopping with mother.

If the と meaning 'and' is used, then one gets a sentence like:

> 母と私はいっしょに買物をします。
> My mother and I will go shopping together.

9.7 Noun + に行く

休みには友達と旅行に行きます。

This pattern is very commonly used to express the idea of going 'to do something':

旅行に行く。	go on a trip
買物に行く。	go shopping
ピクニックに行く。	go on a picnic
キャンプに行く。	go camping
ジョギングに行く。	go jogging

9.8 Verbal nouns

ピアノの練習をします。 仕事をします。 散歩します。

In the previous lesson you were introduced to native Japanese verbs. There is in addition a large set of verbs that are formed by taking a noun, usually one of Chinese origin, and adding the verb する 'do'. (From now on when verbs are discussed in these notes they will usually be quoted in their plain form.) We shall call these verbal nouns. They include the following:

勉強 (べんきょう) する	study
旅行 (りょこう) する	travel
料理 (りょうり) する	cook
練習 (れんしゅう) する	practise
散歩 (さんぽ) する	go for a walk
質問 (しつもん) する	ask a question
運動 (うんどう) する	take exercise
発音 (はつおん) する	pronounce
買物 (かいもの) する	do the shopping
病気 (びょうき) する	be ill
仕事 (しごと) する	work
電話 (でんわ) する	telephone
運転 (うんてん) する	drive

Provided that no other object is present, these verbal nouns can also be treated as the object of the verb する and marked with を:

日曜日も仕事をする。
Work on Sundays as well

日本語の発音の練習をする。
Practise Japanese pronunciation

毎日三十分運動をする。
Take exercise half an hour a day

However, when there is an object marked by を already present in the sentence these verbal nouns must remain intact. For instance, both 日本語の歌を練習する and 日本語の歌の練習をする are correct, but one cannot say: *日本語の歌を練習をする.[1]

1. Note the convention that any sentence marked with an asterisk in this textbook is ungrammatical and is being used purely for illustrative purposes.

Key to passage

Romanisation

Watakushi no kazoku wa minna de gonin desu. Chichi to haha no hoka ni otōto ga hitori to imōto ga hitori imasu. Chichi wa enginia desu. Ichinen ni nikai shigoto de Igirisu ni ikimasu. Chichi no heya ni wa konpyūtā ga nidai mo arimasu. Otōto wa nijūissai desu. Kyōto daigaku no gakusei desu. Yasumi ni wa tomodachi to ryokō ni ikimasu. Imōto wa mada kōkōsei desu. Mainichi sanjikan mo piano no renshū o shimasu. Watakushi wa isha desu. Asa kara ban made daigaku byōin de hatarakimasu. Tokidoki yoru mo shigoto o shimasu. Yasumi no hi ni wa yoku haha to sanpo shimasu.

Translation

Altogether there are five people in my family. As well as my father and mother, I have a younger brother and a younger sister. My father is an engineer. Twice a year he goes to Britain on business. There are *two* computers in my father's room. My younger brother is twenty-one years old. He is a a student at Kyōto University. During the holidays he goes on trips with his friends. My younger sister is still a high school student. She practises the piano for at least three hours every day. I am a doctor. I work from morning to night at the university hospital. Sometimes I even work at night. On days off I often go for a walk with my mother.

Lesson 10

John goes to a JR reservation office (みどりの窓口 *midori no madoguchi*) in Tōkyō Station to buy a ticket on the Super Express (*shinkansen*) to Kyōto.

駅員	次の方どうぞ。
ジョン	京都までの新幹線のきっぷを下さい。
駅員	指定席ですか、自由席ですか。
ジョン	指定席券はいくらですか。
駅員	五百円です。
ジョン	それでは指定席をお願いします。
駅員	はい。いつのきっぷですか。
ジョン	来週の水曜日の午前十時発ひかり11号をお願いします。
駅員	ええと、来週の水曜日は十月十日ですね。午前中のひかりは全部いっぱいです。
ジョン	それでは十一日はどうですか。
駅員	ひかり11号はいっぱいですが、次のひかり79号はどうですか。十時四分発です。京都へは十二時四十六分着です。
ジョン	はい、それでけっこうです。
駅員	お一人ですか。
ジョン	はい、そうです。
駅員	はい、どうぞ。乗車券と指定席特急券で 1,2970 円になります。
ジョン	どうも。

John pays 1,5000 yen.

駅員	それでは 2030 円のおつりです。ありがとうございました。

Comment

When the Japanese rail network was 'privatised' in 1988, the overall name devised for the group that emerged was JR (pronounced ジェーアール), which stands for Japan Rail. The national system had previously been known as 国鉄 (こくてつ). JR is divided into regions, each with its own extended name: JR 東日本 (read ひがしにほん), for example, which serves Tōkyō and its region.

Despite the fact that this particular phonetic combination of foreign letters is definitely un-Japanese and awkward to pronounce, it seems to have been accepted because of its 'modern' feel. The privatisation is only partial, of course, and one can still buy tickets to anywhere in Japan on the national network at any JR station. The same is not true for the many truly private railways in Japan, which are more localized. To buy tickets for the Super Express (新幹線), you either have to go to a travel bureau or to a station that has a *midori no madoguchi* ('green window'). This system of high-speed lines is gradually expanding throughout the country, because it brings such a dramatic reduction in travel times. The express that runs between Tōkyō and Kyōto (and on to Ōsaka) is known as the 東海道新幹線, named after the Tōkaidō, the old trunk road along the Eastern seaboard.

In the example here, John needs three types of ticket: a Tōkyō–Kyōto fare (乗車券), an express fare (特急券) and a seat reservation (指定席), although the last two may be combined. If he did not want to bother with a reservation and preferred to trust to luck that he could get a free seat (自由席), and if he was actually in Tōkyō station, he could obtain a ticket at an automatic machine. If he wants a non-smoking seat, he will have to ask for a 禁煙車 (きんえんしゃ).

10.1 Noun + を下さい

きっぷを下さい。

下(くだ)さい is the imperative form of the verb 下さる, which will be dealt with in detail in a later lesson. At this point simply learn that when 下さい is added to a noun or nouns it means 'please give me...' The particle を, which marks the object, may well disappear in colloquial speech. Observe the use of numerical classifiers in the following examples:

たまご(を)一ダース下さい。
Please give me a dozen eggs.

220円の切手を八枚下さい。
Please give me eight 220 yen stamps.

あしたの六時ごろお電話を下さい。
Please give me a ring tomorrow around six thirty.

10.2 Noun + をお願いします

それでは指定席をお願いします。

We saw お願いします in 3.3 meaning 'please'. It works in a similar fashion to 下さい, coming directly after a noun with the object marker を.

コーヒーをお願いします。
Please give me a cup of coffee.

コピーを十六枚お願いします。
Please make sixteen copies.

10.3 'When'

いつのきっぷですか。

いつ is an interrogative noun meaning 'when?' You can see here how useful the particle の can be at times. Here it is linking the interrogative to the noun 'ticket' in economical fashion: *lit*. 'when ticket?' The closest English equivalent is probably: 'A ticket for when?'

10.4 Train names and numbers

午前十時発ひかり11号

First of all, take note of the way 'departing at' is expressed. The time is followed immediately by the character 発 (はつ) 'leaving', read in the *on*. Most express trains are known by a name, which tells you their route, and a number. The trains on the 東海道新幹線 are called either ひかり, 'Light', stopping at Nagoya and Kyōto only, or こだま, 'Echo', stopping at many intermediate stations. The word for 'number' in this context is 号 (ごう), not 番. There is not much difference between these two words for 'number' and the decision to use one rather than the other is more a matter of usage; lines and platforms will need 番 for instance. Both words are short for the word you have already learned in connection with telephone numbers: 番号. Do *not* make the mistake of thinking that these are actually numerical classifiers: they are different ways of expressing the concept of 'number X'; they are not a way of counting the object concerned. The usual classifier for trains (rather than the engines themselves) is in fact 本, based on the way trains are listed vertically in the timetables.

10.5 Dates

来週の水曜日は十月十日ですね。

Months are expressed by adding the suffix 月(がつ) to the number, and there are no irregular sound changes.

一月	いちがつ	January	五月	ごがつ	May
二月	にがつ	February	六月	ろくがつ	June
三月	さんがつ	March	七月	しちがつ	July
四月	しがつ	April	八月	はちがつ	August

九月	くがつ	September	十一月	じゅういちがつ	November
十月	じゅうがつ	October	十二月	じゅうにがつ	December

Be careful! 一月 does *not* mean 'one month' but 'January'. Refer back to 9.1 to find out how to say 'one month'.

Days of the month are somewhat more complicated and involve a second set of numbers, two of which (よん and なな) we have already met. You will see that they are simple to write:

一日	ついたち	1st	十六日	じゅうろくにち	16th
二日	ふつか	2nd	十七日	じゅうしちにち	17th
三日	みっか	3rd	十八日	じゅうはちにち	18th
四日	よっか	4th	十九日	じゅうくにち	19th
五日	いつか	5th	二十日	はつか	20th
六日	むいか	6th	二十一日	にじゅういちにち	21st
七日	なのか	7th	二十二日	にじゅうににち	22nd
八日	ようか	8th	二十三日	にじゅうさんにち	23rd
九日	ここのか	9th	二十四日	にじゅうよっか	24th
十日	とおか	10th	二十五日	にじゅうごにち	25th
十一日	じゅういちにち	11th	二十六日	にじゅうろくにち	26th
十二日	じゅうににち	12th	二十七日	にじゅうしちにち	27th
十三日	じゅうさんにち	13th	二十八日	にじゅうはちにち	28th
十四日	じゅうよっか	14th	二十九日	にじゅうくにち	29th
十五日	じゅうごにち	15th	三十日	さんじゅうにち	30th

The first term in this series is quite irregular. It is not in fact a number at all but means 'moon rising'. 2nd to 10th are formed by adding the suffix 日, read か here rather than にち, to what is in fact a set of original Japanese numbers that will be studied in more detail in due course. Note that this か also appears in 14th and 24th, and that 20th is again quite irregular. 'What day (of the month) is it?' is expressed as 何日 (なんにち) ですか, and 'What month is it?' is expressed as 何月 (なんがつ) ですか.

Make sure that you differentiate clearly between the two concepts of date on the one hand and duration of time on the other.

date:

九月一日 (ついたち) です。

It's September 1st.

duration:

一日 (いちにち) 四時間勉強する。

I study four hours a day.

十月十日から十ヶ月フランスに行きます。
I'll go to France from October 10th for ten months.

10.6 どう

それでは十一日はどうですか。

どう means 'how'. Learn this example as an idiomatic phrase, 'In that case, how about...?'

10.7 が as a conjunctive marker

ひかり11号はいっぱいですが、次のひかり79号はどうですか。

が can be used as a sentence particle to link two clauses which contrast with each other in some way. Note how it comes at the end of the first phrase, straight after the verb. It is usually translatable as 'but'. Almost every conjunctive operates at the end of the phrase in this way, and as a result it is not difficult to add on further sections. You will find that Japanese sentences have a tendency to keep expanding.

10.8 Two more idioms with で

> それでけっこうです。
> 乗車券と指定席特急券で 1,2970 円になります。

Note the use of the particle で in these two phrases. In the first case we are dealing with それで in the sense of 'with that, it's fine'. Distinguish this from the idiomatic use of それでは 'in that case' in 10.6 above. In the second example it is a question of adding up and 'making something': 'with X and Y, that comes to...' This use of the verb になる in this sense of 'comes to' with figures is quite common.

Key to conversation

Romanisation

Ekiin	Tsugi no kata dōzo.
Jon	Kyōto made no shinkansen no kippu o kudasai.
Ekiin	Shiteiseki desu ka, jiyūseki desu ka.
Jon	Shiteisekiken wa ikura desu ka.
Ekiin	Gohyaku en desu.
Jon	Sore de wa shiteiseki o o-negai shimasu.
Ekiin	Hai. Itsu no kippu desu ka.
Jon	Raishū no suiyōbi no gozen jūji hatsu Hikari jūichigō o o-negai shimasu.
Ekiin	Ēto, raishū no suiyōbi wa jūgatsu tōka desu ne. Gozenchū no hikari wa zenbu ippai desu.
Jon	Sore de wa jūichinichi wa dō desu ka.
Ekiin	Hikari jūichigō wa ippai desu ga, tsugi no Hikari nanajūkyūgō wa dō desu ka. Jūji yonpun hatsu desu. Kyōto e wa jūniji yonjūroppun chaku desu.
Jon	Hai, sore de kekkō desu.
Ekiin	O-hitori desu ka.
Jon	Hai, sō desu.

Ekiin	Hai, dōzo. Jōshaken to shiteiseki tokkyūken de ichiman nisen kyūhyaku nanajūen ni narimasu.
Jon	Dōmo.
Ekiin	Sore de wa nisen sanjūen no o-tsuri desu. Arigatō gozaimashita.

Translation

Attendant	Next please.
John	A Super Express ticket to Kyōto please.
Attendant	With a seat reservation or without?
John	How much is a reserved seat ?
Attendant	Five hundred yen.
John	In that case I'll have a reserved seat please.
Attendant	Certainly. When is the ticket for?
John	For Wednesday of next week. Hikari No. 11 departing at ten a.m. please.
Attendant	Let me see now. Wednesday of next week is October the tenth, isn't it? All the morning Hikari are full.
John	What about the eleventh then?
Attendant	Hikari No. 11 is full, but how about the next one, No. 79? Departing at four minutes past ten and arriving in Kyōto at twelve forty-six.
John	That will do fine.
Attendant	Just one, is it?
John	Yes please.
Attendant	Here you are then. With the ticket and an express seat reservation that comes to 12,970 yen.
John	Thank you.
Attendant	That makes change of 2,030 yen. Thank you very much.

Lesson 11

John visits Yamakawa's younger brother Minoru in Kyōto. They meet each other in front of Kyōto University.

ジョン	失礼ですが、山川正さんの弟さんの実さんですか。
実	はい、山川実です。
ジョン	始めまして、ジョン・スミスです。どうぞよろしく。
実	始めまして、こちらこそどうぞよろしく。京都は初めてですか。
ジョン	そうです。古い町ですね。
実	そうですね。でも新しいビルやアパートもたくさんありますよ。
ジョン	実さんの家はどこですか。
実	私の下宿まではここから車で二十分ぐらいかかります。
ジョン	実さんの車はこれですか。
実	いいえ、私のはあの赤いのです。
ジョン	ずいぶん大きな車ですね。
実	ジョンさんのはどんな車ですか。
ジョン	私のはとても小さい車です。
実	何色ですか。
ジョン	青です。

11.1 'Excuse me...'

失礼ですが

You have already met 失礼 in 5.11 and 6.7. This is just another polite way of interrupting someone or catching their attention.

11.2 Descriptive verbs

(京都は) 古い町ですね。

There is a temptation to assume that because the word 'old' in the English sentence 'Kyōto is an old town' is an adjective, its Japanese counterpart here, 古い, is also an adjective; but this temptation should be resisted. It is in fact a kind of verb and inflects accordingly: 古い means 'is old' and so 古い町 is literally 'a town which is old'. As explained in 2.1, modifiers precede the noun. You should have no difficulty distinguishing these verbs from other verbs because they all end in the vowel い. We shall call them 'descriptive verbs'. Study the following examples:

新しいビル	new building
赤い車	red car
高い山	high mountain
高いコンピューター	expensive computer
安い時計	cheap watch
大きいつくえ	large desk
大きな川	large river
小さいかぎ	small key

Note that the descriptive verbs 大きい and 小さい sometimes become 大きな and 小さな when they are used in the noun-modifying position as seen above (see 13.1 for further details).

11.3 の as a noun substitute, 'the one'

実さんの車はこれですか。
私のはあの赤いのです。

In Japanese, just as in English, it is common practice to avoid constant repetition of nouns; the particle の can be used in such cases as a substitute. Look at the following example:

木村:	これは和子さんの車ですか。
Kimura:	Is this car yours, Kazuko?
和子:	いいえ、それは正さんのです。あの古いのが私のです。
Kazuko:	No, that is Tadashi's. The old one over there is mine.

First make sure you understand the difference between the use of の as a possessive here (in 和子さんの車 'Kazuko's car') and as a noun substitute (in あの古いのが 'that old one'). But then what about the use of の in 正さんのです and 私のです? This usage has already been touched on in 2.1, where it was explained that the second noun (here 車) has been omitted. 古い, being a descriptive verb, can modify the nominal の directly but 正さん and 私, being nouns, cannot; they need an 'extra' の to be able to act as modifier. Hence 正さんのです can be analysed as 正さんの (の) です, where the first の is possessive ('Tadashi's') and the second, which always drops, is the noun substitute ('one').

11.4 Colours

あの赤いのです。
何色ですか。青です。

Colour terms, as we have seen above, are often found as descriptive verbs but many also often have a nominal equivalent.

verb	*nominal*	*meaning*
青い	青 (あお)	blue
赤い	赤 (あか)	red
白い	白 (しろ)	white

黒い	黒 (くろ)	black
黄色い	黄色 (きいろ)	yellow
茶色い	茶色 (ちゃいろ)	brown

These nominal equivalents must be used in the following cases:

(a) When the colour itself is actually named.

山下さんの自動車は何色ですか。
What colour is Yamashita's car?

黒です。
Black.

(b) When one colour is itself modified.

うすい青のびんせん
light-blue letter-paper

こい赤のセーター
dark-red jersey

By no means all colours, however, can be found in this group of descriptive verb/noun sets. Many others appear purely in the form of nouns and they are of two main types:

(c) those that must be formed in conjunction with the word 色 (いろ)

灰 (はい)	ash	灰色	grey	灰色の空	a grey sky
桃 (もも)	peach	桃色	pink	桃色の花	a pink flower
水 (みず)	water	水色	light blue	水色のシャツ	light-blue shirt

(d) those that may have the word 色 omitted.

紫 (むらさき)	purple	むらさきの着物	a purple kimono
紺 (こん)	dark blue	こんの制服	dark-blue uniform
緑 (みどり)	green	緑の山	green mountain
茶 (ちゃ)	brown	茶のくつ	brown shoes

11.5 'What colour?'

何色ですか。

Note that the word 何色 is pronounced なにいろ in this particular context, where it means 'what colour?' As a general rule, the character 何 followed by another noun is pronounced なに. Only when combined with a numerical classifier or a suffix denoting time, date etc. (see 9.1), is it pronounced なん. For example:

何人 read なんにん means 'how many people?'
何人 read なにじん means 'which nationality?'
何色 read なんしょく means 'how many colours?'
何色 read なにいろ means 'what colour?'

11.6 Adverbial modifiers (1)

ずいぶん大きな車ですね。
私のはとても小さい車です。

There is a class of Japanese words which operates much in the same fashion as adverbs in English. Three are introduced here because they are often used to modify descriptive verbs: とても 'very', ずいぶん 'very' and だいぶ 'fairly'. See 15.2 for further uses of these adverbial modifiers.

これはとてもおいしいお酒ですね。
This is a very tasty sake, isn't it!

ずいぶん長い小説ですね。
This is a fairly long novel, isn't it!

だいぶ古いビルですね。
This is a fairly old building, isn't it!

11.7 どんな

ジョンさんのはどんな車ですか。

どんな means 'what kind?' It is another form of prenoun, in that it can be linked to nouns without an intervening particle. Other words in the same set, such as こんな, そんな and あんな, will be introduced in due course.

Key to conversation

Romanisation

Jon	Shitsurei desu ga, Yamakawa Tadashi san no otōto-san no Minoru-san desu ka.
Minoru	Hai, Yamakawa Minoru desu.
Jon	Hajimemashite, Jon Sumisu desu. Dōzo yoroshiku.
Minoru	Hajimemashite. Kochira koso dōzo yoroshiku. Kyōto wa hajimete desu ka.
Jon	Sō desu. Furui machi desu ne.
Minoru	Sō desu ne. Demo atarashii biru ya apāto mo takusan arimasu yo.
Jon	Minoru-san no ie wa doko desu ka.
Minoru	Watakushi no geshuku made wa koko kara kuruma de nijuppun gurai kakarimasu.
Jon	Minoru-san no kuruma wa kore desu ka.
Minoru	Iie, watashi no wa ano akai no desu.
Jon	Zuibun ōki na kuruma desu ne.
Minoru	Jon-san no wa donna kuruma desu ka.
Jon	Watakushi no wa totemo chiisai kuruma desu.
Minoru	Nani iro desu ka.
Jon	Ao desu.

Translation

John	Excuse me, are you Yamakawa Tadashi's younger brother Minoru?
Minoru	Yes, I'm Yamakawa Minoru.
John	How do you do? I'm John Smith. Pleased to meet you.
Minoru	How do you do? Pleased to meet you too. Is this your first time in Kyōto?
John	That's right. It's an old city isn't it?
Minoru	Yes, it is. But there are a lot of new buildings and apartments too you know.
John	Where do you live?
Minoru	It takes about twenty minutes to get to my lodgings from here by car.
John	Is this your car here?
Minoru	No, mine is that red one.
John	It's a pretty big car isn't it!
Minoru	What about yours?
John	Mine is a very small car.
Minoru	What colour is it?
John	Blue.

Lesson 12

John and Minoru visit a temple in Kyōto.

ジョン	京都はいいところですね。 美しいお寺や神社がたくさんありますね。
実	そうですね。京都は花の季節が特にいいですね。 でも冬は寒いですよ。
ジョン	このお寺の拝観料はいくらですか。
実	三百五十円です。ちょっと高いですね。 このお寺はあまり大きくありませんが庭がおもしろいですよ。
ジョン	木も花もありませんね。
実	そうです。白い小石と岩だけの庭です。

They arrive in front of a souvenir shop.

実	絵はがきを買いますか。
ジョン	うーん。でもこの絵はがきは色があまりよくありませんね。
実	こちらのはどうですか。
ジョン	それはいいですね。秋の京都ですね。こちらの冬のお寺の庭 の絵はがきはずいぶん大きいですね。
実	すみません。この絵はがきはおいくらですか。
店員	小さいのは一枚五十円、大きいのは一枚七十五円です。
ジョン	それではこれとそちらのを二枚づつ下さい。
店員	はい、ありがとうございます。全部で二百五十円 いただきます。

12.1 Descriptive verbs as main verbs

> 花の季節が特にいいですね。
> 冬は寒いですよ。

In the light of the explanation in 11.2, it should come as no surprise to find that these words can occur as main verbs on their own without the addition of a copula. So 青い海 'sea which is blue', hence 'blue sea', yields 海は青い 'the sea is blue'; and 寒い冬 'winter which is cold', hence 'cold winter', yields 冬は寒い 'winter is cold'. Study the following:

> 京都はいいところです。
> Kyōto is a pleasant place.
>
> 花の季節はいいですね。
> Blossom time is pleasant, isn't it?

It is one special feature of these 'descriptive verbs' that they do not have a polite form of their own. In other words, although they often behave like other verbs, they do not have the simple ある/あります transformation that we have met in 7.2. You will often feel the need, however, to use these words in normal polite conversation; the answer is simply to append です as in some of the examples above.

It is worth noting that this is something of a grammatical anomaly because, as a rule, inflected words cannot be followed directly by the copula, namely だ, and certainly the plain citation form of the copula must *never* be used after a descriptive verb: *多いだ or *高いだ are not only unnecessary, they are also ungrammatical. Great care must be taken to understand this point. You will be tempted to produce such ungrammaticalities by analogy with the 'noun + copula' pattern, because both アンナ・カレニーナは長い小説です and アンナ・カレニーナは長い小説だ are grammatically correct. Remember: in the case of descriptive verbs, です is being used *purely in order to make the sentence polite;* the plain form of 冬は寒いです is merely 冬は寒い.

12.2 Stative constructions with は…が

京都は花の季節が特にいいですね。

Study the following examples:

あの女の子は	目が青い。 せが高い。 かみの毛が長い。 頭がいい。

京都は	お寺が多い。 歴史が古い。 工場が少ない。 山が近い。 水がよくない。 物が高い。

Here we introduce one of the most productive structures in Japanese, where topic and subject combine. The overall sense of this structure is 'whole + part' where the part is a comment on the topic. Note again how English finds it difficult to express the concept of topic.

京都はお寺が多い。
lit: As for Kyōto, temples are many.
Kyōto has many temples.

あの女の子は頭がいい。
lit: As for that girl, her brain is good.
She is a clever girl.

What in English is expressed as a possessive relationship with a subject followed by a transitive verb of possession, 'have', is expressed in Japanese as a *stative construction* of the topic + comment variety. You will find that descriptive verbs operate in this kind of environment because they are all stative in nature.

あの女の子はかみの毛が長い。
That girl has long hair.

京都は歴史が古い。
Kyōto has a long (i.e. old) history.

象ははなが長い。
Elephants have long trunks.

This pattern is also one of the very few occasions when the verb ある can be used with animate subjects, in the sense of 'to have'. We touched on this matter in 8.1.

清子さんは妹さんがありますか。
Kiyoko, do you have a younger sister?

Given the English translation here, you might be tempted to use the verb 持つ (もつ), which means 'to have' in the sense of 'possess', 'hold' or 'own'. This is in fact possible in many contexts, but not here, where you have absolutely no control over the 'possession'. You cannot choose whether or not to have a younger sister or parents, for example, so you must use ある here.

12.3 Negative of descriptive verbs

> このお寺はあまり大きくありません。
> この絵はがきは色があまりよくありませんね。

To form the plain negative of these descriptive verbs, first change the final い to く and then add ない. For the polite negative replace ない with ありません.

plain positive	*meaning*	*plain negative*	*polite negative*
大きい	big	大きくない	大きくありません
小さい	small	小さくない	小さくありません
新しい	new	新しくない	新しくありません
古い	old	古くない	古くありません
おもしろい	interesting	おもしろくない	おもしろくありません
高い	high	高くない	高くありません

安い	cheap	安くない	安くありません
長い	long	長くない	長くありません
短かい	short	短かくない	短かくありません
よい (いい)	good	よくない	よくありません

Note particularly how the polite negative of these descriptive verbs is formed, with the ～く form of the verb plus ありません, *not* with the copula でありません. This needs stressing, because yet again you may well be tempted at this early stage to produce a form like *古いではありません, by analogy with 古い → 古いです. This is *incorrect*. Remember that in this latter case です is not being used as a copula; it is merely a convenient way of forming politeness. There is in fact an alternate form of the polite negative, 古くないです, but learn the form listed above first to avoid any confusion. Note the alternate listed in the last line; in modifying position 'good' can be either よい or いい, although in final position いい is the more normal, especially in spoken Japanese.

12.4 Adverbial modifiers (2)

> 特にいいですね。
> ちょっと高いですね。

The adverbial modifiers that were introduced in 11.6 were related to descriptive verbs that were themselves modifying nouns: ずいぶん長い小説. They can also be found related to descriptive verbs when those verbs are at the end of the main sentence. Study the following examples:

特に 'particularly'	とても 'very'
たいへん 'very'	だいぶ 'fairly'

奈良は京都にとても近い。
Nara is very close to Kyōto.

この子はとても頭がいい。
This child is very clever.

日本の夏はたいへん暑い。
Japanese summers are very hot.

駅から家まではだいぶ遠い。
It's quite a long way from the station to my home.

The following adverbs link to negative verb forms only:

あまり 'not very'　　　ちっとも 'not in the least'

この小説はあまりおもしろくない。
This novel is not very interesting.

この写真はあまりよくありませんね。
This photograph is not very good, is it!

今年の冬はちっとも寒くない。
This winter is not in the least cold.

この文法の本はちっともよくない。
This grammar book is not at all satisfactory.

12.5 A note on orthography

絵はがき

This word may look a little odd to you at first because it is half in *kanji* and half in *kana*. It is read *ehagaki*. It would be possible to write it all in *kanji* but this is not common today. Although there are rules of orthography published by the Ministry of Education, such is the complexity of the writing system that you will have to be prepared for a good deal of flexibility. In a textbook such as this one, for instance, it is inevitable that some words that are usually written in *kanji* will in fact be presented to you in *kana* first; but we have tried to reduce these oddities to a minimum.

12.6 The prefix お

この絵はがきはおいくらですか。

You have met the prefix お applied to a variety of nouns for formality or politeness (3.2 and 4.1). お is also sometimes used as here with the two interrogatives いくつ 'how many?' or 'how old?' and いくら 'how much?'

12.7 'per unit'

一枚五十円

To express the idea of 'for' or 'per' there is usually no need for a particle between the unit and the price, especially with simple calculations such as here. With a more complicated situation, however, for example '500 yen per 100 sheets', it is common to insert the particle で: コピーは百枚で五百円です.

12.8 いただきます

全部で二百五十円いただきます。

いただく is a verb meaning 'receive'. Verbs of giving and receiving in Japanese need special treatment because they are intimately bound up with matters of status and speech levels. For the moment just learn this verb as one which means 'receive from a superior'. The shopkeeper uses it here as an equivalent of the English 'that'll be 250 yen please, sir'. It is also used when accepting an offer, or when asking politely for something. The phrase いただきます is also what

Japanese say at the beginning of a meal to express their general gratitude: 'we (are about to) partake'.

Key to conversation

Romanisation

Jon	Kyōto wa ii tokoro desu ne. Utsukushii o-tera ya jinja ga takusan arimasu ne.
Minoru	Sō desu ne. Kyōto wa hana no kisetsu ga toku ni ii desu ne. Demo fuyu wa samui desu yo.
Jon	Kono o-tera no haikanryō wa ikura desu ka.
Minoru	Sanbyaku gojū-en desu. Chotto takai desu ne. Kono o-tera wa amari ōkiku arimasen ga niwa ga omoshiroi desu yo.
Jon	Ki mo hana mo arimasen ne.
Minoru	Sō desu. Shiroi koishi to iwa dake no niwa desu.
Minoru	Ehagaki o kaimasu ka.
Jon	Ūn. Demo kono ehagaki wa iro ga amari yoku arimasen ne.
Minoru	Kochira no wa dō desu ka.
Jon	Sore wa ii desu ne. Aki no Kyōto desu ne. Kochira no fuyu no o-tera no niwa no ehagaki wa zuibun ōkii desu ne.
Minoru	Sumimasen. Kono ehagaki wa o-ikura desu ka.
Ten'in	Chiisai no wa ichimai gojū-en, ōkii no wa ichimai nanajūgo-en desu.
Jon	Sore de wa kore to sochira no o nimai zutsu kudasai.
Ten'in	Hai, arigatō gozaimasu. Zenbu de nihyaku gojū-en itadakimasu.

Translation

John	Kyōto is a lovely place isn't it? There are so many beautiful temples and shrines.
Minoru	So there are. Blossom-time in Kyōto is especially good. But winter is cold.
John	How much is the entrance fee to this temple?
Minoru	350 yen. It's a bit expensive isn't it? This temple isn't very big but the garden is interesting.
John	There aren't any trees or flowers, are there?

Minoru	That's right. It's a garden of just rocks and white pebbles.

Minoru	Will you buy some postcards?
John	Hmm. But the colours on this postcard aren't very good, are they?
Minoru	What about this one here?
John	That's a nice one. It's Kyōto in autumn, isn't it? This postcard of the temple garden in winter is very big, isn't it?
Minoru	Excuse me. How much are these postcards?
Assistant	The small ones are 50 yen each and the large ones are 75 yen each.
John	In that case I'll have two each of this one and that one.
Assistant	Certainly. Thank you very much. That will be 250 yen altogether.

Lesson 13

John visits Minoru's lodgings.

ジョン	実さんの下宿はずいぶん静かなところにありますね。
実	前は静かでしたが、このごろはそうでもありません。
	あまりきれいな部屋ではありませんが、どうぞ。
ジョン	失礼します。
実	こちらへどうぞ。
ジョン	いいお部屋ですね。
実	ええ、でもあまり明るくありません。
	お茶をどうぞ。
ジョン	ありがとうございます。今日はいいお天気でしたね。
実	そうですね。割にあたたかかったですね。
ジョン	実さんは京都が好きですか。
実	ええ、東京も好きですが京都も好きです。
ジョン	時々東京へ帰りますか。
実	二ヶ月に一度ぐらいですね。新幹線がとても便利です。
	ジョンさんは旅行が好きですか。
ジョン	大好きです。でもひまな時間があまりありません。
	正さんは山登りが上手ですが実さんは。
実	ぼくは山は全然だめです。休みの日に近くの公園やお寺に散歩には行きますが。

13.1 Adjectival nouns

静かなところ
きれいな部屋

In addition to the descriptive verbs that we met in lesson 11, there is another set of words that translate into English as adjectives but that operate in a rather different manner in Japanese; these are nouns that modify other nouns by means of the link な. な is a form of the classical copula なる and so the underlying pattern is again one of 'noun which is X': きれいな花 'a flower which is pretty', hence 'a pretty flower'. Do not be misled by the fact that きれい ends in い and so looks at first sight like a descriptive verb. As you will see, this is somewhat of an exception and should cause you no problems. Note that not all nouns can be transformed into descriptive expressions in this way: you will have to learn them as you proceed. Many are Chinese compounds, but there are also some native Japanese expressions and the occasional word of European origin. It is probable that this kind of expression, which we shall call 'adjectival nouns', arose in response to the need for the language to absorb a large number of non-native descriptive words that it could not accomodate within traditional grammatical structures. Some common examples are as follows:

便利 (べんり)	convenient	きれい	pretty, clean
元気 (げんき)	good health	ていねい	polite
丈夫 (じょうぶ)	sturdy	いや	unpleasant
立派 (りっぱ)	splendid	ひま	free time
静か (しずか)	quiet	だめ	no good
変 (へん)	strange	ナンセンス	nonsense
正直 (しょうじき)	honest	ゴージャス	gorgeous
大切 (たいせつ)	important	ショッキング	outrageous
平和 (へいわ)	peace	好(す)き	like
自由 (じゆう)	free	きらい	dislike
上手 (じょうず)	good at	下手 (へた)	bad at

Note that in certain rare cases this form can be found with native Japanese descriptive verbs, so that together with phrases such as 大きい町 we can also have 大きな町, and 小さい村 can also be expressed as 小さな村.

13.2 Adjectival nouns in main verb position

京都が好きですか。
新幹線がとても便利です。

These adjectival nouns can also appear at the end of a clause somewhat like descriptive verbs (12.1): but because they are in essence nouns, they must be followed directly by the modern copula だ or です (depending on whether the context demands a plain or a polite form). This is definitely *not* the case with descriptive verbs, so beware (refer back to 12.3).

あの花はとてもきれいだ。
That flower is very beautiful.

この教室は静かです。
This classroom is quiet.

The negative forms of these expressions are created quite simply by changing だ to ではない and です to ではありません.

このワープロはあまり便利ではありません。
This word processor is not very useful.

この作家は日本ではあまり有名ではない。
This writer is not very well known in Japan.

13.3 The perfective form of the copula and adjectival nouns

前は静かでした

You must now learn another set of inflections, which will allow you to produce sentences that refer to completed actions or states. We shall call this the perfective, in distinction to the form you have already learnt: the imperfective. Often, but not always, this form also marks a past tense. Because it ends in ～た, we shall also call it the ～た form. The first table is for the copula:

	imperfective	*perfective*	
		positive	*negative*
plain	だ	だった	ではなかった
polite	です	でした	ではありませんでした

As you have just learned above, the copula must be used when adjectival nouns appear in final position. The perfective of adjectival nouns is formed as follows:

	imperfective	*perfective*	
		positive	*negative*
plain	静かだ	静かだった	静かではなかった
plain	丈夫だ	丈夫だった	丈夫ではなかった
plain	立派だ	立派だった	立派ではなかった
polite	きれいです	きれいでした	きれいではありませんでした
polite	自由です	自由でした	自由ではありませんでした
polite	上手です	上手でした	上手ではありませんでした

13.4 'Not really the case'

> このごろはそうでもありません。

The phrase そうでもない or そうでもありません should be learned as an idiom. What is in fact happening is that the usual は that you find with the negative has here been replaced by も. The effect of this is to soften the impact of the negation, as with the slightly hesitant English 'really'.

13.5 The perfective form of descriptive verbs

> 割にあたたかかったですね。

To form the ～た form of descriptive verbs, change the final い to かった. Similarly, to form the negative ～た form, change ない to なかった. Study the following examples where both imperfective and perfective have been listed in both plain and polite forms.

Plain forms

imperfective		*perfective*	
positive	*negative*	*positive*	*negative*
新しい	新しくない	新しかった	新しくなかった
古い	古くない	古かった	古くなかった
高い	高くない	高かった	高くなかった
安い	安くない	安かった	安くなかった

Polite forms

The polite forms are by and large what you would expect, but there are a number of points which need care. Pay particular attention to the positive in both the imperfective and the perfective. In both cases you will find that です is simply added to the plain form. In the imperfective this should cause you no trouble, but the perfective can cause problems. A very common mistake is for beginners to try and create the form *新しいでした. This is simply wrong and should be avoided. First create the perfective and then make it polite with a simple です.

imperfective		*perfective*	
positive	*negative*	*positive*	*negative*
新しいです	新しくありません	新しかったです	新しくありませんでした
古いです	古くありません	古かったです	古くありませんでした
高いです	高くありません	高かったです	高くありませんでした
安いです	安くありません	安かったです	安くありませんでした

Now turn your attention to the negative of both the imperfective and the perfective: 新しくありません and 新しくありませんでした. There is in fact an alternative form, but it is not listed here for fear of making the list look even more complicated. Learn this set, but be aware of the alternatives, which are 新しくないです and 新しくなかったです.

13.6 The stative construction with adjectival nouns

実さんは京都が好きですか。

This is an extension of what you learned in 12.2. The は…が construction is also commonly found with adjectival nouns expressing the concept of 'whole + part'. Note how many of these expressions involve a strong possessive relationship between the は and が parts of the sentence. Study the following sets.

あの学生は言葉がていねいです。
That student speaks politely.

あの学生は数学がだめです。
That student is hopeless at maths.

あの学生は体が丈夫ではありません。
That student is not very fit.

あの学生はかみの毛がきれいです。
That student's hair is beautiful.

パリは地下鉄が便利です。
The Paris Metro is very convenient.

パリは春と秋がきれいです。
Spring and autumn in Paris are lovely.

パリは建物が立派です。
Paris has splendid buildings.

13.7 Use of が as a sentence particle

東京も好きですが京都も好きです。 休みの日に近くの公園やお寺に散歩には行きますが。

You saw in lesson 10 how が can be used as a sentence particle to link two clauses which contrast with each other. Given two sentences such as (a) 東京も好きです and (b) 京都も好きです, you can join them with が: 東京も好きですが京都も好きです, 'I like Tōkyō, but I like Kyōto as well.'

Take careful note of the second example sentence, where it might seem that が is in fact ending a sentence. You will come across many situations like this where the sentence has indeed just been left hanging, just as we might end a sentence with 'but' if we are not too sure of how to continue. This kind of truncation is quite common, since it can lend a kind of hesitancy that is taken for politeness.

13.8 近くの

近くの公園

There are a few important exceptions to the rule given in 12.1, that descriptive verbs occur in noun-modifying and predicate position in the same form. The major exceptions are as follows:

as predicate	*as noun-modifier*	*meaning*
近い	近くの or 近い	near, nearby
遠い	遠くの or 遠い	far
多い	多くの	many

So one gets pairs such as the following:

> 私の家は海に近い。
> My home is close to the sea.

but

> 近くの郵便局で切手を買う。
> I buy my stamps at the nearby post office.

Note that the word 少ない meaning 'few' or 'little' can never be used as a noun modifier.

13.9 More on the marker は

ぼくは山は全然だめです。

There are two はs in this sentence. How do they differ? Take the following example:

この小説は長いがおもしろかった。
This novel is long but it was interesting.

This kind of contrast is a simple one, where the topic remains the same and only the descriptive statement about the topic is contrasted. Now look what happens when the contrasted elements multiply.

(a)	象の耳は大きい。
(b)	象の目は小さい。
(a)+(b)	象の耳は大きいが目は小さい。 Elephants' ears are large but their eyes are small.

The function of は in (a) and (b) is that of a simple topic marker; but when the statements are juxtaposed and hence contrasted, は can be seen as having a dual role, that of topic marker within its own clause and that of contrast marker in the context of the whole statement. It is this latter use that takes precedence in such cases. Now observe what happens when the clauses being contrasted are of the は…が, 'whole + part' type.

(c)	和子さんはピアノが上手です。
(d)	夏子さんはピアノが上手ではありません。

(c)+(d) 和子さんはピアノが上手ですが夏子さんは (ピアノが) 上手ではありません。
Kazuko is good at playing the piano but Natsuko is not.

First of all, make absolutely sure that you understand the difference between が used as a subject marker and が used as a sentence marker (here underlined). In (c)+(d), the fact that two clauses are linked in a contrastive relationship again shifts the は in 和子さんは and 夏子さんは from topic marker to contrast marker. Now observe what happens when the elements being contrasted are other than the topic of each clause.

(e) 和子さんはピアノが上手です。
(f) 和子さんはヴァイオリンがあまり上手ではありません。
(e)+(f) 和子さんはピアノは上手ですがヴァイオリンはあまり上手ではありません。
Kazuko is good at playing the piano but she is not very good at playing the violin.

In this case 和子さんは remains as the single topic and a contrast is newly introduced between piano and violin, a contrast which is effected by transforming が into は. This transformation highlights the contrast between the two elements and the use of は here should not hide from you the fact that the underlying structure of the clauses is still the は…が of 'whole + part'.

Key to conversation

Romanisation

Jon	Minoru-san no geshuku wa zuibun shizuka na tokoro ni arimasu ne.
Minoru	Mae wa shizuka deshita ga, kono goro wa sō de mo arimasen. Amari kirei na heya de wa arimasen ga, dōzo.
Jon	Shitsurei shimasu.
Minoru	Kochira e dōzo.
Jon	Ii o-heya desu ne.

Minoru	Ē, demo amari akaruku arimasen. O-cha o dōzo.
Jon	Arigatō gozaimasu. Kyō wa ii o-tenki deshita ne.
Minoru	Sō desu ne. Wari ni atatakakatta desu ne.
Jon	Minoru-san wa Kyōto ga suki desu ka.
Minoru	Ē, Tōkyō mo suki desu ga, Kyōto mo suki desu.
Jon	Tokidoki Tōkyō e kaerimasu ka.
Minoru	Nikagetsu ni ichido gurai desu ne. Shinkansen ga totemo benri desu. Jon-san wa ryokō ga suki desu ka.
Jon	Daisuki desu. Demo hima na jikan ga amari arimasen. Tadashi-san wa yamanobori ga jōzu desu ga, Minoru-san wa.
Minoru	Boku wa yama wa zenzen dame desu. Yasumi no hi ni chikaku no kōen ya o-tera ni sanpo ni wa ikimasu ga.

Translation

John	Your lodgings are in a really quiet area aren't they?
Minoru	It used to be quiet, but these days that's not really the case. It's not such a nice room, but do please come in.
John	Thank you.
Minoru	Come this way.
John	What a lovely room!
Minoru	Maybe, but it's not very light. Have some tea.
John	Thank you very much. It was good weather today, wasn't it?
Minoru	Yes it was. It was relatively warm, wasn't it?
John	Do you like Kyōto?
Minoru	Well, I like Tōkyō, but I like Kyōto as well.
John	Do you go back to Tōkyō sometimes?
Minoru	About once every couple of months. The Super Express is very convenient. Do you like travelling?
John	Very much. But I don't have much free time. Tadashi is very good at mountain climbing; how about you?
Minoru	I'm hopeless when it comes to mountains. On my days off I do go for a walk in the nearby park or temple though.

Lesson 14

John's short account of his trip to Kyōto

十月の半ばに京都へ行った。ユースホステルに二泊、京都大学の近くのお寺に三泊した。正君の弟さんの実君に会った。いっしょにお寺を見たり、郊外をドライブしたりした。木下さんにも会った。去年は同じころ北海道へ行ったがとても寒かった。今年の京都はまだかなりあたたかかった。最後の日は一日中雨が降ったりやんだりしたが、それ以外の日はよいお天気だった。京都は初めてだったがとても気に入った。毎日楽しく過ごした。イギリスの両親と祖母に秋の京都の絵はがきを出した。

14.1 The ～た form of true verbs

十月の半ばに京都へ行った。

We saw in 13.3 that the ～た perfective form expresses both the idea of completed actions or states and the 'past'. You should be clear in your mind about the distinction between tense and aspect. *Tense* specifies the relationship between the time when an action, event or state of affairs occurs and some other time. When that 'other time' is the actual moment of utterance then we talk of absolute tense; when the 'other time' is essentially unconnected to the moment of utterance we talk of relative tense. As we shall see, tense in Japanese can be explained as a combination of the two. At this stage you can assume that a verb in the ～た form is referring to something in the past as seen from the moment of utterance, although later on you will come across grammatical structures where this is clearly not the case. Verbal *aspects*, on the other hand, are different ways of viewing the internal make-up of a situation, irrespective of the position of the speaker; expressions of habitual, progressive or resultative action, for example. The plain citation and the ～た forms of the Japanese verbal system cover both tense and aspect, depending upon context. It is for this reason that we have given them the general titles of imperfective versus perfective. The differences in usage should become clearer as you proceed.

	imperfective		*perfective*
group I	ending in *-u*, *-ru*, *-tsu*		ends in *-tta*
	言う	say	言った
	買う	buy	買った
	会う	meet	会った
	使う	use	使った
	ある	exist	あった
	入る	enter	入った
	乗る	ride	乗った
	待つ	wait	待った
	ending in *-ku*		ends in *-ita*
	書く	write	書いた
	歩く	walk	歩いた
	聞く	listen, ask	聞いた
	ending in *-mu*, *-nu*		ends in *-nda*
	飲む	drink	飲んだ
	読む	read	読んだ
	死ぬ	die	死んだ
	ending in *-su*		ends in *-shita*
	話す	talk	話した
	貸す	lend	貸した
	ending in *-gu*		ends in *-ida*
	泳ぐ	swim	泳いだ
	かぐ	smell, sniff	かいだ
exception:	行く	go	行った

	imperfective		*perfective*
group II	ending in *-ru*		ends in *-ta*
	いる	exist	いた
	出る	go out	出た
	かける	hang	かけた
	見る	see	見た
	寝る	go to bed	寝た
	起きる	get up	起きた
	食べる	eat	食べた

	imperfective		*perfective*
irregular	来る	to come	来(き)た
	する	to do	した

As you will see from these lists, the perfective form of group II and irregular verbs is obtained by adding ～た to the conjunctive form that you met in 7.2. This is also in fact the case with group I verbs, although a number of sound changes have taken place in the modern language that obscure this fact.

The polite form of the perfective is obtained by simply adding ～ました to the conjunctive form.

Examples where it is clearly a matter of past tense:

きのうロンドンへ行きました
Yesterday I went to London.

おとといおもしろい映画を見ました。
The day before yesterday I saw an interesting film.

Examples where the ～た form is being used more for an aspectual marker denoting perfectivity.

もうその新聞は読みました。
I have already read that newspaper.

昔はそろばんで計算しましたが今は電卓を使います。
We used to count on the abacus but we use the calculator these days.

14.2 に会う

正君の弟さんの実君に会った。

As we saw in 7.6, the verb 会う takes に. Take note here that this is the verb that you should use when translating the English 'see' in a sentence such as 'I went to see Mr Yamada', where 'see' in fact means 'meet'. To use the Japanese 見る in such a context would be wrong and might not be understood at all.

14.3 The alternative form

いっしょにお寺を見たり、郊外をドライブしたりした。

The alternative form ～たり is produced by adding り after the ～た form:

会う	→ 会った	→ 会ったり	行く	→ 行った	→ 行ったり
話す	→ 話した	→ 話したり	買う	→ 買った	→ 買ったり
出る	→ 出た	→ 出たり	見る	→ 見た	→ 見たり
来る	→ 来た	→ 来たり	する	→ した	→ したり

This form is used when you wish to link verbs together in an 'I do (did) this and/or this' fashion, the final verb always being followed by する 'to do'.

夏休みには海で泳いだり、山に登ったりする。
During the summer holidays I go swimming in the sea, climbing mountains and so on.

きのうの日曜日は手紙を書いたり、散歩をしたりした。
Yesterday, Sunday, I wrote letters, went for a walk, and so on.

14.4 More on years and dates

> 去年は同じころ北海道へ行ったがとても寒かった。
> 今年の京都はまだかなりあたたかかった。

今年 (ことし) is 'this year', 来年 (らいねん) 'next year', and 去年 (きょねん) or 昨年 (さくねん) 'last year'. 'Which year?' is 何年 (なんねん). Years are counted in two different ways in Japan. You will find the Western system is understood; the numbers are simply followed by the word for year, 年 (ねん): 千九百九十年 (せん きゅうひゃく きゅうじゅう ねん) 'one thousand nine hundred ninety year'. Note that the number 4 coming before 年 is pronounced よ rather than よん, so 1984 is read せん きゅうひゃく はちじゅう よ ねん. Much more common, however, is the indigenous system which operates on what are known as 年号 (ねんごう) 'era names'. Prior to the Meiji Restoration the habit was to change the name of the era frequently because calamities could be warded off by choosing a new auspicious name; but post-Meiji the era name has been coterminous with the Emperor's reign. 1868 was the first year of Meiji, 明治元年 (めいじ がんねん), and the name did not change until he died in 1912, 明治四十五年 (めいじ よんじゅうご ねん). With the accession of his son, the era was renamed 大正 (たいしょう). 1912 is therefore 明治 45 and 大正元年. When Emperor Hirohito came to the throne in 1926, the era was renamed 昭和 (しょうわ); 1988 was 昭和 63. The new era name is 平成 (へいせい). 昭和 dates are quite easy to transform into the Western equivalent: just add 25. For 平成 dates you will have to add 88.

明治	めいじ	(1868–1912)
大正	たいしょう	(1912–1926)
昭和	しょうわ	(1926–1989)
平成	へいせい	(1989–

Study the following synoptic chart:

		past	*present*	*future*
days	*kanji*	昨日	今日	明日
	reading	さくじつ	こんにち	みょうにち
	[colloquial	きのう	きょう	あした]
weeks	*kanji*	先週	今週	来週
	reading	せんしゅう	こんしゅう	らいしゅう
months	*kanji*	先月	今月	来月
	reading	せんげつ	こんげつ	らいげつ
years	*kanji*	去年, 昨年	今年	来年
	reading	きょねん, さくねん	ことし	らいねん

14.5 Adverbial use of descriptive verbs

毎日楽しく過ごした。

The adverbial form of the descriptive verbs is obtained by replacing the final い with く. In this form the descriptive verb can be used to modify other verbs, much in the manner of English adverbs.

きのうの晩は早く寝ました。
I went to bed early last night.

この子はまだ三歳ですが、よく歩きます。
This child is still only three, but he walks well.

You will often find this adverbial く form in conjunction with the verb なる 'to become', in the sense of 'getting...':

このごろ、めっきり寒くなりました。
It's turned really cold recently.

Key to passage

Romanisation

Jūgatsu no nakaba ni Kyōto e itta. Yūsu hosuteru ni nihaku, Kyōto daigaku no chikaku no o-tera ni sanpaku shita. Tadashi-kun no otōto san no Minoru-kun ni atta. Issho ni o-tera o mitari, kōgai o doraibu shitari shita. Kinoshita-san ni mo atta. Kyonen wa onaji koro Hokkaidō e itta ga totemo samukatta. Kotoshi no Kyōto wa mada kanari atatakakatta. Saigo no hi wa ichinichijū ame ga futtari yandari shita ga, sore igai no hi wa yoi o-tenki datta. Kyōto wa hajimete datta ga totemo ki ni itta. Mainichi tanoshiku sugoshita. Igirisu no ryōshin to sobo ni aki no Kyōto no ehagaki o dashita.

Translation

In mid-October I went to Kyōto. I stayed two nights at a youth hostel, and three nights at a temple near Kyōto University. I met Tadashi's younger brother Minoru. We looked at temples together, and went driving into the surrounding countryside. I also saw Miss Kinoshita. Last year at the same time I went to Hokkaidō but it was very cold. This year Kyōto was still quite warm. On the last day it rained on and off all day, but apart from that the weather was good. It was my first visit to Kyōto and I liked it very much. I enjoyed myself every day. I sent postcards of Kyōto in the autumn to my parents and grandmother in England.

Lesson 15

Yamakawa Tadashi's account of his climbing trip to the Japan Alps

朝七時発の急行アルプス二号に新宿駅から乗った。昼前に松本に着いた。そこからバスで上高地まで行った。途中トンネルをたくさん通った。このルートは昔はとても時間がかかったが最近便利になった。上高地からなだらかな道を二時間半ほど歩いたがほとんど人に会わなかった。五時半ごろ山小屋に着いた。そこで偶然に大学時代の友達に会った。次の日は朝とても早く起きた。すばらしいお天気だった。五時すぎに山小屋を出た。その友達といっしょに登った。私達はあまり話をしなかったがとても楽しかった。めずらしい鳥やあざやかな色の高山植物をたくさん見た。昼ごはんにはおにぎりを食べた。途中のどがかわいたが頂上に着くまでほとんど水を飲まなかった。八時間以上も山道を歩いたが少しも疲れなかった。頂上近くの山小屋で泊まった。立派な宿ではなかったが気持がよかった。夜空の星が美しかった。

Comment
Both the last lesson and this one are cast entirely in the plain perfective. Note that this is not a form you will encounter much in polite conversation; this is why the context has been shifted to a written record. As there are no polite endings used here, the effect is of reading a diary entry.

15.1 More on negatives

> ほとんど人に会わなかった。
> 私達はあまり話をしなかった。

So far we have touched on how to form the negative of the copula, of descriptive verbs (12.3, 13.5) and adjectival nouns (13.3). You have also learned that the negative of あります is ありません, and of います is いません. So how are the negatives of true verbs formed? In the polite ～ます form this is very easy: for the imperfective change ～ます to ～ません; for the perfective change ～ました to ～ませんでした.

Polite forms

imperfective		perfective
positive	*negative*	*negative*
会います	会いません	会いませんでした
買います	買いません	買いませんでした
見ます	見ません	見ませんでした
食べます	食べません	食べませんでした
来ます	来ません	来ませんでした
します	しません	しませんでした

The plain forms however undergo different inflections:

	imperfective		perfective
	positive	*negative*	*negative*
group I	ending in *-ru*, *-ku*, etc.	ends in *-ranai*, *-kanai* etc.	ends in *-ranakatta* *-kanakatta* etc.
	入る	入らない	入らなかった
	乗る	乗らない	乗らなかった
	書く	書かない	書かなかった
	聞く	聞かない	聞かなかった
	飲む	飲まない	飲まなかった
	死ぬ	死なない	死ななかった
	話す	話さない	話さなかった
	ending in *-u*	ends in *-wanai*	ends in *-wanakatta*
	会う	会わない	会わなかった
	買う	買わない	買わなかった
exception:	ある	ない	なかった

	imperfective		*perfective*
	positive	*negative*	*negative*
group II	ending in *-ru*	ends in *-nai*	ends in *-nakatta*
	いる	いない	いなかった
	出る	出ない	出なかった
	見る	見ない	見なかった
	食べる	食べない	食べなかった

	imperfective		*perfective*
	positive	*negative*	*negative*
irregular	来(く)る	来(こ)ない	来(こ)なかった
	する	しない	しなかった

15.2 Adverbial use of adjectival nouns

> このルートは…最近便利になった。

We have seen in 14.5 how descriptive verbs are used as adverbs. The same kind of adverb can be obtained from adjectival nouns by changing the ～な to ～に.

急な出発 a sudden departure	急に電車が止まった。 Suddenly the train stopped.
静かな村 a quiet village	あの方はいつもとても静かに話す。 That person always talks very quietly.
便利な道具 useful tool	このあたりは最近とても便利になった。 This area has recently become very convenient.

Note that the meaning of the words can sometimes change. For example, 大切な means 'important' but 大切に used as an adverb means 'with care'.

これは大切な手紙です。
This is an important letter.

兄のカメラは大切に使います。
I use my elder brother's camera with care.

Some adverbs are used only or mainly with negatives:

ほとんど	'hardly', 'almost'
少しも	'not in the least', 'not at all'

祖母はこのごろほとんど外出しません。
My grandmother hardly goes out these days.

その雑誌はもうほとんど読みました。
I have read almost all of that magazine.

かぜが少しもよくならない。
My cold does not get better at all.

少しもおなかがすかない。
I don't feel hungry at all.

15.3 Noun + に as adverb

偶然に大学時代の友達に会った。

The term 'adjectival noun' is reserved for those nouns that take な when they modify other nouns, and we have just seen how these can become adverbs with the addition of に. It is important to remember, however, that only a limited number of nouns can become adjectival in this way. The rest must be linked to another noun by means of の. The word 偶然 'accidental' here is a case in point.

Although it can become an adverb with the addition of に, as here, it cannot act adjectivally with な; it needs to link with の. There are no easy rules to tell you into which category a noun will fall, but you should at least be on your guard.

15.4 Use of the particle に meaning 'for'

昼ごはんにはおにぎりを食べた。

We have met に in 7.1, 7.6, 9.3 and 14.2. A further use of に, meaning 'for' is introduced here:

姉のお誕生日のプレゼントにレコードを買った。
I bought a record for my elder sister's birthday present.

テープレコーダーを発音の練習に使う。
We use a tape recorder for our pronunciation practice.

このくつは私の足にぴったり合う。
These shoes fit my feet perfectly.

Key to passage

Romanisation

Asa shichiji hatsu no kyūkō Arupusu nigō ni Shinjuku eki kara notta. Hiru mae ni Matsumoto ni tsuita. Soko kara basu de Kamikōchi made itta. Tochū tonneru o takusan tōtta. Kono rūto wa mukashi wa totemo jikan ga kakatta ga saikin benri ni natta. Kamikōchi kara nadaraka na michi o nijikanhan hodo aruita ga hotondo hito ni awanakatta. Gojihan goro yamagoya ni tsuita. Soko de gūzen ni daigaku jidai no tomodachi ni atta. Tsugi no hi wa asa totemo hayaku okita. Subarashii o-tenki datta. Goji sugi ni yamagoya o deta. Sono tomodachi to issho ni nobotta. Watashitachi wa amari hanashi o shinakatta ga totemo tanoshikatta. Mezurashii tori ya azayaka na iro no kōzan shokubutsu o takusan mita. Hiru gohan ni wa o-nigiri o tabeta. Tochū nodo ga kawaita ga chōjō ni tsuku made hotondo mizu o nomanakatta. Hachijikan ijō mo yamamichi o aruita ga sukoshi mo tsukarenakatta. Chōjō chikaku no yamagoya de tomatta. Rippa na yado de wa nakatta ga kimochi ga yokatta. Yozora no hoshi ga utsukushikatta.

Translation

At Shinjuku station I boarded the Alps No. 2 express which departs at seven o'clock in the morning. We arrived at Matsumoto before noon. From there I went by bus to Kamikōchi. We passed through many tunnels along the way. In the past this route used to take a very long time but recently it has become easier. From Kamikōchi I walked up a gently sloping path for two and a half hours but I met almost no one. At about half past five I reached the mountain lodge. Quite by chance I met a friend from university days there. The next day I got up very early. The weather was superb. I left the lodge just after five o'clock. I climbed with that friend. We didn't talk much but it was a lot of fun. We saw many unusual birds and much brightly-coloured alpine vegetation. For lunch we ate riceballs. I became thirsty along the way but I hardly drank any water until we reached the summit. We walked in the mountains for more than eight hours but I wasn't a bit tired. We stayed at a mountain lodge near the summit. It wasn't very well equipped but there was a pleasant feeling about it. The stars in the night sky were beautiful.

Lesson 16

Tadashi and John meet again after John's trip to Kyōto

正	今晩は。
ジョン	やあ、正さん、今晩は。おととい京都からもどりました。
正	そうですか。お天気はどうでしたか。
ジョン	最後の一日は雨でしたがあとはいいお天気でした。 正さんは相変わらず週末も仕事をしていましたか。
正	僕もこの週末は仕事がなかったのから久しぶりに山登り に行きました。
ジョン	山はもう寒くありませんでしたか。
正	いや、すばらしい秋晴れだったのでいい週末を過ごしました。
ジョン	正さんの弟さんにも京都で会いましたよ。
正	それはよかった。よく勉強していましたか。
ジョン	さあ...。でもとても元気でした。
正	そうですか。ジョンさん、夕食はまだですか。
ジョン	ええ、これからです。
正	きょうはめずらしくたくさんお金を持っているので私が ごちそうします。
ジョン	ありがとうございます。それは嬉しいですね。

16.1 'Good evening/night'

> 今晩は。

Unlike its English equivalent, this phrase is only used for greeting people in the evening; it is not used when parting. It is complementary in usage to the phrase 今日は, 'hello'.

16.2 The 〜て form

To obtain this form simply replace the perfective 〜た by 〜て.

	plain citation		〜て *form*
group I	ending in *-u, -ru, -tsu*		ends in *-tte*
	言う	say	言って
	買う	buy	買って
	会う	meet	会って
	使う	use	使って
	ある	exist	あって
	入る	enter	入って
	乗る	ride	乗って
	待つ	wait	待って
	ending in *-ku*		ends in *-ite*
	書く	write	書いて
	歩く	walk	歩いて
	聞く	listen, ask	聞いて
	ending in *-mu, -nu*		ends in *-nde*
	飲む	drink	飲んで
	読む	read	読んで
	死ぬ	die	死んで
	ending in *-su*		ends in *-shite*
	話す	talk	話して
	貸す	lend	貸して
	ending in *-gu*		ends in *-ide*
	泳ぐ	swim	泳いで
	かぐ	smell, sniff	かいで
exception:	行く	go	行って

	plain citation		〜て *form*
group II	ending in *-ru*		ends in *-te*
	いる	exist	いて
	出る	go out	出て
	かける	hang	かけて
	見る	see	見て
	寝る	go to bed	寝て
	起きる	get up	起きて
	食べる	eat	食べて

	plain citation		〜て *form*
irregular	来る	to come	来(き)て
	する	to do	して

16.3 Meaning and uses of the 〜て form

> 週末も仕事をしていましたか。

As you will discover, the 〜て form is used in a wide range of constructions. In this lesson we shall investigate the form 〜て + いる. The meaning of 〜ている depends on the nature and semantic properties of the verb and so we shall first have to analyse the verbal system in more detail. Japanese verbs can be divided into two major categories: stative and dynamic.

16.4 Stative verbs

Stative verbs refer to states rather than actions. They include all potential forms (which you will meet later), most descriptive verbs, and the following:

ある	be (existential, inanimate)
いる	be (existential, animate)

要る	be in need of, be necessary
ちがう	be different, differ
分かる	understand
出来る	be capable of

These verbs are not found in the 〜ている form when they are used in a stative sense, because their simple imperfective form indicates present situation. You will see later, however, that in certain circumstances a few of them can be used in dynamic senses too.

16.5 Dynamic verbs

Dynamic verbs refer to actions or processes and they comprise the majority of Japanese verbs. Their imperfective form indicates either future or generic action, but never present situation, which is expressed with 〜ている. Dynamic verbs can in turn be subdivided into two sets: *durative* and *punctual*. Only durative verbs will be dealt with in this lesson.

16.6 Durative verbs

When durative verbs are in the 〜ている form they express progressive action, and when in the 〜ていた form they express progressive action in the past. This set includes such verbs as 待つ, 読む, 書く, and 話す. The point about these verbs is that the action they describe in their basic form is seen as taking place over a period of time. Waiting, reading, writing and talking all take some time to complete, so that when the verb いる, which has the basic meaning of 'being', is added to the 〜て form the progressive nature of the verb is highlighted.

父はタイムスを読む。
My father reads *The Times* (as a habit).

父は新聞を読んでいる。
My father is reading a newspaper (actual action going on).

父は新聞を読んでいた。
My father was reading a newspaper.

あしたシェフィールド大学で日本の政治について話します。
I will talk on Japanese politics tomorrow at Sheffield University.

今ラジオでドイツの首相が貿易について話しています。
The German Prime Minister is talking on foreign trade on the radio now.

16.7 Use of ので and から

この週末は仕事がなかったから久しぶりに
山登りに行きました。
きょうはめずらしくたくさんお金を持って
いるので私がごちそうします。

ので and から are sentence particles denoting causal relation. ので is used either following verbs directly or following nouns and adjectival nouns with な. Note this use of な. Do *not* use だ in this construction.

高かったのでその洋服は買わなかった。
I did not buy that dress because it was expensive.

とてもよいお天気なので散歩に行きます。
As the weather is fine I am going for a walk.

音楽が好きなのでよくレコードを聞きます。
As I like music I often listen to records.

から is used either following verbs directly or following noun + だ.

この洋服は安かったから買った。
I bought this dress because it was cheap.

今日は土曜日だから町はかなり混んでいる。
The town is rather crowded because it is Saturday today.

このワープロはとても便利だから毎日使う。
This word processor is very convenient and so I use it every day.

Both ので and から can be translated 'because', but there are differences, differences which have to do more with style than anything else. In general から is less formal and is much used in conversation. ので is far more common in written Japanese and its use in conversation imparts a slight formal stiffness. It is for this reason that から can be said to carry with it a slightly more assertive tone, as if the connection is being made crystal clear. It may help you to catch the difference in nuance if you remind yourself that ので literally means 'with the fact of…' and から '(starting out) from the fact that…'

Key to conversation

Romanisation

Tadashi	Konban wa.
Jon	Yā, Tadashi-san, konban wa. Ototoi Kyōto kara modorimashita.
Tadashi	Sō desu ka. O-tenki wa dō deshita ka.
Jon	Saigo no ichinichi wa ame deshita ga, ato wa ii o-tenki deshita. Tadashi-san wa aikawarazu shūmatsu mo shigoto o shite imashita ka.
Tadashi	Boku mo kono shūmatsu wa shigoto ga nakatta kara hisashiburi ni yamanobori ni ikimashita.
Jon	Yama wa mō samuku arimasen deshita ka.
Tadashi	Iya, subarashii akibare datta no de ii shūmatsu o sugoshimashita.
Jon	Tadashi-san no otōto-san ni mo Kyōto de aimashita yo.
Tadashi	Sore wa yokatta. Yoku benkyō shite imashita ka.
Jon	Saa…Demo totemo genki deshita.
Tadashi	Sō desu ka. Jon-san, yūshoku wa mada desu ka.
Jon	Ē, kore kara desu.
Tadashi	Kyō wa mezurashiku takusan o-kane o motte iru no de watashi ga gochisō shimasu.
Jon	Arigatō gozaimasu. Sore wa ureshii desu ne.

Translation

Tadashi	Good evening.

John	Hello Tadashi, good evening. I got back from Kyōto the day before yesterday.
Tadashi	Really? How was the weather?
John	It rained the last day but apart from that it was good weather. Were you working over the weekend as usual?
Tadashi	I didn't have any work this weekend either, so I went hiking in the mountains, which I haven't done for a long time.
John	Wasn't it already cold in the mountains?
Tadashi	Not at all. It was marvellous fine autumn weather and so I had a great weekend.
John	Tadashi, I also met your younger brother in Kyōto, you know.
Tadashi	That's good. Was he studying hard?
John	Hm...He was very well though.
Tadashi	I see. John, have you eaten dinner yet?
John	No, not yet.
Tadashi	I've got an unusually large amount of money with me today, so I'll buy you dinner.
John	Thank you very much. That sounds wonderful.

Lesson 17

A telephone conversation between John and Tadashi's mother

ジョン	もしもし。
山川	はい、山川ですが…。
ジョン	今日は。ジョン・スミスです。
山川	あら、ジョンさん、お久しぶり。お元気ですか。
ジョン	はい、おかげさまで。正さんはいますか。
山川	正は朝から病院へ行っていますが。
ジョン	日曜も仕事ですか。
山川	ええ、先週は休んでいましたけれど。病院の新しい電話番号は知っていますか。
ジョン	古いのは知っていますが新しいのはまだ知りません。
山川	ええと、新しいのは…。ここにありました。3772-9514 です。
ジョン	3772-9514 ですね。内線番号は。
山川	さあ、それは分かりません。
ジョン	それじゃ、けっこうです。ありがとうございました。
山川	どういたしまして。
ジョン	それでは失礼します。
山川	さようなら。

Comment

The first word in this passage tells you that John is talking on the 'phone. もしもし is the normal way to open a telephone conversation. In fact it is only encountered in one other situation: when you are trying to get the attention of a waiter or have just entered a shop and no one is at the counter. The fact that it is Mrs Yamakawa who answers the 'phone is made clear in her second response: あら is an exclusively female exclamation.

The conversation above is intentionally simple and is restricted to normal polite forms. In fact, you will find that in Japan people are extremely formal on the telephone and use a plethora of polite formulae, which you will have to learn in due course. The main reason for this is that you cannot see the person on the other end of the line and so you 'overdo' it on purpose. You will notice a high frequency of truncated phrases, typical of natural speech. This is what is happening in Mrs Yamakawa's first response はい、山川ですが, where が (usually pronounced quite lightly with a falling intonation) creates a prefatory statement indicating that the speaker is waiting for the next words of the listener.

17.1 The ～ている form continued: punctual verbs

> 正は朝から病院へ行っています。
> 新しい電話番号は知っていますか。

When punctual verbs are in the ～ている form they express resultative action. In the ～ていた form they express resultative action in the past, although the results of the action need not be still operative at the time of utterance. This set includes verbs like:

知(し)る	know
着(つ)く	arrive
始(はじ)まる	begin
帰(かえ)る	return
覚(おぼ)える	remember, memorise

The point about these verbs is that the action is seen as taking place as an indivisible whole, hence it cannot be analysed any further. Interestingly, and quite at variance with English, some verbs of motion in Japanese such as 行く, 出る and 来る are included in this category; this suggests that motion tends to be seen as a change of state in Japanese rather than something continuous.

(a) 兄は今アメリカに行っています。
My elder brother is now in America.

(b) 兄は去年アメリカに行っていました。
My elder brother was in America last year.

(c) 兄はアメリカにいます。
My elder brother is in America.

(a) does not mean that my elder brother is at this moment on the plane, but that he has arrived there and is still there: he 'has gone'. On the other hand (b), which is set in the past, implies that my elder brother went to America but is no longer there. (c) is simply stating the fact that he is in America. More will be said about this stative/dynamic analysis in due course.

17.2 The verb 知る 'to know'

古いのは知っていますが、新しいのは知りません。

Note that the verb 知る 'to know' is not stative as it is in English (we do not need to say 'I am knowing') but is a punctual verb. 'I know' is therefore expressed in Japanese as 知っています, 'I am now in a state of having got to know.' 知る is also unusual in that the negative is *never* *知っていません but always either 知らない or 知りません, presumably because 'not-knowing' is itself a state.

川田さんの住所は知っていますが電話番号は知りません。
I know Kawada's address but not his telephone number.

17.3 The verbs 聞く and 着る

Some verbs can appear in more than one category, which tells us that these verbs have multiple meanings dependent upon context. Observe that the verbs 聞く and 着る, for instance, can be either durative or punctual.

ラジオで音楽を聞いている。
I am listening to the music on the radio.
[*durative*, hence progressive action]

そのことは聞いています。
I have heard about that.
[*punctual,* hence resultative action]

あの子はとなりの部屋で洋服を着ています。
The child is dressing in the next room.
[*durative,* hence progressive action]

母はめずらしく着物を着ている。
My mother is wearing a kimono, unusually for her.
[*punctual,* hence resultative action]

17.4 The verbs ちがう, 出来る, and 分かる

It is here that we can treat the three verbs ちがう, 出来る and 分かる, which were listed under the stative heading in 16.4.

ちがう. When it means 'to differ' it is stative and is *not* used with ～ている. When it means 'to be wrong' it is punctual and *can* be used with ～ている.

私の考えとあなたの考えはちがう。
My ideas and yours differ.

きみの考えはちがっている。
Your ideas are wrong.

出来る. When it means 'capable of' it is stative and is *not* used with ～ている. When it means 'to be complete, finished' it is punctual and *can* take ～ている.

君はら、り、る、れ、ろ、の発音がちゃんと出来ますか。
Can you pronounce *ra, ri, ru, re, ro* properly?

この作文はとてもよく出来ている。
This composition is very well written.

分かる. When it means 'to understand, to be clear' it is stative and is *not* used with ～ている. When it means 'to be aware of something' it is punctual and takes ～ている.

あの学生は日本語がよく分かります。
That student understands Japanese well.

危険はよく分かっています。
I am well aware of the danger.

17.5 'Thanks to you'

おかげさまで。

This phrase, which literally means something like 'in your shade', is often used as a simple polite answer to a question about the health of you and your family. Try to learn it as an automatic response to such solicitous enquiries.

17.6 けれど

休んでいましたけれど。

In the classical form of the language けれど was a particular verb ending, but now it is best to regard it as a kind of conjunctive marker which is simply added to the verb. It signifies 'although'. You will also find it often contracted to けど.

17.7 Perfective of discovery

ここにありました。

If you are searching for something and have just found it, or if you are standing on the platform and a train arrives, you will use the perfective form of the verb to express the discovery or the surprise. This is either because an action has now been completed or because, as here, the object was there all along; compare the English 'it was here all the time!'

17.8 'Goodbye'

さようなら。

This word must have the distinction of being the best known, and most mispronounced, Japanese word in the West. You must therefore take particular care to pronounce it properly, with a long *yō* and a long rising tone. It is in fact a survival from the classical language and literally means 'so if it be thus'. Note that さようなら is not actually that polite and so will not be used by a junior talking to his superior. In the telephone conversation Mrs Yamakawa can say さようなら but John really has to use something a little more humble, such as 失礼します. Refer back to the business conversation in 6.7. さようなら is not used in such a context.

Key to conversation

Romanisation

Jon	Moshi moshi.
Yamakawa	Hai, Yamakawa desu ga…
Jon	Konnichi wa. Jon Sumisu desu.
Yamakawa	Ara, Jon-san, o-hisashiburi. O-genki desu ka.
Jon	Hai, o-kagesama de. Tadashi-san wa imasu ka.
Yamakawa	Tadashi wa asa kara byōin e itte imasu ga.
Jon	Nichiyō mo shigoto desu ka.
Yamakawa	Ē, senshū wa yasunde imashita keredo. Byōin no atarashii denwa bangō wa shitte imasu ka.

Jon	Furui no wa shitte imasu ga atarashii no wa mada shirimasen.
Yamakawa	Ēto, atarashii no wa...Koko ni arimashita. San-nana-nana-ni no kyū-go-ichi-yon desu.
Jon	San-nana-nana-ni no kyū-go-ichi-yon desu ne. Naisen bangō wa.
Yamakawa	Sā, sore wa wakarimasen.
Jon	Sore ja, kekkō desu. Arigatō gozaimashita.
Yamakawa	Dō itashimashite.
Jon	Sore de wa shitsurei shimasu.
Yamakawa	Sayōnara.

Translation

John	Hello?
Yamakawa	Hello! Yamakawa speaking.
John	Hello. This is John Smith.
Yamakawa	John! It's been ages. How are you?
John	Very well thank you. Is Tadashi there?
Yamakawa	Tadashi's been at the hospital since this morning.
John	He's working even on Sunday?
Yamakawa	Yes, though he did take a day off last week. Do you know the new telephone number of the hospital?
John	I know the old one but I don't know the new one yet.
Yamakawa	Let me see now, the new one is...Here it is. It's 3772-9514.
John	That's 3772-9514, right? What's the extension number?
Yamakawa	Now that I don't know.
John	Never mind then. Thank you very much.
Yamakawa	Not at all.
John	Well then, goodbye.
Yamakawa	Goodbye.

Lesson 18

時	十二時半	長谷川	男	35歳
場所	東西銀行	藤本	女	26歳

長谷川	藤本さん、あの仕事はもう出来ましたか。
藤本	いいえ、二番目のがまだ出来ていませんので ちょっと待って下さい。
長谷川	ええ、かまいませんよ。ところでもう昼ごはんは 食べましたか。
藤本	いいえ、朝から忙しかったのでまだ食べていません。
長谷川	僕もこれからですが、いっしょにどうですか。
藤本	はい。私もここで一休みします。

場所　　東西銀行の近くのレストラン

長谷川	何にしますか。
藤本	私はカレー・ライスにします。
長谷川	僕は今日はおなかがすいているから、ランチ・セット のA にします。すいません、カレーを一つとランチ・ セットのA を一つ下さい。
藤本	あしたのミーティングの準備はもうすみましたか。
長谷川	いや、まだ始めていませんよ。
藤本	今月は特に忙しいですね。
ウェイトレス	お待ちどうさまでした。ランチ・セットA のお客さまは どちらですか。
長谷川	あ、こちらです。

Comment

Japanese eat lunch at midday and most office workers in Tōkyō will go to one of the numerous small restaurants in the vicinity of their office. Depending on the area, this could be on the street, or in a large office block, or in one of the huge underground arcades that now honeycomb the large cities. Most small restaurants of this kind will have the main dishes on show in the window in the form of plastic models. Some will offer only *tenpura* or *sushi*, but most will have a fairly large selection. The menu is liable to be a tremendous mixture of Japanese, Chinese and Japanised-English terminology. Here Fujimoto is having a curry. The term for curry is カレー・ライス. Note that despite the plethora of words for 'rice' in Japan, they choose to use the English word, writing it in *katakana*; this is because the dish as a whole is foreign. Hasegawa decides on a 'set lunch A', which will be a tray with one meat or fish dish, together with rice, pickles and soup. If they want coffee or tea afterwards, they might well move on somewhere else.

18.1 The negative forms of ～ている and ～ていた

まだ出来ていません。
まだ食べていません。

Study and learn the following forms:

	plain negative	*polite negative*
～ている	～ていない	～ていません
～ていた	～ていなかった	～ていませんでした

18.2 Question and answer with もう and まだ

あの仕事はもう出来ましたか。
いいえ、二番目のがまだ出来ていません。

Note that although a positive response to this question would simply be: はい出来ました, 'Yes, I've finished it', the negative response with the word まだ 'not yet' must be put into the ～ている form. A further example:

Question:

もう昼ごはんを食べましたか。
Have you already had your lunch?

Positive response:

ええ、さっき近くのきっさ店でサンドイッチを食べました。
Yes, I had some sandwiches in a nearby cafe a few minutes ago.

Negative response:

いいえ、(昼ごはんは) まだ食べていません。
No, I have not eaten (my lunch) yet.

The reason for this shift is that when the meal is over and done with, a perfective form is appropriate. In the negative reply, however, the word まだ, 'still', shows that we are concerned with being in a negative state, hence the ～ている form must be used: 'I am still in a state of not having eaten.' If you answer with negative imperfective form, いいえ、昼ごはんは食べません, you are actually saying 'No, I do not eat lunch.'

Some more examples:

日本航空 908 便はまだ着いていない。
Japan Airline's Flight 908 has not arrived yet.

山田さんにまだお金を返していません。
I have not yet returned the money to Mr Yamada.

18.3 Ordinal numbers

二番目のがまだ出来ていません。

Ordinals are created by adding the suffix 目 (め) to the cardinal number + the word 番 'number'.

一番	number one	一番目	first
二番	number two	二番目	second
十番	number ten	十番目	tenth
何番	which number?	何番目	where in the order?

18.4 Native Japanese numbers

カレーを一つとランチ・セットのAを一つ下さい。

If you are dealing with an object that has no specific classifier, or if you have forgotten which classifier is appropriate, you can, at a pinch, fall back on the following set of numbers. The numbers you met in 4.7 were of Chinese origin. This new set that you must now learn is of native Japanese origin. It only goes as far as ten.

一つ	ひとつ	六つ	むっつ
二つ	ふたつ	七つ	ななつ
三つ	みっつ	八つ	やっつ
四つ	よっつ	九つ	ここのつ
五つ	いつつ	十	とお

The question word with this set is いくつ.

藤本さんの子供はまだ二つです。
Mrs Fujimoto's child is only two years old.

りんごを十下さい。
Ten apples please.

18.5 ～て下さい

ちょっと待って下さい。

下さい is the imperative form of the verb 下（くだ）さる 'to hand down', which will be dealt with in detail later on in the course. In 10.1 we introduced the pattern noun + (を) +下さい meaning 'please give me', を sometimes disappearing in colloquial speech. The same effect can be achieved by adding 下さい to the ～て form of a verb. Some examples:

もう一度言って下さい。	Please say it again (please repeat).
この本を貸して下さい。	Please lend me this book.
よく注意して下さい。	Please be very careful.

Negative requests of this type are produced by adding 下さい to the ～て form of the negative ない which is ないで. Study the following examples:

ここでタバコをすわないで下さい。
Please do not smoke here.

大きな声で話さないで下さい。
Don't talk in a loud voice.

18.6 Two more useful phrases

ええ、かまいませんよ。
ところでもう昼ごはんは食べましたか。

The first of these means 'Yes, I don't mind' and can be used in most situations where you need to express willingness to fall in with the other party. The second,

ところで, is used either when you have just remembered something or when you wish to change the subject of the conversation. Here a simple 'but…' would do, but you will come across situations when it has to be translated 'that reminds me' or 'by the way'.

18.7 An idiomatic use of する

何にしますか。
私はカレー・ライスにします。

An idiomatic use of the verb する is introduced here. When you choose something you can often use the expression X にします, where にする means 'decide on', or 'want'. More examples:

今度の旅行はどこにしますか。
So where shall we go for our next trip?

ミーティングはいつにしますか。
When shall we have our meeting?

どれにしますか。
Which one will you take?

安いのにします。
I'll take the cheap one.

18.8 'Sorry to have kept you waiting'

お待ちどうさまでした。

Yet again, you will have to wait until the grammar of this phrase is properly explained. In the meantime learn it as a set phrase. The use of the term さま is similar to the phrase おかげさま (17.5).

Key to conversation

Romanisation

Toki	Jūnijihan	Hasegawa	otoko	sanjūgo-sai
Basho	Tōzai ginkō	Fujimoto	onna	nijūroku-sai

Hasegawa	Fujimoto-san, ano shigoto wa mō dekimashita ka.
Fujimoto	Iie, nibanme no ga mada dekite imasen no de chotto matte kudasai.
Hasegawa	Ē, kamaimasen yo. Tokoro de mō hirugohan wa tabemashita ka.
Fujimoto	Iie, asa kara isogashikatta no de mada tabete imasen.
Hasegawa	Boku mo kore kara desu ga, issho ni dō desu ka.
Fujimoto	Hai. Watakushi mo koko de hitoyasumi shimasu.

Basho	Tōzai ginkō no chikaku no resutoran

Hasegawa	Nani ni shimasu ka.
Fujimoto	Watakushi wa karē raisu ni shimasu.
Hasegawa	Boku wa kyō wa o-naka ga suite iru kara, ranchi setto no A ni shimasu.
	Suimasen, karē o hitotsu to ranchi setto no A o hitotsu kudasai.
Fujimoto	Ashita no mītingu no junbi wa mō sumimashita ka.
Hasegawa	Iya, mada hajimete imasen yo.
Fujimoto	Kongetsu wa toku ni isogashii desu ne.
Ueitoresu	O-machidōsama deshita. Ranchi setto A no o-kyakusama wa dochira desu ka.
Hasegawa	A, kochira desu.

Translation

Hasegawa	Fujimoto, have you finished those jobs yet?
Fujimoto	No. The second one isn't finished yet, so please wait a bit.

Hasegawa	No matter. By the way, have you eaten lunch yet?
Fujimoto	No. I've been busy all morning and so I haven't eaten yet.
Hasegawa	I haven't eaten yet either, so how about going together?
Fujimoto	All right. I'll take a break now too.

Place	A restaurant near the Tōkai Bank

Hasegawa	What will you have?
Fujimoto	I'll have curry and rice.
Hasegawa	I'm hungry today, so I'll have the A set menu. Excuse me! One curry and rice, and one A set menu please.
Fujimoto	Have you finished the preparation for the meeting tomorrow?
Hasegawa	No. I haven't even started yet.
Fujimoto	We're really busy this month aren't we!
Waitress	Sorry to keep you waiting. Which one of you is having the A set menu?
Hasegawa	Me please.

Lesson 19

John met his old friend Nicholas.

きのうは夕方から銀座へ行って、大学時代の友達ニコラスに会った。彼は今イギリスの会社で働いているが、今年の春から東京に来ている。同じカレッジだったのでいっしょに映画に行ったり、休みには旅行をしたりした。私は医学部にいて毎日毎日忙しかったが、彼は英文学を勉強していたので、私が実験をしている間に本を読んだり音楽を聞いたりしていた。私達が大学を卒業してからもう七年になる。彼は最近小説を書いてかなり有名になった。私達はまずカメラ屋へ行ってレンズを買ってからすし屋へ行った。思い出話をしたり、彼からイギリスの友達のことを聞いたりして楽しい一時を過ごした。雨が降っていたのでタクシーに乗って帰った。

19.1 More on the uses of the 〜て form

You will find in later lessons that the 〜て form is used widely in the creation of verbal aspects and various expressions of respect. Here we shall study its fundamental role, which is to subordinate one clause or phrase to another. In the patterns introduced here *the subject of the two parts must be the same.*

(a) Actions in sequence

> きのうは夕方から銀座に行って
> 大学時代の友達ニコラスに会った。

Although you will see the 〜て form described as indicating '...and...', complete balance between the two clauses is not possible in Japanese; the first one is always to some extent subordinate to the one that follows, on the basic principle that what precedes modifies. The problem for the student of Japanese is that the degree of subordination varies.

おふろに入ってかみの毛を洗った。
I had a bath and washed my hair.

上着をぬいでハンガーにかけた。
I took off my jacket and put it on a hanger.

Here the balance is as close as one can get, but there is still the feeling that the jacket was taken off so that it could be hung up; certainly the actions are not fortuitously connected.

(b) Cause or reason

彼は最近小説を書いてかなり有名になった。

At the other end of the scale one has contexts where the ～て expresses a clear causal connection.

雨にぬれてかぜをひいた。
I have got a cold because I was soaked in the rain.

かぜをひいて学校を休んだ。
I stayed away from school because I had a cold.

おふろに入ってさっぱりした。
Having had a bath, I felt refreshed.

(c) 'Adverbial' modification

タクシーに乗って帰った。

It is often the case that the clause ending in ～て is best understood in an adverbial sense, modifying the action of the final verb. The sense of subordination is so strong here that English dispenses with a verb altogether: 'I returned home by taxi.' Some more examples:

犬を連れて散歩した。
I went for a walk with my dog.

その子は私の方へ走って来た。
The child came running towards me.

ヘレンは赤いセーターを着て来た。
Helen came wearing a red jersey.

19.2 Use of the verb なる

私達が大学を卒業してからもう七年になる。

We saw an instance of the idiomatic use of になるin 10.8. Here is another example. Try and pay particular attention to this manner of phrasing things because the sense of 'becoming' is not always given overt expression in English; you would not normally translate this sentence as 'It has already become seven years since…', although that is how the Japanese puts it.

あの計画はだめになりました。
That plan came to naught.

いとこが北京へ行ってから十年になります。
It is ten years since my cousin went to Beijing.

19.3 The form ～てから

私達はまずカメラ屋へ行ってレンズを買ってから すし屋へ行った。

(a) ～てから meaning 'after...'. This is in a sense an extension of the ～て form when used in a temporal sequence and it emphasises the subordination.

きのうは夕ごはんを食べてからテレビを見ました。
Yesterday, I watched television after having had supper.

宿題をしてから出かけます。
I'll go out after I've finished my homework.

(b) ～てから meaning 'since...' This is essentially the same as (a) but is listed separately here merely because the English expression is different.

この前東京であなたに会ってから、もう三ヶ月たちました。
Three months have already passed by since I last saw you in Tōkyō.

この子は小学校に入ってから体がとても丈夫になった。
This child has become very healthy since he started going to primary school.

19.4 Alternative form ～たり in multiple series

友達のことを聞いたりして楽しい一時を過ごした。

The pattern ～たり, ～たり, する that we saw in 14.3 can be subordinated to another verb by means of して as follows:

ローマでは名所をまわったり、買物をしたりして一週間を過ごしました。
In Rome, we spent one week looking around the sights and shopping.

郵便局でアルバイトをしたり、おじの農場で働いたりしてお金をためた。
I saved up money by taking a temporary job in a post office and working on my uncle's farm.

19.5 間 (pronounced あいだ)

私が実験をしている間に本を読んだり音楽を聞いたりしていた。

This word means 'period of time' and is often used with the ～ている progressive aspect.

> 田中さんが電話をかけている間私は車の中で待っていました。
> While Mr Tanaka was telephoning I waited in the car.
>
> 日本にいた間はよくあちこち旅行した。
> While I was in Japan I travelled around a lot.

When 間 is used by itself it merely means 'during the said space of time' and both activities could begin and end at the same time. If に is added the meaning changes somewhat:

> 五時から九時までの間に来て下さい。
> Please come at some point between five and nine.

In this case, the second activity is seen to occur at a specific point within the said space of time. Compare this sentence with the following:

> きのうは五時から九時までの間ずっと駅でおばを待っていました。
> Yesterday I was waiting for my aunt at the station all the time from five to nine.

The use of 間に also involves a sense of taking advantage of the time allowed to do something. Observe the following sentences:

> 子供が昼寝をしている間私は本を読みました。
> While the child was having his nap, I read my book.

子供が昼寝をしている間に私は本を読んだり手紙を書いたりしました。
While the child was having a nap, I took the opportunity to read my book and write some letters.

その婦人が電車の中でいねむりをしている間に男は彼女からさいふをぬすんだ。
While the woman was dozing off in the train, the man took the chance to steal her purse.

Note also the following phrases, which are based on a 'prenoun + 間' pattern:

(a) この間 'the other day'

この間デパートの入口で山野さんに会いました。
The other day, I met Mrs Yamano at the entrance of the department store.

(b) その間 or あの間 'during that time'

その間にどろぼうが家に入った。
The burglar went into my house during that time.

19.6 は and が again

私は医学部にいて毎日毎日忙しかったが、彼は英文学を勉強していたので、私が実験をしている間に本を読んだり音楽を聞いたりしていた。

Take careful note of how the particles は and が behave here. The two はs here are clearly being used to contrast 'I' and 'he'. Being also a topic marker, は often has influence over a longer stretch of the sentence than が. So it is that here 彼は

controls all the verbs up to and including the 聞いたりしていた at the end, with the sole exception of 実験をしている, which is governed by 私が. A little tip, therefore, to help you find your way in what will seem at first labyrinthine sentences: by and large が extends its influence no further than the next verb.

Key to passage

Romanisation

Kinō wa yūgata kara Ginza e itte, daigaku jidai no tomodachi Nikorasu ni atta. Kare wa ima Igirisu no kaisha de hataraite iru ga, kotoshi no haru kara Tōkyō ni kite iru. Onaji karejji datta no de issho ni eiga ni ittari, yasumi ni wa ryokō o shitari shita. Watakushi wa igakubu ni ite mainichi mainichi isogashikatta ga, kare wa eibungaku o benkyō shite ita no de, watakushi ga jikken o shite iru aida ni hon o yondari ongaku o kiitari shite ita. Watakushitachi ga daigaku o sotsugyō shite kara mō shichi nen ni naru. Kare wa saikin shōsetsu o kaite kanari yūmei ni natta. Watakushitachi wa mazu kameraya e itte renzu o katte kara sushiya e itta. Omoidebanashi o shitari, kare kara Igirisu no tomodachi no koto o kiitari shite tanoshii hitotoki o sugoshita. Ame ga futte ita no de takushī ni notte kaetta.

Translation

Yesterday evening I went to Ginza and met Nicholas, a friend from university days. He is now working for an English firm and has been in Tōkyō since spring this year. We were at the same college, so we went to films and in the holidays we went on trips together. I was in the Faculty of Medicine and busy every day, but he was studying English literature and so while I was doing experiments he was reading books and listening to music. It is now seven years since we graduated from university. Recently he has written a novel and has become quite well known. First of all we went to a camera shop and bought a lens. Then we went to a sushi shop. I spent a pleasant few hours, talking about old times and hearing about friends in England. As it was raining, I came home by taxi.

Lesson 20

ジョン	もしもし。
マリー	ジョンさん、マリーです。今晩は。
ジョン	あ、マリーさん、今晩は。新しいアパートはどうですか。
マリー	引っ越しはとても大変でしたが、やっと落ち着きました。
ジョン	片付けはもうすっかり終わりましたか。
マリー	ええ、おかげさまでほとんど終わりました。
ジョン	無理はしないで下さいね。ところで、部屋数はいくつですか。
マリー	台所とおふろ場のほかに二つあります。
ジョン	いいですね。
マリー	ええ、あまり大きくはありませんが何も文句はありません。明るくて気持のいいところです。
ジョン	それはよかった。JR 線の高円寺駅の近くですか。
マリー	いいえ、JR 線ではなくて地下鉄の駅のそばです。歩いて十分ぐらいかかりますが、お店や郵便局に近くて便利です。今度うちでごちそうを作りますから正さんといっしょに来て下さいね。
ジョン	ありがとう。楽しみにしています。
マリー	それじゃ、又近いうちに。お休みなさい。
ジョン	お休みなさい。

20.1 Linking descriptive verbs and adjectival nouns

> 明るくて気持のいいところです。
> お店や郵便局に近くて便利です。

(a) Descriptive verbs

Here we investigate how one descriptive verb can be linked to another. The first verb must be changed into its ～て form, which is achieved by changing the final い to く + て. These then link in the normal way, modifier preceding nouns:

大きい	→	大きくて	小さい	→	小さくて
高い	→	高くて	安い	→	安くて
悲しい	→	悲しくて	嬉しい	→	嬉しくて
楽しい	→	楽しくて	若い	→	若くて
おいしい	→	おいしくて	まずい	→	まずくて

あの店のコーヒーは安くておいしい。
The coffee in that shop is cheap and tasty.

あの山はけわしくて危ない。
That mountain, being steep, is dangerous.

Take particular care to note this transformation. You might be tempted to produce the form *大きいで instead of 大きくて. This is a common mistake. Occasionally the 〜て form brings with it that sense of subordination that we met in the last lesson, but this is not always the case with these descriptive verbs. On the one hand 安くておいしい does not mean 'tasty because it is cheap', but on the other hand the word けわしくて 'being steep' in あの山はけわしくて危ない is indicating a reason why the mountain is dangerous. You should be able to tell whether subordination is present by context more than anything else.

(b) Adjectival nouns

The copula is used to express A = B as in これは本です(1.3), and it is also used when adjectival nouns appear in final position at the end of the sentence, as in この教室は静かです (13.2). To link nouns and adjectival nouns followed by the copula, use the 〜て form of the copula, which is で.

この村は静かで平和だ。
This village is quiet and peaceful.

小寺さんの話し方はとてもていねいで正確です。
Mrs Kodera's way of talking is very polite and precise.

今日は七月七日で七夕祭り(たなばたまつり)です。
Today is the seventh of July, the festival of Tanabata.

(c) Descriptive verbs can be linked to adjectival nouns and vice versa:

このコンピューター・ゲームは簡単でおもしろい。
This computer game is both easy and interesting.

このコンピューター・ゲームはおもしろくて簡単です。
This computer game is both interesting and easy.

(d) Both descriptive verbs and adjectival nouns can in turn be linked to verb phrases.

(i) あの映画はむずかしかった。
(ii) 私はあの映画がよく分からなかった。
(i)+(ii) あの映画は難しくて分からなかった。
I did not understand that film because it was difficult.

(i) 祖母はこのごろとても元気だ。
(ii) 祖母はよく外出する。
(i)+(ii) 祖母はこのごろとても元気でよく外出する。
Grandmother has been feeling very well recently, so goes out a lot.

Note that unlike the pattern that we saw in 19.1, where the subject of the two clauses had to be the same, the pattern introduced here can involve two different subjects.

(e) Linking modifiers

When a descriptive verb and an adjectival noun, or two descriptive verbs, or two adjectival nouns appear as noun modifiers in the same sentence, they can link in two different ways. Observe the following, where (i)+(ii) can be joined in two ways.

(i) 私のふるさとは静かな村です。
(ii) 私のふるさとは美しい村です。

(i)+(ii) 私のふるさとは静かで美しい村です。

or

(i)+(ii) 私のふるさとは静かな美しい村です。
The place where I grew up is a quiet, pretty village.

In the first case the modifiers are, as it were, on equal terms. In the second case, however, the balance is slightly different because 静かな is seen to be modifying not 村 as such but rather 美しい村 as a whole.

20.2 Interrogative noun + (particle) + も…ない

何も文句はありません。

This pattern is used to express the idea of absolute negation: 'I don't have any complaints.' Take note of how it is used in the following sentences:

きのうは一日中何も食べませんでした。
I did not eat anything yesterday all day long.

だれも話をしませんでした。
Nobody talked.

だれとも話をしませんでした。
I did not talk to anyone.

きのうは日曜日でしたがどこへも行きませんでした。
It was Sunday yesterday but I did not go anywhere.

20.3 The ～て form of the negative

JR 線ではなくて地下鉄の駅のそばです。

(a) The copula

positive	*negative*	〜て *negative*
だ	ではない	ではなくて
です	ではありません	ではなくて

木村さんは医者ではなくて数学者です。
Mr Kimura is not a doctor but a mathematician.

これではなくてあちらのを下さい。
Please give me not this one but the one over there.

(b) Descriptive verbs

positive	*negative*	〜て *negative*
安い	安くない	安くなくて
よい(いい)	よくない	よくなくて

あまり暑くなくていい気持だ。
It is not so hot and (so) I am comfortable.

この小説はちっともおもしろくなくてしかも長い。
This novel is not interesting at all and, what's more, it's long.

(c) Pure verbs

We have already met this form in 18.5 in connection with how to say 'please don't': 〜ないで. Some more examples:

百円玉以外は使わないで下さい。
Please do not use other than 100 yen coins.

文句を言わないで少しは手伝って下さい。
Help me a little without complaining.

父はかさを持たないで出かけた。
My father went out without taking an umbrella with him.

The alternative form 〜なくて also exists and must be used in certain contexts with certain verbs instead of 〜ないで, but its use will be introduced later.

20.4 'Goodnight'

お休みなさい。

Another set phrase; it can be used either on the telephone or simply when leaving company.

Key to conversation

Romanisation

Jon	Moshi moshi.
Marī	Jon san, Marī desu. Konban wa.
Jon	A, Marī san, konban wa. Atarashii apāto wa dō desu ka.
Marī	Hikkoshi wa totemo taihen deshita ga, yatto ochitsukimashita.
Jon	Katazuke wa mō sukkari owarimashita ka.
Marī	Ē, o-kagesama de hotondo owarimashita.
Jon	Muri wa shinaide kudasai ne. Tokoro de, heyakazu wa ikutsu desu ka.
Marī	Daidokoro to o-furoba no hoka ni futatsu arimasu.
Jon	Ii desu ne.
Marī	Ē, amari ōkiku wa arimasen ga nani mo monku wa arimasen. Akarukute kimochi no ii tokoro desu.
Jon	Sore wa yokatta. JR-sen no Kōenji-eki no chikaku desu ka.
Marī	Iie, JR-sen de wa nakute chikatetsu no eki no soba desu. Aruite juppun gurai kakarimasu ga, o-mise ya yūbinkyoku ni chikakute benri desu. Kondo uchi de gochisō o tsukurimasu kara Tadashi-san to issho ni kite kudasai ne.
Jon	Arigatō. Tanoshimi ni shite imasu.

Marī	Sore ja, mata chikai uchi ni. O-yasumi nasai.
Jon	O-yasumi nasai.

Translation

John	Hello?
Marie	John, it's Marie. Good evening.
John	Oh, Marie, good evening. How are you finding your new flat?
Marie	The move was very tiring, but I'm settled at last.
John	Have you finished tidying up completely?
Marie	Yes thanks, I've almost finished.
John	Don't overdo it will you. How many rooms do you have, by the way?
Marie	There are two, in addition to the kitchen and the bathroom.
John	That sounds good.
Marie	Yes, it's not very big but I have no complaints. It's light and the place has a pleasant feeling about it.
John	That's great. Are you close to the JR Kōenji station?
Marie	No, it's not near the JR line but the underground station. It takes about ten minutes to walk there, but it's conveniently close to shops and the post office. I'll cook you a meal here sometime, so do come over with Tadashi.
John	Thank you. I look forward to that.
Marie	Well then, see you again soon. Good night.
John	Good night.

Lesson 21

Yamakawa Minoru and Kinoshita Akiko are in a cafe near the Kyōto International Conference Centre.

山川	きょうはずいぶん混んでますね。
木下	そうですね。きのうから物理学の国際学会が始まりましたから。
山川	ああ、そう言えば僕も新聞で読みました。
木下	あそこに座わっている女の人は最近ノーベル賞をもらった有名な学者ではありませんか。
山川	そうですね。確かポーランドの人ですね。
木下	ところで、山川さんは将来何をするつもりですか。
山川	まだ決めていませんが。木下さんは。
木下	私もまだはっきりは決めていませんが、もう少し英語を勉強するために、一、二年イギリスへ行くつもりです。
山川	それはいいですね。イギリスのどこですか。
木下	さあ、まだ分かりません。でもロンドンではなくて小さな町を選ぶつもりです。

21.1 Contractions in everyday speech

> 混んでますね。

Just as in English, it is quite common to drop certain sounds in fast speech. Here we have an example in the opening phrase: instead of 混んでいます, Yamakawa says 混んでます. Once you hear this a number of times, it will become second nature to you.

21.2 'Come to mention it'

そう言えば

Learn this as an idiom. It literally means 'if (or when) you say thus'.

21.3 Noun modification

あそこに座わっている女の人は最近ノーベル賞をもらった有名な学者ではありませんか。

(a) Noun modification revisited

As you now know, Japanese descriptive verbs directly precede the noun which they modify:

黒い自動車	a black car
青白い顔	a pale face

In order to explain this pattern it was suggested in 11.2 that the literal meaning of 黒い自動車 was 'a car which is black' and this is indeed an example of the Japanese equivalent of English relative clauses. Unlike English, the Japanese construction is simple and involves few changes; just follow the rule that the modifying word or clause comes *before* the noun being modified. Observe the following:

(i)	きのう映画を見た。
(ii)	その映画はとてもおもしろかった。
(i)+(ii)	きのう見た映画はとてもおもしろかった。 The film which I saw yesterday was very interesting.

When the modifying clause includes a subject, either が or の can be used as a subject marker within the clause.

私が/のきのう見た映画はとてもおもしろかった。

Study another example:

(i)	駅の前に女の人が立っています。
(ii)	その女の人は私の日本語の先生です。
(i)+(ii)	駅の前に立っている女の人は私の日本語の先生です。 The woman who is standing in front of the station is my Japanese teacher.

(b) Shedding polite forms

One major change that does occur to the verb when it is shifted into the modifying position is that it will normally shed any polite ending such as 〜ます; the plain form is used instead.

(i)	兄は大学で医学を勉強しています。
(ii)	その兄は二十三歳です。
(i)+(ii)	大学で医学を勉強している兄は二十三歳です。 My elder brother who is studying medicine at the University is twenty-three years old.

It is possible to retain the 〜ます ending sometimes, but this is only when you wish to be particularly polite. For the time being you should stick to the rule that such verbs in modifying position should be in the plain form.

(c) What modifies what?

Occasionally, because of the very simplicity of the Japanese pattern here, you may find yourself faced with an apparent ambiguity when, for example, the noun that is modified could be the subject of the modifying verb. 今読んでいる小説 can only mean 'the novel X is now reading', but 待っていた人 could mean either 'the person for whom X was waiting' or 'the person who was waiting'. Context will usually tell you which interpretation is correct, but you should be aware of the tremendous range and flexibility of this construction.

21.4 Using the negative for politeness

> 有名な学者ではありませんか。

The negative form is very commonly used when asking questions or making suggestions.

これはあなたのかぎではありませんか。
Isn't this your key?

いっしょに行きませんか。
How about going together?

21.5 つもり

> ところで、山川さんは将来何をするつもりですか。

つもり is a noun which means a range of things from intention to opinion, from pretension to belief. It is modified by a whole range of words and is usually followed by the copula, although you will also find が (は) ある / ない after it, especially in negative expressions. It is usual to use this word about oneself, and about the second person if asking a question, but it is not normally found referring to a third person on the principle that other people's intentions can never be known.

この手紙に返事を書くつもりですか。
Do you intend to reply to this letter?

ええ、そのつもりですが。
Yes, I do but...

ええ、そのつもりでした。
Yes, that was my intention.

その学会に参加するつもりはありません。
I have no intention of attending that conference.

今年は日本へは行かないつもりです。
I do not intend to go to Japan this year.

21.6 'I haven't decided yet'

> 将来何をするつもりですか。
> まだ決めていませんが。

Study this response carefully. If you were talking in English, you might also respond with 'I don't know, yet.' Do *not* be tempted to say まだ知りません in Japanese. The verb 知る cannot be used in this way; 決める is the right word in this context.

21.7 ために

> 私もまだはっきり決めていませんが、もう少し英語を勉強するために、一、二年イギリスへ行くつもりです。

ため is a noun meaning 'sake' or 'benefit'. It is used together with に to express the idea of 'for the purpose of', 'in order to' or 'because of'. It can be attached either to another noun with の or to the plain form of verbs. In this example it obviously means 'in order to', but study the following sentences:

(a) meaning 'in order to'

日本へ行くためにお金をためています。
I am saving up money (in order) to go to Japan.

(b) meaning 'because'

楽しみにしていた秋の遠足は雨のために中止になりました。
The autumn trip to which we had been looking forward was cancelled because of the rainy weather.

(c) meaning 'because'

ケンブリッジからロンドンまでの電車が遅れたために飛行機に間に合わなかった。
Because the train from Cambridge to London was late, I missed the plane.

In the context of (a) ため must be followed by に; in the context of (b) and (c) に is optional.

Key to conversation

Romanisation

Yamakawa	Kyō wa zuibun kondemasu ne.
Kinoshita	Sō desu ne. Kinō kara butsurigaku no kokusai gakkai ga hajimarimashita kara.
Yamakawa	Ā, sō ieba boku mo shinbun de yomimashita.
Kinoshita	Asoko ni suwatte iru onna no hito wa saikin Nōberu-shō o moratta yūmei na gakusha de wa arimasen ka.
Yamakawa	Sō desu ne. Tashika Pōrando no hito desu ne.
Kinoshita	Tokoro de, Yamakawa-san wa shōrai nani o suru tsumori desu ka.
Yamakawa	Mada kimete imasen ga. Kinoshita san wa.
Kinoshita	Watakushi mo mada hakkiri wa kimete imasen ga, mō sukoshi Eigo o benkyō suru tame ni, ichi-ni nen Igirisu e iku tsumori desu.
Yamakawa	Sore wa ii desu ne. Igirisu no doko desu ka.
Kinoshita	Sā, mada wakarimasen. Demo Rondon de wa nakute chiisa na machi o erabu tsumori desu.

Translation

Yamakawa	It's pretty crowded today isn't it?
Kinoshita	Yes it is. It's because an international physics conference started yesterday.
Yamakawa	Oh yes, now that you mention it I read about it in the newspaper.
Kinoshita	Isn't that woman sitting over there the famous scholar who recently won a Nobel prize?
Yamakawa	So it is. A Pole I think.
Kinoshita	What are you thinking of doing in the future?
Yamakawa	I haven't decided yet. What about you?
Kinoshita	I haven't made any firm plans either yet, but I plan to go to England for one or two years so I can study English a bit more.
Yamakawa	That sounds good. Where in England?
Kinoshita	Hm, I don't know yet. But not London. I plan to choose a small town.

Lesson 22

A telephone conversation between John and Tadashi.

ジョン	マリーさんが引っ越しをしたのを知っていますか。
正	ええ、二週間ぐらい前に杉並区へ移ったのは知っていますが、電話番号はまだ聞いていません。なぜ引っ越したんですか。
ジョン	よく知りませんが、前のアパートはとてもせまかったし、それに車の音もうるさかったからではありませんか。
正	そうでしたね。今度のところはどんなですか。
ジョン	割りに広いし、静かでいいところでした。
正	それはよかったですね。
ジョン	僕が行ったのは水曜日の午後だったので、となりの小学校の校庭で子供達がさわいでいるのが時々聞こえましたが…。
正	まあ、そのくらいは仕方がないですね。ところでジョンさん、あしたの晩はあいてますか。ちょっと話があるのですが…。
ジョン	ええと、あしたは夕方五時から七時ごろまでは会議がありますが、七時半ごろからあいています。
正	それじゃ、七時半から八時の間にいつものきっさ店でどうですか。
ジョン	いいですね。それじゃ又その時に。さようなら。
正	さようなら。

Comment

In Tadashi's first reply we come across the name of a district in Tōkyō called 杉並区. The centre section of the capital is divided into twenty-three such districts called 区. The larger metropolitan area of Tōkyō is known as 東京都 Tōkyō-to, and it is the only prefecture in Japan so designated. Ōsaka and Kyōto are both prefectures, known as 府 (ふ) in this case, and cities, known as 市(し). All the other prefectures in Japan are called 県 (けん), except for 北海道. The all-inclusive term for Japan as an administrative whole is therefore 都道府県.

22.1 Nominalisation using の

マリーさんが引っ越しをしたのを知っていますか。

When の is added to the plain form of the verb the whole preceding clause is transformed into a noun clause that can then act the role of subject, object or topic with the appropriate particles:

> 一人で山に登るのは危険です。
> Climbing alone is dangerous.
>
> 木村さんが時間通りに来ないのはめずらしい。
> It is very unusual for Mr Kimura not to come on time.
>
> 言うのは易しいが行うのは難しい。
> Saying is easy but doing is difficult.

This use of の nominalising a whole clause should be clearly distinguished from those occasions when の is simply substituting directly for another noun (refer back to の as a noun substitute 'the one' in 11.3). In that pattern a sentence such as フランスで買ったハンドバッグは安かった can be changed into フランスで買ったのは安かった, which means 'the one I bought' not 'the buying'. What we are dealing with here is something very different: the transformation of a whole verb phrase into its nominal equivalent.

22.2 The pattern のです/んです

なぜ引っ越したんですか。
ちょっと話があるのですが…。

You will frequently come across sentences which end in のだ or んだ (informal), のです or んです (polite), のである(formal). This addition of のです, the literal meaning of which is 'it's that', gives a simple statement certain overtones. It is often employed when the speaker wishes to explain reasons, causes or circumstances to the listener.

あしたは八時過ぎまで会社にいるつもりです。仕事が山ほどあるのです。
I think I shall be in my office until after eight tomorrow. I have a mountainous load of work.

顔色が悪いですね。
You look pale.

今朝からとても頭が痛いんです。
I have had a really bad headache since this morning.

テニスをしませんか。
Shall we have a game of tennis?

ええ、でも下手なんです。
Yes, but I'm not very good.

お仕事は何ですか。
What's your job?

まだ学生なんです。
I'm still a student.

This pattern often occurs in a question, particularly with the interrogatives なぜ and どうして, both meaning 'why?', and the assumption is that the speaker is seeking some kind of explanation. Look at the sentence なぜ引っ越したんですか again. It has a similar effect to the English 'why is it that she moved?', although it is used far more often and is somewhat less conspicuous as a result. In fact you will find that this explanatory のです used much more in Japanese than its literal English equivalent might lead you to expect. Notice how the pattern appears in both question and response in the following exchanges.

どうしてきのうは来なかったんですか。
Why didn't you come yesterday?

すみませんでした。急に用事が出来たのです。
Sorry about that. Some business turned up unexpectedly.

なぜだまって行ったんですか。
Why did you go without telling me?

なぜ and どうして are more or less interchangable and so can be used in both formal and colloquial contexts. If there is any difference, it is that なぜ is slightly less direct and so sounds more polite.

22.3 The particle し

前のアパートはとてもせまかったし、それに車の音もうるさかったからではありませんか。

し can be used as a conjunctive particle when one is listing a series of factors that lead to some sort of conclusion. し in this usage can be found after any of the following: the copula, descriptive verbs, verbs and adjectival nouns.

彼は健康だし、頭はいいし、礼儀正しいし、全く理想的な青年ですね。
He is healthy, intelligent and polite; he is really an ideal young man.

この部屋は明るいし、つくえやいすやコンピューターもそろっているし、事務所として申し分ありません。
This room is really ideal for an office because it is light, and it's well equipped with a desk, a chair and a computer.

22.4 こんな/そんな/あんな/どんな

今度のところはどんなですか。

Here is another set of prenouns. こんな 'this kind of', そんな 'that kind of', あんな 'that kind of'. The corresponding interrogative is どんな 'what kind of?', which you have already met in 11.7

どんな色が好きですか。
What kind of colour do you like?

あんな人はきらいです。
I don't like people like that.

そんな話は信じません。
I won't believe such a story.

22.5 The emphatic construction using のは…です

僕が行ったのは水曜日の午後だった

In 11.3 you were introduced to the use of の as a noun substitute. This usage of の can be effective when you wish to invert a sentence in order to emphasise something. Study the following transformations:

金子さんは去年インドへ行きました。
Mr Kaneko went to India last year.

去年インドへ行ったのは金子さんです。
It was Mr Kaneko who went to India last year.

金子さんがインドへ行ったのは去年です。
It was last year that Mr Kaneko went to India.

Similarly,

日本で初めて生の魚を食べた。
I ate raw fish for the first time in Japan.

初めて生の魚を食べたのは日本でだった。
It was in Japan that I first ate raw fish.

Take special care to understand that the の is being used as a substitute for 'person', 'year' and 'place' in these examples. It is *not* creating the kind of generalised 'going' or 'eating', for which we have reserved the term nominalisation. Note how は is being used here, acting as a kind of pivot, de-emphasising its own phrase and drawing attention to what follows.

22.6 Noun clause as the object of perception

> となりの小学校の校庭で子供達がさわいでいるのが
> 時々聞こえました。

As an extension of its role as nominaliser, の is often used with verbs of perception, seeing and hearing, when it can often be translated as the English gerund '…ing'.

(私は)その男が部屋を出るのを見た。
I saw him going out of the room.
lit. I saw his going...

みんなが笑っているのを聞いて私も楽しくなった。
Hearing the others laughing, I also became happy.

さっき、部長が電話でどなっているのが聞こえました。
A little while ago, I could hear our head of department shouting on the telephone.

22.7 仕方がない

> そのくらいは仕方がないですね。

仕方がない is a phrase meaning 'there's nothing to be done'. It is commonly used when expressing resignation of the 'well, we'll just have to put up with it' variety. Take note that in fact we have another example of the stative は…が construction here.

Key to conversation

Romanisation

Jon	Marī san ga hikkoshi o shita no o shitte imasu ka.
Tadashi	Ē, nishūkan gurai mae ni Suginami-ku e utsutta no wa shitte imasu ga, denwa bangō wa mada kiite imasen. Naze hikkoshitan desu ka.
Jon	Yoku shirimasen ga, mae no apāto wa totemo semakatta shi, sore ni kuruma no oto mo urusakatta kara de wa arimasen ka.
Tadashi	Sō deshita ne. Kondo no tokoro wa donna desu ka.
Jon	Wari ni hiroi shi, shizuka de ii tokoro deshita.
Tadashi	Sore wa yokatta desu ne.
Jon	Boku ga itta no wa suiyōbi no gogo datta no de, tonari no shōgakkō no kōtei de kodomotachi ga sawaide iru no ga tokodoki kikoemashita ga…
Tadashi	Mā, sono kurai wa shikata ga nai desu ne. Tokoro de Jon san, ashita no ban wa aitemasu ka. Chotto hanashi ga aru no desu ga…
Jon	Ēto, ashita wa yūgata goji kara shichiji goro made wa kaigi ga arimasu ga, shichijihan goro kara aite imasu.
Tadashi	Sore ja, shichijihan kara hachiji no aida ni itsumo no kissaten de dō desu ka.
Jon	Ii desu ne. Sore ja mata sono toki ni. Sayōnara.
Tadashi	Sayōnara.

Translation

John	Do you know that Marie has moved?
Tadashi	Yes, I knew she had moved to Suginami ward about two weeks ago, but I haven't got her telephone number yet. Why did she move?
John	I don't really know, but wasn't it because her previous flat was too small and also

	noisy from the traffic?
Tadashi	So it was. What kind of a place does she have now?
John	It's comparatively spacious, and it's nice and quiet.
Tadashi	That is good isn't it.
John	It was Wednesday afternoon when I went there, and so from time to time I could hear children making a lot of noise in the primary school playground next door...
Tadashi	Well, not much you can do about that kind of thing. John, I was wondering, are you free tomorrow night? There's something I want to talk to you about...
John	Let me see now, tomorrow from five until about seven I have a meeting, but I'm free after seven thirty.
Tadashi	In that case, how about between seven thirty and eight in the usual coffee shop?
John	That sounds's fine. I'll see you then then. Good-bye.
Tadashi	Good-bye.

Lesson 23

A postcard from Minoru to his mother.

おかあさん、お元気ですか。京都はこの三、四日ぐっと気温が下がり、すっかり秋らしくなりました。東京はいかがですか。きょうは朝から友達と奈良に遊びに行きました。駅前から鹿を見ながら奈良公園を通り、大仏殿まで歩きました。春日神社の近くでお弁当を食べてから久しぶりに新薬師寺まで行ってきました。もう十年も前にみんなでいっしょに行ったのを覚えていますか。萩の花が見事にさいていました。一日中歩き回り、少し疲れたので帰りは新薬師寺前からバスに乗りました。今度の休みには紅葉を見に嵐山に行くつもりです。おとうさん、正おにいさん、それに国子にもよろしく伝えて下さい。では、さようなら。実

Comment

Minoru is a university student, but Japanese of all ages make these kind of trips. The habit of tourism within the country is an old one that has roots far back in Japanese history, when people would visit shrines and places famous for their spiritual atmosphere. For a Japanese today the habit begins with school trips to the major centres of historical and cultural importance. Kyōto and Nara are, of course, the main destinations. Kyōto is famous for its temples and for its position, surrounded on three sides by heavily wooded mountains. Nara, to the south, is somewhat older, and is similarly visited for its temples and shrines; above all, however, it is famous for the *shika* deer that roam the parks. One of the results of tourism being old and well established is that particular places are always visited at particular times of the year, and so in the popular mind place names become linked with seasons, and often with particular flowers. The temple at Hase, for instance, is famous for its tree peonies (*botan*) and Arashiyama, on the western edge of Kyōto, is prized for the show of autumn leaves and so in a sense signifies autumn. The habit of visiting certain sights at fixed periods means that you may find them well-nigh deserted at others. Note that in this short postcard to his mother Minoru uses generally polite verb forms.

23.1 The conjunctive form linking clauses

この三、四日ぐっと気温が下がり、すっかり秋らしくなりました。 駅前から鹿を見ながら奈良公園を通り、大仏殿まで歩きました。

We have already met the conjunctive form of the verb in 7.2 in the context of forming the polite ～ます form. This conjunctive form itself can be found in numerous other contexts. It can, for example, be used simply to link two clauses. Such a link can be interpreted quite widely: '…and then', '…and so', 'and yet'.

上着をぬぎハンガーにかけた。
I took my jacket off and hung it up.

The main difference between this kind of link and the use of the ～て form that was introduced in 19.1, namely 上着をぬいでハンガーにかけた, is that the conjunctive form is more likely to appear in formal written Japanese than in everyday speech.

23.2 '-like', and '-ish'

秋らしくなりました。

らしい is a suffix which inflects in the manner of a descriptive verb. The basic meaning is 'seeming' or '-like' and here it follows directly after the noun: 秋らしい 'autumnlike'. When used like this with a noun, the extended nuance may be 'typical of' or 'as befits'. Later on in the course you will meet it appended to verbs.

彼は留守らしい。
He seems to be out.

彼は医者らしい。
It seems that he is a doctor.

日本人らしいですね。
That's very Japanese.

23.3 Verb in conjunctive + に + verb of motion.

きょうは朝から友達と奈良に遊びに行きました。
今度の休みには紅葉を見に嵐山に行くつもりです。

In 9.7 you were introduced to the pattern 'noun + に + 行く'. The conjunctive form can be also used in a similar construction. The second verb is invariably a verb of motion and the pattern signifies 'to move for the purpose of doing something'. Usually the subject of both verbs is the same and the first verb must represent a single action, not a state or a habit. Stative verbs, therefore, such as いる, ある, ちがう and all potential forms cannot be used in this pattern. Furthermore, those dynamic verbs that express actions that cannot be fully controlled by the self such as 理解する, 知る and most expressions of emotion such as 笑う, 泣く or 喜ぶ cannot be used in this pattern either, for what should be obvious reasons: you cannot 'move with the intention of doing something' that you cannot actually control. Other verbs of motion that can be used with に in this way include 帰る, もどる, 出る, 入る, 登る and 向かう.

何をしに駅へ行ったのですか。
What did you go to the station for?

指定席のきっぷを買いに行ったんです。
I went to buy a seat reservation.

山田さんは電話をかけにもどりました。
Mrs Yamada went back (home, or to her office) to make a telephone call.

Note that with verbal nouns such as 勉強する, the する can be dropped in this pattern so that we end up with 'noun + に + 行く' again.

図書館へ勉強(し)に行く。
To go to the library to study.

23.4 Conjunctive + ながら

駅前から鹿を見ながら奈良公園を通り、大仏殿まで歩きました。

The word ながら, attached to the conjunctive form, connects two actions in the sense of 'while':

父はいつも朝刊を読みながら朝ごはんを食べる。
My father always has his breakfast while reading the morning papers.

Note that the actions must be two *separate* actions so that there is some kind of contrast between them. Hence a sentence like テレビを見ながら勉強した cannot be used, for instance, about an Open University student studying via the TV. The major restrictions on the use of ながら are as follows:

(a) The actions in both clauses must be performed by the same person.

(b) The actions must be either simultaneous or concurrent.

その青年は昼間は工場で働きながら、夜は法律の勉強を続けた。
That youth worked in a factory during the day while studying law in the evening.

23.5 ～てくる

新薬師寺まで行ってきました。

Later on in this course you will be introduced to a number of verbs which have special significance when they follow a ～て form. Among these will be ～てくる, which has more than one function. More will be said about this combination in due course. In this particular context it marks simple direction, but you will notice that where in English you would simply say 'went to Shin-Yakushi-ji', in Japanese you are more likely to say 'went and came (back)'. Try and remember this because you will have a natural tendency to leave the second verb out.

This kind of construction is very common. When you leave the house in the morning, you will usually say 行ってきます as you go out the door, whereas in English you would be more likely to say 'I'm off.' Indeed you will find occasions when you will actually have to translate ～てくる as simply 'go and...' Take special note that くる in this idiomatic usage is usually written in *hiragana*. For example:

見てきます。
I'll go and have a look (and then return).

肉や野菜は私が買ってきます。
I'll go and buy the meat and vegetables.

23.6 Deverbals

帰りは新薬師寺前からバスに乗りました。

The conjunctive is also used to derive nouns from verbs, so-called deverbals; not all verbs can be transformed into nouns in this way. Do not try and invent them yourself. Some examples:

verb		*noun*	
休む	rest	休み	a rest, holiday
笑う	laugh	笑い	a laugh
答える	answer	答え	an answer
話す	talk	話 (はなし)	a story, a talk

この電車は名古屋行きです。
This train is bound for Nagoya.

行き is sometimes pronounced ゆき and sometimes いき in a context like this where it forms a compound; いき is becoming more common. When the word 行き is used in a sentence such as 電車は行きも帰りもとても混んでいました 'both the train going and coming back were very crowded', the reading いき is mandatory.

This kind of nominal transformation also occurs with the descriptive verbs 近い and 遠い that we introduced in 11.2. The ～く form can be treated as the conjunctive of the descriptive verb in this case. An example taken from the text of this lesson is 春日神社の近くでお弁当を食べてから...

図書館はこの近くです。
The library is near here (*lit.* in this vicinity).

23.7 How to 'sign off'

よろしく伝えて下さい。

You will be introduced to proper letter writing later on. Here Minoru has written a simple postcard, and one does not usually bother with formal set phrases on such a card. This phrase よろしく伝えて下さい, however, is a very useful and general way to finish a letter or short note like this: 'please give my best to...'

Key to passage

Romanisation

O-kāsan, o-genki desu ka. Kyōto wa kono san yokka gutto kion ga sagari, sukkari aki rashiku narimashita. Tōkyō wa ikaga desu ka. Kyō wa asa kara tomodachi to Nara ni asobi ni ikimashita.

Ekimae kara shika o minagara Nara Kōen o tōri, Daibutsuden made arukimashita. Kasuga Jinja no chikaku de o-bentō o tabete kara hisashiburi ni Shin-Yakushi-ji made itte kimashita. Mō jūnen mo mae ni minna de issho ni itta no o oboete imasu ka. Hagi no hana ga migoto ni saite imashita. Ichinichi-jū arukimawari, sukoshi tsukareta no de kaeri wa Shin-Yakushi-ji mae kara basu ni norimashita. Kondo no yasumi ni wa kōyō o mi ni Arashiyama ni iku tsumori desu. Otōsan, Tadahi o-niisan, sore ni Kuniko ni mo yoroshiku tsutaete kudasai. De wa, sayōnara. Minoru

---

Translation

Mother, how are you? In Kyōto the temperature has dropped like a stone these past three or four days, and it has become very autumnal. How is it in Tōkyō? Today I spent relaxing in Nara with friends. From just in front of the station we walked to the Daibutsuden through Nara Park looking at the deer. After we had eaten a boxed lunch near Kasuga Shrine we went as far as Shin-Yakushi-ji, where I haven't been for ages. Do you remember going there with everyone more than ten years ago? The *hagi* were blooming spectacularly. Walking around all day, we were a bit tired and so on the way home we boarded the bus in front of Shin-Yakushi-ji. Next holiday I plan to go to Arashiyama to see the autumn leaves. Please give my regards to father, Tadashi and Kuniko. That's enough for now. Minoru

---

Lesson 24

A conversation between Kuniko and her mother.

国子	ねえ、おかあさん、この前京都へ行った時、どこに泊まったの。
母	あの時は学会がたくさんあってホテルはどこも空いていなかったので、実おにいさんの下宿のそばのお寺に泊まったけれど。
国子	今ごろも宿はどこもいっぱいかしら。
母	そうね。秋は観光客も多いし、学会に来る外国人も多いからいっぱいかもしれないわね。
国子	きょう、学校の帰りに指定席のきっぷを買いに駅に行ってみたけど、来週の木曜のはもう一枚も残っていなかったわ。
母	それじゃあ、宿もきっといっぱいね。京都のホテルがいっぱいの時も奈良のホテルは時々空いていますよ。
国子	おかあさん達の泊まったお寺はよかった。
母	そうね。静かで清潔なところでしたよ。
国子	行く前に予約をした。
母	いいえ、あの時はおにいさんの下宿へ行ってから捜したのよ。
国子	おにいさんに電話をかけて聞いてみるわ。

Comment

Japanese may not have any 'masculine' or 'feminine' genders for its nouns, but this does not mean that the language lacks a sense of gender. Far from it, gender is very strongly marked in everyday speech; men and women speak in different tones and use different words. It is immediately obvious from the words alone here that this conversation is between two women. Note in particular the use of ねえ as a way of catching someone's attention, and a whole series of female specific sentence ending markers: かしら for 'I wonder', and わね, わ, のよ etc. Since the conversation is an intimate one between mother and daughter, the plain form is used. You will however notice that the mother does use ～ます and でした on two occasions. In this particular context, such a change marks a very slight shift: from talking on an equal footing to a more 'kindly' tone. Study this conversation very carefully. Ask yourself, for example, why both the mother and Kuniko use the word おにいさん to refer to Minoru. It is because he is Kuniko's *elder* brother.

24.1 The noun 時

この前京都へ行った時、どこに泊まったの。
あの時は学会がたくさんあってホテルはどこも空いていなかった。

時, here pronounced とき, is a noun meaning 'time' and when modified by a verb it can function as a subordinating conjunction meaning 'when'. Being a noun, it can also appear directly after prenouns (この, その, あの), descriptive verbs, adjectival nouns + な, and true verbs; but to be linked to another noun, of course, it needs the particle の. 時 can also be found with or without the particle に. When に is used, a certain amount of stress is being put on 時. We shall classify the use of this word into three categories.

(a) A specific identifiable *moment* in perfective and imperfective contexts

その時電話がなった。
At that moment the telephone rang.

三時に電話をかけた時には彼は留守でした。
When I telephoned him at three o'clock he was out.

十年前、広島に住んでいた時ひどい台風にあいました。
Ten years ago, when we were living in Hiroshima, we experienced a terrible typhoon.

帰る時には戸にかぎをかけて下さい。
When you go home, please lock the door.

(b) A specific identifiable *period of time*, usually in a perfective context but occasionally in an imperfective context

子供の時にピアノを習いました。
I learned the piano when I was a child.

今が大切な時です。
Now is the important time.

仕事を捜していた時には毎月二十通以上いろいろな会社に手紙を書いた。
While I was looking for a job, I wrote more than twenty letters a month to various companies.

(c) A moment or a period of time or an occasion which is *generic*, hence unspecific. Consequently the ～た form is not used here.

火事の時にはエレベーターを使わないで下さい。
In the event of fire, please don't use the lift.

暑い時には冷たいビールがおいしい。
When it's hot, cold beer tastes good.

24.2 The use of の in sentence-final position

どこに泊まったの。

The sentence particle の is here being used to signify an informal question. Remember that it is by and large a 'female' ending.

24.3 前

この前京都へ行った時、 行く前に予約をした。

前 is another noun used in time clauses; it means 'before'.

(a) Noun + の + 前, or prenoun + 前:

その前はどこにいたのですか。
Where were you before that?

この前三ヶ月ぶりに山田さんが遊びに来ました。
The other day Mr Yamada came to visit for the first time in three months.

試験の前は少なくとも一日 (に) 八時間勉強しました。
Before the examination I studied at least eight hours a day.

(b) Verb + 前

The verb preceding 前 can *never* occur in the perfective ～た form. This is an instance of relative tense in Japanese: the meaning of 前 makes it inevitable that the action of the verb in the 前 clause occurs after the verb in the main clause, so it must be imperfective with reference to the final verb.

お金を払う前に金額をよく確かめて下さい。
Please make sure of the sum before you pay.

ベトナムは独立する前はフランスの植民地だった。
Vietnam was a French colony before its independence.

24.4 Tense agreement

The use of time expressions raises the matter of tense agreement between clauses in Japanese. Students are often confused to find mixtures of perfective and imperfective where they expect a measure of 'tense agreement', and this gives rise to the common but erroneous impression that Japanese is generally lax in such matters. It is probably wiser to say that 'tense agreement', as it is usually applied to European languages, does not exist in Japanese. But this should not lead you to assume that you can just mix imperfective and perfective at random; it is just that decisions are made on somewhat different criteria. The problem for the student is that these criteria are still not sufficiently understood. The following example should at least give you some idea of what can be involved:

去年中国へ行く時空港で橋本さんに会いました。
去年中国へ行った時空港で橋本さんに会いました。

Both of these sentences are correct and both can be translated as 'When I went to China last year I met Hashimoto at the airport.' But the first sentence with the imperfective 行く indicates that the meeting with Hashimoto occurred prior to the act of going, hence the speaker probably met Mr Hashimoto at London Airport. The second sentence with the perfective 行った implies that the speaker probably met Mr Hashimoto having gone to China, so the meeting could well have taken place in Beijing Airport.

24.5 かしら

宿はどこもいっぱいかしら。

かしら or のかしら is used, usually by women, at the end of a statement to express a rhetorical question, as though one were half-way addressing oneself. かしら can be added directly to nouns or verbs; のかしら, however, needs the copula な to link to nouns.

あしたは雨かしら。
Will it rain tomorrow, I wonder?

来ないのかしら。
Perhaps he's not coming?

便利なのかしら。
I wonder if it might be convenient.

24.6 かもしれない

いっぱいかもしれないわね。

This is a colloquial expression meaning 'perhaps' or 'maybe'. It can be used directly after the plain form of a verb, or directly after a noun.

さっき来たのは山田さんかもしれない。
Maybe it was Mr Yamada who came a few minutes ago.

工事のため電車は遅れるかもしれません。
Due to construction work, trains may be delayed.

山の上は寒いかもしれないのでセーターを持っていきます。
I will take my jumper with me because it may be cold on top of the mountain.

24.7 The ～て form + みる

指定席のきっぷを買いに駅に行ってみたけれど、
電話をかけて聞いてみるわ。

As we saw in lesson 16, the ～て form of the verb can be used in combination with a number of other verbs. These combinations often need special attention because they are used idiomatically; in other words, their meaning is not immediately obvious from the constituent elements. This ～てみる pattern means 'do something and see how it goes' or 'try to...'

彼に手紙を書いてみましたが、今のところ返事がありません。
I have written to him, but so far there is no reply.

三時ごろに電話をかけてみましたが、彼女は留守でした。
I tried to call her around three o'clock but she was not in.

Look at the phrase 電話をかけて聞いてみる again. There is a series of two ～て forms in a row. Such series may seem a bit complicated at first but they are quite commonly used. Here she is saying 'I'll try calling and asking him'.

家にもどってもう一度捜してみます。
I'll go home and try looking for it again.

24.8 一 + numerical classifier + も…ない

来週の木曜のはもう一枚も残っていなかったわ。

This pattern expresses 'not a single...'

今週は授業に一度も出なかった。
This week I did not attend lectures even once.

先週は一回も授業を休まなかった。
Last week I did not miss a single lecture.

彼からは一通も手紙が来ない。
Not even a single letter has arrived from him.

24.9 Unmarked questions

おかあさん達の泊まったお寺はよかった。 行く前に予約をした。

Although neither of these phrases have either a か or a の to show that they are questions, the context will tell you that they must be. In live speech the question would be clear from the rising intonation. The same kind of thing happens in English, but we have the help of a question mark to help us out when writing such a sentence down. In Japanese it is not the habit to use such a symbol. You will undoubtedly be thrown by this a few times before you learn to anticipate it.

Key to conversation

Romanisation

Kuniko Nē, o-kāsan, kono mae Kyōto e itta toki, doko ni tomatta no.

Haha	Ano toki wa gakkai ga takusan atte hoteru wa doko mo aite inakatta no de, Minoru o-niisan no geshuku no soba no o-tera ni tomatta keredo.
Kuniko	Imagoro mo yado wa doko mo ippai kashira.
Haha	Sō ne. Aki wa kankōkyaku mo ōi shi, gakkai ni kuru gaikokujin mo ōi kara ippai ka mo shirenai wa ne.
Kuniko	Kyō, gakkō no kaeri ni shiteiseki no kippu o kai ni eki ni itte mita kedo, raishū no mokuyō no wa mō ichimai mo nokotte inakatta wa.
Haha	Sore jā, yado mo kitto ippai ne. Kyōto no hoteru ga ippai no toki mo Nara no hoteru wa tokidoki aite imasu yo.
Kuniko	Okāsantachi no tomatta o-tera wa yokatta.
Haha	Sō ne. Shizuka de seiketsu na tokoro deshita yo.
Kuniko	Iku mae ni yoyaku o shita.
Haha	Iie, ano toki wa o-niisan no geshuku e itte kara sagashita no yo.
Kuniko	O-niisan ni denwa o kakete kiite miru wa.

Translation

Kuniko	Mother, when you last went to Kyōto, where did you stay?
Mother	There were a lot of conferences on then and all the hotels were full, so we stayed at a temple next door to Minoru's lodgings.
Kuniko	I wonder if all the inns are full now too.
Mother	Yes, I wonder. There are lots of tourists in the autumn and lots of foreigners coming for conferences, so they might all be full.
Kuniko	Today on the way home from school I went to the station to see if I could buy a reserved seat, but there wasn't a single ticket left for next Thursday.
Mother	In that case all the inns will be full too. Sometimes when Kyōto hotels are full, hotels in Nara have vacancies though, you know.
Kuniko	Was the temple where you stayed good?
Mother	Yes. It was quiet and clean.
Kuniko	Did you book before you left?
Mother	No, we found it after we had got to Minoru's lodgings.
Kuniko	I'll try ringing him to ask.

Lesson 25

Mr and Mrs Yamakawa are having tea in the afternoon.

信子	おとうさん、お茶が入りました。
一	ああ、ありがとう。庭の柿の木もずいぶん色づいてきたね。
信子	そうですね。あの木を植えたのはいつごろでしたっけ。
一	国子が生まれたすぐ後じゃなかったかい。
信子	そうそう、そうでした。
一	あのころはずいぶん大変だったな。
信子	そうでしたね。子供が三人いましたし、お金もあまりありませんでしたし、それにあなたはお仕事がとてもお忙しかったから…。
一	正はきょうも仕事か。
信子	ええ、朝早くから病院へ行っていますが、そろそろもどるころです。
一	国子は。
信子	お友達と連休を利用して、京都、奈良へ行っています。
一	ああ、そうだったね。そういえば、きょうは六時ごろ会社の大山君が来る。
信子	夏にも一度いらっしゃった方ですね。
一	そうだ。お酒はあるか。
信子	はい。それでは何か簡単なおつまみでも用意します。

Comment:
Note the difference between this conversation and the one in lesson 24. There, mother and daughter were talking in a relaxed manner. Here we have wife and husband; a totally different situation that will demand different language. When mother becomes wife, the persona changes. As the wife, Nobuko regularly uses polite です/ます endings, whereas the husband uses brusque masculine forms in return. In a Japanese context the husband is not being rude; he is merely talking as a husband is expected to talk, and the wife is being 'wifely'. You may wish to argue on this basis that Japanese society is extremely sexist, and that the sexism is rooted in the language. To a certain extent this is true: both status and

gender are overtly present in the grammatical forms to a degree that we find unsettling. This means that whenever the Japanese communicate they can hardly avoid the fact that they are playing a particular role. But whatever the rights and wrongs of the matter, it is important for you as a student of the language and the culture to realise that the wife would normally interpret this language as something intimate. If the husband were polite, then something would be wrong!

You will find in the passage a number of specifically 'male' markers, such as かい, だったな, and the abrupt use of か directly after a noun. Study them carefully.

25.1 More about ～てくる

色づいてきたね。

In addition to the meaning explained in 23.5, the form ～てくる is used to indicate two types of verbal aspect.

(a) Inception. It marks a process (often a natural process) that is beginning to happen.

東の方から夜が明けてきました。
Dawn is starting to break from the east.

雨が降ってきました。
It's come on to rain (started raining).

(b) It can also mark the continuation of a process up to a particular point, usually, but not necessarily, the present.

日本語を上手に話す外国人が増えてきましたね。
There are now more and more foreigners who speak Japanese well, aren't there?

森林保護の重要性を理解する人が少しづつ多くなってきている。
There has been a gradual increase in the number of people who understand the importance of protecting forests.

25.2 ころ

あの木を植えたのはいつごろでしたっけ。 あのころはずいぶん大変だったな。 そろそろもどるころです。

ころ is a noun meaning 'approximate time' and it is sometimes used in similar ways to 時. There are, however, cases where 時 cannot be simply replaced by ころ, so you should be careful.

(a) A less specific moment in a perfective context

初めてイギリスへ来たのは水仙の花のころでした。
It was daffodil time when I first came to England.

(b) Speculation about a moment both in perfective and imperfective contexts

父は一時の電車で行ったのでもうそちらへ着くころです。
Father went on the one o'clock train, so he should be there about now.

日本への小包は一ヶ月前に出しましたからもう着いたころです。
I sent the parcel to Japan a month ago, so it's about time it arrived.

(c) A period of time which is not clearly identifiable or specific, used in a perfective context only. In these sentences 時 can be used instead of ころ with only slight change in meaning. ころ is more commonly used when the speaker is talking about his past with a certain nostalgia.

戦争のころはお米の代わりにさつまいもを食べた。
During the war, we had sweet potatoes instead of rice.

若いころはよく友達と議論をした。
When I was young, I often used to have debates with my friends.

大学で日本語を勉強していたころはとても楽しかった。
I enjoyed myself very much while I was studying Japanese at university.

25.3 でしたっけ

いつごろでしたっけ。

っけ marks a rhetorical question. It normally occurs with the perfective form and in such a context brings with it a sense of retrospection: 'now, when was that?' It also gestures towards the other person and invites them to participate in your thoughts.

25.4 後

国子が生まれたすぐ後じゃなかったかい。

後, pronounced あと, is a noun meaning 'after'. It is used to produce time clauses in much the same way as 前.

(a) Noun + の + 後, or prenoun + 後. When it is combined with a prenoun, 後 can be pronounced either あと or ご.

その後どうなりましたか。
And then what happened?

試合の後でみんなと飲みに行きました。
After the match, I went drinking with everyone.

(b) Verb + 後:

友達が帰った後、私は洗いものをした。
After my friends had returned home I did the washing up.

大きな事故が起こった後で人々はその道路が危険なのに気がついた。
They noticed how dangerous the road was after a serious accident had occurred.

Note here that the verb that precedes 後 or 後で is *always* in the ～た form for reasons of relative tense. This is the case even when the tense of the main clause is present or future.

25.5 The question marker かい

じゃなかったかい。

かい is best treated as a simple variant for the ending かね. It marks a slightly softer question than the direct か, so much so that it will be used when you are asking yourself a question: 'Let me see, wasn't it...' Since it is colloquial, you will find that the copula is often omitted: そうかい 'Oh, was it really?' It is by and large, but not exclusively, male.

25.6 Noun + か

正はきょうも仕事か。

If the father had been using the polite です form here, he would have said 正はきょうも仕事ですか, but the copula is omitted entirely when asking this type of question in the plain form. The interrogative equivalent of 正はきょうも仕事だ is therefore *not* *正はきょうも仕事だか. Study the following examples:

一男が来たのはきのうか。
Was it yesterday that Kazuo came?

弟さんは元気か。
Is your younger brother well?

あの音は風か。
Is that noise the wind?

25.7 早くから

朝早くから

You will perhaps recognize the word 早く as the adverbial form of the descriptive verb 早い. Here it means 'early', so the phrase above means 'from early this morning'. When using the particle から with descriptive verbs take great care to distinguish between those occasions when it follows the plain form meaning 'because': まだ朝早いからお店はどこも開いていない, 'None of the shops are open because it's still too early' (see also 16.7), and those occasions when it follows the adverbial form く, as above, and means 'from'.

25.8 Honorific language versus politeness

一度いらっしゃった方ですね。

This is the first example we have given of a verb that expresses respect. From now on you will have to keep clear in your mind the somewhat different concepts of honorific language on the one hand and politeness on the other. *Honorific* language relates to the question of the status of people or objects in the real world that are mentioned in conversation; decisions here on what is known as the 'level of reference' are governed by the speaker's attitude towards the subject or topic of discourse. *Politeness*, however, relates to whether your language in any particular situation is polite, neutral or actively rude. This is known as the 'level of address' because decisions here are governed by the speaker's attitude towards the addressee. In this case, the wife's normal speech level when conversing with her husband is polite. When the husband introduces a friend from work into the conversation, she refers to him with a verb of *respect*, いらっしゃった, the perfective form of the verb いらっしゃる, the respectful equivalent of 行く, 来る, or いる 'be'. More will be said about these verbs and their humble equivalents in due course. Just note that a verb like いらっしゃる here *raises the status of its subject*. This is not always the same thing as being polite to the person with whom you are conversing.

You were introduced to the polite prefix お in 4.1. You will see that it is used on a number of occasions, and each time the nuance is slightly different; when the wife says お茶, for instance, the sense of politeness is very weak because the prefix has become habitually attached to the word for tea. Later on the husband will say お酒 in an entirely neutral manner. When the wife says あなたはお仕事がとてもお忙しかったから, however, she actually repeats the prefix; this gives one the feeling that here she is being particularly solicitous. When she says お友達 about Kuniko's friends, the prefix takes on the attributes of honorific language.

25.9 More on names

会社の大山君が来る。

Note how the husband refers to one his fellow employees. If he had used さん, it would mean that they were not particularly close and that Ōyama was either older or senior to him in the company. Because he uses the intimate suffix 君

(くん), we know immediately that Ōyama is either younger or the same age, and that he is either below him in the company hierarchy or at roughly the same level.

25.10 何か…でも

何か簡単なおつまみでも用意します。

The use of an interrogative followed by か expresses the idea of *indeterminacy;* so here 何か means 'something'. The whole sentence is given a further self-deprecating flavour by the substitution of でも for the object marker を. 'Well then, I'll prepare something: (even something as insignificant as) some simple snacks to go with the drinks.' You will find this でも used quite often when people are offering you something to eat or drink; it reminds one of the English usage 'would you like a little…' お茶でもどうぞ 'Would you like a little tea?'

Key to conversation

Romanisation

Nobuko	Otōsan, o-cha ga hairimashita.
Hajime	Ā, arigatō. Niwa no kaki no ki mo zuibun irozuite kita ne.
Nobuko	Sō desu ne. Ano ki o ueta no wa itsu goro deshitakke.
Hajime	Kuniko ga umareta sugu ato ja nakatta kai.
Nobuko	Sō sō, sō deshita.
Hajime	Ano koro wa zuibun taihen datta na.
Nobuko	Sō deshita ne. Kodomo ga sannin imashita shi, o-kane mo amari arimasen deshita shi, sore ni anata wa o-shigoto ga totemo o-isogashikatta kara…
Hajime	Tadashi wa kyō mo shigoto ka.
Nobuko	Ē, asa hayaku kara byōin e itte imasu ga, sorosoro modoru koro desu.
Hajime	Kuniko wa.

Nobuko	O-tomodachi to renkyū o riyō shite, Kyōto, Nara e itte imasu.
Hajime	Ā, sō datta ne. Sō ieba, kyō wa rokuji goro kaisha no Ōyama kun ga kuru.
Nobuko	Natsu ni mo ichido irasshatta kata desu ne.
Hajime	Sō da. O-sake wa aru ka.
Nobuko	Hai. Sore de wa nani ka kantan na o-tsumami de mo yōi shimasu.

Translation

Nobuko	Hajime. There's some tea, if you'd like.
Hajime	Oh, thank you. The persimmon tree in the garden has really turned hasn't it!
Nobuko	So it has. When was it that we planted it?
Hajime	Wasn't it just after Kuniko was born?
Nobuko	Yes, yes, so it was.
Hajime	Those were tough times!
Nobuko	So they were. Three children, not much money, and then you were so busy at work...
Hajime	Tadashi working today too?
Nobuko	Yes, he's been at the hospital since early this morning but he'll be back any moment now.
Hajime	Where's Kuniko?
Nobuko	She's taking advantage of the long weekend and is spending it in Kyōto and Nara with a friend.
Hajime	Oh yes, I remember. That reminds me, about six o'clock today young Ōyama from the company is coming over.
Nobuko	The one who came over once during the summer?
Hajime	Thats right. Is there any sake in?
Nobuko	Yes. Well then I'll prepare something simple to go with it.

Lesson 26

Mr Ōyama visits Mr Yamakawa at his home.

大山　　ごめん下さい。
信子　　あ、大山さん。お待ちしていました。どうぞ。
大山　　おじゃまします。
信子　　さ、どうぞこちらへ。

大山　　来年の一月から三年の予定でサウジアラビアへ行くことになりました。
一　　そうか。それで君一人で行くのかい。
大山　　はい。最初の二、三ヶ月はまず私が一人で行って、その後で家族をよぶことにしました。
一　　そうか、それがいいかもしれないな。君は前にも外国で仕事をしたことはあったね。
大山　　はい、アジアの国には長期滞在したことがありますが、中近東の国へはまだ行ったことがありません。
一　　ところで、アラビア語は少しは出来るのか。
大山　　この話はだいぶ前からありましたから勉強を始めたことは始めたのですが...。まあ、話すことは何とか少しは出来ますが、読んだり、書いたりするのはまだまだです。
一　　それは大変だな。

Comment

When Mr Ōyama arrives at the house he is greeted at the door by Mr Yamakawa's wife. All Japanese houses, and most apartments, have a space at the front door known as the 玄関 (げんかん) where the necessary formalities of greeting and saying farewells can be carried out. During this first exchange, Mr Ōyama is probably still standing at the entrance, preparing to take off his shoes. Normally there will be a step up into the house and the wife would be kneeling down on the wooden floor of the house proper, putting out the house slippers that are always provided for guests. You should try and memorise all these phrases, because they are very useful.

Once the men settle down for a chat, their relationship becomes a little clearer. You will notice that Ōyama uses the polite ～ます form, whereas Mr Yamakawa does not. This tells you that Ōyama is probably junior to Yamakawa in the company; but if he were working directly under Yamakawa, it is likely that his language would be more formal still. You still cannot be a hundred per cent certain of their exact relationship.

26.1 'Please excuse me'

ごめん下さい。

This phrase literally means 'may I receive your indulgence', めん meaning 'indulgence' or 'exemption'. ご (御) is similar to お in that it is prefixed to nouns and signifies politeness. Generally speaking ご is used when the characters are being pronounced in their *on* reading; お when the *kun* reading is being used. 酒 'alcoholic drink', for example, takes お when read さけ, but ご when pronounced しゅ. You have also met combinations such as お金 and お寺. This 'rule', however, has many common exceptions: you have already come across a word like お電話, where the expected *ご電話 does *not* occur. You will have to learn each case as and when you meet it.

26.2 Humble verbs

お待ちしていました。
おじゃまします。

In 25.8 we touched on the subject of levels of speech. Here is another example. We can tell that the sentence is *polite* because it ends in ～ました, but it also contains an example of honorific language. Honorific language either works by raising the status of the subject of the verb, in which case we call it respect, or by lowering the status of the subject of the verb, in which case we call it humble. The previous lesson had the example of いらっしゃる, which was an example of respect being shown for the subject, Ōyama-san. Here we have the opposite, two humble constructions: 'We have been waiting for you' and 'I am about to interfere.' There are a number of ways of producing a humble form, but this is the simplest: prefix お + conjunctive form + する.

> メッセージは確かにお伝えしました。
> I definitely passed on the message.
>
> あの本はもう先生にお返ししました。
> I have already returned that book to the teacher.

You may be surprised to see お being used in a humble construction, but these statements always involve another person to some extent. The お is present in order to show an element of respect to that other person. Look, for instance, at the following sentence:

> あの本はもう先生にお返しした。
> I have already returned that book to the teacher.

Here there is no politeness expressed between speaker and hearer, perhaps because they are close friends, but the verb お返しした both humbles its subject (the student speaking) and expresses respect to the teacher by means of お.

26.3 Uses of こと

> サウジアラビアへ行くことになりました。
> 君は前にも外国で仕事をしたことはあったね。
> アジアの国には長期滞在したことがありますが、
> 中近東の国へはまだ行ったことがありません。

We have seen how の can be used to transform a verb or clause into a noun. こと has a similar function. This process is known by the general term nominalisation, although in this course the word nominalisation is being used in a somewhat more restricted sense (see 22.5). In the following expressions, the use of こと is obligatory. Note how you can in fact analyse these sentences in two ways. 外国で仕事をしたことはあった could be seen as 'the working abroad has existed' or 'the fact that X has worked abroad has existed', depending on whether you wish to see こと as a kind of empty word that has a nominalising function, or as an abstract noun in its own right meaning 'fact', 'activity' or 'behaviour'.

26.4 Verb in citation form + ことになる

三年の予定でサウジアラビアへ行くことになりました。

This pattern means 'It has been decided that...' or 'It has been arranged that...'; its use implies that you had little or nothing to do with making the decision.

今度出張で九州に行くことになりました。
It has now been decided that I will go to Kyūshū on business.

その仕事は島田さんが担当することになりました。
It has been decided that Mr Shimada will be in charge of that job.

26.5 Verb in citation form + ことにする

その後で家族をよぶことにしました。

This pattern means 'to decide to...' and implies that the subject has made a conscious decision to do something.

これからは毎日軽い運動をすることにします。
I've decided to exercise a little every day from now on.

あの人とはもう話をしないことにしました。
I have decided not to talk to that person any more.

26.6 ことがある

> アジアの国には長期滞在したことがありますが、
> 中近東の国へはまだ行ったことがありません。

The phrase ことがある, literally 'there exists a matter', is used in the following ways:

(a) When the verb preceding こと is in the perfective form as here, the phrase means 'doing X happened', i.e. 'one has had the experience of...'

日本語で小説を読んだことがありますか。
Have you ever read a novel in Japanese?

生れてから雪を見たことがない子供が世界には案外たくさんいます。
There is a surprisingly large number of children in this world who have never seen snow in their life.

(b) When the verb preceding こと is in the imperfective form the phrase means 'doing X does happen', i.e. 'there are times when'.

この時計は時々進むことがあります。
There are times when this watch runs fast.

このごろとても忙しいので夜八時過ぎまで会社にいることがよくあります。
These days I am so busy that there are many times when I stay at the office until after eight.

26.7 ことが出来る

アラビア語は少しは出来るのか。 話すことは何とか少しは出来ますが

In the first of these examples, the 出来る is short for 話すことが出来る, which makes its full appearance in the second example. が has changed to は at this point because we are dealing with a contrast leading up to the hesitant 'yes, but' at the end. This pattern means 'to be able to...' Here again, こと nominalises the clause that precedes it. Study the following examples:

彼は優秀な科学者だが、自分の研究を平易な言葉で説明することが出来ない。
He is an outstanding scientist but cannot explain his research simply.

御意見はよく分りましたが残念ながら賛成することは出来ません。
I understood your opinion perfectly well but I regret to say that I cannot agree with you.

26.8 Verb + ことは + verb

勉強を始めたことは始めたのですが

As a follow-on from 26.6 above, we also have a fully-fledged example here of the hesitant 'Well, it *does...*, but' or 'Well, I *have...*, but'.

もう昼ごはんは食べましたか。
Have you already had lunch?

ええ、食べたことは食べたのですが、まだおなかがすいています。
Well yes, I *have had* lunch, but I'm still hungry.

この本はもう読みましたか。
Have you read this book?

はい、読んだことは読みましたが、あまりよく分かりませんでした。
Well yes, I *have read* the book, but I didn't really understand it.

26.9 The particle で

最初の二、三ヶ月はまず私が一人で行って、

We have met で meaning 'by means of'. With words denoting people, で is used to express 'by' as in:

せんたくやそうじは全部自分でします。
Washing and cleaning, I do it all by myself.

フランスまでは妹と行きます。そしてそこからエジンバラへは一人で行きます。
I will go as far as France with my younger sister. And then from there I will go on to Edinburgh by myself.

By implication, this use of で tends to exclude other people:

この仕事は母と私とでします。
lit. As for this work, my mother and I will do it (and need no other help).

Key to conversation

Romanisation

Ōyama Gomen kudasai.
Nobuko A, Ōyama-san. O-machi shite imashita. Dōzo.
Ōyama O-jama shimasu.
Nobuko Sa, dōzo kochira e.
Ōyama Rainen no ichigatsu kara sannen no yotei de Sauji Arabia e iku koto ni

	narimashita.
Hajime	Sō ka. Sore de kimi hitori de iku no kai.
Ōyama	Hai. Saisho no ni-sankagetsu wa mazu watakushi ga hitori de itte, sono ato de kazoku o yobu koto ni shimashita.
Hajime	Sō ka, sore ga ii ka mo shirenai na. Kimi wa mae ni mo gaikoku de shigoto o shita koto wa atta ne.
Ōyama	Hai, Ajia no kuni ni wa chōki taizai shita koto ga arimasu ga, chūkintō no kuni e wa mada itta koto ga arimasen.
Hajime	Tokoro de, Arabiago wa sukoshi wa dekiru no ka.
Ōyama	Kono hanashi wa daibu mae kara arimashita kara benkyō o hajimeta koto wa hajimeta no desu ga... Mā, hanasu koto wa nan to ka sukoshi wa dekimasu ga, yondari, kaitari suru no wa mada mada desu.
Hajime	Sore wa taihen da na.

Translation

Ōyama	May I come in?
Nobuko	Oh, Mr Ōyama. We've been looking forward to your visit. Please come in.
Ōyama	Sorry to disturb you.
Nobuko	Please, this way.
Ōyama	It's been decided that I'll go to Saudi Arabia for three years from January next year.
Hajime	Really? So, are you going alone?
Ōyama	Yes. I've decided that I'll go by myself for the first two or three months, and then I'll bring my family over.
Hajime	I see, that sounds like a good idea. You've worked abroad before haven't you?
Ōyama	Yes, I've had long postings in Asian countries, but I've never been to a Middle Eastern country before.
Hajime	Can you understand a bit of Arabic?
Ōyama	I've known about this for quite a while, so I have at least *begun* studying...Well, somehow or other I can get by in speaking; but reading and writing, not yet.
Hajime	What a chore!

Lesson 27

A short letter from John to Tadashi.

正君
先日会った時に伝えるのを忘れましたが、マリーさんが十一月二十三日にいっしょに遊びに来ないかと言っていました。この日は祭日だと思いますが、ちがいますか。都合を知らせて下さい。
この間の話のことですが、まだ決心がつきません。大学の調査隊の医師としてネパールへ行くというのはとても興味のある話ですが、実は来年はイギリスへ帰ることも考えているのです。調査目的、方法、日程などについては読んでみましたが、分からないことが一つ、二つあるので今度会った時に説明して下さい。いずれにしても今年中に決めるつもりです。では又近いうちに。ジョン

27.1 Quoting and reporting

マリーさんが十一月二十三日にいっしょに遊びに来ないかと言っていました。

What Marie actually said was:

(a) 十一月二十三日の土曜日に正さんといっしょに遊びに来ませんか。

If you were to quote this as direct speech, you would enclose the actual words in quotation marks and add と言った.

(b) マリーさんが「十一月三十日の土曜日に正さんといっしょに遊びに来ませんか」と言った。

If you were to report this as indirect speech, the result would be a little different:

(c) マリーさんが十一月三十日の土曜日にいっしょに遊びに来ないかと言っていました。

From this it should be clear that と is the quotative particle. It is used with verbs of saying and thinking and marks both direct and indirect speech. In the latter case it has the same effect as 'that' in English: it nominalises the quoted clause. Unlike English, however, there is a minimum of morphological change between the content of direct and indirect speech; often the only marker identifying direct speech is either the typographical one of quotation marks or the presence of polite verb endings and other sentence particles that denote 'raw' speech. Quoted material in indirect speech is usually minus these. Note that the particle と often emerges as って in ordinary speech:

一郎君がよろしくって言っていました。
Ichirō said to send his best.

27.2 言った as opposed to 言っていた

Why does (b) above end in と言った and (c) in と言っていました? Observe the following exchange:

I am talking to Hayashi:

私: 今晩、山田さんのうちの集まりに行きますか。
Are you going to the meeting at Yamada's tonight?

林: ええ、もちろん行きますよ。
Yes, of course.

Later, in conversation with Yamada, I report what Hayashi said (note that both 'I' and Yamada are female; you can tell this from the final particles):

山田: 今晩の集まりに林さんはいらっしゃるかしら。
Do you think Hayashi will come tonight?

私: さっき会った時、もちろん行くって言ってたわよ。
I've just met him and he said of course he'd come.

山田: それはよかったわ。
Oh good.

That evening:

山田: 林さんずいぶん遅いわね。もう来ないと思うわ。
Hayashi's very late isn't he? I don't think he'll come now.

私: でも今日の午後会った時には来ると言っていたわよ。
But he said he would come when I met him this afternoon.

Three hours later:

山田: やっぱり林さんは来なかったわ。あなたの聞きちがいじゃない。
You see, Hayashi didn't come did he? Didn't you mishear him?

私: そんなことはないわよ。私には「行きます」ってはっきり言ったわよ。 or 私には来るってはっきり言ったわよ。
No, honestly. He definitely said he was coming.

When you are simply *reporting* what someone said it is normal to use the ～ている form of the verb. Such and such was said and you are reporting what was said and the fact that it was said. However, when you actually *quote* what was said or wish to stress that something was definitely said 'in so many words' then you would tend to use the perfective instead. The ～ていた suggests the present relevance of something that has occurred; the ～た pinpoints it in the past. There is a certain parallel in the English 'he said that the other day' versus 'he was saying just that the other day', although this analogy should not be pushed too far.

27.3 'I think that...'

この日は祭日だと思いますが、ちがいますか。

The two verbs that normally occur in this pattern are ～と思う 'I think that...' and ～と考える 'I consider that...' Here too, as in indirect speech, the clause containing the thought content normally takes the plain form:

まちがっているのは彼だと思う。
I think it is he who is wrong.

On the principle that one cannot really know what other people are thinking, the subject of the verb 思う or 考える is usually the speaker. Thus, a sentence like

山田さんは来ないと思います。

can only mean 'I don't think Mr Yamada will come' and *not* 'Mr Yamada thinks he won't come.' To express speculation about other people's thoughts you need to use different forms that will be introduced later in the course. Note that we translated 山田さんは来ないと思います as 'I don't think Mr Yamada will come.' The literal English version, 'I think Mr Yamada will not come', sounds stilted and old-fashioned, and if used at all today would suggest that I was convinced Yamada would not come.

27.4 知らせる

都合を知らせて下さい。

The verb for 'tell or inform' here is 知らせる. You may learn it as a verb in its own right, but you will also probably recognise part of it as the verb 知る 'know'. It is in fact the causative form of this verb and so should be analysed as 'cause to know'. You will be introduced to causatives in a more systematic manner in a later lesson.

27.5 Noun + のことですが...

この間の話のことですが、まだ決心がつきません。

This phrase is used to introduce a topic of conversation, but in a more roundabout way than simply marking it with は.

明日のことですが、朝の会議は何時から始めますか。
About tomorrow; at what time shall we start the morning session?

山田さんのことですが、このごろ元気がありませんね。
By the way, about that Mr Yamada; he doesn't look well these days, does he?

The second phrase in the box above is a good example of how Japanese tends to avoid passives when possible. You will be introduced to the passive form later, but note here how what we would put as a passive, 'there's no decision been made yet', is expressed intransitively in Japanese.

27.6 という as an identification marker

大学の調査隊の医師としてネパールへ行くというのは
とても興味のある話ですが、

という is used to identify or to give further information about a noun. Quite often, as in the above example, it serves to nominalise a rather long clause:

他人と共同生活をするというのは難しい。
It is difficult to lead a communal life with strangers.

林田さんと結婚するといううわさは本当ですか。
Is the rumour that you are going to get married to Hayashida true?
社会における男の役割と女の役割はちがうという考え方は日本では一般的ですか。
Is the idea that man's role and woman's role in society are different common in Japan?

You will find that this explanatory pattern is used far more often in Japanese than you might expect, and as a result it does not have the rather precious feel that a literal translation would suggest. One fairly literal use of という can be found in the pattern 'noun + という + noun' meaning '...called...'

> 黒沢明という人を知っていますか。
> Do you know someone called Kurosawa Akira?
>
> これは何という花ですか。
> What is this flower called?
>
> 山口というところで生まれました。
> I was born in a place called Yamaguchi.

Again, you will find that, as a general rule, という is used far more than the English 'called', which can sound pedantic if used too often. Conversely, this means that you may find yourself forgetting to use という in contexts where a Japanese would expect it.

27.7 More on こと

分からないことがひとつ、ふたつあるので今度会った時に説明して下さい。

分からないこと in this context must be translated as '(there are one or two) things I don't understand', *not* as 'the lack of understanding'. The context tells you that こと is best interpreted here as an abstract noun meaning 'things' rather than as a nominaliser. Take, for instance, the following pair of sentences:

(a) その作家にとって書くことは社会批判だ。
For that author writing means social criticism.

(b) その作家の書くことは平凡だ。
What that author writes is trite.

In (a) it is the activity of writing that is in question, and so we can say that 書く

is being nominalised; in the second case it is what is being written that is in focus, and so こと means 'the things that'.

27.8 Choice of tense or aspect

今度会った時に説明して下さい。

Note the use of the ～た form here. You might, on the pattern of English 'please explain when next we meet', be tempted to produce an imperfective at this point. Remember, however, that the logic of time in a Japanese sentence works more within the sentence than without. The verb for 'meet' is in the perfective here, because the explanation will take place *after* the actual moment of meeting. Think of it as 'please explain when we (will) have met.' Conversely, in a sentence such as:

今度来る時に持ってきて下さい。
Please bring it when next you come.

the imperfective is used, because the 'bringing' is an integral part of the 'coming' and does not happen either before or after.

Key to passage

Romanisation

Tadashi-kun
Senjitsu atta toki ni tsutaeru no o wasuremashita ga, Marī-san ga jūichigatsu nijūsannichi ni issho ni asobi ni konai ka to itte imashita. Kono hi wa saijitsu da to omoimasu ga, chigaimasu ka. Tsugō o shirasete kudasai.
Kono aida no hanashi no koto desu ga, mada kesshin ga tsukimasen. Daigaku no chōsatai no ishi toshite Nepāru e iku to iu no wa totemo kyōmi no aru hanashi desu ga, jitsu wa rainen wa Igirisu

e kaeru koto mo kangaete iru no desu. Chōsa mokuteki, hōhō, nittei nado ni tsuite wa yonde mimashita ga, wakaranai koto ga hitotsu futatsu aru no de kondo atta toki ni setsumei shite kudasai. Izure ni shite mo kotoshi-jū ni kimeru tsumori desu. Dewa mata chikai uchi ni. Jon.

Translation

Dear Tadashi,
When we met the other day I forgot to tell you that Marie asked us to come over to her place together on 23 November. I think it's a public holiday, but correct me if I'm wrong. Please let me know whether you're free or not.
Concerning that other business, I still haven't been able to make up my mind. It sounds interesting to go to Nepal as the doctor on a university survey team, but to tell the truth I am also thinking of going back to England next year. I read about the purpose, method and schedule of the survey, but there are one or two things I'm not clear about so I'd like you to explain them next time we meet. In any case, I intend to decide before the end of the year. Hope to see you again soon. John.

Lesson 28

John and Tadashi visit Marie's new flat.

正	今晩は。
マリー	今晩は、正さん。どうぞこちらへ。
正	ずいぶんながめのいいところですね。
マリー	ええ、六階ですから。
正	このまどから西の方を見ると遠くに富士山も見えますね。
マリー	そうなんです。まわりには木もたくさんあるし、朝は鳥が鳴くのも聞こえるんですよ。
正	それはいいですね。あの辺にあるのは桜の木ですね。
マリー	ええ、近所の人が春になるときれいな花がさくと言っていました。
ジョン	ごめん下さい。
マリー	ジョンさん、どうぞ。
ジョン	やあ、正君。もう来ていたんですか。
正	いや、僕も今来たところです。
マリー	何か飲み物はいかがですか。
正	ビールをお願いします。
ジョン	いいですね。僕もとてものどがかわいているのでビールをいただきます。
マリー	はい、どうぞ。

28.1 Subjects in subordinate clauses

> ずいぶんながめのいいところですね。

In 21.3 we touched on the fact that subjects of subordinate clauses may be marked with の instead of が. This happens particularly when the subordinate clause modifies the noun very closely, as here. ながめのいいところ is literally 'a place whose view is good' hence 'a place with a good view'.

28.2 Further uses of と

> このまどから西の方を見ると遠くに富士山もみえますね。
> 春になるときれいな花がさく

When the sentence particle と is added to a verb, either in plain or 〜ます form, the result is a pattern meaning 'when...' There are a number of restrictions on its use, however, and its range is not nearly as wide as you might expect from the translation. It will never, for instance, be found following a 〜た form but is rather associated with the imperfective. Study the following:

(a) When the second clause is either a habitual occurrence or a natural consequence of the first clause, the feeling is that of a general statement, and the translation 'whenever' may perhaps be used:

秋になると木の葉が散る。
When autumn comes the leaves fall.

かぜをひくと必ず高い熱が出ます。
Whenever I catch cold, I always get a high temperature.

(b) と may also be used in more specific circumstances, but here too it is subject to a number of constraints. In this context the verb in the first clause is often found in the 〜ている progressive form and the verb in the second clause in the perfective. This particular pattern often brings with it an element of surprise:

ピアノをひいていると電話がなった。
The telephone rang, while I was playing the piano.
(or) There I was playing the piano when the telephone rang.

知子さんのうわさをしていると彼女が入ってきた。
As we were gossiping about Tomoko she (unexpectedly) turned up.

(c) Verb in plain form + と + verb in perfective. In this pattern, the action indicated by the second verb is either a direct and immediate reaction to that of the first verb, or both actions occur one after the other in rapid succession.

その話を聞くと青年は真っ赤になっておこった。
Hearing that story, the young man was absolutely furious.

私のすがたを見るとポチはしっぽをふりながら走って来た。
As soon as he saw me, Pochi (a dog) came running towards me wagging his tail.

品物を受け取ると男は大急ぎで店を出て行った。
On receiving the goods, the man left the shop in a hurry.

私がおはようと言うと彼女は「もう午後ですよ」とそっけなく答えた。
When I said good morning to her, she replied coldly saying 'it's already afternoon'.

(d) Verb in plain form + と + verb in past progressive or perfective.
In this pattern, the action indicated by the first verb makes the subject realise what had been going on.

外に出ると雨が降っていた。
On going out, I found it was raining.

家へ帰ると食事の支度が出来ていた。
On going home, I found that dinner had been prepared.

ふと目を上げると外は雪で真っ白だった。
I looked up and I found that outside everything was quite white with snow.

28.3 The verbs 見える and 聞こえる

> 富士山も見えますね。
> 鳥が鳴くのも聞こえるんですよ。

Both these sentences would normally be expressed in English using a transitive verb: 'you can even see Fujisan' and 'you can hear the birds sing too'. In Japanese these are best expressed intransitively. The whole question of transitive versus intransitive will be given more detailed coverage later. Note here that the verb 見える, being the intransitive equivalent of 見る, literally means 'is visible', and the verb 聞こえる, being the intransitive equivalent of 聞く, literally means 'is audible'. It is worth pointing out perhaps that the 'can' of the English translations does not really indicate ability, but rather possibility.

28.4 Uses of ところ

> 僕も今来たところです。

The noun ところ, which means 'place', is used as a grammatical tool as follows.

(a) Added to the imperfective, ところです means 'to be just on the point of...'

これから実験を始めるところです。
I am just about to start an experiment.

(b) added to the ～ている form, it means 'to be just now in the process of...'

今その本を読んでいるところです。
I am in the process of reading that book now.

(c) Added to the perfective, ところです means, as you might expect, 'to have just done something'.

今お茶を入れたところです。
I have just made some tea.

山田さんは今帰ったところです。
Yamada has just gone home.

28.5 Interrogative word + か

何か飲み物はいかがですか。

This is an extension of note 25.10. When か is added to an interrogative noun such as だれ 'who', 何 'what', どこ 'where', いくつ 'how many', it has the effect of transforming it into an *indefinite noun*. だれか 'someone', 何か 'something', どこか 'somewhere', いくつか 'some (number/amount)'. Note that syntactic particles such as が are often omitted with these words. Where numerical classifiers are involved, the pattern is 何 + numerical classifier + か.

その話はどこか (が) おかしい。
Something is wrong with that story.

冬休みにはどこかへ行くつもりですか。
Do you have any plans to go somewhere during the winter holiday?

私がいない間にだれかがこのコンピューターを使ったことはまちがいない。
There is no doubt that someone has used this computer during my absence.

このクラスには何人か剣道の得意な人がいる。
There are some in this class who are good at kendō.

Key to conversation

Romanisation

Tadashi	Konban wa.
Marī	Konban wa, Tadashi-san. Dōzo kochira e.
Tadashi	Zuibun nagame no ii tokoro desu ne.
Marī	Ē, rokkai desu kara.
Tadashi	Kono mado kara nishi no hō o miru to tōku ni Fujisan mo miemasu ne.
Marī	Sō nan desu. Mawari ni wa ki mo takusan aru shi, asa wa tori ga naku no mo kikoerun desu yo.
Tadashi	Sore wa ii desu ne. Ano hen ni aru no wa sakura no ki desu ne.
Marī	Ē, kinjo no hito ga haru ni naru to kirei na hana ga saku to itte imashita.
Jon	Gomen kudasai.
Marī	Jon-san, dōzo.
Jon	Yā, Tadashi-kun. Mō kite itan desu ka.
Tadashi	Iya, boku mo ima kita tokoro desu.
Marī	Nani ka nomimono wa ikaga desu ka.
Tadashi	Bīru o o-negai shimasu.
Jon	Ii desu ne. Boku mo totemo nodo ga kawaite iru no de bīru o itadakimasu.
Marī	Hai, dōzo.

Translation

Tadashi	Good evening.
Marie	Good evening Tadashi. Do come in please.
Tadashi	Your place has a wonderful view hasn't it?
Marie	Well, that's because it's on the sixth floor.
Tadashi	When you look to the west from this window you can even see Mt Fuji in the distance.
Marie	That's right. And there are lots of trees around, and you can hear the birds singing in the morning.
Tadashi	That's nice. Those ones over there are cherry trees aren't they?
Marie	Yes, one of my neighbours said that in spring there are lots of beautiful flowers in bloom.

John	May I come in?
Marie	John! Come in.
John	Tadashi! You're already here.
Tadashi	No no, I've only just arrived too.
Marie	Would you like something to drink?
Tadashi	A beer please.
John	That sounds good. I'm very thirsty so I'll have a beer too.
Marie	Here you are then.

Lesson 29

John, Tadashi and Marie go on talking in Marie's flat.

正	もうすっかり落ち着きましたか。
マリー	ええ、おかげさまで。一応片付け終わりました。
ジョン	日本にはまだしばらくいるつもりですか。
マリー	友達といっしょに日本の小説を一つフランス語に訳し始めたので、来年三月に大学が終った後もその仕事を続けるつもりにしています。
正	だれの小説ですか。
マリー	安部公房のです。
ジョン	難しくありませんか。
マリー	ええ、初めは引き受けるつもりはなかったんですが、いい勉強になると思ってやってみることにしました。
正	いつでも手伝いますよ。
マリー	ありがとう。
正	マリーさんが日本語を習い出したのは何年前ですか。
マリー	もう八年になります。
正	それじゃあ、きっと大丈夫だ。
マリー	そうだといいのですが、あまり自信がありません。話は割に分かりやすいのですが、フランス語に訳しにくい表現がたくさんあります。
正	細かいところは気にし過ぎない方がいいのではありませんか。
ジョン	いや、僕は小説の場合は細かいところも大切だと思いますね。
マリー	この訳し終ったところを読んでみて下さい。

29.1 Compound verbs using the conjunctive form

> もうすっかり落ち着きましたか。
> 一応片付け終わりました。

There are in Japanese a large number (over 1,000) of compound verbs which express complex action or states in single units. They are a combination of two verbs, the first one ending in the conjunctive form.

(a) It is useful to distinguish a subset of these compound verbs where the second element is not tied exclusively to one verb but can link to almost any verb. The major examples that you will come across are:

Verb + 出す	-	start...
Verb + 始める	-	begin...
Verb + 終わる	-	finish...
Verb + 続く	-	continue...(intrans.)
Verb + 続ける	-	continue...(trans.)

(b) With the majority of compound verbs it is a simple matter to predict the meaning from the constituent parts, but this is not always the case. There is, for example, a set of verbs which act as the second element in a compound the meaning of which may not be immediately obvious.

Verb + 合う (*lit.* to bring something together, mutually)

話し合う	-	discuss
出し合う	-	contribute
落ち合う	-	meet at a pre-arranged place
知り合う	-	get to know each other

Verb + 上げる (*lit.* to raise)

仕上げる	-	complete
読み上げる	-	complete reading, to read out aloud
切り上げる	-	wind up, to finish

Verb + 取る (*lit.* to take)

書き取る	-	write down
引き取る	-	take over

NB: 読み上げる in the second list is similar in meaning to 読み終わる but 読み

上げる emphasises the action that has been completed. The verbs *食べ上げる, *飲み上げる or *話し上げる do not exist, although 食べ終わる, 飲み終わる or 話し終わる are all very common.

(c) You will also come across some compound verbs where the meaning is even more idiomatic.

落ち着く	-	settle down
立ち寄る	-	drop by
見合わす	-	put off until later
見送る	-	see someone off
引き受ける	-	take on (a job)
割り切る	-	give a clear solution for, adopt a clear-cut attitude
張り切る	-	be in high spirits

Some compounds, however, appear to mean somewhat *less* than their constituent parts: つみおろす, for example, means not 'to load and then unload' but merely 'to unload', although the first verb may in fact refer to piling the load on the backs of labourers. Note also that although you may well find compounds being used which are not listed in dictionaries, you are not free to invent them at will. Restrict yourself to ones that you have heard and learned.

29.2 と producing conditionals

> そうだといいのですが。

You will find this phrase in the shorter form だといいのですが or だといいんだが as well. Literally the phrase means 'good if it were thus', and so we are dealing with a pattern that uses the particle と to produce conditional statements. In 28.2 this particle was treated as a temporal particle and was translated exclusively as 'when', but the distinction between 'when' and 'if' does not always hold in Japanese. The main difference is that English concentrates on certainty versus uncertainty, whether the speaker knows an action will or will not happen; Japanese, on the other hand, concentrates on the connection between two events, whether the second event is expected or arbitrary, natural or forced. The use of と in this example sentence should cause you no problems, but this particle will have to be discussed in more detail later when we introduce more ways of producing conditionals, because Japanese usage does not always coincide with English.

For the time being, we shall state the following: the implication of と in a conditional sentence is that the second clause is an *inevitable* consequence of the first: 'if..., then X is bound to happen'. Furthermore, there is a sense of immediacy and continuity attached to と, i.e. the action mentioned in the second clause follows straight after the first action almost automatically.

眠くなるとあくびが出る。
Whenever I become sleepy, I yawn.

今すぐ出発しないと飛行機に乗り遅れますよ。
Unless you leave right now you will miss the flight.

29.3 Verb + やすい, にくい

話は割に分かりやすいのですが、フランス語に訳しにくい表現がたくさんあります。

The descriptive verbs やすい 'is easy' and にくい 'is difficult' are often linked to verbs in the same way as these compounds.

Conjunctive + やすい	'...is easy to...'
Conjunctive + にくい	'...is difficult to...'

高速道路は運転しやすい。
It is easy to drive on motorways.

一度ついたくせはなかなか直しにくい。
Once one falls into a habit it is difficult to get out of it.

In such compounds the final product is treated as a descriptive verb for the purposes of further agglutination.

29.4 Use of + 過ぎる

気にし過ぎない方がいいのではありませんか。

The verb 過ぎる 'to exceed' 'to over…' can be linked not only to verbs but also to the stem of descriptive verbs and adjectival nouns.

きのうのパーティーでは飲み過ぎた。
I drank too much at yesterday's party.

正直過ぎる人はよく損をする。
Those who are too honest are often losers.

専門家の考え方は時々視野がせま過ぎる。
Experts think too narrow-mindedly on occasions.

29.5 方がよい/いい

気にし過ぎない方がいいのではありませんか。

方(ほう)がよい/いい is an expression meaning 'It would be better if…' 方(ほう) is a noun meaning 'direction' or 'alternative' and so the literal meaning of this phrase is 'the…alternative is good/preferable'. More will be said later about the various grammatical uses of this useful word 方(ほう).

練習を続ける方がいいですよ。
It would be better to carry on practising.

彼は来ないかもしれないので待たない方がよい。
It would be better not to wait because he may not come.

そんなことは言わない方がよい。
It would be better if you didn't say such a thing.

Key to conversation

Romanisation

Tadashi	Mō sukkari ochitsukimashita ka.
Marī	Ē, o-kagesama de. Ichiō katazuke owarimashita.
Jon	Nihon ni wa mada shibaraku iru tsumori desu ka.
Marī	Tomodachi to issho ni Nihon no shōsetsu o hitotsu Furansugo ni yakushihajimeta no de, rainen sangatsu ni daigaku ga owatta ato mo sono shigoto o tsuzukeru tsumori ni shite imasu.
Tadashi	Dare no shōsetsu desu ka.
Marī	Abe Kōbō no desu.
Jon	Muzukashiku arimasen ka.
Marī	Ē, hajime wa hikiukeru tsumori wa nakattan desu ga, ii benkyō ni naru to omotte yatte miru koto ni shimashita.
Tadashi	Itsu de mo tetsudaimasu yo.
Marī	Arigatō.
Tadashi	Marī san ga Nihongo o naraidashita no wa nannen mae desu ka.
Marī	Mō hachi nen ni narimasu.
Tadashi	Sore jā, kitto daijōbu da.
Marī	Sō da to ii no desu ga, amari jishin ga arimasen. Hanashi wa wari ni wakariyasui no desu ga, Furansugo ni yakushinikui hyōgen ga takusan arimasu.
Tadashi	Komakai tokoro wa ki ni shisuginai hō ga ii no de wa arimasen ka.
Jon	Iya, boku wa shōsetsu no baai wa komakai tokoro mo taisetsu da to omoimasu ne.
Marī	Kono yakushiowatta tokoro o yonde mite kudasai.

Translation

Tadashi	Have you completely settled in now?
Marie	Yes thank you. I've finished tidying up for the time being.
John	Do you intend to stay on in Japan for a bit longer?
Marie	I've begun translating a Japanese novel into French together with a friend and so even after university finishes in March of next year I intend to continue with that project.
Tadashi	Whose novel is it?
Marie	One of Abe Kōbō's.
John	Isn't it difficult?
Marie	Yes, so in the beginning I didn't intend to take it on, but I decided to give it a go because I thought I would learn a lot.
Tadashi	I'll help you whenever you wish.
Marie	Thank you.
Tadashi	How many years ago did you begin learning Japanese?
Marie	It's already eight years now.
Tadashi	Well in that case you'll have no problems.
Marie	It would be good if that were true, but I'm not so confident. The story is comparatively easy to understand, but there are many expressions which are difficult to translate into French.
Tadashi	Wouldn't it be better not to worry too much about the finer details?
John	On the contrary, I think that in the case of novels the finer details are important too.
Marie	Please have a look at these passages I've finished translating.

Lesson 30

A conversation between John and Tadashi

正	ネパールのこと決めましたか。
ジョン	ええ…。とても行きたいとは思っているんですが…。
正	何か問題があるんですか。
ジョン	一つは時期の問題で、十月からイギリスの病院で働くことが決まったので四月から九月末までネパールに行くというのはちょっと時間的にきついと思うのです。
正	そうですね。
ジョン	それに、イースターまでには帰ると母に手紙を書いたばかりなので両親ががっかりすると思うんです。
正	ジョンさんは日本へ来てもう三年目ですね。
ジョン	そうです。その間一度も帰っていませんし…。それに新しい仕事を始める前にイギリスやアメリカで最近出た医学雑誌なども読んでおきたいと思っているんです。
正	僕達医者の仕事は忙しいからゆっくり本を読んだり、考えたりする時間が本当にほしいですね。調査隊の責任者の人が二十五日までに決めてほしいと言っていましたけど…。

30.1 The ～たい form

> とても行きたいとは思っているんですが…。
> 最近出た医学雑誌なども読んでおきたいと思っているんです。

When the suffix ～たい is added to the conjunctive form of the verb the result is a descriptive verb signifying 'I want to…'

行く	行きたい	I want to go…
する	したい	I want to do…
買う	買いたい	I want to buy…

As the ～たい suffix transforms the whole compound into a descriptive verb, the pattern of inflections is as follows:

	positive	*negative*
imperfective	～たい	～たくない
perfective	～たかった	～たくなかった
imperfective	行きたい	行きたくない
perfective	行きたかった	行きたくなかった
imperfective	勉強したい	勉強したくない
perfective	勉強したかった	勉強したくなかった

30.2 が or を?

A verb form such as 買いたい 'I want to buy' being a descriptive verb is of course stative, so that when the 'object' bought is expressed, a stative construction should be used. This kind of construction was first introduced in 12.2, where it was explained in terms of a は + が combination. It might help to see this pattern in the same terms, although the は phrase is almost always suppressed:

(私は) 自転車が買いたい。
I want to buy a bike.

(私は) さっぱりした物が食べたい。
I want to eat something simple.

There is one important constraint about this pattern that you must always keep in mind. The general rule with such words that express desire or internal feeling in Japanese is that they can only be used in the affirmative *about the first person,* on the grounds that it is not possible to state anything about anyone else's feelings. They refer to individually experienced desires or wishes and cannot be used to assert anything about someone else. The only time you may use this construction about a second person is when you are asking a question. When you do so, however, you are specifically asking about their desires and feelings. It is for this reason that you should try to avoid as far as possible saying things like 行きたいですか, for 'do you want to go?' It is preferable to use some other phrase such as 行きませんか, or 行きましょうか ('shall we go', a form that will be introduced in due course).

Despite what has just been said above about stative intransitive constructions, you will, however, find sentences such as the following:

帰りに買物をしたい。
I would like to do the shopping on my way home.

パンダのよい写真をとりたかったが天気がよくなかったので難しかった。
I wanted to take good pictures of pandas but it was difficult because the weather was bad.

These are quite clearly simple transitive constructions with を. What seems to be happening is that the dynamic nature of the verb in question is achieving greater prominence than the stative nature of the construction itself. The construction shifts ground accordingly. You must be prepared to meet both kind of sentences, because the situation is at present fluid.

There will also be times, however, when this が/を conversion is *not* automatic, times when only を is acceptable. The rule here seems to be that if the 'object' is animate, or is being treated as being animate (for example in metaphorical usage), then を must be used.

敵を殺したい。
I want to kill my enemy.

私達のパーティーに原先生を招待したい。
I would like to invite Professor Hara to our party.

その指導者は人民の眠っている精神を呼び起こしたいと言っていた。
The leader said that he wanted to awaken the people's dormant spirit.

30.3 のですが and ～たいと思います(が)

とても行きたいとは思っているんですが...。

Just as in English, only more so, it is considered rather rude to state one's wishes in a blunt manner. You should take care to use this ～たい construction as sparingly as possible. When you need to say 'I want to…' get in the habit of softening the demand by adding のですが…, or ～たいと思います(が).

> 頭が痛いので今日は少し早目に帰りたいと思います(が)。
> As I have a headache I should like to go home slightly early today.
>
> ちょっと御相談したいのですが…
> I would like to talk to you...

30.4 The suffix 的

ちょと時間的にきつい

This suffix 的 (てき) can be appended to many nouns to form the Japanese equivalent of '-like', '-wise' or '-ish'. It is as ubiquitous as its English counterparts and you will find it cropping up in both adjectival position, taking the form 的な, or in adverbial position as here, taking the form 的に. Because it originates in Chinese, you will find it restricted, by and large, to nouns of Chinese origin.

30.5 Use of ばかり with the perfective

イースターまでには帰ると母に手紙を書いたばかりなので がっかりすると思うんです。

You will find the word ばかり normally used as an adverb meaning 'only' or 'just'. When the ～た form of a verb is followed by ばかり, it signifies that the action expressed by the verb has been completed only a short while ago. This construction is very similar to perfective + ところ (28.4).

父は中国から帰って来たばかりです。
My father has only just returned from China.

その点についてはつい先日説明したばかりです。
I explained to you about that point only the other day.

聞いたばかりの話をもう忘れた。
I have already forgotten the story I just heard.

木村さんのうちでは赤ちゃんが生まれたばかりだ。
They've just had a baby at the Kimura's.

30.6 ～て + おく

医学雑誌なども読んでおきたいと思っているんです。

This is another example of a ～て form being combined idiomatically with another verb. In this case the second verb is おく 'put', and so literally the pattern means 'do something and put (leave) it' hence 'do something in advance of something'. John uses it here because he will be studying the journals to help him with future research. This is a very useful construction, but we tend to forget to use it because it has no direct counterpart in English. Observe the following:

今日の午後停電があるかもしれないと話しておきました。
I have warned (them) that there might be a power cut this afternoon.

あしたのミーティングまでにこのレポートを読んでおいて下さい。
Please make sure you read this report before tomorrow's meeting.

彼女には三時ごろ行くと電話しておきました。
I have telephoned to tell her we'll be there around three.

Note that ておく can be abbreviated to とく: this produces forms such as 電話しときました. Note in particular the two forms 置いておく, meaning 'leave it, let it be' (usually abbreviated to 置いとく) and とっておく, meaning 'to set aside, to reserve for, to keep back' (usually abbreviated to とっとく).

30.7 Noun + が + ほしい

> ゆっくり本を読んだり、考えたりする時間がほしいですね。

There is another descriptive verb ほしい, which signifies 'want, desire'. This can be used in two patterns: noun + が + ほしい or ～て form + ほしい. Noun + が + ほしい is used when one wants an object or something that is seen to be an 'object': 'I am desirous of obtaining...' Again note the use of が here, going with the stative nature of the expression.

クリスマス・プレゼントにカメラがほしい。
I want a camera for my Christmas present.

自由がほしい。
I want freedom.

私がほしかったレコードは売り切れでした。
The record which I wanted was sold out.

Note that this descriptive verb *never* takes the nominalised form of a verb. Thus you cannot say either *行くことがほしいです or *食べるのがほしいです.

30.8 ～て form + ほしい

> 調査隊の隊長の人が二十五日までに決めてほしいと
> 言っていましたけど。

When ほしい is linked with the ～て form this pattern signifies 'I want *you* to…' Take particular care to compare this with 30.6. Because this form expresses a direct request for someone to do something for you, you should be careful when you use it. It can sound very pushy in the wrong situation.

あしたまでこの本を貸してほしい。
I would like you to lend me this book until tomorrow.

希望をもってほしい。
I want you to have hope.

約束は守ってほしい。
I want you to keep your promises.

Key to conversation

Romanisation

Tadashi	Nepāru no koto kimemashita ka.
Jon	Ē…Totemo ikitai to wa omotte iru no desu ga…
Tadashi	Nani ka mondai ga arun desu ka.
Jon	Hitotsu wa jiki no mondai de, jūgatsu kara Igirisu no byōin de hataraku koto ga kimatta no de shigatsu kara kugatsu matsu made Nepāru ni iku to iu no wa chotto jikanteki ni kitsui to omou no desu.
Tadashi	Sō desu ne.
Jon	Sore ni, Īsutā made ni wa kaeru to haha ni tegami o kaita bakari na node ryōshin ga gakkari suru to omoun desu.
Tadashi	Jon-san wa Nihon e kite mō sannenme desu ne.
Jon	Sō desu. Sono aida ichido mo kaette imasen shi…Sore ni atarashii shigoto o hajimeru mae ni Igirisu ya Amerika de saikin deta igaku zasshi nado mo yonde okitai to omotte irun desu.
Tadashi	Bokutachi isha no shigoto wa isogashii kara yukkuri hon o yondari kangaetari suru jikan ga hontō ni hoshii desu ne. Chōsatai no sekininsha no hito ga nijūgonichi made ni kimete hoshii to itte imashita kedo…

Translation

Tadashi	Have you decided about Nepal?
John	Yes... I do very much want to go, but...
Tadashi	Is there some sort of problem?
John	One is the problem of timing. It's been decided that I'll work at a hospital in England from October, so to go to Nepal from April to the end of September is cutting it a bit fine I think.
Tadashi	It is indeed.
John	And then I have just written a letter to my mother saying that I'll be back before Easter and so I think that my parents would be very disappointed.
Tadashi	This is the third year since you arrived in Japan isn't it?
John	Yes. And I haven't been back even once during that time. And then before I start my new job I've been thinking that I want to read up on recently published English and American medical journals and so forth.
Tadashi	Our work as doctors keeps us so busy that we really do want some time to read and think, don't we? The man in charge of the survey team said that he'd like you to decide by the twenty-fifth.

Lesson 31

Some more conversations

交換手	東西銀行でございます。
林田	内線402をお願いします。
藤本	外国為替課でございます。
林田	長谷川様はいらっしゃいますか。
藤本	誠に申し訳ございませんが、長谷川はただ今席をはずしております。失礼ですが、どちらさまでいらっしゃいますか。
林田	中野商事の林田と申します。長谷川様がお帰りになりましたらお電話をいただきたいのですが...。
藤本	はい、承知いたしました。中野商事の林田様ですね。もどりましたらすぐにこちらからお電話を差し上げます。

正	国子、僕のフランス人の友達のマリーさんには会ったことがあるね。
国子	ええ、だいぶ前にジョンさんとうちにいらっしゃった時にお会いしたわ。
正	来週の日曜日は彼女のお誕生日なのだけれど、プレゼントには何がいいかな。
国子	そうね。何か日本的なものを上げるのはどうかしら。
正	それはいい考えだけれど、たとえばどんなもの。
国子	うーん。なかなか難しいわね。でも考えておくわ。
正	ありがとう。それから僕はあしたから五日間、学会で留守をするから、僕の部屋の植木に一日おきに水をやってほしいんだけど。
国子	いいわよ。そういえば、そろそろポチにえさをやる時間だわ。

原	山川君、今度の水曜日の晩はひまですか。
山川	ええ、あいてますが、何か御用ですか。

原	いや、そうではなくて、音楽会の券が二枚あるので上げますよ。
山川	それは、ありがとうございます。よろしいんですか。
原	もちろん。人からもらった券なんですが、その日は残念ながら先約があるので。山川君は確か音楽が好きでしたね。
山川	ええ、大好きです。
原	それはよかった。

ジョン	もしもし。
正	もしもし、正です。
ジョン	ああ、正君。お元気ですか。
正	おかげさまで。急な話ですが、あさっての晩はひまじゃありませんか。
ジョン	うん。特に予定はありませんけれど。
正	原先生が音楽会の券を二枚下さったので、いっしょに行きませんか。ドイツ人のピアニストの演奏です。
ジョン	僕に一枚くれるんですか。それは嬉しいですね。どうもありがとう。

Comment

The purpose of these conversations is to investigate further the workings of language in its social context. The two main elements that affect the use of different speech levels are (a) the superior/inferior distinction that has reference to matters of age, sex, level of education, profession and rank or position in a company and (b) the inside/outside distinction that has reference to one's group. We have already seen how you must be ready to shift your vocabulary at all times to respond to these changes in the context in which you are speaking. One area that may give you some trouble is the use of what are known as 'donatory verbs', namely verbs of giving and receiving. By their very nature, these verbs involve questions of status and of interpersonal relations, questions that simply cannot be avoided when speaking Japanese.

31.1 The deferential copula

東西銀行でございます。
外国為替課でございます。

You have already met the word ございます in such phrases as ありがとうございます and おはようございます. It is in fact a super-polite form of the verb ある. Here, in the form でございます, it is a super-polite or 'deferential' form of the copula. It is extremely common, particularly in business situations. Note, therefore, that the copula has the following forms:

	plain	*polite*	*deferential*
neutral	だ	です	でございます
formal	である	であります	でございます

31.2 Talking on the phone

林田　長谷川様はいらっしゃいますか。
藤本　誠に申し訳ございませんが、長谷川はただ今、席をはずしております。失礼ですが、どちらさまでいらっしゃいますか。
林田　中野商事の林田と申します。長谷川様がお帰りになりましたらお電話をいただきたいのですが...。

By now you should be used to the fact that people are referred to differently in different contexts. Remember, for example, that when addressing your father you must use the word おとうさん or おとうさま. The same word can be used when talking about your father to others within the family circle, but as soon as the situation shifts and you find yourself talking about your father *outside* that circle, the word must change to 父. This ability to shift register quickly is especially important when talking on the phone; after all, such a context forces you to rely entirely on the nuances of language because there is no visual contact. This is why people tend to use extremely polite language in such a situation. The conversation quoted above contains hardly a single neutral word; not only is it all in the polite ～ます form, but it also contains a succession of subject-raising and subject-lowering verbs. When Hayashida rings the bank, he asks for 長谷川様 (さま), using a suffix that is one notch higher than a simple さん. He also uses the respectful verb いらっしゃいます for 'is'. Fujimoto, however, is in a completely different situation. If she were either talking directly to Hasegawa or talking about him to his other colleagues in the company, she too would use the suffix さん. But when talking to someone outside the company circle, she cannot possibly use an honorific about Hasegawa, *no matter how important Hasegawa may be inside the company*. The 'inside' versus 'outside' relationship will always take precedence over the more parochial relationship.

Note how the conversation proceeds. In her reply, Fujimoto first of all apologizes with 申し訳ございません. This phrase, which means roughly the same as すみません, is made up of the humble verb 申(もう)す 'respectfully say' compounded with the noun わけ 'reason', hence 'excuse': 'there is no excuse'. She then leaves off the さん suffix and uses a humble equivalent for はずしています, namely はずしております 'he has left his seat'. Note this verb おる, which is often found in place of いる, when a humble expression is called for. This is followed by a very polite どちらさまでいらっしゃいますか 'Who are you please?' でいらっしゃいます is a somewhat specialised form of the copula, which you will only really meet when you find yourself referring directly to the addressee or to someone closely connected to the addressee: 'Who are you?' When Hayashida in his turn speaks, he uses a humble equivalent about himself and a respectful equivalent when he refers to Hasegawa.

31.3 Giving and receiving

長谷川様がお帰りになりましたらお電話をいただきたいのですが...。
もどりましたらすぐにこちらからお電話差し上げます。

There is in this sentence a verb form that will be treated in detail somewhat later in the course: なりましたら. It can be translated here as 'when...' But our main concern here is with the verbs of giving and receiving. This section will range across all the rest of the conversations. During this discussion you will have to keep in mind the concept of being either 'inside' or 'outside' a closed circle.

31.4 Giving 'out'

There are three verbs meaning 'give': 差し上げる 'offer up', 上げる 'give', and やる 'offer down'. In the following examples Tadashi is on the same level as Marie, his teacher Hara is treated as being superior to him and, linguistically at least, he can look down on his younger brother, the dog and any inanimate object. Remember that it is Tadashi who is doing the 'giving' here, so the subject of the quoted sentences is 'I'.

正 giving to 原教授, says 「原先生にお電話を差し上げたが、お留守だった。」
'I gave Professor Hara a call, but he was out.'

正 giving to マリー, says 「マリーさんのお誕生日にプレゼントを上げるつもりだ。」
'I intend to give Marie a present for her birthday.'

正 giving to 実, says 「この自転車はもう使わないから上げる/やる。」
'I'm not using this bicycle any more so I'll give it to you.'

正 giving to his dog or his plant, says 「水をやる。」
'I'll give it some water.'

So Tadashi must 'offer up' things to the teacher, he can simply 'give' things to Marie, and he can 'offer down' things to the rest if he feels like it. The first thing is to remember that he has a choice of three verbs. The decision as to which one he actually uses will, of course, depend on the social context.

31.5 Giving 'in'

This situation is in some ways the reverse of the above. Tadashi is being given things by other people, but there is no passive here because the subject is not 'I' but 'he', the donor. So when Tadashi wants to say 'he gave me' he has a choice of two verbs: 下さる 'bestow, present' and くれる 'let have'.

原教授 giving to 正, 正 says 「原先生が音楽会の券を下さった。」
'Professor Hara gave me a concert ticket.'

山川一 giving to 正, 正 says 「父がとてもいいカメラをくれた。」
'Father gave me a very good camera.'

ジョン giving to 正, 正 says 「ジョンがいいアドバイスをくれた。」
'John gave me some good advice.'

実 giving to 正, 正 says 「京都にいる弟がはがきをくれた。」
'My younger brother in Kyōto sent me a postcard.'

31.6 Receiving

This situation is similar to the above in that the action occurs 'inwards', but the point of view shifts as Tadashi now becomes the subject, so it is no longer an act of 'giving' but an act of 'receiving'. Again he has a choice of two verbs, depending on his relationship to the donor: いただく 'receive from above, be granted' and もらう 'get'. The agent can be marked by either に or から.

正 receiving from 原教授 says 「原先生から音楽会の券をいただいた。」
'I received a concert ticket from Professor Hara.'

正 receiving from 山川一 says 「父にとてもいいカメラをもらった。」
'I received a very good camera from father.'

正 receiving from ジョン says 「ジョンにめずらしい切手をもらった。」
'I got a rare stamp from John.'

正 receiving from 実 says 「京都にいる弟からはがきをもらった。」
'I got a postcard from my younger brother in Kyōto.'

Again, the decision as to which of these verbs to use will hang on the precise relationship of donor to receiver.

31.7 Donatory verbs with expressions of hope and desire

> お電話をいただきたい、
> 植木に一日おきに水をやってほしいんだけど。

These verbs of giving and receiving can be combined with those expressions of hope and desire that we met in the last lesson. In such cases, of course, the subject must be 'I'. But take care to note the difference between these two sentences. The first one simply means 'I would like to be granted a telephone call.' The second one means 'I would like *you* to give the plant some water every other day.' (see 30.7)

Key to conversations

Romanisation

Kōkanshu	Tōzai ginkō de gozaimasu.
Hayashida	Naisen yon-zero-ni o o-negai shimasu.
Fujimoto	Gaikoku kawase-ka de gozaimasu.
Hayashida	Hasegawa-sama wa irasshaimasu ka.
Fujimoto	Makoto ni mōshiwake gozaimasen ga, Hasegawa wa tadaima, seki o hazushite orimasu. Shitsurei desu ga, dochira sama de irasshaimasu ka.
Hayashida	Nakano shōji no Hayashida to mōshimasu. Hasegawa-sama ga o-kaeri ni narimashitara o-denwa o itadakitai no desu ga...
Fujimoto	Hai, shōchi itashimashita. Nakano shōji no Hayashida-sama desu ne. Modorimashitara sugu ni kochira kara o-denwa sashiagemasu.

Tadashi	Kuniko, boku no Furansujin no tomodachi no Marī san ni wa atta koto ga aru ne.
Kuniko	Ē, daibu mae ni Jon-san to uchi ni irasshatta toki ni o-ai shita wa.
Tadashi	Raishū no nichiyōbi wa kanojo no o-tanjōbi na no da keredo, purezento ni wa nani ga ii kana.
Kuniko	Sō ne. Nani ka Nihonteki na mono o ageru no wa dō kashira.

Tadashi	Sore wa ii kangae da keredo, tatoeba donna mono.
Kuniko	Ūn. Nakanaka muzukashii wa ne. Demo kagaete oku wa.
Tadashi	Arigatō. Sore kara boku wa ashita kara itsukakan, gakkai de rusu o suru kara, boku no heya no ueki ni ichinichi oki ni mizu o yatte hoshiin da kedo.
Kuniko	Ii wa yo. Sō ieba, sorosoro Pochi ni esa o yaru jikan da wa.

Hara	Yamakawa-kun, kondo no suiyōbi no ban wa hima desu ka.
Yamakawa	Ē, aitemasu ga, nani ka goyō desu ka.
Hara	Iya, sō de wa nakute, ongakkai no ken ga nimai aru no de agemasu yo.
Yamakawa	Sore wa, arigatō gozaimasu. Yoroshiin desu ka.
Hara	Mochiron. Hito kara moratta ken nan desu ga, sono hi wa zannen nagara senyaku ga aru no de. Yamakawa-kun wa tashika ongaku ga suki deshita ne.
Yamakawa	Ē, daisuki desu.
Hara	Sore wa yokatta.

Jon	Moshi moshi.
Tadashi	Moshi moshi, Tadashi desu.
Jon	Ā, Tadashi-kun. O-genki desu ka.
Tadashi	O-kagesama de. Kyū na hanashi desu ga, asatte no ban wa hima ja arimasen ka.
Jon	Un. Toku ni yotei wa arimasen keredo.
Tadashi	Hara sensei ga ongakkai no ken o nimai kudasatta no de, issho ni ikimasen ka. Doitsujin no pianisuto no ensō desu.
Jon	Boku ni ichimai kurerun desu ka. Sore wa ureshii desu ne. Dōmo arigatō.

Translation

Operator	Tōzai Bank.
Hayashida	Extension 402 please.
Fujimoto	Foreign exchange department.
Hayashida	Is Mr Hasegawa there please?
Fujimoto	I'm terribly sorry but Hasegawa is not at his desk just at the moment. May I ask who is calling?
Hayashida	It's Hayashida from Nakano Trading. When Mr Hasegawa returns, I'd be very grateful if he could ring me please.

Fujimoto	Certainly. That's Mr Hayashida of Nakano Trading. He'll ring you as soon as he returns.

Tadashi	Kuniko, you've met my French friend Marie haven't you?
Kuniko	Yes, I met her some time ago when she came here with John.
Tadashi	It's her birthday next Sunday, and so I was wondering what would be a good present.
Kuniko	I see. What about giving her something Japanese?
Tadashi	That's a good idea, but what sort of thing for example?
Kuniko	Hmm. It's hard isn't it? But I'll give it some thought.
Tadashi	Thanks . Oh and I'll be away from home at a conference for five days as of tomorrow, so would you water the potplants in my room every other day?
Kuniko	That's OK. That reminds me, it's almost time to feed Pochi.

Hara	Yamakawa, are you free next Wednesday evening?
Yamakawa	Yes, I'm free. Is there something you need me for?
Hara	No, it's not that. It's just that I've got two tickets to a concert that I'd like to give you.
Yamakawa	Thank you very much. Are you sure that's alright?
Hara	Of course. They're tickets someone gave me, but unfortunately I have a prior engagement that day. If I remember rightly, you're fond of music aren't you?
Yamakawa	Yes, I do enjoy it.
Hara	That's good.

John	Hello?
Tadashi	Hello, it's Tadashi.
John	Oh, Tadashi. How are you?
Tadashi	Very well thank you. It's very short notice, but you wouldn't be free tomorrow night would you?
John	Yes. I don't have anything in particular on.
Tadashi	Professor Hara kindly gave me two tickets to a concert, so would you like to come with me? It's a recital by a German pianist.
John	You'll give me a ticket? That sounds wonderful. Thanks very much.

Lesson 32

Ōyama goes into Yamakawa's office.

大山	部長、失礼いたします。
山川	やあ、大山君。何だね。
大山	実はブリティシュ・エンジニアリングのブラウンさんが交通事故にあって入院されましたのでお知らせに来ました。
山川	それは大変だ。けがはひどいのか。
大山	詳しいことはよく分かりませんが、タクシーに乗っていた時に大きなトラックが横からぶつかってきたらしいんです。幸い命に別条はないみたいですが、体全体に相当ひどい打撲傷を受けたようです。
山川	もうお見舞いには行ったのかね。
大山	ええ、きのう会社の帰りに行ってきました。案外元気そうでしたけれど、動くたびにあちこち痛がっていました。
山川	もうイギリスの家族には連絡したんだろうね。
大山	ええ、こんな時に一人では心細いらしくて、おくさんやお子さんにとても会いたがっていました。
山川	それはそうだろう。それで病院はどこ。
大山	渋谷の川里病院です。地下鉄の神宮前駅からすぐです。
山川	そうか、分かった。どうもありがとう。
大山	それでは私はこれで失礼いたします。

32.1 Use of the passive for respect

> 入院されましたのでお知らせに来ました。

される is the passive form of the verb する. The passive will be dealt with in detail in lesson 35. All you need to do at this point is to learn the form される

and take note of the fact that it raises the status of its subject; Ōyama is using it to show respect for Mr Brown, because Mr Brown is 'outside' the circle. The fact that the respect/humble system is separate from the politeness system means that he can do this without being impolite to his boss Yamakawa. Take care to study the regular alternation of polite verb endings from Ōyama with brusque ones from Yamakawa. お知らせに: here we have the conjunctive form of the verb 知らせる 'to inform', followed by に + a verb of motion, a pattern that was explained in 23.3. 知らせる is literally 'to cause to get to know': this causative form of the verb will be introduced in 37.2. The prefix お shows respect to his boss.

32.2 Seeming

> トラックが横からぶつかってきたらしいんです。
> 幸い命に別条はないみたいですが
> 打撲傷を受けたようです。
> 元気そうでしたけれど、

All these expressions, らしい, みたい, ようだ and ～そうだ have to do with some kind of speculation on the part of the speaker: 'it seems that...' らしい, in the form らしくなりました, was introduced in 23.2. To repeat: it is a suffix which inflects in the manner of a descriptive verb; it is added either to the plain form of the verb or directly after a noun: 彼は医者らしい 'It seems he's a doctor.' When らしい is used, it is not clear whether the speculation is based on the speaker's own observation or not. Note how らしい attaches to various words:

大雪で列車が遅れているらしい。
Due to heavy snow, trains seem to be delayed.

橋本さんは行きたくなかったらしい。
It seems that Mr Hashimoto did not want to go.

清水さんは病気らしい。
It seems that Miss Shimizu is ill.

彼はおとうさんがこわいらしい。
He seems to be afraid of his father.

近藤さんの弟さんはドイツ語が得意らしい。
It seems that Mr Kondō's younger brother is good at German.

みたい is somewhat similar to らしい in that it links directly to verbs and nouns. Note, however, that unlike らしい it does *not* act like a descriptive verb: it takes だ, more like an adjectival noun. Also take great care not to confuse it with the word 見たい 'I wish to see'; both words are obviously closely connected but should be treated as being distinct.

よう is the *on* reading of 様, a noun meaning 'shape' or 'appearance'. Being a noun, it attaches directly to verbs but needs an intervening の when linked to another noun. It can be described as a slightly more formal equivalent to みたい, which is colloquial and often heard in the conversation of children or close friends. Note that with either of these patterns there is no inherent indication of whether the statement is based on the speaker's own observation or from information taken from another source.

Observe the following:

まだ分からないよう /or みたい/ ですね。
It seems you still don't understand.

どこかで事故があったよう /or みたい/ だ。
I think there has been an accident somewhere.

ブラウンさんのけがは相当ひどいみたい /or よう/ ですね。
It appears that Mr Brown's injury is rather serious.

彼も共産主義者みたい /or のよう/ ですね。
It appears that he is also a communist.

このごろ割にひまみたい /or なよう/ ですね。
You seem to be relatively free nowadays.

〜そうだ is added to the conjunctive form of verbs, the base of descriptive verbs and directly to most adjectival nouns. Note two irregular formations:

よい (いい) + そう → よさそう　　　　ない + そう → なさそう

Compared to ようだ, ～そうだ gives a stronger sense of the speaker's direct observation of something. It implies in fact that that you have good reason for your speculation. There is less distance between observer and event, and more personal involvement.

このケーキはおいしそうだ。
This cake looks delicious.

心配しない方がよさそうです。
It seems to me that it is best not to worry.

日焼けして子供達はみんな丈夫そうだ。
All the children look healthy with their suntans.

頭が痛くて死にそうだ。
I have such a bad headache that I feel I am almost dying.

病人は何も食べたくなさそうですね。
The patient looks as if he does not want to eat anything.

When used with a verb, ～そう sometimes suggests that something is about to occur.

その子は大切なノートをなくして今にも泣き出しそうだった。
Having lost her favourite notebook, that child was about to start crying.

あっ、雨が降りそうだ。
Oh dear, it's going to rain!

Note that one cannot express speculation about an event in the past using this conjunctive + ～そう construction. In this case ようだ has to be used, because the speaker by definition can have had no direct observation of the particular event.

このあたりは道路にまだ水たまりが残っているのできのうの夜は相当雨が降ったようですね。
There are still some puddles around here, so it must have rained quite a lot last night.

cf. モンスーンの季節には一日に何回かザーッと雨が降るようですね。
It seems that there are showers several times a day during the monsoon season.

32.3 Citation form + たびに (度に) + verb

動くたびに

You have already been introduced to the use of 時に in this kind of position, signifying simply 'when'. Using たびに puts stress on the recurrent nature of the event.

この写真を見る度に母のことを思い出します。
Whenever I see this picture it brings back memories of mother.

日本へ行くたびに地震にあいます。
Whenever I go to Japan, I meet up with an earthquake.

32.4 The suffix がる

あちこち痛がっていました。 会いたがっていました。

We have here two examples of the suffix がる. We saw in the previous lesson how the suffixes ～たい and ほしい could only be used with reference to one's own desires or wishes, on the principle that one cannot really know someone else's desires. This principle also operates with reference to people's feelings and emotions, expressed in Japanese by descriptive verbs (and adjectival nouns on occasion). When, for instance, Ōyama describes how Mr Brown felt after his accident, he cannot simply say 'it hurts' 痛い, because he can only say that about himself. Just as in English we would be likely to say 'he feels pain', so in Japanese you need something extra: the suffix がる. It is assumed that this suffix actually stems from 気 (げ) + ある 'to have an appearance (feeling) of'. がる attaches to the stem of descriptive verbs, so producing 痛 (いた) がる, 痛がっている. Note that がる transforms a descriptive (hence stative) verb into a true verb of group I, hence any intransitive が sentence is transformed into a transitive sentence with を:

> そのおばけの話がこわい。
> I'm scared by that ghost story.

but

> 子供達はそのおばけの話をこわがった。
> The children were scared by that ghost story.

> このねこはとてもかわいいですねえ。
> This cat is really sweet, isn't it!

but

> むすめはこのねこをとてもかわいがっています。
> My daughter really spoils this cat (finds it sweet).

Unlike English, however, wishes are treated in exactly the same way as feelings and emotions; so that when Ōyama wants to say 'he wants to see his wife and children' he cannot simply use the ～たい form, he must use ～たがる.

> 弟はスポーツカーを買いたがっている。
> My younger brother is keen to buy a sports car.

32.5 だろう/でしょう

連絡したんだろうね。 それはそうだろう。

Uncertainty is expressed by adding the suggestive form of the copula, plain

だろう, polite でしょう, to the plain form of the verb.

北海道は今ごろもう寒いでしょうね。
I suppose it's already cold in Hokkaidō now.

この天気では飛行機はだいぶ遅れるだろう。
In this weather, the flight will probably be considerably delayed.

Note that if pronounced with a rising and hence questioning intonation here, でしょう will indicate a rhetorical question.

大丈夫でしょう。↗
It's OK, isn't it?

分かるでしょう。↗
You understand, don't you?

The form でしょうか can be used instead of ですか if you wish to ask a polite question.

すみませんが、今何時でしょうか。
Excuse me, what time is it now?

東京駅はどこでしょうか。
Where is Tōkyō Station?

仙台行きの新幹線は何番線からでしょうか。
From which platform does the Shinkansen for Sendai leave?

It can also be used to show sympathy. The following sentence expresses sympathetic understanding rather than any real sense of uncertainty.

今日は十時間以上も山道を歩いてきっと疲れたでしょう。
You must be tired out, having walked over mountain tracks for more than ten hours today.

Key to conversation

Romanisation

Ōyama	Buchō, shitsurei itashimasu.
Yamakawa	Yā, Ōyama-kun. Nan da ne.
Ōyama	Jitsu wa Buritisshu Enjiniaringu no Buraun-san ga kōtsū jiko ni atte nyūin saremashita no de o-shirase ni kimashita.
Yamakawa	Sore wa taihen da. Kega wa hidoi no ka.
Ōyama	Kuwashii koto wa yoku wakarimasen ga, takushī ni notte ita toki ni ōkina torakku ga yoko kara butsukatte kita rashiin desu. Saiwai inochi ni betsujō wa nai mitai desu ga, karada zentai ni sōtō hidoi dabokushō o uketa yō desu.
Yamakawa	Mō o-mimai ni wa itta no ka ne.
Ōyama	Ee, kinō kaisha no kaeri ni itte kimashita. Angai genkisō deshita keredo, ugoku tabi ni achikochi itagatte imashita.
Yamakawa	Mō Igirisu no kazoku ni wa renraku shitan darō ne.
Ōyama	Ē, konna toki ni hitori de wa kokorobosoi rashikute, okusan ya o-kosan ni totemo aitagatte imashita.
Yamakawa	Sore wa sō darō. Sore de byōin wa doko.
Ōyama	Shibuya no Kawazato byōin desu. Chikatetsu no Jingūmae-eki kara sugu desu.
Yamakawa	Sō ka, wakatta. Dōmo arigatō.
Ōyama	Sore de wa watakushi wa kore de shitsurei itashimasu.

Translation

Ōyama	Do you have a minute sir?
Yamakawa	Oh, Ōyama. What is it?
Ōyama	I've come to tell you that Mr Brown of British Engineering was involved in a car accident and has been admitted to hospital.
Yamakawa	That's terrible. Is he badly injured?
Ōyama	I don't know the details, but apparently he was hit from the side by a big truck as he was in a taxi. Happily it appears that he won't suffer any after-effects, but it seems that he has been quite badly bruised all over his body.
Yamakawa	Have you been to see him already?

Ōyama	Yes, I went yesterday on my way home from work. He looked surprisingly well, but he appeared to be in pain in various places whenever he moved.
Yamakawa	Someone's already informed his family in England I suppose.
Ōyama	Yes, he seems a bit forlorn by himself at a time like this, and he wanted to see his wife and children.
Yamakawa	Yes, I imagine he would. Where is the hospital?
Ōyama	It's the Kawazato Hospital in Shibuya. Not far from the Jingūmae underground station.
Yamakawa	Right then, understood. Thanks very much.
Ōyama	Well then, I'll be on my way now. Excuse me.

Lesson 33

A conversation between Mr and Mrs Yamakawa

一	今日、大山君から聞いたんだが、ブリティッシュ・エンジニアリングのブラウンさんが交通事故にあって、入院されたそうだ。
信子	まあ、それはいけませんね。おけがはひどいんですか。
一	いや、そうでもないらしいが、あしたいっしょにお見舞いに行ってみよう。
信子	はい。何を持っていって差し上げるのがよろしいでしょうか。
一	そうだな。一人でさびしがっているようだから、僕は英語の雑誌でも持っていって上げるつもりなんだが。
信子	そうですね。それでは私はくだものでも買っておきましょうか。

The doctor visits Mr Brown's ward.

医者	具合はどうですか。
ブラウン	まだ動くとあちこち痛みますが、少しづつ楽になってきました。
医者	頭痛はどうですか。
ブラウン	まだ頭の後ろの方がズキズキしますが。
医者	それでは、痛み止めをもう一度上げましょう。御家族とは連絡がつきましたか。
ブラウン	おかげさまで。今朝も家内が電話してくれました。 あのう、まだしばらく退院は無理でしょうか。
医者	二、三日中に検査の結果が出ますから、もう少し待って下さい。あと困ったことはありませんか。
ブラウン	いいえ、看護婦さん達にはとても親切にしてもらっています。
医者	そうですか。それでは、お大事に。

A conversation between John and Tadashi

ジョン	正君、この間書いていた論文はどうなりました。
正	今、原先生に読んでいただいているところです。
ジョン	そうですか。ひまな時に最近僕が書いたものも読んでくれますか。
正	もちろん。論文ですか。
ジョン	いや、実はある雑誌の依頼で、日本とイギリスの子供の育て方のちがいについて書いたんですが。
正	それじゃあ、日本語でですか。
ジョン	ええ、自信がないんですけど。
正	そんなことはないでしょう。いつも僕の英語を直してもらっているから、いつでも読んで上げますよ。
ジョン	ありがとう。さっそく郵便で送ります。手書きですがいいですか。
正	ジョン君の字はきれいだから大丈夫です。国子が週末にでもワープロでうってくれると思いますよ。

33.1 Hearsay

入院されたそうだ。

Hearsay, of the type 'it is said that' or 'I heard that', is expressed by adding the phrase そうだ (そうです), to the plain form of the verb.

日本では新学期は四月に始まるそうです。
I hear that in Japan the beginning of the school year is in April.

東京の物価は世界一だそうです。
It is said that the cost of living in Tōkyō is the highest in the world.

Take care to note the difference between this plain form of the verb + そうだ and the conjunctive form of the verb + ～そう that we saw in 32.2, meaning 'seems that'.

今晩からぐっと寒くなるそうだ。
They say it's going to get much colder tonight.

and

今晩からぐっと寒くなりそうだ。
It looks to me as though it's going to get much colder tonight.

33.2 Expressions of suggestion and intention

お見舞いに行ってみよう。

Suggestions of the type 'let's...' are made by using yet another verb inflection, this time ending in *-ō*. The rules for these sound changes are as follows:

	plain citation		*suggestive form*
group I	ending in *-u, -ru, -tsu, -ku* *-mu, -nu, -su, -gu*		ends in *-ō, -rō, -tō, -kō* *-mō, -nō, -sō, -gō*
	言う	say	言おう
	買う	buy	買おう
	会う	meet	会おう
	使う	use	使おう
	ある	exist	***
	入る	enter	入ろう
	乗る	ride	乗ろう
	待つ	wait	待とう
	行く	go	行こう
	書く	write	書こう
	歩く	walk	歩こう
	聞く	listen, ask	聞こう
	飲む	drink	飲もう

	読む	read	読もう
	死ぬ	die	死のう
	貸す	lend	貸そう
	泳ぐ	swim	泳ごう
	かぐ	smell, sniff	かごう
	plain citation		*suggestive form*
group II	ending in *-ru*		ends in *-yō*
	いる	exist	いよう
	出る	go out	出よう
	かける	hang	かけよう
	見る	see, look	見よう
	寝る	go to bed	寝よう
	起きる	get up	起きよう
	食べる	eat	食べよう
	plain citation		*suggestive form*
Irregular	する	do	しよう
	来る	come	来よう (こよう)

The polite version of this suggestive form is obtained adding ～ましょう to the conjunctive.

Study the following to see how the polite form is used:

遅くなったのでタクシーで行こう (or 行きましょう)。
It's already late, so let's go by taxi.

成功するかもしれないのでやってみよう。
We may succeed, so let's try and see.

まどを開けて新鮮な空気を入れましょう。
Let's open the window and let in some fresh air.

僕が木村君の代わりに行こうか。
Shall I go instead of Kimura?

If sentence-final particle か is added to this form, the suggestion expressed becomes less direct and more formal, and in some cases the emphasis changes from suggestion to offer:

そろそろお茶にしましょう。
Let's have a cup of tea.

そろそろお茶にしましょうか。
Shall I make some tea?

33.3 Donatory verbs used with the ～て form

何を持っていって差し上げるのがよろしいでしょうか。
ワープロでうってくれると思いますよ。
原先生に読んでいただいているところです。

All the verbs met in lesson 31 can be used with the ～て form of other verbs in order to indicate the giving or receiving of favours, and almost exactly the same constraints apply as described in that lesson. These forms are sometimes difficult for English speakers to use correctly, mainly because they involve instant reference to social status among a number of people, and this can at times get very complicated. When you have studied this section, go back to the main conversations and analyse each example that you find.

33.4 To do a favour for someone else

Operating on the same principle as 'giving out' discussed in 31.4, three verbs are used to express the concept.

(a) ～て差し上げる

ブラウンさんが入院されているのでお見舞いに行って差し上げるつもりです。
As Mr Brown is in hospital, I intend to visit him (offer him a visit).

(b) 〜て上げる

きのうは兄の論文をタイプして上げました。
I typed my elder brother's essay for him yesterday.

(c) 〜てやる

この話は子供には少し難しいかもしれませんが易しい言葉で話してやります。
This story may be a little difficult for a child, but I will tell it to her in easy words.

33.5 Someone else does you a favour

Operating on the giving 'in' principle (31.5), we have again two verbs here which can act as auxiliaries.

(a) 〜て下さる

このパーティに山本先生は遠くからわざわざ来て下さいました。
Mr Yamamoto came all the way specially for the party.

(b) 〜てくれる

おかあさんがこの手ぶくろを編んでくれた。
Mother knitted me these gloves.

おにいさんが宿題を手伝ってくれた。
Brother helped me with my homework.

33.6 Receiving favours

The next two verbs may cause you somewhat more difficulty, because the subject is not the giver but the receiver. This is not a normal form of expression in English. The person who does the giving is therefore marked not by が but by the agent marker に, and the whole situation is seen from the point of view of the receiver.

(a) 〜ていただく

子供のころ近くのお寺のおしょうさんにお習字を教えていただきました。
When I was a child, I was kindly taught calligraphy by the Buddhist priest from the nearby temple. (*lit*. I received the favour of his teaching)

(b) 〜てもらう

ガソリン・スタンドでガソリンを入れてもらった。
I had them put petrol in the car at a petrol station.
(*lit*. I received the favour of them putting…)

Key to conversation

Romanisation

Hajime	Kyō, Ōyama-kun kara kiitan da ga, Britisshu Enjiniaringu no Buraun san ga kōtsū jiko ni atte, nyūin sareta sō da.
Nobuko	Mā, sore wa ikemasen ne. O-kega wa hidoin desu ka.
Hajime	Iya, sō de mo nai rashii ga, ashita issho ni o-mimai ni itte miyō.
Nobuko	Hai. Nani o motte itte sashiageru no ga yoroshii deshō ka.
Hajime	Sō da na. Hitori de sabishigatte iru yō da kara, boku wa eigo no zasshi demo motte itte ageru tsumori nan da ga.
Nobuko	Sō desu ne. Sore de wa watakushi wa kudamono demo katte okimashō ka.

Isha	Guai wa dō desu ka.
Buraun	Mada ugoku to achikochi itamimasu ga, sukoshi zutsu raku ni natte kimashita.
Isha	Zutsū wa dō desu ka.
Buraun	Mada atama no ushiro no hō ga zukizuki shimasu ga.
Isha	Sore de wa, itamidome o mō ichido agemashō. G-okazoku to wa renraku ga tsukimashita ka.
Buraun	O-kagesama de. Kesa mo kanai ga denwa shite kuremashita. Anō, mada shibaraku tai'in wa muri deshō ka.
Isha	Ni-sannichi-chū ni kensa no kekka ga demasu kara, mō sukoshi matte kudasai. Ato komatta koto wa arimasen ka.

Buraun	Iie, kangofusan-tachi ni wa totemo shinsetsu ni shite moratte imasu.
Isha	Sō desu ka. Sore de wa, o-daiji ni.

Jon	Tadashi kun, kono aida kaite ita ronbun wa dō narimashita.
Tadashi	Ima, Hara sensei ni yonde itadaite iru tokoro desu.
Jon	Sō desu ka. Hima na toki ni saikin boku ga kaita mono mo yonde kuremasu ka.
Tadashi	Mochiron. Ronbun desu ka.
Jon	Iya, jitsu wa aru zasshi no irai de, Nihon to Igirisu no kodomo no sodatekata no chigai ni tsuite kaitan desu ga.
Tadashi	Sore jā, Nihongo de desu ka.
Jon	Ē, jishin ga nain desu kedo.
Tadashi	Sonna koto wa nai deshō. Itsumo boku no Eigo o naoshite moratte iru kara, itsu de mo yonde agemasu yo.
Jon	Arigatō. Sassoku yūbin de okurimasu. Tegaki desu ga ii desu ka.
Tadashi	Jon-kun no ji wa kirei da kara daijōbu desu. Kuniko ga shūmatsu ni de mo wāpuro de utte kureru to omoimasu yo.

Translation

Hajime	Today I heard from young Ōyama that Mr Brown from British Engineering has been involved in a car accident and has apparently been admitted to hospital.
Nobuko	Dear me, that is unfortunate. Are his injuries serious?
Hajime	No, apparently not that serious, but let's go and see him tomorrow.
Nobuko	Yes let's. What should we take as a present?
Hajime	Let me see now... He seems to be lonely by himself, so I'm thinking of perhaps taking some English language magazines to give him.
Nobuko	Yes. In that case shall I get some fruit?

Doctor	How are you feeling?
Brown	It still hurts in various places when I move, but bit by bit I'm feeling more comfortable.
Doctor	What about your headache?
Brown	The back of my head still throbs.
Doctor	In that case I'll give you some more pain-killer. Have you been in touch with your family?

Brown	Yes thank you. My wife gave me a call again this morning. Ah, will it be a while still before I'm well enough to leave?
Doctor	In two or three days we'll have the results of the tests, so please be patient. Is there anything else troubling you?
Brown	No, I'm being treated very kindly by the nurses.
Doctor	Good. Well then, look after yourself.

John	Tadashi, what happened to that thesis you were writing a little while ago?
Tadashi	I'm just having it read by Professor Hara now.
John	I see. When you've got some free time, would you be good enough to read something I wrote recently too?
Tadashi	Of course. Is it a thesis?
John	No, actually I was asked by a certain magazine to write about the differences between the way Japanese and English children are brought up.
Tadashi	So it's in Japanese then?
John	Yes, but I'm not very confident about it.
Tadashi	You shouldn't feel that way. I'm always having you correct my English, so I'll read it whenever you like.
John	Thank you. I'll put it in the post right away. It's handwritten but is that all right?
Tadashi	Your handwriting is neat so it'll be fine. Kuniko will type it up for you on the word processor over the weekend perhaps.

Lesson 34

Mr and Mrs Yamakawa visit Mr Brown in hospital. At the entrance

山川信子	あのう、すいませんがブラウンさんという方の病室はどちらでしょうか。
受付けの人	何科の患者さんですか。
山川信子	さあ、よく分かりませんが交通事故にあって入院している人です。
受付けの人	そうですか。ちょっとお待ち下さい。ああ、マーク・ブラウンさん、イギリスの方ですね。病室は六階の628号です。
山川信子	どうもありがとうございました。

Mr and Mrs Yamakawa go into room 628.

山川一	おじゃまします。ブラウンさん、今回は大変な目にあいましたね。
ブラウン	あ、山川さん。どうも。
山川信子	おかげんはいかがですか。
ブラウン	これは、奥様も。わざわざおいでいただきましてありがとうございます。
山川信子	いいえ、どういたしまして。お花とくだものを少し持って参りましたのでどうぞ。
山川一	それから、これは英語の新聞と雑誌です。
ブラウン	どうも御心配をおかけして申し訳ありません。
山川一	いやいや。それより具合の方はどうですか。
ブラウン	幸い骨は折れていないので歩けるのですが、動くとまだ痛みます。
山川一	打撲傷だけですか。
ブラウン	まだよく分かりませんが、頭をひどく打ったのでそちらの方はまだ検査中です。
山川信子	そうですか。それは御心配ですね。
ブラウン	ええ、でもこの病院はお医者さんも看護婦さんもとても親切ですし英語を話せる人も多いのでその点では安心

	していられます。
山川信子	それはとても心強いですね。
山川一	そろそろ面会時間の終りなので失礼しよう。
山川信子	そうですね。近いうちに又参りますので何か必要なものがありましたらどうぞ遠慮なくおっしゃって下さい。ブラウンさんのアパートとうちはお近くですから。
ブラウン	ありがとうございます。それでは誠に申し訳ありませんがトランジスター・ラジオを持ってきていただけますか。居間のテーブルの上にあると思います。
山川信子	はい、分かりました。
山川一	それでは又。お大事に。
山川信子	早くよくなって下さいね。

Comment

If you have an accident on the street in Japan, an ambulance will take you to the nearest hospital. But what if you just happen to feel ill? There is no system of general practitioners as there is in the UK, and so you would probably end up either at the nearest chemist's shop (薬局) or a clinic. Normally this would be a clinic for internal medicine (内科), but if you knew more specifically what was wrong with you, you might head straight for one of the more specialised clinics: ear, nose and throat (耳鼻咽喉科), eye (眼科), pediatric (小児科), or dental (歯科). If you had broken your arm, you would go to a 外科, and if you were pregnant, you would go to a 産婦人科. Small clinics and hospitals are common all over the major cities. There is also, of course, traditional Chinese medicine and practice available, known generally as 漢方, and offering a range of remedies from massage (指圧), to acupuncture (鍼) or moxa (灸).

34.1 'Please wait a moment'

ちょっとお待ち下さい。

The phrase ちょっと待って下さい was introduced in 18.5. Here we have a more formal variation with the prefix お added to the conjunctive form of the verb + 下さい. Expect also the similar expression 少々お待ち下さい. Note that this is a polite phrase. Politeness and respect coalesce when the person you are addressing is the subject of the sentence.

ここにお名前と御住所をお書き下さい。
Please write your name and address here.

料金はあちらの窓口でお払い下さい。
Please pay the fare at the counter over there.

どうぞお上がり下さい
Please come in.

34.2 Expressing surprise

これは、奥様も。

これは is here used as an interjection: 'My goodness. Mrs Yamakawa too!' Note how this statement is entirely adequate on its own; the truncation has nothing to do with being impolite. Mr Brown correctly gives the wife a very polite さま when he addresses her.

34.3 More on verbs of respect

おいでいただきましてありがとうございます。

The question of honorific language and levels of speech was mentioned in 25.8 and 26.2. Here we have a further example of a way of raising the status of the subject. The word おいで is made up from the prefix お and the conjunctive form of the verb いでる, which itself is a remnant of the older language. Here it is almost exactly the same as いらっしゃる and acts as a respectful equivalent of either 行く, 来る, or いる, meaning something like 'your coming'. Added to this we find いただく 'receive'; the whole phrase is very similar to the 〜ていただく just mentioned in 33.6. It could be literally translated as 'receiving your deigning to come, thank you', although this stilted English should not lead you to think that the Japanese expression is anything out of the ordinary. There is another place in the conversation where a respectful equivalent is used: 遠慮なくおっしゃって下さい. おっしゃる is the respectful equivalent of 言う 'to say'. More will be said about these equivalents in due course.

34.4 More on being humble

> 持って参りました
> 御心配をおかけして申し訳ありません。
> 近いうちにまた参ります

Remember that the normal way of making a humble equivalent is with お + conjunctive form + する (see 26.2). We have another example here with 御心配をおかけして, from the phrase 心配をかける 'to cause someone worry'. The verb 参る is a humble equivalent of 行く or 来る. The subject in both of these cases is 'I'. We met 申し訳 in 31.2.

34.5 の方 (ほう) は

> それより具合の方はどうですか。

There are two phrases here that need explanation. より is a comparative 'than'. We will meet it later when comparatives are discussed in greater detail. The phrase is being used to change subject radically: 'rather than that...' or 'now we're not here to talk about that, are we?' As far as the other phrase, 具合の方は, is concerned, note first that 方 is pronounced ほう, rather than かた. It occurs again a few lines later in そちらの方は. Meaning 'direction' or 'alternative', it in a sense strengthens the effect of the は as a contrast marker and functions in this kind of context as a kind of vague pointer: 'let's concentrate on *this* for a moment'. The reasons for vagueness could range from embarrassment to assumed nonchalance. Although it is not an exact parallel, think of the use of the word 'old' in 'so how's the old foot then?'

34.6 The potential form

> 歩けるのですが
> 英語を話せる人も多い

The idea that 'someone can do (is able to do) something' can be expressed with a pattern you have already met: verb + ことが出来る (see 17.4 and 26.7).

> 木下さんは中国語を話すことが出来ます。
> Mr Kinoshita can speak Chinese.

Here こと nominalises the verb, and 出来る, originally meaning something like 'to be forthcoming', means 'is possible'. Note the stative は + が construction again: 'As for Mr Kinoshita, speaking Chinese is possible.' In addition to this construction, however, there is a special form of the verb itself, known as the potential. It is created as follows:

	plain citation		*potential form*
group I	ending in -*u*		ends in-*eru*
	会う	meet	会える
	言う	say	言える
	買う	buy	買える

	ending in *-ru*		ends in *-reru*
	入る	enter	入れる
	乗る	ride	乗れる
	ある	exist	***
	ending in *-tsu*		ends in *-teru*
	待つ	wait	待てる
	ending in *-ku*		ends in *-keru*
	書く	write	書ける
	聞く	ask	聞ける
	[聞く	listen, hear	聞こえる]
	行く	go	行ける or 行かれる
	ending in *-mu*		ends in *-meru*
	読む	read	読める
	飲む	drink	飲める
	ending in *-nu*		ends in *-neru*
	死ぬ	die	死ねる
	ending in *-su*		ends in *-seru*
	話す	talk	話せる
	plain citation		*potential form*
group II	ending in *-ru*		ends in *-rareru*
	いる	exist	いられる
	出る	go out	出られる
	かける	hang	かけられる
	見る	look, see	見られる or 見える
	食べる	eat	食べられる
	寝る	go to bed	寝られる
	起きる	get up	起きられる

	plain citation		*potential form*
irregular	来る	come	来られる (こられる)
	する	do	出来る

Note that for group II verbs the potential form is in fact the same as the passive form, which you will meet in the next lesson.

The meaning of the sentences この子はもう歩くことが出来ます and この子はもう歩けます is exactly the same and in most cases these two forms are interchangeable. The only difference is that ことが出来る sounds slightly more formal and is more often used in the written language.

All potential forms are *stative* in character and hence are used with the same kind of construction that you have met in 12.2. As with ～たい constructions (30.1), however, you will often find that the dynamic nature of the verb takes precedence over the stative nature of the potential form itself, with the result that a transitive construction is often found. Either of the following sentences is perfectly acceptable (although see lesson 43 for further comments on the two verbs 聞ける and 見られる).

(あなたは) この漢字が読めますか。

(あなたは) この漢字を読めますか。

34.7 Polite requests with いただける

トランジターラジオを持ってきていただけますか。

For an explanation of the grammar of this construction turn back to 33.6. It comes up again here because it involves the potential form of いただく. The potential of both もらう and いただく are combined with the ～て form to express polite requests.

明後日まで待ってもらえますか (or いただけますか)。
Could you please wait until the day after tomorrow?

And by using this pattern with the negative form, one can be even more polite.

> あしたもう一度連絡してもらえませんか (or いただけませんか)。
> Could you please contact me again tomorrow?

Key to conversation

Romanisation

Nobuko	Anō, suimasen ga, Buraun-san to iu kata no byōshitsu wa dochira deshō ka.
Uketsuke	Nanika no kanja-san desu ka.
Nobuko	Sā, yoku wakarimasen ga kōtsū jiko ni atte nyūin shite iru hito desu.
Uketsuke	Sō desu ka. Chotto o-machi kudasai. Ā, Māku Buraun san, Igirisu no kata desu ne. Byōshitsu wa rokkai no roku-ni-hachi gō desu.
Nobuko	Dōmo arigatō gozaimashita.
Hajime	O-jama shimasu. Buraun-san, konkai wa taihen na me ni aimashita ne.
Buraun	A, Yamakawa san. Dōmo.
Nobuko	O-kagen wa ikaga desu ka.
Buraun	Kore wa, okusama mo. Wazawaza o-ide itadakimashite arigatō gozaimasu.
Nobuko	Iie, dō itashimashite. O-hana to kudamono o sukoshi motte mairimashita no de dōzo.
Hajime	Sore kara kore wa Eigo no shinbun to zasshi desu.
Buraun	Dōmo go-shinpai o o-kake shite mōshiwake arimasen.
Hajime	Iya iya. Sore yori guai no hō wa dō desu ka.
Buraun	Saiwai hone wa orete inai no de arukeru no desu ga, ugoku to mada itamimasu.
Hajime	Dabokushō dake desu ka.
Buraun	Mada yoku wakarimasen ga, atama o hidoku utta no de sochira no hō wa mada kensa-chū desu.
Nobuko	Sō desu ka. Sore wa go-shinpai desu ne.
Buraun	Ē, de mo kono byōin wa o-isha-san mo kangofu-san mo totemo shinsetsu desu shi, Eigo o hanaseru hito mo ōi no de sono ten de wa anshin shite iraremasu.
Nobuko	Sore wa totemo kokorozuyoi desu ne.
Hajime	Sorosoro menkai jikan no owari na no de shitsurei shiyō.
Nobuko	Sō desu ne. Chikai uchi ni mata mairimasu no de nani ka hitsuyō na mono ga

	arimashitara dōzo enryo naku osshatte kudasai. Buraun-san no apāto to uchi wa o-chikaku desu kara.
Buraun	Arigatō gozaimasu. Sore de wa makoto ni mōshiwake arimasen ga toranjisutā rajio o motte kite itadakemasu ka. Ima no tēburu no ue ni aru to omoimasu.
Nobuko	Hai, wakarimashita.
Hajime	Sore de wa mata. O-daiji ni.
Nobuko	Hayaku yoku natte kudasai ne.

Translation

Nobuko	Excuse me, could you tell me which is the room of a Mr Brown?
Receptionist	Which section is he in?
Nobuko	Well now, I'm not really sure, but he's in hospital because he was involved in a car accident.
Receptionist	I see. Just a moment please. Ah, Mr Mark Brown, from England. He's room number 628 on the sixth floor.
Nobuko	Thank you very much.
Hajime	May we disturb you? Mr Brown, this is a dreadful business.
Brown	Oh, Mr Yamakawa. How good to see you.
Nobuko	How are you feeling?
Brown	My goodness! Mrs Yamakawa too! How very kind of you to go out of your way.
Nobuko	Not at all. I've brought flowers and a little fruit for you.
Hajime	And this is an English newpaper and a magazine.
Brown	I'm terribly sorry to have put you to so much trouble.
Hajime	Nonsense. More importantly, how are you feeling?
Brown	Happily I haven't broken any bones and so I'm able to walk, but it still hurts whenever I move.
Hajime	Is it just bruising?
Brown	That's not clear yet. I hit my head badly and so that's still being investigated.
Nobuko	I see. That's a worry isn't it?
Brown	Yes, but the doctors and nurses at this hospital are very kind and there are many who can speak English, so I've no worries on that score.
Nobuko	That is very reassuring isn't it?
Hajime	It's almost the end of visiting hours, so let's be on our way.
Nobuko	Yes. We'll come again soon, so if there's something you need please don't hesitate

	to say so. Our house is very close to your flat so...
Brown	Thank you very much. In that case I wonder if I might ask you to bring my transistor radio. I think it's on the table in the living room.
Nobuko	Yes, of course.
Hajime	Well then, until next time. Look after yourself.
Nobuko	Do get better soon.

Lesson 35

John goes to the police station by Ueno Station to report a robbery.

ジョン	あのう、ほんの数分前に駅のホームで若い男に手さげかばんをひったくられたんですけど…。
巡査	何が入ってたんですか。
ジョン	お金はズボンのポケットに入れていたので大丈夫だったんですが、パスポート、外人登録証明書、銀行の通帳それに仕事関係の書類をとられました。
巡査	すりやひったくりは残念ながらほとんどの場合犯人はつかまらないんですが、一応正式の届けを出して下さい。
ジョン	はい、分かりました。
巡査	まず、名前、年齢、住所、電話番号、勤務先をここに記入して下さい。

John starts filling in the form.

巡査	ひったくりにあった時間と場所は。
ジョン	場所はJR線上野駅の三番線ホームです。時間は今から二十分ぐらい前ですから、五時半ごろですね。
巡査	どんな男だったか覚えていますか。
ジョン	だれかに背中をおされて、アッと思った瞬間にやられたのであまりよく覚えてませんが中肉中背の黒いセーターを着た男でした。
巡査	そうですか。年は。
ジョン	多分、二十四、五歳だと思います。
巡査	分かりました。それでは届けのコピーを一枚お渡ししますからこれを持っていって、パスポートと外人登録証明書の再発行を受けて下さい。
ジョン	はい。
巡査	このごろはすり、ひったくりが多いのでよく気を付けてください。

Comment

The first place to go if you get into trouble is the police. They will not be difficult to find, as there are more police per population than in any other country. Apart from the main stations, there is a network of small neighbourhood kiosks known as 交番. You will often find them at major intersections. A 交番 is a useful place to go if you have lost your way because it is the job of these local police to know what is going on in their area. You should not be surprised, however, if they in turn seem inquisitive. Japanese police are permitted to carry firearms.

35.1 The passive form

> 若い男に手さげかばんをひったくられた
> 書類をとられました。

The passive form is created as follows:

	plain citation		*passive form*
group I	ending in *-u*		ends in *-wareru*
	会う	meet	会われる
	言う	say	言われる
	買う	buy	買われる
	ending in *-ru*		ends in *-rareru*
	入る	enter	入られる
	乗る	ride	乗られる
	ある	exist	***
	ending in *-tsu*		ends in *-tareru*
	待つ	wait	待たれる

	ending in *-ku*		ends in *-kareru*
	書く	write	書かれる
	聞く	listen, ask	聞かれる
	行く	go	行かれる
	ending in *-mu*		ends in *-mareru*
	読む	read	読まれる
	飲む	drink	飲まれる
	ending in *-nu*		ends in *-nareru*
	死ぬ	die	死なれる
	ending in *-su*		ends in *-sareru*
	話す	talk	話される
	plain citation		*passive form*
group II	ending in *-ru*		ends in *-rareru*
	いる	exist	いられる
	出る	go out	出られる
	かける	hang	かけられる
	見る	look,see	見られる
	食べる	eat	食べられる
	寝る	go to bed	寝られる
	起きる	get up	起きられる
	plain citation		*passive form*
irregular	来る	come	来られる (こられる)
	する	do	される

The polite form of the passive is obtained by replacing る with 〜ます, and all passives become group II verbs for the purposes of further inflection.

35.2 Uses of the passive

In general it is fair to say that Japanese use the passive far less than we do in English. We often use the passive to avoid mentioning the subject of an active verb but, as you have seen, in Japanese the subject is in any case left out wherever possible. Another way of avoiding the passive in Japanese is to use one of the many transitive/intransitive pairs that will be introduced in lesson 42.

Note that, as a rule, Japanese passives are only used when the agent is animate, or at least has animate connotations. Exceptions will be found, but you should be wary of producing such sentences yourself. When a sentence with an active verb is changed into the passive form, observe the changes of particle as subject becomes agent:

(a) When the subject or topic of the passive sentence is animate, the particle marking the agent should be に. The passive of the sentence 親は (が) 子を育てる 'parents bring up chidren' is 子は親に育てられる.

(b) When the subject or topic of the passive sentence is inanimate, によって marks the agent in preference to に, especially in written Japanese. The passive of コロンブスが (は) アメリカ大陸を発見した 'Columbus discovered the American continent' is アメリカ大陸はコロンブスによって発見された.

(c) You will also find から being used to mark the source. The sentence 国民は天皇を尊敬していますか 'Do the people have respect for the emperor?' when put into the passive, 'Is the emperor respected by the people?', can become either 天皇は国民に尊敬されていますか or 天皇は国民から尊敬されていますか.

35.3 Passive with direct and indirect objects

The use of the particle に can give rise to some confusion on occasion, in particular when the sentence to be put into the passive contains both a direct and an indirect object, which also takes に. Take, for instance, the sentence:

(私は) 林さんに和子さんを紹介した。
I introduced Kazuko to Mr Hayashi.

This can be transformed into the passive as

> 和子さんは林さんに紹介された。
> Kazuko was introduced to Mr Hayashi.

but take note that this is highly ambiguous in Japanese and might also mean 'Kazuko was introduced to me (or to some third party) by Mr Hayashi.'

35.4 The 'adversative' passive

As in English, the passive can mark an action which is an intrusion rather than a pleasure. The active sentence

> すりはその婦人からさいふをすった。
> The pickpocket stole the purse from that woman.

would give

> その婦人はすりにさいふをすられた。
> That woman had her purse stolen by the pickpocket.

Note that in Japanese, as in English, the agent can be omitted if so desired:

> その婦人はさいふをすられた。
> That woman had her purse stolen.

and given the Japanese propensity for omitting topics when they are readily understandable from context, this sentence might be further reduced to

> さいふをすられた。
> (She) had her purse stolen.

Now this sentence will probably strike you as a little unusual because if the information had been reduced this far in English, in other words if we only had the words 'purse' and 'steal' to play with, the natural reaction would be to say:

> さいふがすられた。
> The purse was stolen.

In Japanese both sentences are in fact possible: さいふがすられた is a neutral statement and さいふをすられた, as the English translation suggests, carries with it a sense of annoyance. This use of を with a passive normally indicates that someone has been inconvenienced by an action. Compare the following:

となりに家が建てられた。
A house was built next to mine.

となりに家を建てられた。
(I am inconvenienced because) a house was built next to mine.

This form of the verb is known as the *adversative passive*. It can also be used with intransitive verbs, but that will be dealt with in the next lesson.

Key to conversation

Romanisation

Jon	Anō, hon no sūfun mae ni eki no hōmu de wakai otoko ni tesage-kaban o hittakuraretan desu kedo...
Junsa	Nani ga haittetan desu ka.
Jon	O-kane wa zubon no poketto ni irete ita no de daijōbu dattan desu ga, pasupōto, gaijintōroku shōmeisho, ginkō no tsūchō sore ni shigoto kankei no shorui o toraremashita.
Junsa	Suri ya hittakuri wa zannen nagara hotondo no baai hannin wa tsukamaranain desu ga, ichiō seishiki no todoke o dashite kudasai.
Jon	Hai, wakarimashita.
Junsa	Mazu, namae, nenrei, jūsho, denwa bangō, kinmusaki o koko ni ki'nyū shite kudasai.
Junsa	Hittakuri ni atta jikan to basho wa.
Jon	Basho wa JR sen Ueno eki no sanbansen hōmu desu. Jikan wa ima kara nijuppun gurai mae desu kara, gojihan goro desu ne.
Junsa	Donna otoko datta ka oboete imasu ka.
Jon	Dare ka ni senaka o osarete, atto omotta shunkan ni yarareta no de amari yoku oboetemasen ga chūniku chūzei no kuroi sētā o kita otoko deshita.

Junsa	Sō desu ka. Toshi wa.
Jon	Tabun, nijūshi-go sai da to omoimasu.
Junsa	Wakarimashita. Sore de wa todoke no kopī o ichimai o-watashi shimasu kara kore o motte itte, pasupōto to gaijintōroku shōmeisho no saihakkō o ukete kudasai.
Jon	Hai.
Junsa	Kono goro wa suri, hittakuri ga ōi no de yoku ki o tsukete kudasai.

Translation

John	Excuse me, just a few minutes ago my briefcase was snatched by a young man on the platform.
Policeman	What was in it?
John	I had my money in my trouser pocket so that was all right, but my passport, my alien registration card, my bank passbook and papers to do with my work were taken.
Policeman	Unfortunately in the case of pickpockets or bag snatchers we almost never catch the culprit, but for the record please submit an official notification form.
John	Yes, right.
Policeman	First, fill in your name, age, address, telephone number and place of work here.
Policeman	When and where was it snatched?
John	It was on platform 3 of the JR line at Ueno station. About twenty minutes ago, so that would make it about half-past five.
Policeman	Do you remember what sort of man he was?
John	It all happened very suddenly, just as someone pushed me in the back, so I don't remember very clearly, but he was a man of medium build and medium height wearing a black sweater.
Policeman	I see. How old was he?
John	Probably about twenty-four or five I think.
Policeman	Right. I'll give you a copy of the form so take it with you and arrange for the reissue of your passport and alien registration card.
John	Thank you.
Policeman	Pickpockets and bag snatchers are everywhere these days. Please take care.

Lesson 36

John tells Tadashi about his unfortunate day.

正	この間はひどい目にあったそうですね。
ジョン	どうして知っているんですか。
正	おとといマリーさんと電話で話した時に聞きました。
ジョン	そうですか。あの日は一日中運の悪いことばかりあったんですよ。
正	かばんをとられただけではなかったんですか。
ジョン	それが、交番に行って、届けを出したりしていたので大切なミーティングに遅れてしまったんです。
正	でもそれは仕方がないんじゃありませんか。
ジョン	と、僕も思ったんです。でもその集まりに来ていた人の一人に、ひったくりにあったのはボンヤリしていたからだろうなどといやみを言われました。
正	ずいぶん同情心のない人がいるもんだなあ。
ジョン	バカにされたみたいな気がしましたよ。
正	まあ、いろいろな人がいるから気にしない方がいいな。
ジョン	その上、帰りには雨に降られてびしょぬれになったんですよ。そのおかげでかぜをひいてしまいました。
正	かさは持っていなかったんですか。
ジョン	それが持ってはいたんですが…。多分ひったくりにあって気が転倒していたからだと思うのです。かさは交番に置き忘れたんですよ。
正	それは全くふんだりけったりでしたね。ところで、交番のお巡りさんは親切にしてくれましたか。
ジョン	ええ、住所や名前の他いろいろなことを聞かれましたけれどとても親切にしてくれました。

36.1 'Well yes, but...'

それが、

This phrase is hanging in mid-air. Do not mistake it for the subject of the following verb. It takes up what has just been said in the previous sentence and tries to put a gloss on it.

36.2 ～てしまう

ミーティングに遅れてしまったんです。 かぜをひいてしまいました。

(a) ～てしまう expresses the completion of an action or an event (not, of course, a state which cannot be 'completed'), and it often carries with it a sense of regret, or annoyance at something you (or someone else) might have done, or at something that has happened.

長い間かっていた犬が死んでしまった。
(Sadly) the dog which we had had for a long time died.

車のワイパーが急に動かなくなってしまった。
My car's windscreen wipers suddenly packed in.

As these examples indicate, ～てしまう usually has a negative implication, so a sentence such as

長いこと使わなかったのでドイツ語が下手になってしまった。
My German has become rusty, because I have not used it for a long time.

is quite acceptable; but you cannot really say:

*ドイツ語が上手になってしまった。
My German has gone and got a lot better.

because the negative connotation of ～てしまう contradicts the general sense of the sentence.

However there are cases when ～てしまう can express a strong sense of completion with pride.

木村君はこの本を読むのに一ヶ月もかかったが私は十日で読んでしまった。
Although it took Kimura a whole month to read this book, I finished reading it in ten days.

この仕事は明後日までに仕上げてしまう予定です。
I plan to have this job completed by the day after tomorrow.

(b) ～てしまう is different from the conjunctive form of the verb + 終わる that you met in 29.1. This latter signifies no more than that an action has been completed. Remember that with ～てしまう a sense of regret, or occasionally pride, at having managed to complete something, is normally present.

その本は三日前に読み終わりました。
I finished reading that book three days ago (neutral).

この図書館の本は全部読んでしまいました。
I have read all the books in this library.

This last sentence implies either that the speaker is very pleased at having read all the books in the library or that he is sad because there is nothing left to read. Notice also in this context another compound which was dealt with in 29.1: verb in conjunctive form + 上げる.

とうとう源氏物語を読み上げた。
I've finally got through the *Tale of Genji*.

(c) You will find ～てしまう used quite often, especially in Tōkyō and among young people, so often in fact that its completive force is sometimes lost. In this context note the common abbreviations: ～ちゃう for ～てしまう and ～ちゃった for ～てしまった.

飲んでしまった → 飲んじゃった
来てしまった → 来ちゃった

(d) しまった! used on its own has the force of 'blast!' or 'damn it!'

36.3 'So I thought'

と、僕も思ったんです。

Note the use of the particle と here. You have previously met it as a marker of direct and indirect speech. In this particular context it is standing for the whole of the previous statement, hence the translation 'So I thought, but...'

36.4 Further connotations of the passive

いやみを言われました。
バカにされたみたいでした。

We have seen that the use of the passive form in this kind of sentence where the speaker is directly involved often brings with it a sense that the speaker is being adversely affected by the action of the verb. It is for this reason that when you want to say something like 'they treated me very well' you cannot express it with a passive in Japanese: *私はとても親切にされた. This will have to be rephrased using one of the donatory verbs: 親切にしてもらいました, or 親切にしてくれました, as you see at the end of this conversation. All the following sentences and phrases carry with them a sense of being hard done by:

私は (彼女に) 不愉快なことを言われた。
She said unpleasant things to me.

きのう彼女から気になることを言われたので落ち着きません。
I feel unsettled because she said some disturbing things to me yesterday.

私は笑い者にされた。
I was made a laughing stock.

私は不親切にされた。
I was treated unkindly.

私は意地悪をされた。
They were very unkind to me.

36.5 Verb + もんだ

ずいぶん同情心のない人がいるもんだなあ。

The effect of this pattern もんだ or ものだ is to lend a sense of sympathetic emphasis to the sentence: 'there *are* some unsympathetic people around, aren't there!'

36.6 Two expressions with the noun 気

バカにされたみたいな気がしましたよ。
気にしない方がいい

The noun 気 'feeling' or 'spirit' is used to form a number of idiomatic expressions in Japanese. 気がする means 'have a feeling that'.

彼は来ないような気がする。
I have a feeling that he is not going to come.

その名前は前にどこかで聞いたことがあるような気がします。
I have a feeling that I have heard that name before somewhere.

You will also come across a number of other nouns that combine with the verb する in this intransitive fashion. Many of these phrases can be translated into English using a *transitive* equivalent.

> 台所で変な音がしたような気がしましたが。
> I thought I heard a strange noise in the kitchen.
>
> おかあさん。となりで知らない人の声がするけど、お客さんが来てるの。
> Mother, I hear a stranger's voice next door. Do we have a guest?
>
> 何かがこげているにおいがしますが大丈夫ですか。
> There is a smell of something burning; is it all right?

The second phrase here is 気にする. This means 'worry about', 'be affected by'.

> もう済んだことですから、気にしないで下さい。
> It's all over and done with, so please don't worry about it.

36.7 Verb + 方が…

気にしない方がいいな。

Constructions with 方がいい were introduced in 29.5. The pattern 方が…can be used with either imperfective or perfective forms.

> もう行った方がいい。
> It would be better if you left now.
>
> ケンブリッジからオックスフォードまではバスで行く方が便利です。
> From Cambridge to Oxford, going by bus is more convenient.

When the statement that follows is conditional on the completion of the action of the first verb, the 〜た form is used. The imperfective, on the other hand, is normally used for making general statements.

Some more examples:

よく考えた方がいいですよ。
I think you should think about it carefully.

あまり考え過ぎない方がいいのではありませんか。
Don't you think it would be preferable to stop worrying about it too much?

私が運転した方が安全だと思いますが…。
I really do think it would be safer if I drove…

少しだけですがビールを飲んだので運転しない方がいいと思います。
It was only a little, but I have drunk some beer so I think it would be better if I didn't drive.

36.8 Passive of intransitives

雨に降られてびしょぬれになったんですよ。

From the point of view of an English speaker, another rather 'unusual' use of the passive is with intransitive verbs. Here too there is a strong suggestion that the subject has been adversely affected by the event or situation.

父に死なれた。
My father went and died on me.

急にお客に来られた。
I was suddenly visited by a guest (and it was highly inconvenient).

36.9 Sarcastic use of おかげで

そのおかげでかぜをひいてしまいました。

You have met the phrase おかげさまで meaning 'thanks to you' in 17.5. Just as in English, it can also be used ironically, although it is usual in such a context to drop the polite さま. そのおかげで here means 'and thanks to the rain'.

Key to conversation

Romanisation

Tadashi	Kono aida wa hidoi me ni atta sō desu ne.
Jon	Dōshite shitte irun desu ka.
Tadashi	Ototoi Marī-san to denwa de hanashita toki ni kikimashita.
Jon	Sō desu ka. Ano hi wa ichinichi-jū un no warui koto bakari attan desu yo.
Tadashi	Kaban o torareta dake de wa nakattan desu ka.
Jon	Sore ga, kōban ni itte, todoke o dashitari shite ita no de taisetsu na mītingu ni okurete shimattan desu.
Tadashi	Demo sore wa shikata ga nain ja arimasen ka.
Jon	To, boku mo omottan desu. Demo sono atsumari ni kite ita hito no hitori ni, hittakuri ni atta no wa bonyari shite ita kara darō nado to iyami o iwaremashita.
Tadashi	Zuibun dōjōshin no nai hito ga iru mon da nā.
Jon	Baka ni sareta mitai na ki ga shimashita yo.
Tadashi	Mā, iroiro na hito ga iru kara ki ni shinai hō ga ii na.
Jon	Sono ue, kaeri ni wa ame ni furarete bishonure ni nattan desu yo. Sono o-kage de kaze o hiite shimaimashita.
Tadashi	Kasa wa motte inakattan desu ka.
Jon	Sore ga motte wa itan desu ga...Tabun hittakuri ni atte ki ga tentō shite ita kara da to omou no desu. Kasa wa kōban ni okiwasuretan desu yo.
Tadashi	Sore wa mattaku fundari kettari deshita ne. Tokoro de, kōban no o-mawari-san wa shinsetsu ni shite kuremashita ka.
Jon	Ē, jūsho ya namae no hoka iroiro na koto o kikaremashita keredo totemo shinsetsu ni shite kuremashita.

Translation

Tadashi	I heard you had a pretty bad time the other day.
John	How do you know?
Tadashi	I heard about it when I was talking on the telephone with Marie the day before yesterday.
John	I see. That day I had nothing but bad luck all day long.
Tadashi	Having your case taken wasn't the only thing?
John	What with going to the police station and submitting the complaint, I was late for an important meeting.
Tadashi	But there was nothing you could do about that surely?
John	That's what I thought. But I had the humiliating experience of being told by one of the people at the gathering that I must have been daydreaming to have something snatched.
Tadashi	There are some unsympathetic people around, aren't there!
John	I felt as if I was being laughed at.
Tadashi	Well, it takes all sorts, so don't take it to heart.
John	And then on the way home I was rained on and got completely soaked. Thanks to that I caught a cold.
Tadashi	You weren't carrying an umbrella?
John	Well yes, I was carrying one...I think it must have been because I was upset after my case had been snatched. I left my umbrella at the police kiosk.
Tadashi	Oh that's really adding insult to injury! And was the policeman at the kiosk kind to you?
John	Yes. I was asked all sorts of things, apart from my name and address of course, but he did treat me very kindly.

Lesson 37

Minoru meets Kinoshita in front of the library on a snowy day.

実	木下さん、今日は。寒いですね。
木下	本当に。きのうから降り出した雪はちっともやみそうもありませんね。
実	下宿のそばのお寺は雪化粧をして、とてもきれいでした。
木下	うちの近くでは、子供達が雪だるまを作ってましたよ。
実	卒業試験の前で忙しいですか。コーヒーでも飲みに行きませんか。
木下	そうしましょうか。

They go into a nearby cafe.

実	コーヒー二つ、お願いします。
ウェイトレス	はい、ホットですね。
実	卒論や試験の準備で忙しいでしょう。
木下	ええ、でも先学期は一週間に三回も高校で英語を教えていたので、もっと大変でした。
実	アルバイトですか。
木下	とんでもない。英語教員の資格をとるための実習ですよ。
実	あ、そうか。うまく出来ましたか。
木下	授業を始める前に生徒を静かにさせるのがひと苦労でした。
実	僕も大学から若い先生が来た時は、さわいだ記憶があるな。それで、どんなことをしたんですか。
木下	まあ、テキストを読ませたり、練習問題に答えさせたりしましたけど。
実	宿題も出したんですか。
木下	ええ、作文を一度書かせました。とてもよく出来ているのもありましたよ。
実	木下さんは本当に将来先生になるつもりなんですか。

木下	さあ、何だか自信がなくなってしまいました。
実	四月からはイギリスに行くんでしょう。
木下	ええ、カンタベリーに六ヶ月ほど行くことにしました。
実	そう言えば、妹の国子もヨーロッパに行くみたいですよ。
木下	妹さん、大学へは行かないんですか。
実	父の手紙によると、ドイツの音楽学校へ行ってピアノを続けたいという本人の希望をいれて、留学させることにしたそうです。
木下	そうですか。

Comment

Note the words ホット and アルバイト here. They are typical examples of what can happen to loanwords: their range is often either narrowed or transformed entirely. ホット 'hot' is short for ホットコーヒー 'hot coffee'. It never stands for anything else, not even tea. アルバイト stems from the German *Arbeit* 'work'. In Japanese, however, it refers only to the kind of part-time work that students and others often undertake to help out on their expenses. It could involve working in a shop, a restaurant, or tutoring middle and senior high school students for their exams. It is such a common thing to do that it immediately springs to mind when Minoru hears Kinoshita has been teaching English.

37.1 'You must be joking!'

とんでもない。

Learn this phrase as an idiom. It can mean a range of things from 'absurd' to 'inconceivable' and you will often hear it in this sense of 'far from it'. You may see it written with the *kanji* for *tobu* 'fly', i.e. 'not even if I (could) fly!' but this is based on a somewhat fanciful etymology.

37.2 The causative form

生徒を静かにさせる

Japanese verbs have a further inflection that represents causative constructions, namely 'causing someone do something'. The causative is formed using the 'negative' base (see 15.1) as follows

	plain form	*causative*
group I	ending in *-ru, -ku, -mu, -nu, -su, -gu*	ends in *-raseru, -kaseru, -maseru,* etc.
	入る	入らせる
	乗る	乗らせる
	書く	書かせる
	聞く	聞かせる
	飲む	飲ませる
	死ぬ	死なせる
	話す	話させる
	泳ぐ	泳がせる
	ending in *-u*	ends in *-waseru*
	会う	会わせる
	買う	買わせる

Note that there is no causative for the verb ある.

	plain form	*causative*
group II	ending in *-ru*	ends in *-saseru*
	いる	いさせる
	出る	出させる
	見る	見させる
	食べる	食べさせる

	plain form	*causative*
irregular	来る	来(こ)させる
	する	させる

The polite form of the causative is obtained by replacing る with ～ます. All causatives become group II verbs for the purposes of further inflection.

The basic meaning of this form is 'to make, or let, someone do something'; causatives can span the whole range from permission to coercion. Because it covers 'allowing' as well as 'causing', it is also known as the permissive form. As a general rule both subjects and underlying agents should be animate beings. Both transitive and intransitive verbs may appear in the causative.

37.3 Transitive causatives

> テキストを読ませたり、練習問題に答えさせたりしましたけど。

With transitive verbs the person or animal being made to do something is normally marked by に, so with all the elements present, a sentence might read:

私は	生徒に	テキストを	読ませた
I	the students	text	caused to read
topic/subject	underlying agent	direct object	transitive causative

Incidentally, note that the second に in the sentence in the box (練習問題に) has nothing to do with the causative and is *not* marking the agent. It is part of an idiom whereby 'answering questions' is rendered in Japanese as 'replying *to* questions'. Some more examples of the causative of transitive verbs:

先生は学生に日本語で日記を書かせた。
The teacher made the students write their diary in Japanese.

赤ん坊にミルクを飲ませた。
I fed the baby with milk.

There are, however, some exceptional cases in which the underlying agent of the transitive verb in the causative form is marked not by に but by を:

> 会議が終わるまでタクシーを待たせます。
> I will have the taxi wait (for me) until the meeting is over.
>
> 娘を手伝わせましょう。
> I will have my daughter help (you).

In these sentences the direct objects (the ones in brackets) are omitted because they are obvious from the context, and the subject, 'I' in both cases, is treating the underlying agent (the taxi and the daughter respectively) as an object over which there is complete control. Note that if the direct object is present, then に *must* be used to mark the underlying agent.

> 洗いものを娘に手伝わせましょう。
> I will have my daughter help you wash up.

37.4 Intransitive causatives

静かにさせる

Causatives can also be used with verbs that do *not* have direct objects.

医者は	患者を/に	一日三十分	歩かせる。
The doctor	the patient	30 mins. a day	causes to walk
topic/subject	underlying agent		intransitive causative

With intransitive verbs both に and を are used to mark the underlying agent. に is used when the agent has complete choice or freedom of action:

> その先生は子供達に湖で好きなだけ泳がせた。
> The teacher let the children swim in the lake as long as they liked.

However if the agent is forced to act, or the agent has no ability to perform the act on his or her own, the particle must be を.

その先生は子供達をプールで泳がせた。
The teacher let the children swim in the pool (under his supervision).

When the person (or animal) acts either intentionally or without the aid of the subject, に and を can be employed with little difference in meaning.

この老人ホームでは元気な老人達に/を毎日海岸まで散歩させる。
In this home for the aged, they send healthy old people for a daily walk to the beach.

Either に or を can be used in this case, because the walking is an act controlled by the old people themselves. But in the following case you can only use を, because the baby is still too weak to really help itself.

その若い母親はヨチヨチ歩きの赤ん坊を毎日散歩させる。
That young mother takes her toddler for a walk every day.

私は犬を散歩させる。
I take the dog for a walk.

The particle after 犬 here *must* be を because, although a dog can wander about, it cannot 'go for a walk' on its own. Similarly を is employed in the following example:

温室で真冬にバラをさかせる。
In our greenhouse I get roses to flower in midwinter.

37.5 Agent marked by を with verbs of emotion

With those verbs that express emotion or involuntary action such as 笑う 'to laugh', おこる 'to get angry', 悲しむ 'to be sad' etc., the underlying agent must always be marked by を. This is because these emotions and actions cannot normally be controlled by the individual concerned; they are indeed involuntary.

じょうだんを言ってみんなを笑わせた。
He made people laugh by telling jokes.

弟は無理ばかり言って両親を困らせる。
My younger brother is always coming out with unreasonable statements and causing my parents much worry.

そのニュースは母をとても喜ばせた。
The news delighted my mother.

37.6 Cases when the causative cannot be used

Sentences can often be grammatically correct but still wrong in context. Social considerations come into play here, especially with a form like the causative, which by its very nature, implies the ability to make others do something. The causative is only really used, therefore, when the subject is equal or higher in status to the underlying agent. A sentence such as

私は先生に説明させるつもりだ。
I intend to make my teacher explain.

may be grammatically correct but it is not socially acceptable. So what about the following?

私はがんこな父を病院へ行かせた。
I persuaded my stubborn father to go to hospital.

Usually, your father should be regarded as someone superior to you. In this case, however, the relative positions of speaker and father are reversed, perhaps because of the father's illness or old age: if the speaker can be seen acting as a protector, the sentence is acceptable.

Key to conversation

Romanisation

Minoru	Kinoshita-san, konnichi wa. Samui desu ne.
Kinoshita	Hontō ni. Kinō kara furidashita yuki wa chittomo yamisō mo arimasen ne.
Minoru	Geshuku no soba no o-tera wa yukigeshō o shite, totemo kirei deshita.
Kinoshita	Uchi no chikaku de wa, kodomo-tachi ga yukidaruma o tsukuttemashita yo.
Minoru	Sotsugyō shiken no mae de isogashii desu ka. Kōhī de mo nomi ni ikimasen ka.
Kinoshita	Sō shimashō ka.
Minoru	Kōhī futatsu, o-negai shimasu.
Ueitoresu	Hai, hotto desu ne.
Minoru	Sotsuron ya shiken no junbi de isogashii deshō.
Kinoshita	Ē, demo sengakki wa isshūkan ni sankai mo kōkō de Eigo o oshiete ita no de, motto taihen deshita.
Minoru	Arubaito desu ka.
Kinoshita	Tonde mo nai. Eigo kyōin no shikaku o toru tame no jisshū desu yo.
Minoru	A, sō ka. Umaku dekimashita ka.
Kinoshita	Jugyō o hajimeru mae ni seito o shizuka ni saseru no ga hitokurō deshita.
Minoru	Boku mo daigaku kara wakai sensei ga kita toki wa, sawaida kioku ga aru na. Sore de, donna koto o shitan desu ka.
Kinoshita	Mā, tekisuto o yomasetari, renshū mondai ni kotaesasetari shimashita kedo.
Minoru	Shukudai mo dashitan desu ka.
Kinoshita	Ē, sakubun o ichido kakasemashita. Totemo yoku dekite iru no mo arimashita yo.
Minoru	Kinoshita san wa hontō ni shōrai sensei ni naru tsumori nan desu ka.
Kinoshita	Sā, nan da ka jishin ga nakunatte shimaimashita.
Minoru	Shigatsu kara wa Igirisu ni ikun deshō.
Kinoshita	Ē, Kantaberī ni rokkagetsu hodo iku koto ni shimashita.
Minoru	Sō ieba, imōto no Kuniko mo Yōroppa ni iku mitai desu yo.
Kinoshita	Imōto-san, daigaku e wa ikanain desu ka.
Minoru	Chichi no tegami ni yoru to, Doitsu no ongaku gakkō e itte piano o tsuzuketai to iu honnin no kibō o irete, ryūgaku saseru koto ni shita sō desu.
Kinoshita	Sō desu ka.

Translation

Minoru	Kinoshita san, hello! It's cold isn't it?
Kinoshita	Very. The snow that's been falling since yesterday doesn't look like stopping at all, does it?
Minoru	The temple next to my lodgings has a coat of snow and looked very pretty.
Kinoshita	Near my place, the children were making snowmen.
Minoru	You must be busy just before the final exams. Do you have time for a cup of coffee?
Kinoshita	Let's do that.
Minoru	Two coffees please.
Waitress	Yes, hot coffee?
Minoru	You must be busy preparing your graduation thesis and for the exams.
Kinoshita	Yes, but last term I was teaching English three times a week at a high school, so that was much worse.
Minoru	A part-time job?
Kinoshita	You must be joking! It was practice-teaching in order to get my qualification as an English teacher .
Minoru	I see. Did you do well?
Kinoshita	It was a big effort to get the students quiet before I began a class.
Minoru	I remember making a lot of noise when a young teacher came from university. So, what sorts of things did you do?
Kinoshita	Well, I had them do things like read texts and answer practice questions.
Minoru	Did you give them homework too?
Kinoshita	Yes, I had them write a composition once. Some were very well done, too.
Minoru	Do you really intend to become a teacher in the future?
Kinoshita	Hm, but I'm somehow not so confident about it now.
Minoru	You're going to England in April aren't you?
Kinoshita	Yes, I've decided to go to Canterbury for six months.
Minoru	That reminds me, it looks as though my younger sister Kuniko is going to Europe too.
Kinoshita	Your sister's not going to university?
Minoru	According to father's letters, he says he's agreed to her own wish to continue studying piano at a German music school, so he has decided to let her go abroad to study.
Kinoshita	I see.

Lesson 38

John and Marie are waiting for Tadashi at Shinbashi Station.

ジョン　おかしいなあ。正君はいつも時間に正確なのに…。
マリー　そうですね。もう約束の時間を十五分も過ぎているのに…。アッ、来ましたよ。
正　ごめん、ごめん。寒いところでずいぶん待たせてしまって、悪いことをしました。
マリー　どうしたんですか。
正　八時には用意が出来ていたのに、丁度家を出ようとした時に電話がなったんです。
ジョン　急な用事だったんですか。
正　いや、新しい仕事を頼まれただけなんですが。
マリー　ずいぶん、忙しそうですね。
正　いやあ、このごろとても忙しいのに、また仕事が一つ増えてしまいましたよ。ところで、マリーさん、お誕生日おめでとうございます。
マリー　どうもありがとう。今日の鎌倉行きは前からとても楽しみにしていました。
ジョン　鎌倉にはもう何度も行ったことがあるでしょう。
マリー　ええ、有名な大仏や八幡宮には行ったことがありますけど、冬の鎌倉は初めてです。
正　京都は寒くて、雪が降っているらしいけれど、こちらは割にあたたかいから梅の花がそろそろ咲きかけているかもしれないな。
ジョン　電車が来ましたから乗りましょう。

The three of them are now on the train.

ジョン　日曜日なのに案外混んでるなあ。
正　そうですね。ところで、十二時半に精進料理の店に予約をしておきました。
マリー　わあ、本物の精進料理ですか。
正　今日はマリーさんのお誕生日ですからね。ジョン君と僕から

	のプレゼントです。
マリー	本当にどうもありがとう。すばらしい記念になりそうです。
ジョン	お昼まで時間があるので、どうしましょうか。
正	鎌倉駅の一つ手前の北鎌倉で電車を降りて、円覚寺をぬけて、それから建長寺の方へ下るのはどうですか。
ジョン	寒くないかなあ。
マリー	寒くても私は平気よ。それに今日はとてもカラッとしたいいお天気だし。
正	鎌倉駅からバスに乗って、大塔の宮から瑞泉寺の方を見にいってもいいと思うけれど。
マリー	瑞泉寺は確か水仙のころに一度行きました。
ジョン	それじゃあ、円覚寺から歩くことにしよう。正君は何度も通ったことのある道でしょう。
正	ええ、でも何度通っても飽きない散歩道ですけど。

Comment

As we have explained, tourism in Japan is a habit with a long history. You will find that the commuter trains in the Tōkyō area are only slightly less crowded at the weekend than during the week, and it seems at times as though everyone is forever on the move. Kamakura, the old seat of power in the thirteenth century, is about one hour's train ride south of the capital and is a favorite for 'days out'. It is possible to follow mountain routes from temple to temple, and there is nowhere better to get some feel of Japan as it was in pre-modern times; if, that is, you can avoid the crowds.

38.1 Concessions with のに

> 正君はいつも時間に正確なのに...。
> もう約束の時間を十五分も過ぎているのに...。
> 八時には用意が出来ていたのに、

のに here means 'despite the fact that...' or 'although'. It is added directly to the plain form of verbs. When the copula is present, it takes the form な.

> 試験が近いのに遊んでばかりいる。
> Despite the fact that the exams are close, he does nothing but play around.
>
> わざわざ彼の家まで訪ねて行ったのに留守だった。
> We went to his house specially to see him, but he was out.

As you will see from the above examples, のに can express either surprise at something unexpected or disappointment at an unwelcome outcome.

> せっかくケーキを焼いたのにだれも食べようとしなかった。
> Although I baked a cake specially, nobody tried it.

38.2 'Forgive me'

ごめん、ごめん。

ごめん is here a colloquial abbreviation of ごめんなさい, 'I do apologise' or 'Please forgive me.' For a somewhat different use of this word in the phrase 御免下さい, meaning 'excuse me' but used when entering a room, refer back to 26.1.

38.3 Concessions with 〜ても

寒くても私は平気よ。 でも何度通っても飽きない散歩道ですけど。

When a verb in the 〜て form is followed by も, the effect is equivalent to the English 'even though' or 'even if'.

その子は母親の言うことが分かっても分からないふりをします。
That child pretends he doesn't understand what his mother says, even though he does.

その本はずっと前から捜していたので高くても買います。
I have been looking for that book for a long time, so I'll buy it even if it is expensive.

The same construction can be observed with the copula, in which case it appears as でも. In such cases the English equivalent may have to be more idiomatic.

その問題には専門家でも答えられないかも知れません。
It could well be that even a specialist would find it difficult to answer that question.

山田さんがいくら英語から日本語へのほん訳が上手でもこの仕事を三日でするのは無理でしょう。
No matter how good Mr Yamada is at translating English into Japanese, I don't think he can do this job in three days.

38.4 のに and 〜ても compared

So how do these two patterns differ? The difference is often difficult to define and is perhaps best illustrated with some examples. In general the 'if' element in 〜ても is much stronger, and のに cannot be used in a future context.

明日は雨が降っても出かけます。
I'll go out tomorrow even if it rains.

雨が降っているのに出かけるらしい。
It seems that he intends to go out even though it's raining.

あの子はどんなに悪いことをしてもしかられない。
That child never gets a scolding no matter how naughty he is.

あの子は何も悪いことをしないのにしかられてばかりいる。
That child is always being scolded although she never does anything naughty.

38.5 The suggestive form + とする

ちょうど家を出ようとした時に電話がかかってきた。

This pattern means 'to be about to…' or 'to try to…' and often marks an action which is about to be interrupted.

道路を渡ろうとした時に信号が赤に変わった。
I was just about to cross the road, when the traffic lights turned red.

遅れてすみません。出来るだけ早く来ようとしたのですが…。
Sorry I'm late. I tried to come as soon as possible.

38.6 'Congratulations'

お誕生日おめでとうございます。

The form おめでとうございます is used very much like the English 'Congratulations' or 'Happy…' Other common examples are: 御結婚おめでとうございます, for a newly married couple, and 明けましておめでとうございます or 新年おめでとうございます, for the New Year.

38.7 も with a positive verb

何度も行ったことがあるでしょう。

You were introduced to the use of classifier + も with the negative in 24.8. Here we have も marking an indeterminative in a positive sentence. It can be translated 'You must have been many times before.'

彼は一日何杯もコーヒーを飲む。
He drinks many cups of coffee a day.

38.8 The conjunctive form + かける

梅の花がそろそろ咲きかけているかもしれないな。

We saw in lesson 29 how compound verbs could be created by using the conjunctive form of the first verb. Occasionally the second verb in a compound has a special role and かける is one such example. It signifies 'be on the verge of' or 'begin to'. It is broadly the same as 始める in meaning, although 始める has a sense of conscious control about it. With かける the impression is of some process which is about to get underway, and which may be interrupted:

この子は何かやりかけてもすぐに飽きてしまって、途中でやめてしまいます。
This child quickly gets bored with things as soon as he starts them, and so gives up halfway.

Key to conversation

Romanisation

Jon	Okashii nā. Tadashi kun wa itsumo jikan ni seikaku na no ni…
Marī	Sō desu ne. Mō yakusoku no jikan o jūgofun mo sugite iru no ni…A! Kimashita yo.
Tadashi	Gomen, gomen. Samui tokoro de zuibun matasete shimatte warui koto o shimashita.
Marī	Dō shitan desu ka.

Tadashi	Hachiji ni wa yōi ga dekite ita no ni, chōdo ie o deyō to shita toki ni denwa ga nattan desu.
Jon	Kyū na yōji dattan desu ka.
Tadashi	Iya, atarashii shigoto o tanomareta dake nan desu ga.
Marī	Zuibun, isogashisō desu ne.
Tadashi	Iyā, kono goro totemo isogashii no ni, mata shigoto ga hitotsu fuete shimaimashita yo. Tokoro de, Marī-san o-tanjōbi o-medetō gozaimasu.
Marī	Dōmo arigatō. Kyō no Kamakura-yuki wa mae kara totemo tanoshimi ni shite imashita.
Jon	Kamakura ni wa mō nando mo itta koto ga aru deshō.
Marī	Ē, yūmei na Daibutsu ya Hachimangū ni wa itta koto ga arimasu kedo, fuyu no Kamakura wa hajimete desu.
Tadashi	Kyōto wa samukute, yuki ga futte iru rashii keredo, kochira wa wari ni atatakai kara ume no hana ga sorosoro sakikakete iru ka mo shirenai na.
Jon	Densha ga kimashita kara norimashō.

Jon	Nichiyōbi na no ni angai konderu nā.
Tadashi	Sō desu ne. Tokoro de, jūnijihan ni shōjin ryōri no mise ni yoyaku o shite okimashita.
Marī	Wā, honmono no shōjin ryōri desu ka.
Tadashi	Kyō wa Marī-san no o-tanjōbi desu kara ne. Jon-kun to boku kara no purezento desu.
Marī	Hontō ni dōmo arigatō. Subarashii kinen ni narisō desu.
Jon	O-hiru made jikan ga aru no de, dō shimashō ka.
Tadashi	Kamakura eki no hitotsu temae no Kita-Kamakura de densha o orite, Enkakuji o nukete, sore kara Kenchōji no hō e kudaru no wa dō desu ka.
Jon	Samukunai ka nā.
Marī	Samukutemo watakushi wa heiki yo. Sore ni kyō wa totemo karatto shita ii o-tenki da shi.
Tadashi	Kamakura eki kara basu ni notte, Daitō no Miya kara Zuisenji no hō o mi ni itte mo ii to omou keredo.
Marī	Zuisenji wa tashika suisen no koro ni ichido ikimashita.
Jon	Sore jā, Enkakuji kara aruku koto ni shiyō. Tadashi-kun wa nando mo tōtta koto no aru michi deshō.
Tadashi	Ē, demo nando tōte mo akinai sanpomichi desu kedo.

Translation

John	How strange. Tadashi's normally so punctual...
Marie	So he is. It's already fifteen minutes past the time we agreed to meet. Ah, here he comes.
Tadashi	Sorry, so sorry. How bad of me to have kept you waiting so long in the cold.
Marie	What happened?
Tadashi	I was ready by eight, but just as I was about to leave the house the telephone rang.
John	Was it something urgent?
Tadashi	No, I was merely asked to take on a new job.
Marie	You seem very busy.
Tadashi	Yes, and even though I'm really busy at the moment now there's yet another thing I have to do. But Marie. Happy birthday.
Marie	Thank you very much. I've been looking forward to our trip to Kamakura today for some time.
John	You must have been to Kamakura many times before surely?
Marie	Yes, I've been to famous places like the Daibutsu and the Hachimangū, but this is my first time to go to Kamakura in the winter.
Tadashi	It's cold in Kyōto and they say it's snowing there, but here it's comparatively warm, so the plum blossom may be just about coming out.
John	The train's here. Shall we get on?

John	It's rather crowded for a Sunday.
Tadashi	So it is. By the way, I've made a booking at a Buddhist vegetarian restaurant for twelve thirty.
Marie	Oh marvellous! Real vegetarian food?
Tadashi	Because it's your birthday today. It's a present from John and me.
Marie	Really, thank you so much. I'm sure it'll be a meal to remember.
John	We'll have some time before lunch, so what shall we do?
Tadashi	How about getting off one stop before Kamakura at Kita-Kamakura and going through Enkakuji, and then down towards Kenchōji?
John	It won't be too cold?
Marie	I don't mind if it's cold. And today it's such good weather – crisp and dry.
Tadashi	We could also take a bus from Kamakura station and go and have a look at Daitō no Miya and Zuisenji.

Marie	I'm pretty sure I went to Zuisenji when the daffodils were out.
John	Well then, let's walk from Enkakuji. You've done the route many times haven't you Tadashi?
Tadashi	Yes, but it's a path that you never tire of, no matter how many times you do it.

Lesson 39

マリーの日記

二月二十四日(土)　　　　　　　　　　　　　　晴れのち小雨

今日は私の誕生日。ジョンと正さんが鎌倉に連れていってくれた上、本格的な精進料理をごちそうしてくれた。精進料理らしいものは何度も食べたことがあるが、本物は初めてだった。日本料理は何よりも目を楽しませてくれる。いくつかのお寺を見て歩きながら、正さんが十二世紀の終わりに源氏が鎌倉に幕府を開いたころのことを説明してくれた。これから私も少し日本の歴史の本を読んでみようと思う。ジョンは結局、ネパールには行かないことにしたとのこと。
昼間はよいお天気で、春らしくなってきたと思ったのに、夕方から急に寒くなって、小雨が降り出した。留守の間に、高野さんが来てくれたらしい。カードといっしょにプレゼントを置いていってくれた。
夜、フランスの両親から電話がかかってきた。来週の土曜日の朝七時半に成田に着くとのこと。日本語も英語も出来ないので心配していたが、私が空港まで迎えに行くので心配しないようにと言っておいた。

Comment
This short diary entry is in straightforward prose. Note that there is no use of polite forms such as ～ます or です, because Marie is addressing herself. さん is still used where appropriate, however, and the donatory verb くれる is carefully chosen to reflect appropriate status.

39.1 Use of 上

ジョンと正さんが鎌倉に連れていってくれた上

上, read うえ here, simply means 'in addition to' or 'on top of'. Its use is, by and large, restricted to the written language or at least to formal situations.

39.2 Idiomatic use of causative

目を楽しませてくれる。

This phrase looks complicated because it combines a causative with a donatory verb. The sentence means 'Japanese food is above all a delight for the eye' but a more literal rendition would be 'Japanese food above all does us the favour of causing pleasure to the eye.' It may strike you as a little odd that the food does the favour; in a sense it is this personification of the food that lends the phrase a somewhat rhetorical touch.

39.3 ～おうと思う

日本の歴史の本を読んでみようと思う。

We have already met the phrase つもりです 'intend to...' in 21.5. つもり, however, is a little too direct in many situations which call for a milder touch; ～おうと思う also expresses volition and intention, but rather less directly.

> かぜをひいて具合が悪いので今晩は早く寝ようと思う。
> I have a cold and don't feel too well, so I think I'll go to bed early tonight.
>
> 子供のころは汽車の運転手になろうと思っていました。
> When I was a child I wanted to become an engine driver.

In this connection, note the difference between : (a) 行こうと思います and (b) 行くと思います. In (a) the subject of the subordinate clause is in the first person, hence the sentence means 'I think I will go' but in (b) the subject of the two verbs is different and the sentence means 'I think he (she) will go' (see 27.3).

今度の試合では絶対に勝とうと思う。
I am determined to win the next match.

今度の試合ではロシアが勝つと思う。
I think the Russian team will win the next game.

39.4 とのこと

ジョンは結局、ネパールには行かないことにしたとのこと。
来週の土曜日の朝七時半に成田に着くとのこと。

This is another, somewhat more formal, way of expressing hearsay; 'they say that…' or 'he said that…' It may appear as either the full ということだ (です) or as a truncated とのことだ (です). It acts in very much the same way as そうだ (33.1).

木下先生、山下さんは頭痛のため今日は来られないとのことです。
Dr Kinoshita, Yamashita asked me to inform you that she cannot be present today because she has a headache.

メキシコ地震による死者の数は三千人以上ということだ。
It has been reported that the number of casualties in the earthquake in Mexico is more than 3,000.

39.5 〜ていく and 〜てくる

プレゼントを置いていってくれた。
夜、フランスの両親から電話がかかってきた。

Before discussing the forms 〜ていく and 〜てくる, we should perhaps review the use of the verbs 行く and 来る in isolation. Unlike English, in Japanese it is *not* permissible to transfer the point of view to the other person. Observe the following situations:

(a) Both A and B are in A's office.

A: あしたも来られますか。
Can you come again tomorrow?

B: ええ、大丈夫ですよ。九時半までに来ます。
Yes, no problem. I'll come by nine thirty.

(b) A and B are talking on the telephone.

A: あしたの三時にJALの315便で成田に着くのですが...。
I'll be arriving at Narita tomorrow at three o'clock on JAL 315.

B: 分かりました。空港までお迎えに行きます。
Fine, I'll come and meet you at the airport.

In the first case 来る is permissable only because B is in the same place as the person with whom he is speaking and he will be returning to that place; he will be 'coming back'. In the second case, however, 行く must be used because the movement is away from, rather than towards, the speaker.

39.6 ～ていく

～ていく expresses the concept of doing something before leaving. Note, however, that the 'leaving' or 'going' part is treated very much as background information; despite the fact that it is overtly expressed in the Japanese, it is not in any way stressed.

どうぞ、晩ごはんを食べていって下さい。
Please stay for supper.

彼女はめずらしく長いこと話していきました。
She chatted for hours (and then left), which is unusual for her.

出発前にかぎは事務所に置いていって下さい。
Please leave the key at the office before you leave.

〜ていく can also signify an action which is going to proceed and develop into the future.

秋になるとどんどん日が短かくなっていきます。
In autumn the days get shorter and shorter.

これからは大学へ行く人が増えていくでしょう。
There will be more and more people going to university from now on.

39.7 〜てくる

This is in essence a repeat of what was said in 23.5. There are occasions when the 'coming' sense in 〜てくる is weak. The following illustrate similar examples:

秋になってどんどん日が短くなってきた。
Now it's autumn, the days have become shorter and shorter.

もう十二時ですからどこかで昼ごはんを食べてきて下さい。
It's already twelve o'clock, so please go and eat somewhere (and come back).

ごはんは。	もう食べてきました。
A meal?	Oh, I've already eaten.

If you would like to say 'Please eat before you come', ごはんを食べてから来て下さい would be more normal than ごはんを食べてきて下さい.

39.8 With verbs of motion

ジョンと正さんが鎌倉に連れていってくれた。

When 〜ていく and 〜てくる are used in combination with a verb of motion, the verb in the 〜て form is often best understood in an adverbial sense (see 19.1).

飛んでいく	fly off, hurry off

走っていく	run off
タクシーに乗ってくる	come by taxi

For an explanation of 春らしくなってきた turn back to 25.1.

39.9 Indirect requests with ように

> 心配しないようにと言っておいた。

This pattern is quite simple, using the plain form of the verb followed by ように (と言う). A request quoting the actual words to be said would look like this:

山田さんに「電話をかけて下さい」と言って下さい。
Please say to Mr Yamada, 'Please telephone.'

This would be recast indirectly as:

山田さんに電話をかけるように(と)言って下さい。
Please tell Mr Yamada to telephone me.

Note also that verbs other than 言う can be used:

タクシーの運転手さんにちょっと待ってくれるように頼みましょう。
Let's ask the taxi driver to wait a little.

Key to passage

Romanisation

Marī no nikki

Nigatsu nijuyokka (do) Hare nochi kosame

Kyō wa watakushi no tanjōbi. Jon-san to Tadashi-san ga Kamakura ni tsurete itte kureta ue, honkakuteki na shōjin ryōri o gochisō shite kureta. Shōjin ryōri rashii mono wa nando mo tabeta koto ga aru ga, honmono wa hajimete datta. Nihon ryōri wa nani yori mo me o tanoshimasete kureru. Ikutsu ka no o-tera o mite arukinagara, Tadashi-san ga jūniseiki no owari ni Genji ga Kamakura ni Bakufu o hiraita koro no koto o setsumei shite kureta. Kore kara watakushi mo sukoshi Nihon no rekishi no hon o yonde miyō to omou. Jon wa kekkyoku, Nepāru ni wa ikanai koto ni shita to no koto.

Hiruma wa yoi o-tenki de, haru rashiku natte kita to omotta no ni, yūgata kara kyū ni samuku natte, kosame ga furidashita. Rusu no aida ni, Takano-san ga kite kureta rashii. Kādo to issho ni purezento o oite itte kureta.

Yoru, Furansu no ryōshin kara denwa ga kakatte kita. Raishū no doyōbi no asa shichiji ni Narita ni tsuku to no koto. Nihongo mo Eigo no dekinai no de shinpai shite ita ga, watakushi ga kūkō made mukae ni iku no de shinpai shinai yō ni to itte oita.

Translation

Marie's diary

24 February (Sat.) Clear, later drizzle

Today is my birthday. John and Tadashi took me to Kamakura, and on top of that, they took me to eat authentic Buddhist vegetarian cuisine. I've eaten something resembling it many times, but this was the first time I had the real thing. More than anything, Japanese cuisine is a treat for the eyes. While we were walking around looking at a number of temples, Tadashi explained all about the period at the end of the twelfth century when the Minamoto clan set up a military government in Kamakura. I think I'll try and read some books about Japanese history too. John says he has decided not to go to Nepal in the end.

The weather was good during the day, and I was thinking how springlike it had become when in the evening it suddenly became cold and began to drizzle. It appears that Takano-san dropped by while I was out. She left a card with a present.

Tonight there was a telephone call from my parents in France. They said that they would arrive at Narita next Saturday at seven in the morning. They were worried because they can't speak Japanese or English, but I told them not to worry as I would go to meet them at the airport.

Lesson 40

Kuniko comes home from school.

国子　おかあさん、ただいま。
信子　あら、お帰りなさい。今日はいつもより早いのね。
国子　そうでもないわよ。五分ぐらい早いかもしれないけど。
信子　お茶を入れましょう。ケーキが買ってありますよ。
国子　わあ、嬉しい。手を洗って、着がえてくるわ。

Kuniko and her mother are having tea together.

信子　国ちゃんはチョコレート・ケーキとこちらのシュークリームとどちらが好き。
国子　どっちも好きだけど、今日はシュークリームにしようかな。いただきます。
信子　日本茶よりもお紅茶の方がケーキに合うでしょう。
国子　そうね。ミルク・ティーがいいわ。今日は体育の時間に二キロも走ったのよ。
信子　そう。だれが一番だったの。
国子　それがね、クラスで一番背の低い宮坂さんが一番だったの。彼女より背が高くて、足の長い人がたくさんいるのに、宮坂さんが一番走るのが速いから不思議ね。
信子　それで、国ちゃんは。
国子　私は三番。木村さんが二番。百メートル競争では私の方が木村さんより速く走れるんだけど…。
信子　今週は忙しかったわね。
国子　本当に。月曜と水曜にテストがあったし、ピアノのおけいこもあったし。来週は今週ほどは忙しくないと思うわ。
信子　あしたの土曜日は新宿のデパートまで買物に行こうと思っているんだけど、あなたもいっしょに来られない。
国子　そうね。学校が終わるのが十二時半だから、一時ごろには新宿に着けると思うわ。

40.1 ただいま

ただいま。
あら、お帰りなさい。

Two more important idioms to learn here. When you come home it is usual to announce your arrival with the word ただいま 'just now (returned)'. The automatic response will be お帰りなさい. Learn this as a phrase; explanation of the grammar will emerge later.

40.2 Comparing two things

今日はいつもより早いのね。
日本茶よりもお紅茶の方がケーキに合うでしょう。

There is no formal equivalent in Japanese of the comparative adjective or adverb in English, but the same meaning is achieved by the following patterns:

(a) X は Y より (も)...(です). より performs a similar function to the English 'than' or 'compared to', so that this construction is literally 'X compared to Y is Z.'

今日はきのうより寒い。
It is colder today than yesterday.

祖父は祖母より丈夫だ。
My grandfather is healthier than my grandmother.

木下君は山田君より速く走れる。
Kinoshita can run faster than Yamada.

和子さんは道子さんより上手に説明出来る。
Kazuko can explain better than Michiko.

(b) X の方 (ほう) が Y より (も)... The following sentences have the same meaning as the sentences above, but with the noun 方 (ほう), 'direction' or 'alternative', X is slightly emphasised.

エベレストの方がモンブランより高い。
Everest is higher than Mt Blanc.

小包は船便(で出す)よりも航空便で出す方が早く届く。
Parcels get delivered quicker by air than by sea.

茶の間の方が客間より落ち着く。
I feel more relaxed in the living room than in the guest room.

今はお金よりも時間の方が貴重だ。
For the moment, time is more precious than money (for me).

When this kind of comparison is used in a negative sentence, 'not as...as', より is replaced by the nouns ほど 'extent' or 'degree' and contrastive は tends to appear.

山田君は木下君ほど速く走れない。
Yamada cannot run as fast as Kinoshita.
山田君は木下君ほど速くは走れないが泳ぐのは (木下君より) 上手だ。
Yamada cannot run as fast as Kinoshita, but he is a better swimmer.

高橋さんは松本さんほど熱心ではない。
Miss Takahashi is not as keen as Miss Matsumoto.

40.3 ～てある

ケーキが買ってありますよ。

Note that ～てある is usually only found with transitive verbs. It signifies a state that has resulted from someone's action, although the performer of the action is left unspecified. This construction with ～てある rather than ～ている is one with which you may have a little trouble. Note that although the English translation here will probably be transitive 'I bought you a cake' the Japanese is stative and so in essence *intransitive*. So we have a statement the literal rendition of which might be 'a cake, having been bought, exists'. You will find that this construction does not come naturally to you, but it is used quite often in Japanese, precisely because it de-personalises the expression just enough to reduce any sense that you have done someone a favour: to do so would entail imposing a sense of obligation on them. In this context, the mother prefers such an expression to one with a donatory verb such as 上げる. *ケーキを買って上げましたよ would be out of place here. So perhaps a more appropriate English translation for ケーキが買ってありますよ would be 'And there's some cake.' Note the difference between ～てある and ～ておく (see 30.6).

> かぎは山下さんに預けてあります。
> The key has been left with Mr Yamashita.
>
> かぎは山下さんに預けておきました。
> I have left the key (for you) with Mr Yamashita.

With ～ておく, the sense of intention and the presence of a perfomer of an act is far stronger and you would only use it if you wished to make a point. Look at the following sentence:

> 食事の用意はしてありますからおなかのすいた時にあたためて食べて下さい。
> The meal is ready, so please heat it up when you feel hungry.

You might expect ～ておく ('I've prepared you a meal in advance') but in fact ～てある will be preferred because it de-emphasises the favour.

40.4 Familiar ちゃん for さん

国ちゃん

Within the family, and among very close young friends, you will hear this diminutive form of the polite suffix さん. Do not try and use it yourself unless you are absolutely certain that the social situation allows it.

40.5 Question and answer, 'which is ...er?'

チョコレート・ケーキとこちらのシュークリームとどちらが好き。

This is expressed by using the pattern: X と Y と…どちら (の方) が…

スコットランドとウェールズとどちらの方が大きいですか。
Which is bigger, Scotland or Wales?

スコットランドの方が大きいです。
Scotland is bigger.

春と秋とどちらが好きですか。
Which do you prefer, spring or autumn?

春の方が (秋より) 好きです。
I prefer spring (to autumn).

きのうの晩はお兄さんとあなたとどちらが先に帰ってきたの。
Last night who came back earlier, you or your elder brother?

私の方がずっと早く帰ってきたわよ。
I came back much earlier (than my brother).

40.6 Comparing three or more things (superlative)

クラスで一番背の低い宮坂さんが一番だったの。

This pattern makes use of the word 一番 (いちばん) 'number one'. For 'which/who is the best out of...' one can either say: X と Y と Z の中で (は) どれが (だれが) 一番...か or X と Y と Z の 中で 一番...のはどれ(だれ) ですか.

> 'Who is the tallest among Peter, Nick and James?' is either
>
> ピーターとニックとジェームズの中でだれが一番背が高いですか or
> ピーターとニックとジェームズの中で一番背が高いのはだれですか.

and the reply would be either

> ピーターが一番背が高い (です) or
> 一番背が高いのはピーターです.

Occasionally you will come across 一番です or 一番だ on its own with よい or some other obvious words omitted. Study the following examples:

> 健康が一番 (大切) だ。
> Health is the most important (thing).
>
> かぜには薬よりもよく休むのが一番だ。
> For a cold, having a good rest is far better than taking medicine.
>
> このクラスではジョージが一番だ。
> George is the outstanding one in this class.

Here one cannot tell in what George excels without a further context. It could be, for example:

> ジョージが一番背が高い。
> ジョージが一番勉強が出来る。
> ジョージが一番フットボールが上手だ。etc.

40.7 Use of で with comparison

百メートル競争では私の方が木村さんより速く走れる

When one compares things, で is used to indicate the scope or limits within which the comparison is made.

日本では牛肉はぶた肉よりも高い。
In Japan beef is more expensive than pork.

日本で一番人気のあるスポーツは野球です。
The most popular sport in Japan is baseball.

一年のうちで一番美しい季節は春です。
The most beautiful season in the year is spring.

日本で一番高い山は富士山です。
The highest mountain in Japan is Mt Fuji.

世界で一番長い川はどれですか。
Which is the longest river in the world?

Key to conversation

Romanisation

Kuniko	Okāsan, tadaima.
Nobuko	Ara, o-kaeri nasai. Kyō wa itsumo yori hayai no ne.
Kuniko	Sō de mo nai wa yo. Gofun gurai hayai ka mo shirenai kedo.
Nobuko	O-cha o iremashō. Kēki ga katte arimasu yo.
Kuniko	Wā, ureshii. Te o aratte, kigaete kuru wa.
Nobuko	Kuni-chan wa chokorēto kēki to kochira no shūkurīmu to dochira ga suki.
Kuniko	Dotchi mo suki dakedo, kyō wa shūkurīmu ni shiyō ka na. Itadakimasu.
Nobuko	Nihoncha yori mo o-kōcha no hō ga kēki ni au deshō.
Kuniko	Sō ne. Miruku tī ga ii wa. Kyō wa taiiku no jikan ni nikiro mo hashitta no yo.
Nobuko	Sō. Dare ga ichiban datta no.
Kuniko	Sore ga ne, kurasu de ichiban se no hikui Miyasaka-san ga ichiban datta no. Kanojo yori se ga takakute, ashi no nagai hito ga takusan iru no ni, Miyasaka-san ga ichiban hashiru no ga hayai kara fushigi ne.
Nobuko	Sore de, Kuni-chan wa.
Kuniko	Watakushi wa sanban. Kimura-san ga niban. Hyaku mētoru kyōsō de wa

	watakushi no hō ga Kimura-san yori hayaku hashirerun dakedo...
Nobuko	Konshū wa isogashikatta wa ne.
Kuniko	Hontō ni. Getsuyō to suiyō ni tesuto ga atta shi, piano no o-keiko mo atta shi. Raishū wa konshū hodo wa isogashikunai to omou wa.
Nobuko	Ashita no doyōbi wa Shinjuku no depāto made kaimono ni ikō to omotte irun dakedo, anata mo issho ni korarenai.
Kuniko	Sō ne. Gakkō ga owaru no ga jūnijihan dakara, ichiji goro ni wa Shinjuku ni tsukeru to omou wa.

Translation

Kuniko	Mother, I'm back!
Nobuko	Oh! Welcome home. You're earlier than usual today.
Kuniko	Not really. Well, maybe I'm five minutes early.
Nobuko	Let's have a cup of tea. There's some cake.
Kuniko	Great! I'll wash my hands and get changed.
Nobuko	Which do you prefer, the chocolate cake or this choux creme?
Kuniko	Either would be nice, but today I think I'll have the choux creme. Thanks.
Nobuko	English tea would go better with cake than Japanese tea wouldn't it?
Kuniko	Yes. I'd like tea with milk. In games today we ran two kilometres you know.
Nobuko	Really. Who came first?
Kuniko	You'd never guess, but Miyasaka won, the smallest one in the class. There are lots of people who are taller than her and who've got longer legs, but she can run the fastest. It's odd, isn't it?
Nobuko	And what about you?
Kuniko	I was third. Kimura was second. But I can run faster than Kimura in the hundred metre dash...
Nobuko	You've been busy this week haven't you?
Kuniko	Very. Tests on Monday and Wednesday, and there was my piano lesson too. But I don't think next week will be as busy as this one.
Nobuko	Tomorrow's Saturday and I'm thinking of going shopping in the Shinjuku department stores. Can you come too?
Kuniko	Let's see. School finishes at twelve thirty, so I think I can be in Shinjuku by one o'clock.

Lesson 41

Mrs Yamakawa and Kuniko go shopping together.

国子	おかあさん、今日は何を買うの。
信子	おとうさんの会社の方が結婚なさるので、何かお祝いを差し上げようと思って…。
国子	何とおっしゃる方。
信子	ええと、泉谷さん。
国子	どんな方。
信子	それが、お会いしたことがないのよ。
国子	それじゃあ、どうやってお祝いを選ぶの。
信子	おとうさんが何がいいかって聞いて下さったんだけど、結婚式の後すぐにアフリカへ転任することが決まっているので、短波放送の聞けるラジオがほしいっておっしゃるんですって。
国子	ふーん。ずいぶん変わった御希望ね。あまり結婚のお祝いらしくないけど、役に立つものの方がいいのかもしれないわね。
信子	おかあさんもそう思ってるの。

信子	すいませんが、ラジオの売り場はどちらですか。
店員	六階でございます。エスカレーターはこちらのハンカチ売り場の左手になっております。
店員	いらっしゃいませ。
信子	短波放送の入るラジオを捜しているんですが…。
店員	こちらのケースに入っておりますのはどれも短波がついております。
信子	こちらのをちょっと見せていただけますか。
店員	はい、お客様。どうぞ。こちらのはラジオとテープレコーダーが組み合わされておりますのでとても便利です。
国子	FMも聞けるのかしら。
店員	はい、FM、AM両方入ります。
国子	ちょっと、聞いてみてもいいですか。
店員	今、電池をお入れします。お客さま、どうぞ。
国子	いい音がするけど、少し大き過ぎないかしら。

信子	そうね。これと同じようなのでもうちょっと小さいのはありませんか。
店員	こちらのはいかがですか。そちらのと同じようにFM、AMそれに短波も聞けますが、サイズはだいぶ小さくなっております。
信子	こちらの方がいいと思うけど、国ちゃん、どう思う。
国子	初めのほど大きくなくて、機能はみんなそろっているようだから、いいんじゃないかしら。
店員	こちらはとてもよく売れているモデルですが…。
信子	それじゃあ、小さい方にしましょう。おいくらですか。
店員	三万五千円いただきます。
信子	クレジット・カードでお払いしてもいいですか。
店員	はい、お客様。どうぞ。

41.1 'How does one…?'

> どうやってお祝いを選ぶの。

The verb やる is a fairly colloquial equivalent of する and means 'do'. Here we find it combined with どう to give 'doing how'. どうやって is the normal way to express the idea 'how are we going to…?' or 'how does one…?'

41.2 Reported questions

> おとうさんが何がいいかって聞いて下さったんだけど、

Reported questions are very simple to produce in Japanese. As here, と or って is placed between the question and the verb of questioning. Sometimes indeed the quotative particle と can be left out, but の is often added just in front of か.

Any polite ～ます forms used within the quotation are usually changed to the plain forms.

「何時に起きましたか。」
'What time did you get up?'

何時に起きたか聞いた。
I asked at what time he got up.

「いつまでに出来ますか。」 「分かりません。」
'When will this be ready by?' 'I don't know.'

いつまでに出来る(の)かと聞いたが分からないと言われた。
I asked when it would be ready by, but was told that they didn't know.

「きのうはなぜ来なかったのですか。」
'Why didn't you come yesterday?'

きのうはなぜ来なかったのかって聞かれた。
I was asked why I had not come the day before.

41.3 More on reported speech

おとうさんが何がいいかって聞いて下さったんだけど、
結婚式の後すぐにアフリカへ転任することが決まっているので、
短波放送の聞けるラジオがほしいっておっしゃるんですって。

In 27.1, which dealt with と as a quotation marker, it was stated that there is often very little to distinguish direct from indirect speech. There are, however, some occasions when certain changes may obviously have to be made. Look again at what Nobuko has to say above. This is obviously reported speech, although it is made somewhat complicated because Nobuko is actually reporting two levels: what Izumitani said to her husband and then what her husband reported to her. Note how this difference is made explicit in the verbs at the end: おっしゃる referring to Izumitani's words and ですって being her husband's words. What actually went on was something like the following:

山川:　結婚のお祝いにはどんなものがいいのかな。
泉谷:　ありがとうございます。式の後すぐにアフリカへ転任することが決まっておりますので、短波放送の聞けるラジオがいただきたいのですが。

Another occasion when you may find that you will have to change something when you shift from actual speech to reported speech is when demonstratives are involved. Take, for example, the following:

川北:　「ここのコーヒーが京都で一番うまい。」
'The coffee here is the best in Kyōto.'

How would you report this to a third person? If you were both in the coffee shop or at the entrance of the shop at the time, then you would naturally report this as follows:

川北さんがここのコーヒーが京都で一番おいしいと言っていた。

If you were both somewhere near the coffee shop, from where you could perhaps actually point out the shop, you would say:

川北さんがあそこのコーヒーが京都で一番おいしいと言っていた。

If you were both nowhere near the coffee shop, but the name of the shop or something which reminded you of Kawakita's comment came up in the conversation, then you would say:

川北さんがそこのコーヒーが京都で一番おいしいと言っていた。

41.4 Adjectival use of perfective verb forms

ずいぶん変わった御希望ね。

There are quite a large number of words which, although they are usually translated into English as simple adjectives, are in fact the perfective form of a verb used in a descriptive manner. In addition to 変わった 'odd', note:

(a) すぐれた 'distinguished' from すぐれる 'be excellent, excel'

彼はすぐれた科学者だ。
He is a distinguished scientist.

(b) 困った 'troublesome', 'inconvenient' from 困る 'be in difficulty'

和子は本当に困った子だ。何も食べない。
Kazuko is a really troublesome child. She does not eat a thing.

(c) さっぱりした 'clean', 'neat', 'simple' from さっぱりする 'be refreshed'

彼女はいつもさっぱりした洋服を着ている。
She always dressed in a simple but neat dress.

41.5 More on names within the family

おかあさんもそう思ってるの。

You may be a little surprised to see the mother referring to herself as おかあさん here, particularly since we have stressed that you should never use the polite さん about yourself. In English, when speaking to children, parents quite often refer to each other by using names that reflect the child's point of view. It is perhaps a little more unusual to refer to *oneself* in this way in English, but it is a fairly common habit in Japanese families.

41.6 Being welcomed in a shop

いらっしゃいませ。

You will probably never have need to use this word yourself, but you will hear it whenever you enter a shop, bank or restaurant. It tells you that your entry has been noticed and that you will be looked after as soon as possible.

41.7 Asking permission

聞いてみてもいいですか。 クレジット・カードでお払いしてもいいですか。

When ～て is followed by も, the meaning is 'even if'. よい/いい is, of course, the descriptive verb meaning 'is good', 'is all right'. When these are added together in the interrogative form we get literally 'even if I…, is it all right?', the usual way of asking permission to do something in Japanese. You may also find the verb かまいませんか, negative of the verb かまう 'care' or 'bother about something', being used in a similar context:

もう帰ってもいいですか。
May I go home now?

ここでたばこをすってもかまいませんか。
Do you mind me smoking here?

ええ、かまいませんよ。
No, I don't mind.

現金で払わなくてもいいですか。
Is it all right if I don't pay by cash?

41.8 同じ

これと同じようなのでもうちょっと小さいのはありませんか。

同じ functions like a descriptive verb meaning 'be the same as', but, apart from the form 同じく, it does not usually inflect in the modern language. You will, of course, find it meaning 'same' in normal modifying position in sentences like:

> 節子さんと孝子さんは同じ学校に行っています。
> Setsuko and Takako go to the same school.

but the usage can be somewhat more idiomatic. Observe the following:

> あの兄弟は同じぐらいの背の高さだ。
> Those brothers are the same height.
>
> セーラはジェーンと同じようにおしゃべりです。
> Sarah is as talkative as Jane.

41.9 Idiomatic use of それに

> FM、AM それに短波も聞けますが、

When enumerating things, it is common to slip a に or それに in before the last item. It usually means very little more than just 'and' in a series, but here with the addition of も there is a definite sense of 'and what is more…'

41.10 ほど

> 初めのほど大きくなくて、

ほど is a noun meaning 'limit', 'extent' or 'degree'. The reason it needs special comment here is that it has a number of grammatical functions. As you will see from the example, it can occur by itself without a particle meaning 'to the extent', and it is found in expressions of comparison. The best translation of the above would be 'It's not as large as the first one', although the Japanese is literally saying 'It's not large (to the) extent of the first (one).' Since it is a noun, you should in fact be tempted to surround this word with particles; it is unusual in that it hardly ever needs them. Study the following sentences:

仕事が山ほどたまっています。
A mountain of work has accumulated.

イギリスの春ほど美しい季節はない。
There is no season as beautiful as an English spring.

彼女ほど気の短い人はいない。
There is no-one as short-tempered as she.

これほどがっかりしたことはない。
I have never been so disappointed.

Key to conversation

Romanisation

Kuniko	Okāsan, kyō wa nani o kau no.
Nobuko	Otōsan no kaisha no kata ga kekkon nasaru no de, nani ka o-iwai o sashiageyō to omotte…
Kuniko	Nan to ossharu kata.
Nobuko	Ēto, Izumitani san.
Kuniko	Donna kata.
Nobuko	Sore ga, o-ai shita koto ga nai no yo.
Kuniko	Sore jā, dō yatte o-iwai o erabu no.
Nobuko	Otōsan ga nani ga ii ka tte kiite kudasattan da kedo, kekkonshiki no ato sugu ni Afurika e tennin suru koto ga kimatte iru no de, tanpa hōsō no kikeru rajio ga hoshii tte osshrun desu tte.
Kuniko	Fūn. Zuibun kawatta gokibō ne. Amari kekkon no o-iwai rashikunai kedo, yaku ni tatsu mono no hō ga ii no kamo shirenai wa ne.
Nobuko	Okāsan mo sō omotteru no.

Nobuko	Suimasen ga, rajio no uriba wa dochira desu ka.
Ten'in	Rokkai de gozaimasu. Esukarētā wa kochira no hankachi uriba no hidarite ni natte orimasu.
Ten'in	Irasshaimase.
Nobuko	Tanpa hōsō no hairu rajio o sagashite irun desu ga...
Ten'in	Kochira no kēsu ni haitte orimasu no wa dore mo tanpa ga tsuite orimasu.
Nobuko	Kochira no o chotto misete itadakemasu ka.
Ten'in	Hai, o-kyaku-sama. Dōzo. Kochira no wa rajio to tēpurekōdā ga kumiawasarete orimasu no de totemo benri desu.
Kuniko	FM mo kikeru no kashira.
Ten'in	Hai, FM, AM ryōhō hairimasu.
Kuniko	Chotto, kiite mite mo ii desu ka.
Ten'in	Ima, denchi o o-ire shimasu. O-kyaku-sama, dōzo.
Kuniko	Ii oto ga suru kedo, sukoshi ōki suginai kashira.
Nobuko	Sō ne. Kore to onaji yō na no de mō chotto chiisai no wa arimasen ka.
Ten'in	Kochira no wa ikaga desu ka. Sochira no to onaji yō ni FM, AM sore ni tanpa mo kikemasu ga, saizu wa daibu chiisaku natte orimasu.
Nobuko	Kochira no hō ga ii to omou kedo, Kuni-chan, dō omou.
Kuniko	Hajime no hodo okiku nakute, kinō wa minna sorotte iru yō da kara, iin ja nai kashira.
Ten'in	Kochira wa totemo yoku urete iru moderu desu ga...
Nobuko	Sore jā, chiisai hō ni shimashō. O-ikura desu ka.
Ten'in	Sanman gosen-en itadakimasu.
Nobuko	Kurejitto kādo de o-harai shite mo ii desu ka.
Ten'in	Hai, o-kyaku-sama. Dōzo.

Translation

Kuniko	Mother, what are you going to buy today?
Nobuko	Someone in your father's company is getting married, so I thought I'd give him some sort of present.
Kuniko	What's his name?
Nobuko	Let me see now, Mr Izumitani.
Kuniko	What sort of person is he?
Nobuko	That's it you see, I've never met him.
Kuniko	Well then, how are you going to choose a present?

Nobuko	Your father was good enough to ask him what he'd like, and since it's been decided that he'll be transferred to Africa soon after his wedding, he apparently said he'd like a radio that will get shortwave broadcasts.
Kuniko	Hm. That's a funny request isn't it? It's not the usual sort of thing one gives as a wedding present, but then again it might be better to get him something practical mightn't it?
Nobuko	That's what I think too.

Nobuko	Excuse me, where is the radio sales department?
Assistant	On the sixth floor. The escalator is to the left of the handkerchief department here.
Assistant	How can I help you?
Nobuko	I'm looking for a radio that will receive shortwave broadcasts.
Assistant	All of the ones in this display case have a shortwave function.
Nobuko	Could you please show me this one?
Assistant	Certainly madam. Here you are. This one combines a tape recorder and a radio and so it's very convenient.
Kuniko	Can you listen to FM too I wonder?
Assistant	Yes, it's got both FM and AM.
Kuniko	May we listen to it just for a bit?
Assistant	I'll just put the batteries in. Here you are madam.
Kuniko	It sounds good, but I wonder if it isn't a little large.
Nobuko	Yes. Do you have one just like this only a little smaller?
Assistant	How about this one? As with that one, you can listen to FM, AM as well as shortwave, but it's much smaller.
Nobuko	I think this one is better but, Kunichan, what do you think?
Kuniko	It's not as big as the first one, and it seems to have all the functions, so I think it might do.
Assistant	This one is a best-selling model...
Nobuko	In that case, let's take the small one. How much is it?
Assistant	35,000 yen please.
Nobuko	May I pay by credit card?
Assistant	Certainly madam. By all means.

Lesson 42

A 'grammar' lesson

ジョン	正君、動詞の使い方でどうもよく分からないことがあるんですけど...
正	僕に説明出来るかな。どんなことですか。
ジョン	動詞には自動詞と他動詞がありますね。この二つの使い方がちがうということは分かるんです。例えば、「りんごを落とす」と「りんごが落ちる」は 'Drop an apple' と 'An apple drops' ですね。
正	そうですよ。大切なことは初めの例では「りんご」は目的語ですから、助詞の「を」がつきます。次の文では「りんご」は主語ですから助詞は「が」ですね。
ジョン	ええ、そこまでは問題はないんです。「授業を始める」と「授業が始まる」、「方向を変える」と「方向が変わる」など、よく分かります。
正	それでは、難しい点というのは何ですか。
ジョン	きのうの朝刊に、大阪で起きた事件の犯人が三日後に、ホノルルでつかまった、と書いてありました。なぜ、受け身を使って、つかまえられたと言わないんですか。
正	それは、「つかまえられた」と言うと、状況を犯人の立場から見ることになるからです。
ジョン	次に分からないのは他動詞と使役動詞のちがいなんです。「授業を終らせた」と「授業を終えた」は同じ意味ですか。
正	いや、全く同じだとは言えませんね。結果的には同じですが、前者の方が話し手が「そのようにした」という意味合いがずっと強くなります。
ジョン	その上、自動詞と可能を表す動詞の形が同じなのもあるでしょう。
正	そうですね。でもそれは意味の上から明らかだからあまり問題はないんじゃありませんか。何だかうまく説明できなくて、申し訳ないな。質問はそれだけですか。
ジョン	まだあるんです。

Comment

This conversation spans two lessons. It is a little unusual in that it represents a discussion about Japanese grammar. It concentrates on verbs and deals in particular with the existence in Japanese of a large number of transitive and intransitive sets of verbs. There are two problems here for the learner. One is that there are no easy rules to help you decide whether a verb is transitive or intransitive: you simply have to learn them in context. The other is that the pairing is not replicated in English, so that you will find yourself translating the intransitive verb with an English passive. So how does an intransitive differ from a passive? Such nuances might better be left until later, but they are unavoidable. We begin with a recap on stative verbs.

42.1 Use of には with stative verbs

僕に説明出来るかな。

In 16.4 you were introduced to the idea that there are two major categories of verb in Japanese: stative and dynamic. To repeat: although the overwhelming majority of Japanese verbs is dynamic, there is a small set of stative verbs which are rather important. 出来る is one of these verbs. Remember that they do not need to be in the ～ている form to indicate present situation, and that they are often found in the は + が construction, with which you are now familiar. Sometimes, as in the example sentence, in order to make the stative nature of these patterns absolutely clear, you will find the person or object involved is followed not by the particles は or が but by に (は). Observe the following:

この仕事は子供には出来ません。
This work cannot be done by a child.

私にはそれは出来ない。
I couldn't possibly do that.

私には彼の気持がよく分かりません。
I find his feelings difficult to understand.

この電卓には電池が要らない。
For this pocket calculator batteries are not necessary.

The use of には in contexts such as these is definitely emphatic, putting stress on the person or object involved.

42.2 Transitive and intransitive pairs

「りんごを落とす」と「りんごが落ちる」

As we have already explained, there are a large number of transitive and intransitive pairs, such as ...を落とす and ...が落ちる. You will find a representative list of them at the end of the next lesson. By and large, try to keep to the rule that transitive verbs, because they 'act' on other things, should be restricted to animate subjects:

あのお医者さんが父の難病を治しました。
That doctor cured my father's intractable illness.

Although it is possible to say 'the new medicine cured his illness' in English, you should resist the temptation to say this in Japanese. It should be rephrased using the intransitive equivalent of 治す, namely 治る.

あの新しい薬で (or のおかげで) 父の難病が治りました。
Thanks to that new medicine, my father's intractable illness was cured.

42.3 Choosing between intransitives and the passive

きのうの朝刊に、大阪で起きた事件の犯人が三日後に、
ホノルルでつかまった、と書いてありました。なぜ、
受け身を使って、つかまえられたと言わないんですか。

It was explained in 35.2 that the passive form is not used quite as much in Japanese as in English, partly no doubt because of the existence of these intransitive equivalents. But in the example that John quotes here, an animate subject is involved and so both the intransitive verb つかまる and the passive of the transitive verb つかまえる can in fact be used. So how do they differ? This is particularly troublesome for speakers of English, because we often have to translate *both* verbs with a passive: 'was captured'. The answer to John's question is that the intransitive つかまった simply means that the police caught up with him in Honolulu; つかまえられた, the passive of the transitive equivalent, would only be used if you wish to see the event from the point of view of the criminal. Here you can see the adversative connotations of the passive coming into play. The rule is therefore that if an intransitive equivalent exists, it is normally preferred to the passive of the transitive verb, unless you wish to make a special point.

Study the following sentences in which there is a contrast between usage of the intransitive and usage of the kind of adversative passive construction that was introduced in 35.4:

あそこに新しい家が建ちました。*(intrans.)*
A new house had been built there.

うちの南側に家を建てられたので、日が入らなくなった。*(trans. passive)*
A new house was built on our south side and it blocked the sunlight.

妹にかぜをうつされた。*(trans. passive)*
My younger sister gave me a cold.

妹からかぜがうつった。*(intrans.)*
The cold passed on to me from my younger sister.

この病気はうつりませんよ。*(intrans.)*
This disease is not infectious.

42.4 Differences between transitives and causatives

> 「授業を終らせた。」と「授業を終えた。」

This is the other side of the coin. On a number of occasions you may be uncertain as to which form of the verb should be used: a transitive verb or the causative form of its intransitive equivalent. In general the causative puts much greater stress on the coercive element:

この幼稚園では子供を三時半に帰します。*(trans.)*
At this kindergarten they let the children go home at three thirty.

この幼稚園では子供を三時半に帰らせます。*(intrans. causative)*
At this kindergarten they make the children go home at three thirty.

六時までには仕事をすましります。*(trans.)*
I'll finish the work by six.

六時までには仕事をすませます。*(intrans. causative)*
I'll make sure the work is finished at six.

42.5 Distinguishing the potential from the intransitive

> 自動詞と可能をあらわす動詞の形が同じなのもあるでしょう。

In a number of cases it will seem that the intransitive form of the verb is exactly the same as the potential of the transitive. It will usually be readily apparent from context which is meant:

姉は上手にフランスパンが焼けます。*(potential of transitive)*
My elder sister can bake French bread very well.

こちらの魚ですか。すぐ焼けますからちょっとお待ち下さい。*(intrans.)*
This fish? It won't take long to grill. Please wait for a minute.

あの巨人は手で鉄の棒が割れる。*(potential of transitive)*
That giant can break an iron bar in his hands.

きのうの地震でまどガラスが数枚割れた。*(intrans.)*
A number of window panes were broken in yesterday's earthquake.

42.6 'Somehow or other'

何だかうまく説明できなくて、

何だか, literally 'what is it?', is an idiomatic phrase meaning 'somehow' or 'for some unknown reason'. As a rule it will come at the beginning of the sentence. You may often find it delivered with a little sideways nod of the head: a sign of slight embarrassment in this particular case.

Key to conversation

Romanisation

Jon	Tadashi-kun, dōshi no tsukaikata de dōmo yoku wakaranai koto ga arun desu kedo…
Tadashi	Boku ni setsumei dekiru kana. Donna koto desu ka.
Jon	Dōshi ni wa jidōshi to tadōshi ga arimasu ne. Kono futatsu no tsukaikata ga chigau to iu koto wa wakarun desu. Tatoeba, 'ringo o otosu' to 'ringo ga ochiru' wa 'drop an apple' to 'an apple drops' desu ne.
Tadashi	Sō desu yo. Taisetsu na koto wa hajime no rei de wa 'ringo' wa mokutekigo desu kara, joshi no 'o' ga tsukimasu. Tsugi no bun de wa 'ringo' wa shugo desu kara joshi wa 'ga' desu ne.
Jon	Ē, soko made wa mondai wa nain desu. 'Jugyō o hajimeru' to 'jugyō ga

	hajimaru', 'hōkō o kaeru' to 'hōkō ga kawaru' nado, yoku wakarimasu.
Tadashi	Sore de wa, muzukashii ten to iu no wa nan desu ka.
Jon	Kinō no chōkan ni, Ōsaka de okita jiken no hannin ga mikka go ni, Honoruru de tsukamatta, to kaite arimashita. Naze, ukemi o tsukatte, 'tsukamaerareta' to iwanain desu ka.
Tadashi	Sore wa, 'tsukamaerareta' to iu to, jōkyō o hannin no tachiba kara miru koto ni naru kara desu.
Jon	Tsugi ni wakaranai no wa tadōshi to shieki dōshi no chigai nan desu. 'Jugyō o owaraseta' to 'jugyō o oeta' wa onaji imi desu ka.
Tadashi	Iya, mattaku onaji da to wa iemasen ne. Kekkateki ni wa onaji desu ga, zensha no hō ga hanashite ga 'sono yō ni shita' to iu imiai ga zutto tsuyoku narimasu.
Jon	Sono ue, jidōshi to kanō o arawasu dōshi no katachi ga onaji na no mo aru deshō.
Tadashi	Sō desu ne. Demo sore wa imi no ue kara akiraka da kara amari mondai wa nain ja arimasen ka. Nan da ka umaku setsumei dekinakute, mōshiwake nai na. Shitsumon wa sore dake desu ka.
Jon	Mada arun desu.

Translation

John	Tadashi, there's something I just don't understand about verb usage.
Tadashi	I wonder if I can explain it. What sort of thing is it?
John	There are intransitive and transitive verbs. That there are differences in the way the two are used I understand. For example, the difference between 'ringo o otosu' and 'ringo ga ochiru' is the difference between 'drop an apple' and 'an apple drops'.
Tadashi	That's right. The important thing is that in the first example, 'apple' is the object, and so the particle 'o' is used. In the next sentence, 'apple' is the subject, and so the particle is 'ga'.
John	Yes, up to that point I have no problems. I understand '[someone] begins the class' and 'the class begins', and '[someone] changes direction' and 'the direction changes'.
Tadashi	In that case, what is it that you find difficult?
John	In yesterday's morning paper, it said that the criminal responsible for the incident in Ōsaka was captured 'tsukamatta' three days later in Honolulu. Why didn't they use the passive form and say 'tsukamaerareta'?

Tadashi	That's because if you say 'tsukamaerareta' it means you're looking at the situation from the point of view of the culprit.
John	The next thing I don't understand is the difference between transitive and causative verbs. Is the meaning of 'jugyō o owaraseta' and 'jugyō o oeta' the same?
Tadashi	No, you can't say that they are exactly the same. In the end they mean the same thing, but the former contains a much stronger sense that the speaker is saying 'and I made it happen that...'
John	And then aren't there some verbs the intransitive form of which is exactly the same as the potential form?
Tadashi	That's right. But it's clear from the meaning which is which, so that's not much of a problem is it? Somehow I haven't explained it very well; I'm sorry. Are those the only questions you have?
John	I do have more.

Lesson 43

The 'grammar' lesson continues:

ジョン	何と言っても、一番難しいのは、「見える」と「聞こえる」ですね。「見える」というのは可能も表すし、自動詞の働きもあるんですね。
正	そうです。目の検査の時、お医者さんが「見えますか」と言いますね。けれども、この動詞を自動詞として使う場合には、「富士山が見えている」とか「ジョンさんはアメリカ人に見える」と言うことが出来ます。
ジョン	私はアメリカ人には見えませんよ。
正	いやいや、今のは文法を説明するための例に過ぎませんよ。母国語というのは普段、意識しないで使っているので、気が付きませんが、こうして改めて考えてみると難しいものですね。
ジョン	そうなんですよ。自動詞と他動詞が分かったと思っても、それが「〜ている」の形で使われる時には、とまどうことがあります。
正	たとえば、どんな時ですか。
ジョン	今の病院で働き始めてすぐに、「スミス先生、お電話がかかってますよ」と看護婦さんに言われたんです。はっきり意味が分かるまで、時間がかかりましたね。
正	それは、確かに難しいですね。
ジョン	それから、「柿を並べている」と「柿が並んでいる」のちがいはやっと分かるようになりましたが、後の方の「柿が並んでいる」と「柿が並べてある」のちがいは今でもはっきりしないんですけど。
正	困ったなあ。何だか僕も分からなくなってきてしまった。

43.1 'Say what you will...'

何と言っても、

This is another idiomatic phrase meaning 'say what you will' or a rather vague 'well you know'. Observe the following examples:

何と言っても、ウィスキーはスコッチですね。
Say what you will, but Scotch is really the only whisky.

何と言っても、健康が一番大切だ。
No matter what, good health is the most important thing.

43.2 Forms of 見る and 聞く

一番難しいのは、「見える」と「聞こえる」ですね。

Now that you have met potentials, passives and transitive/intransitive pairs, observe the following forms of the two verbs 見る and 聞く.

43.3 見る

見る *transitive*: 'see' or 'look at something'

きのうおもしろいフランス映画を見た。
Yesterday I saw an interesting French film.

見える *intransitive*: 'be visible' or 'appear to be'

あそこの雲と雲の間に見えている山がキリマンジェロです。
That mountain that is just visible between the clouds is Mt Kilimanjaro.

本物のように見えますがにせ物ですよ。
It may look authentic but it's a fake.

見える *potential*: 'be able to see'

あんな小さな字も見えるんですか。ずいぶんいい目をしてますね。
Can you see such small characters? Very good eyesight, haven't you!

見られる (見れる) *potential*: 'is possible to see'

バカなことをしてしまったので恥ずかしくて父の顔はまともに見られなかった。
I did something really stupid and was so embarrassed that I couldn't bring myself to look my father straight in the face.

この映画館では昔の名画が見られます。
They show old favourites in this cinema.

見られる *passive* : 'be seen'

(私は) 母につまみ食いをしているところを見られた。
Mother found me picking at the food.

There are a number of problems here. Firstly, for teaching purposes, we have created a distinction between 見える as an intransitive equivalent of 見る and 見える as a potential form. Context will usually tell you which one you are dealing with. Note that the intransitive 見える can be seen as a durative verb that can take the ～ている form; it will then mean something like 'being visible'. The potential 見える, on the other hand, is stative and so does not appear with ～ている. The second difficulty is that you will have to distinguish here between two types of potentiality: 'are you physically able to' as opposed to 'is it possible to'. This is a little awkward because both senses are rendered by 'can' in English.

43.4 聞く meaning 'hear'

The situation with 聞く is a little different, mainly because it has two distinct meanings: 'hear' and 'ask'. Let us take them in turn:

聞く *transitive*: 'hear' or 'listen to something'

彼が仕事をやめて外国へ行くといううわさを聞いた。
I heard a rumour that he was going to give up his a job and go abroad.

聞こえる *intransitive*: 'be audible', 'sound'

子供の泣き声が聞こえている間はどうも落ち着けません。
I really cannot relax as long as the child's cries are still audible.

つくり話のように聞こえるかもしれませんが、実際に起こったことなのですよ。
It may sound as if I made it up, but I assure you it really happened.

聞こえる *potential*: 'be able to hear' (physical ability)

先生、よく聞こえません。もう少し大きな声で話して下さい。
Please sir, I can't hear you very well. Please talk a little louder.

聞ける *potential*: 'bear to listen' (possibility)

あなたの願いごとばかりは聞けません。
I can't go on listening to your constant requests any longer.

聞かれる *passive*: 'be heard'

ないしょ話を聞かれた。
Someone heard our private conversation.

43.5 聞く meaning 'ask'

聞く *transitive*: 'ask' or 'question someone'

私には分かりませんから専門家に聞いて下さい。
I don't know, so please ask an expert.

聞ける *potential*: 'be able to ask'

そんな下だらないことを先生に聞けると思いますか。
Do you really think I could ask the teacher such a silly question?

聞かれる *passive*: 'be asked'

市場で時間を聞かれた。
I was asked the time by someone in the market.

43.6 に過ぎない

今のは文法を説明するための例に過ぎませんよ。

This pattern, に過ぎない or に過ぎません, means 'nothing but...'

それが口実に過ぎないことはあなた自身よく分かっているんでしょう。
You yourself must know very well that it is nothing but an excuse.

日本語が出来るといっても、簡単な日常会話が何とか分かるに過ぎない。
Well, I *can* speak Japanese, but all I can really manage is to understand simple everyday conversation.

Note the use of 今 here. Clearly it can refer to something more than just the present moment. You will sometimes find yourself translating it as 'just now': 今のは 'What I just said was...'

43.7 ～て + すぐ(に)

今の病院で働き始めてすぐに

This pattern, where すぐに follows the ～て form of the verb, means 'no sooner than' or 'immediately upon'.

少しかぜ気味なので、おふろに入ってすぐ寝るつもりです。
I have a touch of cold so I'll go to bed immediately after my bath.

こちらの方があなたのおかあさまだということは写真を見てすぐ分かりました。
As soon as I saw the picture I could tell that this person was your mother.

43.8 ～ている revisited

> 「スミス先生、お電話がかかってますよ」

We have already met the ～ている form having either progressive or resultative meaning, depending on the nature of the main verb. These transitive/intransitive pairs provide further interesting examples of how the meaning of ～ている can differ according to context. The transitive verbs in these pairs are usually durative in nature so that the ～ている refers to an ongoing process. The intransitive verb, on the other hand, is often punctual in nature so that ～ている refers to result.

長谷川さんに電話をかけています。
(He) is telephoning Hasegawa.

長谷川さんから電話がかかっています。
There is a telephone call for you from Mr Hasegawa.

戸を閉めています。
He is shutting the door.

銀行は閉まっています。
The bank is shut.

43.9 ～ている versus ～てある

> 「柿が並んでいる」と「柿が並べてある」

Refer back to 40.3 where you were introduced to the form ～てある. There it was explained that ～てある is usually only formed with transitive verbs and signifies the state that has resulted from someone's action. So how does this differ from the intransitive equivalent with ～ている? Observe the following:

(a) 山水画のかけじくが床の間にかけてあります。
A landscape scroll has been hung in the alcove.

(b) 山水画のかけじくが床の間にかかっています。
A landscape scroll is hanging in the alcove.

Both present situations are, of course, the result of an act of hanging a scroll sometime in the past, but the nuances are quite different. Sentence (a) contains the transitive verb and so carries with it a certain emphasis on the act of hanging that resulted in the present state; (b) on the other hand contains the intransitive verb and is devoid of any sense that someone has physically placed the scroll on the alcove; it is just 'there'.

43.10 Transitive/intransitive pairs

The following is a list of the commonest pairs. Do not try to learn all of these immediately, but rather use the list as a reference.

他動詞 *(transitive)*	自動詞 *(intransitive)*
-eru	*-aru*
授業を始める	授業が始まる
電話をかける	電話がかかる
戸を閉める	戸が閉まる
自動車を止める	自動車が止まる
意思を伝える	意思が伝わる
授業を終える	授業が終わる
値段を上げる	値段が上がる
矢を的に当てる	矢が的に当たる
荷物を重ねる	荷物が重なる
予定を決める	予定が決まる
子供を助ける	子供が助かる
方向を変える	方向が変わる
-eru	*-u*
戸を開ける	戸が開く
家を建てる	家が建つ

品物を並べる	品物が並ぶ
子供を自転車に乗せる	子供が自転車に乗る
話を進める	話が進む
ゲームを続ける	ゲームが続く
-u	*-eru*
物を売る	物が売れる
パンを焼く	パンが焼ける
ガラスを割る	ガラスが割れる
-su	*-reru*
水を流す	水が流れる
家を壊す	家が壊れる
着物を汚す	着物が汚れる
顔を隠す	顔が隠れる
-asu	*-u*
仕事をすます	仕事がすむ
車を動かす	車が動く
花を散らす	花が散る
馬車を走らす	馬車が走る
飛行機を飛ばす	飛行機が飛ぶ
赤ん坊を寝かす	赤ん坊が寝る
-su	*-ru*
病気を治す	病気が治る
金を残す	金が残る
人を通す	人が通る
病気をうつす	病気がうつる
六時に子供を帰す	六時に子供が帰る
事件を起こす	事件が起こる
-osu	*-iru*
物を落とす	物が落ちる
父を起こす	父が起きる

same verb	ふえを吹く	風が吹く
different verb	ねこを入れる	ねこが入る

Key to conversation

Romanisation

Jon	Nan to itte mo, ichiban muzukashii no wa 'mieru' to 'kikoeru' desu ne. 'Mieru' to iu no wa kanō mo arawasu shi jidōshi no hataraki mo arun desu ne.
Tadashi	Sō desu. Me no kensa no toki, o-isha-san ga 'miemasu ka' to iimasu ne. Keredomo kono dōshi o jidōshi toshite tsukau baai ni wa 'Fujisan ga miete iru' to ka 'Jon-san wa Amerikajin ni mieru' to iu koto ga dekimasu.
Jon	Watakushi wa Amerikajin ni wa miemasen yo.
Tadashi	Iya iya, ima no wa bunpō o setsumei suru tame no rei ni sugimasen yo. Bokokugo to iu no wa fudan ishiki shinaide tsukatte iru no de ki ga tsukimasen ga, kōshite aratamete kangaete miru to muzukashii mono desu ne.
Jon	Sō nan desu yo. Jidōshi to tadōshi ga wakatta to omotte mo, sore ga '-te iru' no katachi de tsukawareru toki ni wa tomadou koto ga arimasu.
Tadashi	Tatoeba donna toki desu ka?
Jon	Ima no byōin de hatarakihajimete sugu ni 'Sumisu sensei, o-denwa ga kakattemasu yo' to kangofu-san ni iwaretan desu. Hakkiri imi ga wakaru made jikan ga kakarimashita ne.
Tadashi	Sore wa tashika ni muzukashii desu ne.
Jon	Sore kara 'kaki o narabete iru' to 'kaki ga narande iru' no chigai wa yatto wakaru yō ni narimashita ga, ato no hō no 'kaki ga narande iru' to 'kaki ga narabete aru' no chigai wa ima de mo hakkiri shinain desu kedo.
Tadashi	Komatta nā. Nan da ka boku mo wakaranaku natte kite shimatta.

Translation

John	Say what you will, but the most difficult verbs are 'mieru' and 'kikoeru'. 'Mieru' expresses the potential and also works as an intransitive, doesn't it?
Tadashi	Yes. When testing your eyesight, the doctor will say 'miemasu ka?' But when you

	use this verb as an an intransitive verb, you can say 'Fujisan ga miete iru' or 'Jon san wa Amerikajin ni mieru.'
John	I don't look like an American!
Tadashi	No, no! That was just an example to explain the grammar. You normally use your own native language unconsciously, but when you look at it anew like this it is difficult, isn't it?
John	Indeed it is. I had thought I understood intransitives and transitives, but there are times when I still get confused when they are used in the '-te iru' form.
Tadashi	For instance?
John	Very soon after I started working in my present hospital a nurse said to me 'Sumisu sensei, o-denwa ga kakattemasu yo.' It took me some time before I really understood what she meant.
Tadashi	Yes, that is difficult isn't it?
John	And then, I now just about understand the difference between 'kaki o narabete iru' and 'kaki ga narande iru', but I'm still unclear about the difference between the latter phrase 'kaki ga narande iru' and 'kai ga narabete aru'.
Tadashi	Oh dear! I feel completely at sea now!

Lesson 44

マリー	ジョンさん。困ったことが出来てしまったんですが、相談にのって下さい。
ジョン	浮かない顔をしていますね。どうしたんですか。
マリー	実は、結婚を申し込まれてしまったんです。
ジョン	えっ。じょうだんでしょ。
マリー	じょうだんじゃないから困っているんです。
ジョン	僕の知っている人ですか。
マリー	いいえ。私でさえあんまりよくは知らない人なんですから。
ジョン	それじゃあ、マリーさんはその人と結婚する気はないんですか。
マリー	全然…。
ジョン	マリーさんにその気がなければ、仕方がありませんね。断ればいいじゃありませんか。
マリー	ところが、問題はそう簡単じゃないんです。その人は私の気持が変わるまで待つと言うんです。
ジョン	ハッハッハ。それは困りましたね。
マリー	笑いごとじゃないんですよ。どう説明すれば、私の気持は変わらないということが、相手に分かってもらえるでしょうか。
ジョン	言葉を並べて、説明しようとすればするほど、こんがらがってくるのではないでしょうかね。
マリー	それじゃあ、どうすれば一番いいんですか。
ジョン	まあ、よく分かりませんけれど、僕なら相手にはっきりと言いますね。そして、しばらく会わなければ、相手の人の気持も少しずつ落ち着いてくるんじゃありませんか。
マリー	でもとなりの研究室の人ですから、大学に行けば必ず顔を合わせなければならないんです。
ジョン	そんなに深刻になって考えなくても大丈夫ですよ。
マリー	このごろ、気になって夜も眠れないんですよ。
ジョン	寝る前に、ウィスキーをちょこっと飲めば、ぐっすり眠れますよ。
マリー	ジョンさんは私の問題をちっとも真面目に考えてくれないみたい。

ジョン	いやいや、ただこの件に関しては、マリーさんの気持がはっきりしているので、あまり考える余地もありませんからね。相手が絶対にあきらめないというのならば、冷たいようですが、ほっておくより仕方がないでしょう。
マリー	そうかもしれないわ…。

44.1 Conditionals

> マリーさんにその気がなければ、仕方がありませんね。

Conditionals were introduced in 29.2, but we shall restate the points that were made there, because they are important. There are a number of ways of expressing the idea of 'if' or 'when' in Japanese, and the next two lessons will introduce the major patterns. None of them are intrinsically difficult, but they do need careful study because they do not coincide with English constructions. The main difference is that English concentrates on whether or not the speaker knows an action will or will not happen: if you know something is going to happen, then you will use 'when'; if you do not know or are not at all sure, you will use 'if'. Japanese, on the other hand, concentrates on the connection between two events, whether the second event is expected or arbitrary, natural or forced. The patterns involve two further verb inflections, ～えば and ～たら, and two grammatical 'function words': と and なら(ば). ～えば is introduced first.

44.2 Form of ～えば

The verb inflections for positive ～えば are produced as follows:

	plain citation	*meaning*	～えば
group I	ある	exist	あれば
	歩く	walk	歩けば
	会う	meet	会えば
	行く	go	行けば

	入る	enter	入れば
	話す	talk	話せば
	言う	say	言えば
	買う	buy	買えば
	書く	write	書けば
	聞く	listen, ask	聞けば
	待つ	wait	待てば
	飲む	drink	飲めば
	乗る	ride	乗れば
	使う	use	使えば
	読む	read	読めば
group II	いる	exist	いれば
	出る	go out	出れば
	かける	hang	かければ
	見る	see	見れば
	寝る	go to bed	寝れば
	起きる	get up	起きれば
	食べる	eat	食べれば
irregular	来る	come	来(く)れば
	する	do	すれば
descr. verbs	おいしい	tasty	おいしければ
	美しい	beautiful	美しければ

The negative of this form is produced by taking the normal negative of the verb and then transforming the ～ない to ～なければ as follows:

動く	move	動かなければ
もらう	receive	もらわなければ
開ける	open	開けなければ
かわいい	cute, pretty	かわいくなければ
短い	short	短かくなければ

There is no form for the copula listed here; it will be dealt with separately.

44.3 Uses of ～えば

With ～えば, the emphasis is on the conditions under which something will or might occur. The implication of this form is that the second clause is a necessary and natural consequence of the first clause; provided that something happens, something else will then happen. ～えば is usually, but not always, restricted to present or future time.

雨が降れば出かけません。
I won't go out if it rains.

This does not just describe what will happen when or if it rains; it actually gives a condition under which I will not go out.

分からなければ、遠慮をしないで聞いて下さい。
If you don't understand, please don't hesitate to ask me.

その人の立場に立ってみなければ理解出来ないことがたくさんあります。
There are many things you won't understand, unless you try seeing things from their point of view.

44.4 ～えば＋いい

断ればいい。

This pattern literally means 'if..., then good'. It is used as a mild exhortation, the equivalent of the English 'I should..., (if I were you).'

どうすればいいでしょう。
What should I do?

どこで払えばいいでしょう。
Where should I pay?

正直にありのままを言えばいいでしょう。
I think you should tell him honestly how things are.

44.5 The pattern 'the more...the more/the less'

> 説明しようとすればするほど、こんがらがってくるのではないでしょうかね。

The Japanese equivalent of 'the more...the more/the less' is created in a very different way to its English counterpart. In this example sentence ～えば links with the noun ほど 'extent' to produce a first phrase that can be literally rendered 'when I try to explain, to the extent that I explain…'; the second part of the sentence is straightforward, although note that here ～てくる appears, stressing the progressive nature of the construction. Study the following examples:

練習すればするほど、上手になる。
The more you practise, the better you become.

眠ろうとすればするほど、眠れなくなる。
The more I try to go to sleep, the more difficult it becomes.

44.6 Expressing obligation and asking permission

> 大学に行けば必ず顔を合わせなければならないんです。

We have already seen that Japanese often prefer to avoid expressing power or authority over others, by employing some roundabout phrase. Obligations are of course no exception, and the Japanese construction that is the equivalent of the

English 'must' or 'ought to' is oblique in the extreme. 'You must go' is expressed as 'if you do not go, things will not work out'. For this, the 〜えば inflection of 〜ない, namely 〜なければ, is used. Using this form as a question is a good way of asking permission.

〜なければ + ならない (なりません) or
〜なければ + いけない (いけません)

三時までに行かなければなりませんか。
Must I be there by three o'clock?

明日までにレポートを二本書かなければいけない。
I have to write two essays by tomorrow.

彼は子供の時に父親に死なれたので十六歳の時から働かなければならなかった。
He had to start working at the age of sixteen because his father died when he was a child.

地球は丸いということを人々に分からせるために、ガリレオは命をかけなければならなかった。
In order to make people understand that the earth is round, Galileo had to risk his life.

Sometimes ならない and いけない are interchangeable, but it is fair to say that when you oblige someone *else* to do something, いけない is usually the word to choose.

よく休まなければいけませんよ。
You ought to have a good rest.

この記事には知らない単語がたくさんあるので一つ一つ辞書で調べなければならない。
There are many words which I do not know in this article so I have to look them up in a dictionary one by one.

図書館の本は借りてから四週間以内に返さなければいけませんよ。
You must return library books within four weeks after you borrow them.

44.7 なら or ならば

> 僕なら相手にはっきりと言いますね。
> 相手がどうしてもあきらめないというのならば、

The 〜えば form of the copula is created by going back to the classical equivalent of だ/です, namely なり → ならば, which is also shortened to just なら. When it directly follows a noun it can simply mean 'if it were…', as it does in the example sentence, but it often has an extended sense of 'if actually' or 'if it is indeed a question of…', referring to something in context.

ストならば出かけません。
If there's a strike on, I'll stay at home.

そのことならもう聞いています。
If it's a question of that matter, I have already heard about it.

こちらの方が好きならば取り替えて上げますよ。
If you prefer this one, then I'll change it for you.

When it follows a verb, usually in the imperfective, a nominalising の is usually present:

来られないのならば早目にそう言って下さい。
If you cannot come, please let me know soon.

これだけ説明したのに分らないのなら仕方がない。
If you still do not understand after I have explained it at such length, then it's hopeless.

By and large it is fair to say that なら and ならば are interchangeable, although occasionally なら has an extra nuance: it may sometimes imply either will or intention:

ラジオを聞くならあっちで聞いて下さい。
If you want to listen to the radio, please do so over there.

44.8 Uses of さえ

私でさえ

The particle さえ has a number of uses. Here it is operating idiomatically with で meaning 'even'.

子供でさえそんなことはしませんよ。
Even a child wouldn't do such a (stupid) thing.

It can also be used straight after a noun with roughly the same meaning: that of an emphatic も.

あの学生は外国語はもちろん母国語さえまともに書けない。
That student can't write his *own* language properly, never mind a foreign one.

There is also the important pattern さえすれば, which is why we have left this explanation until the end of the lesson, after ～えば.

来(き)さえすればいいんですか。
Is it OK as long as I just turn up?

「ごめんなさい」と言いさえすればいいんですね。
It's all right as long as I just say I'm sorry, isn't it?

Key to conversation

Romanisation

Marī — Jon-san. Komatta koto ga dekite shimattan desu ga, sōdan ni notte kudasai.

Jon — Ukanai kao o shite imasu ne. Dō shitan desu ka.

Marī	Jitsu wa kekkon o mōshikomarete shimattan desu.
Jon	E! Jōdan desho.
Marī	Jōdan ja nai kara komatte irun desu.
Jon	Boku no shitte iru hito desu ka?
Marī	Iie. Watakushi de sae anmari yoku wa shiranai hito nan desu kara.
Jon	Sore jā, Marī san wa sono hito to kekkon suru ki wa nain desu ka?
Marī	Zenzen.
Jon	Marī san ni sono ki ga nakereba shikata ga arimasen ne. Kotowareba ii ja arimasen ka?
Marī	Tokoro ga, mondai wa sō kantan ja nain desu. Sono hito wa watakushi no kimochi ga kawaru made matsu to iun desu.
Jon	Hahaha. Sore wa komarimashita ne.
Marī	Waraigoto ja nain desu yo. Dō setsumei sureba watakushi no kimochi wa kawaranai to iu koto ga aite ni wakatte moraeru deshō ka?
Jon	Kotoba o narabete setsumei shiyō to sureba suru hodo kongaragatte kuru no de wa nai deshō ka ne.
Marī	Sore ja, dō sureba ichiban iin desu ka?
Jon	Mā, yoku wakarimasen keredo boku nara aite ni hakkiri to iimasu ne. Soshite shibaraku awanakereba aite no hito no kimochi mo sukoshi zutsu ochitsuite kurun ja arimasen ka?
Marī	Demo, tonari no kenkyūshitsu no hito desu kara, daigaku ni ikeba kanarazu kao o awasenakereba naranain desu.
Jon	Sonna ni shinkoku ni natte kangaenakute mo daijōbu desu yo.
Marī	Kono goro ki ni natte yoru mo nemurenain desu yo.
Jon	Neru mae ni uisukī o chokotto nomeba gussuri nemuremasu yo.
Marī	Jon-san wa watakushi no mondai o chittomo majime ni kangaete kurenai mitai.
Jon	Iya iya. Tada kono ken ni kanshite wa Marī san no kimochi ga hakkiri shite iru no de, amari kangaeru yochi mo arimasen kara ne. Aite ga zettai ni akiramenai to iu naraba, tsumetai yō desu ga, hotte oku yori shikata ga nai deshō.
Marī	Sō ka mo shirenai wa...

Translation

Marie	John, something awkward has happened. Please give me some advice.
John	You look a bit depressed. What's up?

Marie	Actually, I've had a marriage proposal.
John	What! You're joking.
Marie	No, I'm not joking. That's why it's awkward.
John	Anyone I know?
Marie	No. It's someone I don't know very well myself.
John	Well then, you're not interested in marrying him?
Marie	Not in the slightest.
John	If you don't want to, then that's it. Can't you simply refuse him?
Marie	But it's not that simple. He says he will wait until I've changed my mind.
John	Ah ha. That is a bit of a problem.
Marie	It's no laughing matter. How can I explain so as to get him to understand that I won't change my mind?
John	The more you try to explain by putting it into words, the more entangled it will become, I should think.
Marie	So what's the best thing to do?
John	Well I don't really know, but if I were you, I'd tell him straight. And if you try not to meet him for a while, he may settle down gradually, don't you think?
Marie	But he's in the next seminar room to mine and I'm bound to meet him whenever I go to the university.
John	Surely you don't have to get so worked up about it all.
Marie	I'm so worried I haven't been able to get to sleep recently.
John	Have a little tot of whisky just before you go to bed and you'll sleep like a top.
Marie	It doesn't seem as though you're taking this at all seriously.
John	No, no. It's just that because you feel as certain as you do, there's not much point in worrying about it. If he really won't resign himself, then I know it sounds cruel, but you'll just have to ignore him.
Marie	Yes, I suppose you're right.

Lesson 45

交換手	東西銀行でございます。
ブラウン	内線402をお願いします。
長谷川	外国為替課です。
ブラウン	長谷川様はいらっしゃいますか。
長谷川	私ですが。
ブラウン	ブリティッシュ・エンジニアリングのブラウンです。
長谷川	あ、ブラウンさん。御無沙汰しております。その後、いかがですか。
ブラウン	おかげさまで。もうすっかりよくなりました。
長谷川	それは結構でした。
ブラウン	実は、近々本社から副社長のハミルトンが参ります。つきましては、お忙しいとは存じますが出来ましたら長谷川様にもお目にかかりたいとのことなのですが…。
長谷川	それはそれは。私共の支店長も是非お会いしたいと申すと思います。それで東京に到着されるのは何日ですか。
ブラウン	三月の十二日で、十八日には香港に向けて発つことになっております。
長谷川	ずいぶん短い御滞在ですね。
ブラウン	ええ、しかも後半は名古屋の方へ行くことになっておりますので…。
長谷川	何日にこちらへおいでいただくのが一番よろしいでしょうか。
ブラウン	十三日か十四日でしたら何時にでも伺えますが…。
長谷川	分かりました。それではさっそく支店長と相談いたしまして、おいでいただく日が決まりましたらすぐにお電話を差し上げます。
ブラウン	ありがとうございます。それから、これは仕事のことではないのですが、あまり時間をかけないで、副社長に日本らしいところを見せるとしたら、どこへ行くのがいいでしょうか。
長谷川	日光か鎌倉へいらっしゃったらいかがですか。月並みですが。
ブラウン	そうですね…。実は、副社長はあまり仏教とかお寺に興味がないようなので、もう少し活気のあるところはないでしょうか。

長谷川	それでしたら、築地の魚河岸へお連れになったらいかがですか。朝相当早くお出かけにならなければなりませんけれどとてもおもしろいと思いますよ。
ブラウン	それはいいアイディアですね。
長谷川	もしよろしかったら、私もお伴しましょうか。
ブラウン	ありがとうございます。案内していただけたら、とても助かります。

Comment

It was mentioned earlier that telephone conversations, by their very nature, are often full of respect language. This is particularly the case when calling a company, so this conversation has been written partly to illustrate this phenomenon. Note how combinations of respectful and humble forms fly thick and fast.

45.1 'It's been quite a while'

御無沙汰しております。

'I have had no communication with you (for some time).' This is a very useful phrase, which you can use either on the phone or simply when meeting someone. It is also often found near the beginning of a letter.

45.2 Idiomatic use of the perfective

それは結構でした。

This phrase would probably be translated into English using the present tense:

'That's excellent news!' Note how the perfective is used in Japanese. Brown has just said that he is fully recovered and Hasegawa's reply is cast in the perfective to emphasise that something is over and that we are back to normal.

45.3 'Subjectless' sentences

> お忙しいとは存じますが

This is as good an example as any of the way that explicit subjects are often quite redundant in Japanese. The phrase お忙しい, being respectful in that the subject is raised, could only possibly refer to 'you'; similarly, 存じます, which is a humble form meaning 'think' or 'know' here, could only refer to Brown himself.

45.4 The form of conditional ～たら

> 出来ましたら…
> 十三日か十四日でしたら何時にでも伺えますが…。
> おいでいただく日が決まりましたらすぐにお電話を
> 差し上げます。

The verb inflections for positive ～たら are produced as follows:

	plain citation	*meaning*	～たら
group I	ある	exist	あったら
	歩く	walk	歩いたら
	会う	meet	会ったら
	行く	go	行ったら
	入る	enter	入ったら
	話す	talk	話したら

	言う	say	言ったら
	買う	buy	買ったら
	書く	write	書いたら
	聞く	listen, ask	聞いたら
	待つ	wait	待ったら
	飲む	drink	飲んだら
	乗る	ride	乗ったら
	使う	use	使ったら
	読む	read	読んだら
group II	いる	exist	いたら
	出る	go out	出たら
	かける	hang	かけたら
	見る	see	見たら
	寝る	go to bed	寝たら
	起きる	get up	起きたら
	食べる	eat	食べたら
irregular	来る	come	来(き)たら
	する	do	したら
descr. verbs	おいしい	tasty	おいしかったら
	美しい	beautiful	美しかったら
copula	だ		だったら
	です		でしたら

The negative of this form is produced by taking the normal negative of the verb and then transforming the 〜ない to 〜なかったら as follows:

plain citation	*meaning*	*negative* 〜たら
動く	move	動かなかったら
もらう	receive	もらわなかったら
開ける	open	開けなかったら
かわいい	cute, pretty	かわいくなかったら

短い	short	短かくなかったら
だ、です	[copula]	ではなかったら

45.5 Uses of ～たら

～たら, being based on the perfective, indicates that the action or event in the first clause is completed before the second action or event occurs. The emphasis here is on what happens if or when, but certainly after, something else happens. When the final verb is in the present or the future, you will find yourself translating ～たら as 'if':

雨が降ったら出かけません。
If it rains, I won't go out.

When the final verb is in the past, you will find yourself using the translation 'when':

公園に行ったら田中さんが犬を散歩させていました。
When I went to the park, Mr Tanaka was taking his dog for a walk.

45.6 Plain verb + としたら

見せるとしたら、

This phrase is a little more elaborate than just a simple 'if': 'if it was a case of showing…' or perhaps here 'if you had to show…' The conditional part of the phrase is being stressed. In this kind of context としたら can be replaced by either とすれば or とすると with no real change in meaning.

会社が終ってから来るとしたら、こちらに着くのは八時ごろですね。
If you were to come after work, you'd get here about eight, wouldn't you?

私の給料だけで暮らさなければならないとしたら、生活はかなりきついと思いますよ。
If we really had to survive on my salary alone, I think things would be fairly tight.

45.7 ～たらどうですか; ～たらいかがですか

日光か鎌倉へいらっしゃったらいかがですか。
それでしたら、築地の魚河岸へお連れになったらいかがですか。

Now you have been introduced to the ～たら form, learn these two idiomatic phrases, meaning 'Why don't you...?', or 'How about...?'

人の批判ばかりしないで、少しは自分のことも反省してみたらどうですか。
Why don't you reflect on your own actions a little instead of criticising others all the time?

その問題に関しては日英共同研究を計画してみたらいかがでしょう。
On that issue, how about planning a joint Anglo-Japanese research project?

Another idiomatic phrase appears near the end of this conversation: よろしかったら: 'if it's all right by you' or 'if it's convenient'. よろしい is a polite equivalent of いい.

45.8 More on forms of respect

築地の魚河岸へお連れになったらいかがですか。
早くお出かけにならなければなりません。

You have already come across a number of ways to express respect. Perhaps the commonest of these forms is the one introduced here: prefix お + conjunctive + になる, giving rise to such verbs as お書きになる, and お話になる. Most verbs can be cast in this form. Remember that a respect form is used to raise the status of its subject. Note one anomaly here however: the form お見えになる means only 'put in an appearance' and so 'come', *not* 'see'.

45.9 ～たら and ～えば compared

Now that you have been introduced to both ～たら and ～えば, you will want to know how they differ. This is not an easy matter to explain, and you will have to accept that some aspects of this difference will simply have to be learned through trial and error. Sometimes ～たら and ～えば are interchangeable, especially if the verb in the main clause is in the imperfective. For example:

(a) この薬を飲んだらすぐに熱が下がる。

(b) この薬を飲めばすぐに熱が下がる。

A fitting translation of (a) might be 'When you take this medicine, your temperature will soon drop.' Since a ～たら sentence signifies 'once an action has taken place X will/might occur', the emphasis is on the temporal link between the two events. (b) might be translated 'If and only if you take this medicine, your temperature will soon drop.' The weight of emphasis here is on the taking of the medicine as a prerequisite. It must be admitted, however, that in these examples the difference is minimal. In the following sentences, however, there are noticeable differences.

弟が帰ってきたらすぐに出かけます。
I will go out as soon as my younger brother returns.

弟が帰ってくれば出かけます。
If my younger brother comes back I will go out.

The first sentence is concerned with timing. The second sentence, with ～えば, is more concerned with the conditions under which the speaker will act, and so a word like すぐに which means 'immediately' or 'straight away' seems unnatural.

Further examples:

八百屋の前まで行ったら雨が降ってきた。
When I got to the greengrocer's, it started raining.

This sentence *cannot* be rewritten in the ～えば form because the 'raining' is not a consequence of arriving in front of the greengrocer's. You can, however, say

八百屋の前まで行けばバスの停留所が見えます。
If you go as far as the greengrocer's, you will be able to see the bus stop.

There are some exceptional cases where only ～たら can be used. Observe the following:

京都へ行ったら清水寺を見に行きましょう (行こう)。
When we go to Kyōto, let's visit the Kiyomizu-dera.

京都へ行ったらつけものを買ってきて下さい。
When you go to Kyōto, please buy me some pickles.

～えば cannot be used in any of these sentences because the condition 'a necessary and natural consequence of the first clause' cannot be met.

45.10 ～たら versus ～なら

Refer back to 44.7. Make sure that you can see the difference between uses of ～たら and ～なら.

この本を読む (の) なら上げます。
If you want/intend to read this book, I will give it to you.

この本を読んだら上げます。
I will give you this book when I've finished reading it.

Key to conversation

Romanisation

Kōkanshu	Tōzai ginkō de gozaimasu.
Buraun	Naisen 402 o o-negai shimasu.
Hasegawa	Gaikoku kawase ka desu.
Buraun	Hasegawa-sama wa irrasshaimasu ka.
Hasegawa	Watakushi desu ga.
Buraun	Buritisshu Enjiniaringu no Buraun desu.
Hasegawa	A, Buraun-san. Go-busata shite orimasu. Sono go ikaga desu ka?
Buraun	O-kage sama de. Mō sukkari yoku narimashita.
Hasegawa	Sore wa kekkō deshita.
Buraun	Jitsu wa chikajika honsha kara fukushachō no Hamiruton ga mairimasu. Tsukimashite wa o-isogashii to wa zonjimasu ga dekimashitara Hasegawa-sama ni mo o-me ni kakaritai to no koto na no desu ga...
Hasegawa	Sore wa sore wa. Watakushidomo no shitenchō mo zehi o-ai shitai to mōsu to omoimasu. Sore de Tōkyō ni tōchaku sareru no wa nannichi desu ka?
Buraun	Sangatsu no jūninichi de, jūhachinichi ni wa Honkon ni mukete tatsu koto ni natte orimasu.
Hasegawa	Zuibun mijikai go-taizai desu ne.
Buraun	Ē, shikamo kōhan wa Nagoya no hō e iku koto ni natte orimasu no de...
Hasegawa	Nannichi ni kochira e o-ide itadaku no ga ichiban yoroshii deshō ka?
Buraun	Jūsannichi ka jūyokka deshitara nanji ni demo ukagaemasu ga...
Hasegawa	Wakarimashita. Sore de wa sassoku shitenchō to sōdan itashimashite o-ide itadaku hi ga kimarimashitara sugu ni o-denwa o sashiagemasu.
Buraun	Arigatō gozaimasu. Sore kara, kore wa shigoto no koto de wa nai no desu ga amari jikan o kakenaide fukushachō ni Nihon-rashii tokoro o miseru to shitara, doko e iku no ga ii deshō ka?
Hasegawa	Nikkō ka Kamakura e irashattara ikaga desu ka? Tsukinami desu ga.
Buraun	Sō desu ne... Jitsu wa fukushachō wa amari bukkyō to ka o-tera ni kyōmi ga nai yō na node, mō sukoshi kakki no aru tokoro wa nai deshō ka?
Hasegawa	Sore deshitara, Tsukiji no uogashi e o-tsure ni nattara ikaga desu ka? Asa sōtō hayaku o-dekake ni naranakereba narimasen keredo, totemo omoshiroi to omoimasu yo.

Buraun	Sore wa ii aidia desu ne.
Hasegawa	Moshi yoroshikattara, watakushi mo o-tomo shimashō ka?
Buraun	Arigatō gozaimasu. Annai shite itadaketara totemo tasukarimasu.

Translation

Operator	Tōzai Bank.
Brown	Extension 402 please.
Hasegawa	Foreign Exchange Department
Brown	Is Mr Hasegawa there please?
Hasegawa	Speaking.
Brown	This is Brown from British Engineering.
Hasegawa	Oh, Mr Brown! It's been a long time. How have you been?
Brown	Well, thank you. I've completely recovered.
Hasegawa	That's splendid.
Brown	Actually our Deputy Chairman Hamilton will be coming to Japan soon. I know you're very busy, but if at all possible he would very much like to see you.
Hasegawa	Well, well. I am sure our Branch Manager will want to see him too. What day does he arrive in Tōkyō?
Brown	March 12th and he leaves for Hong Kong on the 18th.
Hasegawa	A very short visit then.
Brown	Yes. And what's more, for the second half he's going to Nagoya.
Hasegawa	What day would it be most convenient to have him come over?
Brown	We could come over any time on either the 13th or 14th.
Hasegawa	Right then. I'll get on to our Branch Manager right away and ring you as soon as we have fixed a day.
Brown	Thank you very much. One more thing. It's not to do with business, but where do you think we should go to show him something typically Japanese; something that would not take up too much time?
Hasegawa	What about going to Nikkō or Kamakura? Mind, that's what everyone does.
Brown	Yes. Actually he doesn't seem to be that interested in Buddhism or temples; isn't there somewhere a little more lively?
Hasegawa	In that case, what about taking him to the fish market at Tsukiji? You'll have to leave fairly early in the morning, but I would have thought it would be most interesting.

Brown	That's a very good idea!
Hasegawa	If you'd like, I'll come along with you.
Brown	Thank you. It would help enormously if you could take us.

Lesson 46

John and Tadashi are talking in a coffee shop in Shibuya.

ジョン　今日はこれから東大へ行かなくてはならないんですが、どうやって行くのが一番便利でしょうか。

正　JR線で行くんだったら、新宿で乗り換えてお茶の水へ出て、そこからバスですね。

ジョン　僕の地図で見ると、新宿まで行かないで一つ手前の代々木で乗り換えた方がいいみたいですが…。

正　いや、代々木乗り換えだとお茶の水まで各駅停車に乗らなければならないので、新宿まで行って、快速に乗った方がいいですよ。

ジョン　お茶の水からは歩けませんか。

正　うーん。歩けなくはありませんが、ちょっとありますよ。やっぱりバスに乗った方が早いと思いますね。お茶の水駅では電車の進行方向前、つまり東京駅よりの改札口から出て下さい。そうすると、目の前に聖橋が見えます。東大構内行きのバスはその橋の上から出ています。

ジョン　どうもありがとう。でも今からだと、丁度ラッシュの時間で道路が相当混むんじゃないでしょうかね。

正　そうだなあ。それなら渋谷から地下鉄の半蔵門線に乗って、大手町まで行って、そこで丸の内線に乗り換えて本郷三丁目まで行った方が早く着けるかもしれませんね。本郷三丁目から東大までは歩いて十分もかかりませんから。

ジョン　僕もその方がよさそうな気がします。どうもありがとう。まだ少し時間がありますが、あまり電車の混まないうちに行くことにします。

正　じゃあ、又近いうちに。

Comment

The content of this conversation has to do with the Tōkyō transportation system, so in order to follow it you will have to refer to the map. The rail network is a

Tōkyō transportation system (simplified)

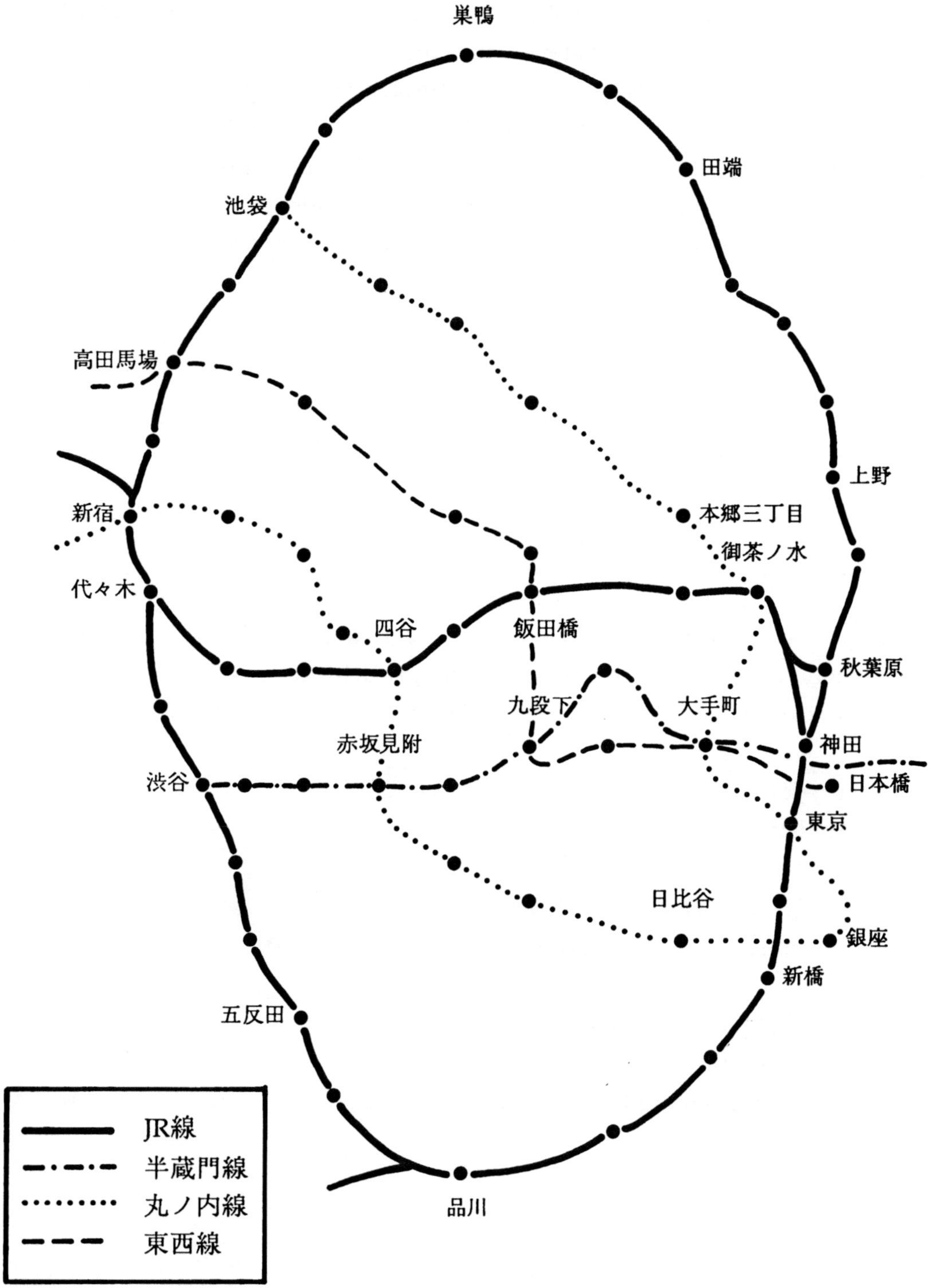

combination of surface lines, the most prominent being the circular Yamanote Line, and a growing number of underground lines. This vast system moves millions daily. It is both clean and efficient, but standing room only is the usual rule. A special feature of the system is the large number of interchanges and connecting corridors, but because it is a conglomeration of private companies, there is only limited common ticketing. As the conversation reveals, a number of surface trains run on the same track but stop at different stations, and each line tends to have its own special name for the various grades from fast to slow. Working out the fastest route is an art best learned as early as possible after your arrival in Tōkyō.

46.1 Expressing obligation again

東大へ行かなくてはならない

In 44.6 you were introduced to the form なければならない. There is a second construction with roughly the same meaning, which employs the 〜て form of 〜ない, namely 〜なくて + は + いけない or 〜なくて + は + ならない.

もう少しよく勉強しなくてはいけない。
You have to work a bit harder.

赤信号の時には止って待たなくてはいけない。
One must stop and wait when the traffic light is red.

出発前にしなくてはならない仕事が山ほどありますので失礼させて下さい。
I have a vast amount of work which must be done before my departure, so please excuse me.

46.2 Use of と for conditionals

> 僕の地図で見ると、
> 代々木乗り換えだとお茶の水まで各駅停車に
> 乗らなければならない

The third pattern for producing conditionals in Japanese involves the sentence particle と that was introduced in lessons 28 and 29. In those lessons it was treated as a temporal particle and was translated exclusively as 'when', but, as we have seen, the distinction between 'when' and 'if' does not always hold in Japanese.

よく考えてみるとその話は本当に妙ですね。
When you really think about it, that story sounds pretty odd, doesn't it?

外国語は使わないとすぐに話せなくなってしまう。
With a foreign language, if you don't use it you soon lose it.

いいかげんなことをしていると大変なことになりますよ。
If you go on taking halfway measures, it will become a very serious problem.

46.3 ～ないで and ～なくて compared

> 新宿まで行かないで

In 20.3 (c) we mentioned that the negative ～て form of pure verbs had in fact two forms: ～ないで or ～なくて. The difference between these two is largely a matter of the type of subordination they mark.

彼はケンブリッジ大学へは行かないでオックスフォード大学へ
行った。
He went to Oxford instead of going to Cambridge.

〜ないで is used when the verb is clearly subordinate to the final statement, but without any suggestion of cause or reason. This is why it appears in phrases such as 〜ないで下さい. In the example from the main text 'going to Shinjuku' is very much part and parcel of 'changing at Yoyogi'.

お金が足りなくてタクシーには乗れなかった。
We didn't have enough money and so couldn't take a taxi.

〜なくて is used when the verb is clearly subordinate to the final statement in such a way as to suggest cause or reason.

46.4 と, 〜たら and 〜えば compared

As you have seen in the previous lessons, sentences with 〜たら and 〜えば are sometimes interchangeable with little difference in meaning. Now observe the following:

(a) 何度も練習すると上手になる。

(b) 何度も練習したら上手になる。

(c) 何度も練習すれば上手になる。

These sentences are all grammatical and they are often used, particularly in the spoken language, without clear distinction. They can all be translated: 'If you practise repeatedly, you will make progress.' There is, however, a subtle difference: (a) implies that your progress is automatic so long as you practise hard, (b) indicates that progress will come after practice and finally (c) gives a condition for progress.

The following three sentences are also correct, with similar slight differences in nuance. They all mean 'He said that by drinking it is possible to forget even unpleasant matters.'

お酒を飲むといやなことも忘れられると彼は言った。

お酒を飲めばいやなことも忘れられると彼は言った。

お酒を飲んだらいやなことも忘れられると彼は言った。

More examples:

お酒を飲むと気分が悪くなります。
Whenever I drink I feel ill.

This sentence describes habitual occurrence and neither ～たら nor ～えば would be suitable. On the other hand, if you want to refer to a particular incident in the past ～たら must be used.

きのう忘年会で日本酒を飲んだら気分が悪くなった。
Yesterday I felt somewhat queasy after having drunk sake at an end-of-year party.

と cannot be used here because the consequences, although perhaps foreseeable, are not strictly inevitable!

46.5 ～なくはない

歩けなくはありませんが、ちょとありますよ。

This is an idiom consisting of two negatives split by は. The effect is similar to the English 'it's not that you can't, but...' or 'well yes, but...' So here we have 'well you *can* walk, but...' Note the idiomatic second part of this phrase, ちょっとありますよ, 'but it's quite a way'. Some more examples of ～なくはない:

この仕事、あしたまでに出来ますか。
Can you do this job by tomorrow?

出来なくはありませんが、他にも仕事が入っておりますので…。
It is not completely impossible, but I do have some other work that's come in…

この時計の修理をお願いしたいんですが。
Would you mend this clock for me?

直らなくはありませんが、新しいのを買った方が安いですよ。
It's not impossible to mend, but it would be cheaper to buy a new one.

46.6 'In other words'

つまり

つまり comes from a verb meaning 'pack tight, shrink' and is often used adverbially in the sense of 'i.e.' or 'in the final analysis'.

私の父の父、つまり私の祖父は戦争前満州に住んでいました。
My father's father, namely my grandfather, lived in Manchuria before the War.

つまり人口問題を解決することが先決だということですか。
Do you mean to say that in the final analysis it is the population problem that must be solved first?

46.7 Uses of うちに

あまり電車の混まないうちに行くことにします。 じゃあ、又近いうちに。

うち is a noun meaning 'inside' or 'within', but occasionally the sense is more akin to 'period of time'. It is similar to 間 (19.5) in that it is used to express the concept of 'while', but it has the added significance of a kind of urgency, as if the second activity must be completed before the time span expires:

熱いうちにお茶を飲んで下さい。
Please drink the tea while it's still hot.

朝のうちに計画をたてて、お昼前にはファックスでお送りします。
I will work out the plan during the morning and send it to you by fax before noon.

When うちに is used with a negative verb this sense of urgency is even stronger:

雨が降り出さないうちに帰りましょう。
Let's go home before it starts raining.

忘れないうちに言っておきますが来週の月曜日の試験は十時からではなくて十二時からです。
I'll tell you before I forget: next Monday's test is not from ten but from twelve.

Note also the following temporal phrases with うち:

そのうち	'in the near future', 'in time'
近いうち (に)	'in the very near future'
今のうち (に)	'while the iron is hot'

Key to conversation

Romanisation

Jon	Kyō wa kore kara Tōdai e ikanakutewa naranain desu ga, dō yatte iku no ga ichiban benri deshō ka?
Tadashi	JR-sen de ikun dattara, Shinjuku de norikaete Ochanomizu e dete, soko kara basu desu ne.
Jon	Boku no chizu de miru to Shinjuku made ikanaide hitotsu temae no Yoyogi de

	norikaeta hō ga ii mitai desu ga...
Tadashi	Iya, Yoyogi norikae da to Ochanomizu made kakueki teisha ni noranakereba naranai no de, Shinjuku made itte, kaisoku ni notta hō ga ii desu yo.
Jon	Ochanomizu kara arukemasen ka?
Tadashi	Ūn. Arukenaku wa arimasen ga chotto arimasu yo. Yappari basu ni notta hō ga hayai to omoimasu ne. Ochanomizu eki de wa densha no shinkō hōkō mae, tsumari Tōkyō eki yori no kaisatsuguchi kara dete kudasai. Sō suru to, me no mae ni Hijiribashi ga miemasu. Tōdai kōnai yuki no basu wa sono hashi no ue kara dete imasu.
Jon	Dōmo arigatō. Demo ima kara da to, chōdo rasshu no jikan de dōro ga sōtō komun ja nai deshō ka ne.
Tadashi	Sō da nā. Sore nara Shibuya kara chikatetsu no Hanzōmon-sen ni notte, Ōtemachi made itte, soko de Marunouchi-sen ni norikaete, Hongō Sanchōme made itta hō ga hayaku tsukeru ka mo shiremasen ne. Hongō Sanchōme kara Tōdai made wa aruite juppun mo kakarimasen kara.
Jon	Boku mo sono hō ga yosasō na ki ga shimasu. Dōmo arigatō. Mada sukoshi jikan ga arimasu ga, amari densha no komanai uchi ni iku koto ni shimasu.
Tadashi	Ja, mata chikai uchi ni.

Translation

John	I've got to go to Tōkyō University today. What's the most convenient way to get there?
Tadashi	If you're going on the JR line, change at Shinjuku, go to Ochanomizu and then get a bus.
John	According to my map it looks better if I don't go as far as Shinjuku but change at Yoyogi, one stop before.
Tadashi	No. If you change at Yoyogi, you'll have to get the slow train to Ochanomizu, so it's better to go as far as Shinjuku and get on the express.
John	Can't I walk from Ochanomizu?
Tadashi	Well you can walk if you want to, but it's a fair way. I really think it'd be quicker by bus. At Ochanomizu Station leave by the exit nearest the front of the train, in other words the exit lying in the direction of Tōkyō Station. Then you'll see Hijiri Bridge right in front of you. The bus for the Tōkyō University campus leaves from that bridge.

John	Thanks. But if I left now wouldn't the roads be jammed with rush hour traffic?
Tadashi	You're right. Well then, it would probably be quicker to get the Hanzōmon underground from Shibuya, go to Ōtemachi, change there onto the Marunouchi Line and go as far as Hongō Sanchōme. From Hongō Sanchōme it's not ten minutes walk to Tōkyō University.
John	I have a feeling that's the best way too. Thank you. I've still got some time, but I think I'll go before the trains get too crowded.
Tadashi	OK. See you soon.

Lesson 47

Kuniko talks to her brother Tadashi.

国子	ねえ、おにいさん。どうしよう…。
正	どうしようっていきなり言われても、何が何だかさっぱり分からないじゃないか。どうしたんだい。
国子	それがね…、実は数学の試験で失敗しちゃって…。
正	落ちたのか。
国子	うん…。
正	おとうさんとおかあさんにはもう話したのか。
国子	ううん…。だって…。
正	ちゃんと話さなくちゃだめだよ。
国子	だって、心配させるだけでしょ。
正	そんなことを言ったって、だまっているわけにはいかないじゃないか。試験を一つ落したら卒業出来ないんだろ。
国子	うん。でもあさって追試があるので、それでまあまあの点がとれれば卒業は大丈夫だろうって、担任の先生はおっしゃるんだけど。
正	それで自信はあるのか。
国子	全然。でも運がよければ30点ぐらいはとれるかもしれないと思うの。
正	国子の数学はそんなにひどいのか。
国子	だって、きらいなんですもの。
正	数学はちゃんと勉強しさえすればだれでも点がとれる学科だと思うんだけどな。
国子	そんなことないわよ。いくら勉強したってちっとも分かるようにならないわ。
正	そんなものかなあ。
国子	おにいさんだってずいぶんピアノを練習したのにちっとも上手にならなかったじゃない。同じことよ。人それぞれ向き不向きがあるんだと思うわ。
正	まあ、それは当たっているかもしれないな。
国子	もし追試がうまくいって、卒業できるようだったら、この数学の試験のことはだまっていてはいけないかしら。

正	うそをついてはいけないと思うけどな。
国子	別にうそをつくわけではないでしょ。どうしても今晩おとうさんに話さなきゃだめ。
正	まあ、今すぐにはおとうさんやおかあさんに話さなくてもいいから、そんなことを心配するより少しはその追試のために勉強しておきなさい。
国子	ありがとう。子供のころからおにいさんはいつも私の味方になってくれたものね。
正	そういうわけでもないんだけど…。

Comment

This exchange between brother and sister reverts to the highly colloquial. Note that at this level of informality と is regularly reduced to って and でしょう, だろう are both 'cut back' to でしょ, and だろ. However informality in no way reduces the gender difference as revealed in speech; indeed in many ways it becomes more pronounced. Kuniko's sentence endings are recognizably female: の, もの, わ; and Tadashi's recognisably male: だい, のか, な and なあ.

47.1 Prohibition

> ちゃんと話さなくちゃだめだよ。
> うそをついてはいけない。

The patterns introduced in 44.6 and 46.1, meaning 'must', all involved the use of a double negative. The first example sentence here is yet another way of saying 'must', this time in colloquial form. いけない or ならない can often be replaced by だめ + (だ/ですよ), or even just simply omitted altogether. ちゃ is, of course, a colloquial form of ては.

早くしなくちゃだめよ。
You have to do it (or finish it) soon!

あら、もう三時だわ。急いで行かなくちゃ。
Oh, it's three o'clock already. I must dash.

The prohibition 'must not' is expressed in Japanese with a similar somewhat roundabout phrase: 'if you do x, it will not do'. Note that this involves only *one* negative and this negative occurs in the second part of the phrase. You may find this a little confusing, so take care to understand what is going on here.

ここでタバコをすってはいけません。
You should not smoke here.

そんな失礼なことを言ってはならない。
You must not say such rude things.

展示品に手をふれてはいけません。
Please do not touch the exhibits.

まだ食べちゃだめですよ。
You mustn't eat it yet!

47.2 わけにはいかない

だまっているわけにはいかない。

The noun わけ means 'reason', 'motive' or 'meaning' (see 31.2) and is often found simply in these senses. It also appears, however, in a number of important idiomatic expressions. わけにはいかない means 'it's impossible to…' 'it's not reasonable to…', or 'there is no way that'.

その件に関しては他言しないように言われているので教える
わけにはいかない。
I have been told to keep that business to myself, so there is no way that I can tell you about it.

安全のためと言われたら飛行機の遅れで迷惑をかけられてもそうやたらに文句を言うわけにはいかない。
Even if we are being inconvenienced by the flight delay, we really can't moan too much when they explain it's for our safety.

47.3 Indefiniteness revisited

だれでも点がとれる学科だ。

In 20.2 we explained the pattern 'interrogative noun + も…ない, meaning 'not any…' Hence:

彼女は外国語は何語も話せない。
She can't speak any foreign languages at all.

When this kind of indefinite statement appears in the positive, the pattern is 'interrogative word + でも':

彼女は外国語は何語でも話せる。
She can speak any foreign language!

そんなことはだれでも出来る。
Anyone can do that!

In this last example でも can be replaced by the more colloquial だって:

そんなことはだれだって出来る。

When an interrogative word like だれ, 何 or いくら appears in a ～ても or のに sentence, the indefiniteness is extended even further:

何回読んでもこの話は分らない。
No matter how many times I read this story, I still don't understand it.

何回も読んだのにこの話は分らない。
Although I have read this story many times, I still don't understand it.

父はいくら説明しても私の気持を分かってくれない。
However much I explain, my father never understands my feelings.

47.4 Some idiomatic uses of ～ても

どうしても今晩おとうさんに話さなきゃだめ。

The following is just a list of some useful phrases:

どうしても	at any cost, by all means
何としても	at any cost (risk), somehow or other
それにしても	but, still, nevertheless

それにしても今年は春が来るのが遅いですね。
And yet, spring is late in coming this year, you know.

何としてもこの実験は成功させたい。
I am determined to make this experiment successful.

47.5 Asking permission

だまっていてはいけないかしら。

You have met one way of asking permission in 41.7. This involved the patterns ～てもいいです and ～てもかまいませんか. Another way of doing this involves ～てはいけない set in the interrogative:

(a) ここに駐車(を)してもいいですか。 or
ここに駐車(を)しても かまいませんか。

(b) ここに駐車してはいけませんか。

(a) is a straightforward question: 'Is it all right if I park here?', but if you use (b), you are showing that your expectation of a negative answer is higher: 'Do I take it that it is prohibited to park here?' For sociological reasons you may find (b) used more in Japanese than you might expect from looking at its English equivalent.

Observe the following:

この報告書は明日書いてもいいですか。
Is it all right if I write this report tomorrow?

この報告書は明日までに書かなくてもいいですか。
Is it all right if I do not write this report by tomorrow?

この報告書は明日までに書かなくてはいけませんか。
Do I have to write this report by tomorrow?

この報告書は明日までに書かなければいけませんか。
Do I have to write this report by tomorrow?

クレジット・カードで払ってはいけませんか。
Can't I pay with a credit card?

どうしても教授からの許可をもらわなくてはいけませんか。
Do I really have to obtain permission from the professor?

47.6 わけではない

うそをつくわけではない。

This phrase literally means 'It is not a case of…', and it can also be found as わけでもない.

君一人が悪いわけではない。
lit: It is not the case that only you were wrong.
You were not the only one who was wrong.

参加したくないわけではありませんが、財政上ちょっと無理だと思います。
It is not that I don't want to participate, but I feel it's just not financially feasible.

組合側の要求が分からないわけでもないんですがね...。
It is not that I don't understand the Union's demands, but...

47.7 Commands

勉強しておきなさい。

Commands in Japanese are a combination of the conjunctive form of the verb plus the word なさい, which is the imperative form of the verb なさる, the respectful equivalent of する 'to do'. Commands of this type should only really be used with people you know very well indeed; their most common use is in fact by parents speaking to their children. They are certainly less polite than forms with 〜て下さい.

おふろに入りなさい。
Get in the bath!

ぐずぐずしていないでさっさと来なさい。
Stop messing around and come here quickly!

Note the following everyday formulae which use this pattern. You will probably have already met all of these in conversation, but they are listed here for convenience:

お帰りなさい。
Welcome back!

お休みなさい。
Sleep well.

ごめんなさい。
Please excuse me.

Key to conversation

Romanisation

Kuniko	Nē, o-niisan. Dō shiyō...
Tadashi	Dō shiyōtte ikinari iwarete mo, nani ga nan da ka sappari wakaranai ja nai ka. Dō shitan dai.
Kuniko	Sore ga ne... Jitsu wa sūgaku no shiken de shippai shichatte...
Tadashi	Ochita no ka.
Kuniko	Un...
Tadashi	Otōsan to okāsan ni wa mō hanashita no ka.
Kuniko	Ūun... Datte...
Tadashi	Chanto hanasanakucha dame da yo.
Kuniko	Datte, shinpai saseru dake desho.
Tadashi	Sonna koto o ittatte damatte iru wake ni wa ikanai ja nai ka. Shiken o hitotsu otoshitara sotsugyō dekinain daro.
Kuniko	Un. Demo asatte tsuishi ga aru no de, sore de mā mā no ten ga torereba sotsugyō wa daijōbu darōtte, tannin no sensei wa ossharun dakedo.
Tadashi	Sore de jishin wa aru no ka?
Kuniko	Zenzen. De mo un ga yokereba sanjutten gurai wa toreru ka mo shirenai to omou no.
Tadashi	Kuniko no sūgaku wa sonna ni hidoi no ka.
Kuniko	Datte, kirai nan desu mono.
Tadashi	Sūgaku wa chanto benkyō shi sae sureba dare demo ten ga toreru gakka da to omoun dakedo na.
Kuniko	Sonna koto nai wa yo. Ikura benkyō shitatte chittomo wakaru yō ni naranai wa.
Tadashi	Sonna mono ka nā.
Kuniko	O-niisan datte zuibun piano o renshū shita no ni chittomo jōzu ni naranakatta ja nai. Onaji koto yo. Hito sorezore muki fumuki ga arun da to omou wa.

Tadashi	Mā, sore wa atatte iru ka mo shirenai na.
Kuniko	Moshi tsuishi ga umaku itte sotsugyō dekiru yo dattara kono sūgaku no shiken no koto wa damatte ite wa ikenai kashira.
Tadashi	Uso o tsuite wa ikenai to omou kedo na.
Kuniko	Betsu ni uso o tsuku wake de wa nai desho. Dōshite mo konban otōsan ni hanasanakya dame.
Tadashi	Mā, ima sugu ni wa otōsan ya okāsan ni hanasanakute mo ii kara, sonna koto o shinpai suru yori sukoshi wa sono tsuishi no tame ni benkyō shite okinasai.
Kuniko	Arigatō. Kodomo no koro kara o-niisan wa itsumo watakushi no mikata ni natte kureta mono ne.
Tadashi	Sō iu wake de mo nain dakedo...

Translation

Kuniko	Well, Tadashi. What shall I do?
Tadashi	You ask me what to do all of a sudden, but I haven't got a clue what you're on about. What's wrong?
Kuniko	Well... Actually I've gone and done badly in my maths exam.
Tadashi	Have you failed?
Kuniko	Yes.
Tadashi	Have you mentioned it to father and mother?
Kuniko	No... Because...
Tadashi	You'll have to tell them you know.
Kuniko	But, it'll only get them worried.
Tadashi	You say that, but you can't just keep quiet about it can you? If you fail one exam you can't graduate, can you?
Kuniko	I know. But I've got a resit tomorrow and the form teacher said that if I got reasonable marks in that I'd be able to graduate.
Tadashi	So are you confident?
Kuniko	Absolutely not. But if I'm lucky I might get about 30.
Tadashi	Your maths that bad?
Kuniko	Well, I hate it.
Tadashi	Surely, maths is the kind of subject that anyone can pass as long as they study.
Kuniko	That's not true! No matter how hard I study I don't seem to understand a thing.
Tadashi	Really?

Kuniko	Look at you. You practised the piano a lot but never got any better. It's the same thing. Everyone has got strengths and weaknesses.
Tadashi	Well, I suppose your right.
Kuniko	If my resit goes well and I can graduate, do you think it would be wrong to say nothing about this exam?
Tadashi	I do think it would be wrong to lie.
Kuniko	It's not really lying at all. Do you think I ought to tell father this evening?
Tadashi	Well, you don't have to tell father and mother immediately, so rather than worrying about that why don't you do some preparation for that resit instead.
Kuniko	Thanks. You always were on my side, ever since we were children.
Tadashi	Well, I don't know about that…

Lesson 48

A conversation between John and Tadashi

ジョン	きのうの新聞に電気製品をつくっているある会社の組合が給料を二十二パーセント上げろと社長に迫ったという記事が出ていましたが、ちょっと要求し過ぎの感じがしませんか。
正	それはすごいなあ。
ジョン	日本の物価上昇率は今のところ五パーセント以下ですからね。
正	まあ、組合側としては自分達の要求がそのまま通るとは思っていないから、実際の目標よりは相当高い数字を出しているのだとは思いますけどね。
ジョン	それにしても必要以上に高い数を出すということは、労使間交渉が始まる前から会社側に悪い印象を与えることになるんじゃないでしょうか。
正	それはそうですね。でも労使関係というのは、もともとそうスムーズにいくものではないし、双方ともどこまで押せるか、どこで妥協すべきかということは案外よく分かっているんだと思いますよ。
ジョン	話し合いが平行線をたどったままだということもなくはないみたいですがね。
正	そう、時にはお互いがああしろ、こうしろと繰り返すばかりで、相手側の立場を理解しようなどという気が全くないように見えることもありますね。
ジョン	正君の病院でも組合運動はさかんですか。
正	ええ、かなり活発にやってますよ。一番大きな問題は看護婦さん達の給料なんですね。彼女達の仕事は内容からいっても勤務時間の上からも相当きついのに信じられないような低い給料で働かされているんですよ。
ジョン	同じ問題をかかえている国はたくさんあると思いますね。私も看護婦さんや病院の雑用をしている人達の収入はもっとよくするべきだと思います。

48.1 Expressing percentage

ある会社の組合が給料を二十二パーセント上げろと社長に迫った。

There are two ways of expressing percentage:

(a) using the loanword パーセント

15 per cent: 十五パーセント
83 per cent: 八十三パーセント

(b) using a combination of ～割 (わり), which means 10 per cent and ～分 (ぶ), which means 1 per cent.

15 per cent: 一割五分
83 per cent: 八割三分

この一年間で学生が習う漢字の数は漢字全体の数の十パーセント以下です。
The number of *kanji* the students will learn in this year is under 10 per cent of the whole.

48.2 Brusque commands

ある会社の組合が給料を二十二パーセント上げろと社長に迫った。

Brusque commands are formed by using yet another verb inflection, the imperative form.

	plain form	*meaning*	*imperative*	*negative imperative*
group I	ある	exist	(あれ)	---------
	歩く	walk	歩け	歩くな
	会う	meet	会え	会うな
	行く	go	行け	行くな
	入る	enter	入れ	入るな
	話す	talk	話せ	話すな
	言う	say	言え	言うな
	買う	buy	買え	買うな
	書く	write	書け	書くな
	聞く	listen, ask	聞け	聞くな
	待つ	wait	待て	待つな
	飲む	drink	飲め	飲むな
	乗る	ride	乗れ	乗るな
	使う	use	使え	使うな
	読む	read	読め	読むな
group II	いる	exist	いろ	いるな
	出る	go out	出ろ	出るな
	かける	hang	かけろ	かけるな
	見る	see	見ろ	見るな
	寝る	go to bed	寝ろ	寝るな
	起きる	get up	起きろ	起きるな
	食べる	eat	食べろ	食べるな
Irregular	来る	come	来(こ)い	来るな
	する	do	しろ or せよ	するな

There is not much to say about the above forms except that they must be used very sparingly indeed, as they are potentially extremely rude. So unless you actually intend to be rude, restrict usage. Study the following examples, however, where it is correct to use this form:

気を付けろ	Be careful!
恥を知れ	For shame!

しっかりしろ	Pull yourself together! Cheer up!
頑張れ	Hold out! Bear up! Keep it up!
英訳せよ	Translate into English!
和訳せよ	Translate into Japanese!

Note that the form せよ is the imperative form of the verb する in the classical language. Its use in the modern language lends the sentence a very stiff, and even at times martial, feel. Although this imperative form is only rarely used in direct speech for the reasons just stated, it is a good way of making a sentence concise in indirect speech. Study the following:

父:「早く来なさい」→ Father: 'Come quickly.'	早く来いと父が言った。 My father told me to come quickly.
先生:「この本を読みなさい」→ Teacher: 'Read this book.'	この本を読めと先生がおっしゃった。 Our teacher told us to read this book.

48.3 Negative commands

The above list included negative commands listed at the end. Note that these are produced quite differently from the positive. Simply take the plain citation form of the verb and add either な or its literary equivalent なかれ. This な is, of course, related to the negative ～ない form.

近寄るな	Don't come near!
あきらめるな	Don't give up!
バカにするな	Don't make fun of me! Don't belittle me!
いい気になるな	Don't get conceited!

48.4 まま

要求がそのまま通る。
平行線をたどったままだ。

ままis a noun which means 'the way it is', and is sometimes translated 'as is'. It signifies a given or unchanging state of affairs. You will find it used in a number of idiomatic ways. Study the following examples:

これは生のまま食べられます。
You can eat this raw.

分からないまま質問もしないでほっておいたんですか。
Did you just leave the matter there without understanding it and not even asking?

ままwill often be found with the preceding verb in the ～た form:

私は人から聞いたままを話しているだけですからそのつもりで聞いてください。
I'm just telling you exactly as I heard it from others; so please remember that as you listen.

むし暑いのでまどを開けたまま寝ます。
It's hot and sticky, so I'll go to sleep with the windows open (as they are).

48.5 Expression of duty with べき

どこで妥協すべきかということは

The word べき is added to the citation form of verbs and means 'should' or 'ought to'. It is in fact a descriptive verb from classical Japanese that remains in use today. With the common verb する be ready to find it in two forms: するべき or すべき; either is correct.

学生はまず第一に勉強するべきだ。
Students should, above all, work.

言うべきことははっきり言わなければならない。
You must say clearly what has to be said.

決める前に両親に相談すべきだ。
You should consult your parents before making a decision.

べき operates slightly differently, depending on whether the context is imperfective or perfective. When the context is imperfective, べき usually refers either to another's duty or to a general obligation. The sentence すぐに関係者に知らせるべきだ, for example, means 'You (or they) should inform those who are concerned straight away.' If you wanted to say 'I should inform those who are concerned straight away' you would have to say すぐに関係者に知らせなければならない. You may well be tempted to produce a sentence such as *私は行くべきだ for 'I should go', but this is not acceptable, at least not as a main sentence. However, べき can be used with the reference to the first person in subordinate sentences or in interrogative contexts.

父が病院へ行く時は私もついて行くべきでしょうか。
Should I accompany my father when he goes to hospital?

私が行くべきだと思いますがその日は都合がつかないので代わりの人に行ってもらいます。
I think I should go but that day is inconvenient for me so I shall get someone to go in my stead.

In a perfective context, however, べき can refer to first, second and third person without the above restriction. It also brings with it the nuance 'should have …but didn't'.

その案は具体的な計画をきちんと立ててから実行に移すべきでした。
That idea should have been put into practice only after we had drawn up proper concrete plans.

彼を批判する前にもう少し注意深く考えてみるべきでした。
I should have thought a little more carefully before criticising him.

48.6 ああしろ、こうしろ

ああしろ、こうしろと繰り返すばかりで

As you might expect there is a set of three such words: こう、ああ、そう. They mean 'in this way', 'in that way', etc. and unlike こんな can stand on their own as here directly before a verb. Another example:

そうしろよ。
Yes, do it!

48.7 ような

信じられないような低い給料

Refer back to 32.2 and the pattern ようだ, meaning 'seems'. When this phrase is found modifying a noun, as in this example, it becomes ような, very much like an adjectival noun. So here the literal sense is 'low wages, which seem unbelievable'.

まるで政治家のような人ですね。
He's just like a politician, isn't he!

彼女は皆から好かれるような性格だ。
She has the kind of character that appeals to everyone.

Key to conversation

Romanisation

Jon	Kinō no shinbun ni denki seihin o tsukutte iru aru kaisha no kumiai ga kyūryō o nijūni pāsento agero to shachō ni sematta to iu kiji ga dete imashita ga, chotto yōkyū shisugi no kanji ga shimasen ka.
Tadashi	Sore wa sugoi nā.
Jon	Nihon no bukka jōshōritsu wa ima no tokoro go pāsento ika desu kara ne.
Tadashi	Mā, kumiaigawa to shite wa jibuntachi no yōkyū ga sono mama tōru to wa omotte inai kara, jissai no mokuhyō yori wa sōtō takai sūji o dashite iru no da to wa omoimasu kedo ne.
Jon	Sore ni shite mo hitsuyō ijō ni takai kazu o dasu to iu koto wa rōshikan kōshō ga hajimaru mae kara kaishagawa ni warui inshō o ataeru koto ni narun ja nai deshō ka.
Tadashi	Sore wa sō desu ne. Demo rōshi kankei to iu no wa motomoto sō sumūzu ni iku mono de wa nai shi, sōhō tomo doko made oseru ka doko de dakyo subeki ka to iu koto wa angai yoku wakatte irun da to omoimasu yo.
Jon	Hanashiai ga heikōsen o tadotta mama da to iu koto mo naku wa nai mitai desu ga ne.
Tadashi	Sō, toki ni wa o-tagai ga ā shiro kō shiro to kurikaesu bakari de, aitegawa no tachiba o rikai shiyō nado to iu ki ga mattaku nai yō ni mieru koto mo arimasu ne.
Jon	Tadashi-kun no byōin de mo kumiai undō wa sakan desu ka.
Tadashi	Ē, kanari kappatsu ni yattemasu yo. Ichiban ōkina mondai wa kangofusan-tachi no kyūryō nan desu ne. Kanojo-tachi no shigoto wa naiyō kara itte mo kinmu jikan no ue kara mo sōtō kitsui no ni shinjirarenai yō na hikui kyūryō de hatarakasarete irun desu yo.
Jon	Onaji mondai o kakaete iru kuni wa takusan aru to omoimasu ne. Watakushi mo kangofu-san ya byōin no zatsuyō o shite iru hitotachi no shū'nyū wa motto yoku surubeki da to omoimasu.

Translation

John	There was an article in yesterday's newspaper about the union in a company that makes electrical goods that had been pressing their boss for a twenty-two per cent

	rise in pay; don't you think they're demanding too much?
Tadashi	That's pretty steep!
John	Because the rate of inflation in Japan at the moment is under 5 per cent.
Tadashi	Well, the union side doesn't believe that their demands will be accepted as it is, so they are undoubtedly presenting a figure much higher than their real target.
John	Even so, to present an unnecessarily high figure surely gives the employer's side a bad impression even before they start negotiating.
Tadashi	That's true. But labour relations never run very smoothly and I think both sides actually know quite well how far they can push and where they should compromise.
John	Mind you, that's not to say there aren't occasions when discussions never seem to converge.
Tadashi	Yes. Sometimes they just go at each other, 'do this' 'do that', and they never seem to want to even try and understand each other's position.
John	Do you have an active union movement at your hospital?
Tadashi	Yes, it's fairly active. The greatest problem is nurses' pay. Their work is pretty tough both in terms of what they do and their hours, and yet they are made to work for unbelievably low wages.
John	I think there are a lot of countries with the same problem. I agree that they ought to improve the pay of nurses and hospital orderlies.

Lesson 49

A telephone conversation between Mrs Yamakawa and Mrs Ōyama

山川　もしもし。
大山　もしもし、山川様でいらっしゃいますか。
山川　はい、さようでございますが。
大山　あのう…、大山でございますが。
山川　ああ、サウジアラビアに行っていらっしゃる大山さんの奥様でいらっしゃいますね。
大山　はい。さようでございます。
山川　御主人様はお元気でいらっしゃいますか。
大山　はい、おかげさまで。やっと新しい環境にも慣れてきたようでございます。実は私共も今月末にサウジの方へ出発することになりましたので、近いうちに一度御挨拶に伺いたいと思いまして。
山川　それは御丁寧にありがとうございます。もし御都合がよろしければ、今度の日曜の午後あたりいかがでしょうか。あいにく主人はまだもどっておりませんが、その日は一日家でゆっくりするようなことを申しておりましたから。
大山　せっかくのお休みの日におじゃまするようで申し訳ございませんが、それでは遠慮なく日曜日に伺わせていただきます。何時ごろがよろしいでしょうか。
山川　三時過ぎでしたら、いつでも結構でございます。
大山　それではそのころに。
山川　御出発の準備で何かと大変でいらっしゃいますでしょう。
大山　ええ、出来るだけ荷物は少なくするように心がけてはいるのですが、子供の本や薬などでずいぶん量が増えてしまいました。
山川　ヨーロッパやアメリカへ出かけるのとはちがいますものね。
大山　ええ、それと言葉の方が心配で…。
山川　御主人様は御出発前に、だいぶアラビア語を勉強していらっしゃったようですが。
大山　ええ、私もカセット・テープなどはいっしょに聞いたりいたしましたので少しは分かるはずなのですが、実際に人々の話

	しているのが聞きとれるかどうかは行ってみないと分かりません。
山川	そうですね。でもあまり御心配なさらなくてもきっと大丈夫だと思いますよ。
大山	まあ、あまり気にしても仕方のないことですから。お電話でとんだ長話をして失礼いたしました。それではまた日曜の午後に。
山川	お目にかかって、御主人様からのニュースなど聞かせていただくのを楽しみにしております。
大山	御主人様にもどうぞよろしくお伝えくださいませ。
山川	承知いたしました。それではまた、ごめん下さいませ。

49.1 でございます and でいらっしゃいます

> 山川様でいらっしゃいますか。
> さようでございます。
> 大山でございますが。

This is a revision section. You have already met both of these forms before. In 31.1 でございます was explained as a super-polite or 'deferential' form of the copula. The more polite you want to be, the more you will find yourself using this form. いらっしゃる, without the で, is the respectful equivalent of the verb いる 'be'. でいらっしゃる, however, is the form of the copula you must use when you are referring to the addressee or to someone connected with the addressee. Its use is therefore fairly restricted, but quite common in telephone conversations and the like, for obvious reasons. Note that for 大山 to say *山川様でございますか would be a mistake.

49.2 Honorific language, a synopsis

By now, you will have already met most of the ways Japanese produces either humble or respectful forms: what follows is essentially for reference. Please look back to specific sections for more details. The first distinction to keep in mind is that between *politeness* and *honorific language*. Politeness is governed by your attitude to the person you are addressing: you can be polite, neutral or rude, as the case may be. The most obvious way to achieve politeness is to keep your verbs in the 〜ます form and to use です as opposed to だ for the copula. Honorific language, on the other hand, is concerned with your attitude to the subject or topic of discourse, and this is achieved by either raising or lowering the status of the subject. Obviously there will be occasions when these two phenomena overlap: when, for instance, the addressee is also the subject of the sentence; but nevertheless the two concepts should be kept separate in your mind.

49.3 Forms expressing respect (by raising the subject)

(a) The prefix お + conjunctive form of the verb + になる (see 45.8). Note that a shorter form of the above can be obtained by replacing になる by a simple です:

お発ちです。
He is leaving.

お帰りですか。
Are you going home?

The honorific nature of this statement can be turned a notch higher by changing です to でいらっしゃいます.

いつお発ちでいらっしゃいますか。
When are you leaving?

(b) Alternatively, the passive form of the verb may also be used to indicate respect (see 32.1).

毛利さんは二、三日前に北海道へ移られました。
Mr Mōri moved to Hokkaidō a few days ago.

鈴木さんは息子さんの先生と話し合われてからこのことを決められました。
Mr Suzuki decided on this matter after having had a discussion with his son's teacher.

(c) Verbal nouns. Although verbal nouns can be used with the passive form, as in 先生が説明された 'the teacher explained', they are usually dealt with in a different fashion They take the prefix 御 (ご) and change する to なさる: 旅行する → 御旅行なさいます.

もう御注文なさいましたか。
Have you already ordered?

(d) The other group is of those verbs that have special honorific equivalents:

いる	いらっしゃる、おいでになる
行く、来る	いらっしゃる、おいでになる
着る	召す、お召しになる
くれる	下さる
見る	ごらんになる
死ぬ	亡くなる、お亡くなりになる
する	なさる
食べる	上がる、お上がりになる、召し上がる
言う	おっしゃる

NB: Remember that ～ます, which is not on the level of reference but of address, need not be used unless the speaker specifically wants or needs to show politeness to the second person; but if the second person is the subject, ～ます is normally obligatory. There will be occasions, however, when you will hear these forms being used both to and about the second person without the expected ～ます. This is a pattern found more widely among women than men, and conveys a feeling of respect combined with a friendly familiarity:

いっしょにいらっしゃらない。
Won't you please come along too?

You have seen the command forms of 来る and 見る, namely 来なさい and 見なさい respectively, in lesson 47. However, おいでなさい or いらっしゃい, and ごらんなさい are also commonly used. The command is considerably softened when such verbs that indicate respect are used.

こちらへいらっしゃい。いっしょにお茶を飲みましょう。
Come this way. Let's have some tea together.

49.4 Forms expressing humility (by lowering the subject)

(a) Formed by the prefix お + conjunctive form of the verb + します/いたします (see 26.2)

お食事の支度が出来ましたらお呼びいたします。
I will call you when the meal is ready.

(b) As with the respect forms, there are two groups of verbs which do not use this construction. One is verbal nouns: 説明する → 御説明します/いたします. Note however that a phrase like *御勉強いたします is not normally used. With all these verbs, the other person being shown respect should be involved in some way or other in the action. The implication is that something is being done 'for' someone else. If no other person is involved, as in the case of 勉強, an ordinary plain form is used.

どうぞこちらへ。工場の中を御案内いたします。
Please come this way, I will show you the factory.

旧友の大野さんを御紹介いたします。
I would like to introduce my old friend Ōno to you.

(c) The following have special humble equivalents:

いる	おる
行く、来る	参る、伺う
言う	申す, 申し上げる
する	いたす

もらう、飲む、食べる	いただく、ちょうだいする
見る	拝見する/いたす
見せる	お目にかける、ごらんにいれる、お見せする
会う	お目にかかる、お会いする
思う、知る	存じる、存じ上げる
かりる	拝借する
やる	上げる、差し上げる
聞く	伺う、承る

NB: The same comment made about respect forms applies here: ～ます is used when the speaker wishes to be polite to his interlocutor; it does not refer to anything within the world of the sentence as such.

49.5 Using causatives for requests

> 日曜日に伺わせていただきます。
> 聞かせていただくのを楽しみにしております。

The causative form (37.2) can often be used to make a request or a demand. As shown in the examples below, some of these expressions are not necessarily designed to express politeness, but there is an advantage in using the causative form to request something for oneself, because it implies the speaker's submission to the will of the person addressed. Such expressions often look very complicated, but they are in common use and should be mastered.

(a) Causative + ～てもらいます

Causative + ～ていただきます

This form is used to announce something one has already decided to do. One is not really asking for permission, merely being polite.

失礼させていただきます。
I will take my leave.
lit: I will receive the favour of your permitting me to be rude (and leave)

It can also be employed as an abrupt parting shot.

それではやめさせてもらいます。
Right then, I'll resign.

(b)

Causative	+	てくれ て下さい てもらいたい てほしい ていただきたい

Here a strong request or even demand is cast in the form of asking for a favour.

その件についてはしばらく考えさせて下さい。
Let me think over the matter for a while.

見合い結婚をするつもりはありません。好きな人と結婚させてもらいたいと思います。
I have no intention of accepting an arranged marriage. Let me marry someone I love.

49.6 出来るだけ

> 出来るだけ荷物は少なくするように

This phrase simply means 'as...as possible'

出来るだけ今日中に仕上げて下さい。
Try as hard as possible to finish this today.

出来るだけ早く来て下さい。
Come as soon as (as early as) possible.

49.7 Some idiomatic uses of ように

出来るだけ荷物は少なくするように

(a) Verb (imperfective) + ようにする, meaning 'to make it so that it becomes...'

道を広げて車が通れるようにしました。
We widened the path so that cars could go through.

この国立公園ではいろいろな設備を整えて一般の人々にも自然の価値が理解出来るようにするつもりです。
We intend to provide various facilities in this National Park so that ordinary people (too) can appreciate the value of nature.

(b) Verb (imperfective) + ようにしている, meaning 'I try to make it a rule that...'

手紙をもらったらすぐに返事を書くようにしている。
I try to reply as soon as I receive a letter.

酒は飲まないようにしている。
I try not to drink any alcohol.

cf. 酒は飲まないことにしている。
I have decided not to drink.

49.8 Idiomatic use of もの

ちがいますものね。

もの or もん can be used at the end of a sentence in this way in order to add a gesture of sympathy directed towards the listener.

彼が自殺したって本当ですか。
They say he's committed suicide; is it true?

うん、分からないもんだな。
Yes, you never know, do you?

49.9 はず

少しは分かるはずなのですが、

はず, a noun meaning 'expectation', usually found at the end of a clause or sentence in the form はずだ (です), expresses a state of general expectation that something will either occur or follow on naturally from something else.

札幌行きの特急はあと十分で出るはずです。
The limited express for Sapporo is due to leave in ten minutes.

義務教育を終えているのだから少なくとも新聞は読めるはずだ。
As he has completed his compulsory education, he should be able to read the newspapers at least.

あしたは祭日なので、学校は休みのはずです。
Tomorrow is a festival day, so there should be a holiday at school.

国子さんはもう十年以上もピアノを習っているのでかなり上手なはずですよ。
Kuniko has been practising the piano for more than ten years now, so you'd expect her to be fairly good.

Note that the English concept of 'expectation' can sometimes suggest intention, as in the sentence 'I expect I'll go to Japan this summer.' はず cannot be used if any element of intention or conscious planning is present. So to translate this as:

*私は今年の夏休みに日本へ行くはずです is wrong. はず refers to something that that is in a sense bound to occur. The sentence 今年彼は日本へ行くはずです is possible, but only if you are saying 'I have reason to believe that he is going to Japan this year.' It cannot mean 'He expects to go to Japan this year.'

49.10 かどうか

> 人々の話しているのが聞きとれるかどうかは
> 行ってみないと分かりません。

Reported questions of the form 'whether or not' are expressed by adding かどうか directly after a verb or a noun.

ロシア語は話せますか。
Can you speak Russian?

ロシア語が話せるかどうか聞いた。
I asked whether he could speak Russian.

明日六時半までに来られますか。
Can you come by six thirty tomorrow?

明日六時半までに来られるかどうか聞いた。
I asked whether she could come tomorrow by six thirty.

人類は進歩しているのかどうか分からない。
I am not sure whether mankind has been progressing or not.

その部屋は静かかどうか聞いて下さい。
Please ask whether that room is quiet or not.

この絵が本物かどうかは私には分かりません。
I cannot tell whether this picture is genuine or not.

As seen in this last example, の is sometimes inserted between the verb and かどうか. This addition of の tends to strengthen the sense of doubt but does not otherwise affect the meaning. Compare the following:

> 人類は進歩しているのか(進歩)していないのか分からない。
> I am not sure whether mankind has been progressing or not.
>
> 人類は進歩しているのか退歩しているのか分からない。
> I am not sure whether mankind has been progressing or regressing.

Key to conversation

Romanisation

Yamakawa	Moshi moshi.
Ōyama	Moshi moshi. Yamakawa-sama de irasshaimasu ka.
Yamakawa	Hai, sayō de gozaimasu ga.
Ōyama	Anō…Ōyama de gozaimasu ga.
Yamakawa	Ā, Sauji Arabia ni itte irassharu Ōyama-san no okusama de irasshaimasu ne.
Ōyama	Hai, sayō de gozaimasu.
Yamakawa	Go-shujin-sama wa o-genki de irasshaimasu ka.
Ōyama	Hai, o-kage sama de. Yatto atarashii kankyō ni mo narete kita yō de gozaimasu. Jitsu wa watakushidomo mo kongetsumatsu ni Sauji no hō e shuppatsu suru koto ni narimashita node, chikai uchi ni ichido go-aisatsu ni ukagaitai to omoimashite.
Yamakawa	Sore wa go-teinei ni arigatō gozaimasu. Moshi go-tsugō ga yoroshikereba kondo no nichiyō no gogo atari ikaga deshō ka. Ainiku shujin wa mada modotte orimasen ga, sono hi wa ichinichi ie de yukkuri suru yō na koto o mōshite orimashita kara.
Ōyama	Sekkaku no o-yasumi no hi ni o-jama suru yō de mōshiwake gozaimasen ga, sore de wa enryo naku nichiyōbi ni ukagawasete itadakimasu. Nanji goro ga yoroshii deshō ka.
Yamakawa	Sanji sugi deshitara, itsu demo kekkō de gozaimasu.
Ōyama	Sore de wa sono koro ni.
Yamakawa	Go-shuppatsu no junbi de nanika to taihen de irasshaimasu deshō.
Ōyama	Ē, dekiru dake nimotsu wa sukunaku suru yō ni kokorogakete wa iru no desu

	ga, kodomo no hon ya kusuri nado de zuibun ryō ga fuete shimaimashita.
Yamakawa	Yōroppa ya Amerika e dekakeru no to wa chigaimasu mono ne.
Ōyama	Ē, sore to kotoba no hō ga shinpai de...
Yamakawa	Go-shujin-sama wa go-shuppatsu mae ni daibu Arabiago o benkyō shite irasshatta yō desu ga.
Ōyama	Ē, watakushi mo kasetto tēpu nado wa issho ni kiitari shimashita no de sukoshi wa wakaru hazu na no desu ga, jissai ni hitobito no hanashite iru no ga kikitoreru ka dō ka wa itte minai to wakarimasen.
Yamakawa	Sō desu ne. De mo amari go-shinpai nasaranakute mo kitto daijōbu da to omoimasu yo.
Ōyama	Mā, amari ki ni shite mo shikata no nai koto desu kara. O-denwa de tonda nagabanashi o shite shitsurei itashimashita. Sore de wa mata nichiyō no gogo ni.
Yamakawa	O-me ni kakatte, go-shujin-sama kara no nyūsu nado kikasete itadaku no o tanoshimi ni shite orimasu.
Ōyama	Go-shujin-sama ni mo dōzo yoroshiku o-tsutae kudasaimase.
Yamakawa	Shōchi itashimashita. Sore de wa mata gomen kudasaimase.

Translation

Yamakawa	Hello.
Ōyama	Hello. Is that the Yamakawas?
Yamakawa	Yes, that's correct.
Ōyama	Ah, this is Ōyama speaking.
Yamakawa	Oh, Mrs Ōyama. Your husband went to Saudi Arabia?
Ōyama	Yes, that's right.
Yamakawa	Is he well?
Ōyama	Yes, thank you. It seems he's finally getting used to the new environment. Actually it's been decided that we are to go out there at the end of the month, so I thought about coming to pay my respects soon.
Yamakawa	How kind of you. If it suits you, how about sometime this Sunday afternoon? Unfortunately my husband is not back yet, but he did say he'd be pottering around the house that day.
Ōyama	Well I'm sorry to interrupt you on the one free day you have, but we'll take you at your word and come on Sunday. What time would be most convenient?
Yamakawa	Any time after three in the afternoon.

Ōyama	We shall see you then, then.
Yamakawa	One way or another, you must be very busy before your departure.
Ōyama	Yes, I'm trying to keep down the amount of luggage as far as possible, but what with the children's books, medicine and the like there's an awful lot of it.
Yamakawa	It's rather different from when you go to Europe or America, isn't it?
Ōyama	Yes, and I'm worried about the language.
Yamakawa	Your husband studied quite a lot of Arabic before he left, didn't he?
Ōyama	Yes, and I listened to the cassette tapes with him so I should understand a little, but I don't know whether I will be able to catch what people are actually saying until I get there.
Yamakawa	Yes, I know. But I'm sure you'll be all right. No need to worry.
Ōyama	Well, there's no point in worrying too much I suppose. I'm sorry to have taken up so much of your time on the telephone. Until next Sunday afternoon then.
Yamakawa	I look forward to seeing you and hearing how your husband is getting on.
Ōyama	Please give my regards to Mr Yamakawa.
Yamakawa	I will indeed. Looking forward to it. Goodbye.

Lesson 50

At Narita Airport. Mr and Mrs Yamakawa are seeing off Kuniko who is leaving for Germany.

信子	途中、道路が混むかもしれないと思ってたっぷり時間をとって来たら、早く来過ぎちゃったわね。
国子	そうね。私の便はまだチェック・インが始まってないみたい。
一	じゃあ、荷物を一時預けに預けて、ゆっくりお茶でも飲もうか。
国子	たった一時間ぐらいでも預かってくれるかしら。
一	そりゃあ、もちろん預かってくれるけど、丁度あそこに手押し車があるから、あれに乗せて持って行こうか。
信子	その方がかえって面倒が少ないと思いますわ。

They sit in a coffee shop.

信子	国ちゃん、ピアノを習い始めたころのこと覚えてる。
国子	うん、あのころは学校から帰って来るとすぐに友達と外に遊びに行きたかったのに、おかあさんに一日一時間必ずピアノの練習をさせられたわね。
信子	そうよ。ピアノをひいていてもちっとも楽しそうじゃなかったから、無理に続けさせても意味がないかしらと思っていたら、急に熱心にひくようになったわね。
国子	そうなの。いやいやながら練習しているうちに何だかすごく楽しくなって…。
一	まあ、これからどのくらい上手になるかは国子の努力と才能次第だな。
国子	あんまりこわい先生じゃないといいけれど…。
一	何だか心細そうな顔をしているじゃないか。
国子	今までの先生が厳しいけれどとてもいい方だったから。
信子	きっと大丈夫ですよ。そんなに気の弱いことを言うのはあなたらしくないわ。それより忘れ物はないのね。
国子	何度も確かめたから大丈夫。あら、手帳を忘れてきたかしら。ハンド・バッグのポケットに入れたつもりだけど…。

信子	困ったわね。あちらでお世話になる方の住所なんかが書いてあるんでしょ。
国子	あった、あった。ポケットが二つあるから見えなかっただけ。
一	そろそろ時間じゃないかな。国子のフライトは南ウィングからだね。
国子	そう。そろそろ行った方がいいかもしれない。
一	その便はモスクワ経由だったっけ、それとも北回りのアンカレッジ経由。
国子	ううん。フランクフルトまでの直行便よ。そこで乗り換えてケルンまでいかなきゃならないけれど。
一	そうか、それじゃあ体にはよく気を付けて頑張るんだぞ。
国子	はい。
信子	着いたらすぐに電話をするんですよ。あなたからの連絡が入り次第、残りの荷物を出しますからね。
国子	はい、分かりました。それじゃあ、行って参ります。
一	気をつけて行ってきなさい。
信子	いってらっしゃい。

50.1 預ける and 預かる

> 一時預けに預けて
> 一時間ぐらいでも預かってくれるかしら。

These verbs look at first sight like a transitive/intransitive pair of the kind we described in 42.2, 43.7 and 43.10, but this is not in fact the case. 預ける means 'entrust something into the custody of another'; 預かる means 'have custody of something'. Both verbs therefore take an object and are transitive. The decision as to which to use will depend on the nature of the subject. Take care to study this pair carefully.

50.2 そりゃあ

そりゃあ、もちろん預かってくれるけど

You have had plenty examples of words being shortened or contracted in speech. Here is another example. そりゃあ is a contraction of それは 'well then'.

50.3 Use of かえって

その方がかえって面倒が少ないと思いますわ。

This word is best treated as an adverb meaning 'on the contrary' or 'contrary to expectations'.

この薬を飲んだらかえって頭痛がひどくなった。
After I took this medicine, my headache in fact got worse.

お金もうけをしようと思って投資をしたのにかえって損をしてしまった。
I thought I'd make a profit so I invested in it, but in fact I came out badly.

50.4 The passive causative

おかあさんに一日一時間必ずピアノの練習をさせられたわね。

The causative can in turn be inflected into the passive, to produce what is known as the passive causative: 練習させる inflects to 練習させられる, which means 'to be forced to practise'.

江戸時代には多くのキリシタンが信仰を捨てさせられた。
During the Edo Period many Christians were forced to renounce their beliefs.

第二次大戦が終わるまでは、日本の小学校の児童は天皇の名前を全部暗記させられた。
Before the end of the Second World War, Japanese children in primary school were made to memorise all the names of the emperors.

50.5 More on ように

急に熱心にひくようになったわね。

Verb (imperfective) + ようになった means 'It has come to be that...'

年のせいか このごろ朝早く目が覚めるようになった。
Perhaps due to my age, I wake up early in the morning these days.

人生は公平ではないということが分かるようになった。
I have come to accept that life is not fair.

Note that this form ようになる cannot be used with a negative verb. To say something like 'Since I had an operation last year I cannot drink as I did before.' you must use the pattern neg. + なくなる. So the Japanese version would be:

去年手術を受けてからは昔のようにはお酒が飲めなくなった.

The last part of this *cannot* be expressed as * 飲めないようになった.

50.6 More on うちに

練習しているうちに何だかすごく楽しくなって...。

This pattern was introduced in 46.7. うちに is also used when an uncontrollable event occurs to the speaker while he or she is doing something.

こたつに入ってウトウトしているうちに本当に眠ってしまった。
Nodding off in the *kotatsu* I actually fell asleep.

その小説を読み始めた時は眠くて仕方がなかったが読んでいるうちにおもしろくてすっかり目が覚めてしまった。
When I started reading that novel I was feeling terribly sleepy, but as I read further it got so interesting that I became fully awake.

50.7 ながら

いやいやながら

In 23.4 we introduced the word ながら. There are occasions when it follows not the conjunctive form of a verb but a noun with no intervening particle. 残念ながら '...I'm afraid' is the commonest of these phrases.

このカメラは小型ながらよく写る。
This camera may be small, but it takes good pictures.

Here we have something similar, although いやいや can hardly be described as a noun. Treat it as an idiom meaning 'reluctantly' or 'against one's will'.

50.8 Uses of 次第 (しだい)

国子の努力と才能次第だな。 あなたからの連絡が入り次第、残りの荷物を出しますからね。

(a) Noun + 次第 means 'depending on'

すべては君の決心次第だ。
It all depends on your decision.

行くか行かないかはお天気次第です。
Whether I go or not depends on the weather.

(b) Conjunctive + 次第 means 'as soon as…'

成田に着き次第連絡します。
I will get in touch with you as soon as I arrive at Narita.

結果が出次第お知らせします。
As soon as the results come out, I will let you know.

出来次第お届けします。
As soon as it is ready, I will deliver it to you.

As you can see in the examples above, 次第 only refers to events in the future. When you want to translate a sentence like 'He started shouting as soon as he came into the room', you will have to use a different pattern, for example:

彼は部屋に入ってくるとすぐにどなり出した。

(c) 次第に as an adverb meaning 'gradually, by degrees'

関東地方では午後から次第に風雨が強まるでしょう。
In the Kantō area, the wind and rain will gradually become stronger from the afternoon onwards.

人々の顔には次第に絶望の色が濃くなっていった。
Gradually the shade of despair became deeper on people's faces.

50.9 More on らしい

あなたらしくないわ。

An extended use of noun + らしい brings with it the meaning of 'typical of' or 'as befits'.

いかにも美智子さんらしい心づかいですね。
Such thoughtfulness is typical of Michiko.

その水色のワンピースはとても夏らしいですね。
That light-blue dress is very summery.

警察官は私生活の上でも警官らしく行動する必要があると思いますか。
Do you think it is necessary for a policeman to behave like a policeman even in his private life?

50.10 つもり after the perfective

ハンド・バッグのポケットに入れたつもりだけど…。

We met つもり in 21.5. When this word is used after the perfective form of a verb it means 'I'm sure that I…' or 'I certainly intended to…, but…'

かぎは確かにここに置いたつもりなんですが...
I am *sure* I left the key here, but…

つもり can also be used with reference to the third person, but then it means something rather different.

あの子はまだ十歳なのにもう大人のつもりだ。
That child is still only ten years old, but he already thinks he's an adult.

父はまだ若いつもりだ。
Father thinks he's still young.

Key to conversation

Romanisation

Nobuko	Tochū, dōro ga komu ka mo shirenai to omotte tappuri jikan o totte kitara, hayaku kisugichatta wa ne.
Kuniko	Sō ne. Watakushi no bin wa mada chekkuin ga hajimattenai mitai.
Hajime	Jā, nimotsu o ichijiazuke ni azukete, yukkuri o-cha de mo nomō ka.
Kuniko	Tatta ichijikan gurai de mo azakatte kureru kashira.
Hajime	Soryā, mochiron azukatte kureru kedo, chōdo asoko ni teoshiguruma ga aru kara, are ni nosete motte ikō ka.
Nobuko	Sono hō ga kaette mendō ga sukunai to omoimasu wa.
Nobuko	Kuni-chan, piano o naraihajimeta koro no koto oboeteru.
Kuniko	Un, ano koro wa gakkō kara kaette kuru to sugu ni tomodachi to soto ni asobi ni ikitakatta no ni, okāsan ni ichinichi ichijikan kanarazu piano no renshū o saserareta wa ne.
Nobuko	Sō yo. Piano o hiite ite mo chittomo tanoshisō ja nakatta kara, muri ni tsuzukesasete mo imi ga nai kashira to omotte itara, kyū ni nesshin ni hiku yō ni natta wa ne.
Kuniko	Sō na no. Iyaiya-nagara renshū shite iru uchi ni nan da ka sugoku tanoshiku natte.
Hajime	Mā, kore kara dono kurai jōzu ni naru ka wa Kuniko no doryoku to sainō shidai da na.
Kuniko	Anmari kowai sensei ja nai to ii keredo...
Hajime	Nan da ka kokorobososō na kao o shite iru ja nai ka.
Kuniko	Ima made no sensei ga kibishii keredo totemo ii kata datta kara.
Nobuko	Kitto daijōbu desu yo. Sonna ni ki no yowai koto o iu no wa anata rashikunai wa. Sore yori wasuremono wa nai no ne.
Kuniko	Nando mo tashikameta kara daijōbu. Ara, techō o wasurete kita kashira. Handobaggu no poketto ni ireta tsumori dakedo...

Nobuko	Komatta wa ne. Achira de o-sewa ni naru kata no jūsho nanka ga kaite arun desho.
Kuniko	Atta, atta. Poketto ga futatsu aru kara mienakkata dake.
Hajime	Sorosoro jikan ja nai ka na. Kuniko no furaito wa minami uingu kara da ne.
Kuniko	Sō. Mō itta hō ga ii ka mo shirenai.
Hajime	Sono bin wa Mosukuwa keiyū dattakke, sore tomo kitamawari no Ankarejji keiyū.
Kuniko	Ūun. Furankufuruto made no chokkōbin yo. Soko de norikaete Kerun made ikanakya naranai keredo.
Hajime	Sō ka. Sore jā karada ni wa yoku ki o tsukete ganbarun da zo.
Kuniko	Hai.
Nobuko	Tsuitara sugu ni denwa o surun desu yo. Anata kara no renraku ga hairi shidai nokori no nimotsu o dashimasu kara ne.
Kuniko	Hai, wakarimashita. Sore jā, itte mairimasu.
Hajime	Ki o tsukete itte kinasai.
Nobuko	Itte irasshai.

Translation

Nobuko	We left plenty of time because we were worried about possible heavy traffic on the way, and now we seem to have arrived too early.
Kuniko	Yes. They don't seem to have started check-in for my flight yet.
Hajime	Well then, why don't we put the bags in the temporary left-luggage and have a nice cup of tea?
Kuniko	But will they take it for only an hour?
Hajime	I'm sure they will, but look, there's a trolley over there; why don't we put it on that?
Nobuko	Yes, I think that would actually be less trouble.

Nobuko	Kuni-chan, do you remember when you first started practising the piano?
Kuniko	Yes, all I wanted to do when I came home from school was to go outside and play with my friends, but you made me practise the piano at least one hour a day.
Nobuko	Yes. Even when you were playing, you didn't seem to be enjoying it in the slightest and I was feeling that perhaps there was no sense in forcing you to carry on. Then suddenly you started playing eagerly.

Kuniko	Yes, I remember. There I was, practising most reluctantly, when somehow I began to enjoy it tremendously.
Hajime	Well, how well you do from now on is entirely up to your effort and your talents.
Kuniko	I do hope my teacher isn't too forbidding.
Hajime	Somehow, you look a little down.
Kuniko	Well, the teacher I have had up to now may have been strict but he was very kind...
Nobuko	I'm sure it'll be all right. It's not like you to say such faint-hearted things. Now you haven't forgotten anything, have you?
Kuniko	No it's all right; I've checked so often. Oh! Have I forgotten my diary? I'm sure I put it in the pocket of my handbag.
Nobuko	Oh dear! It had the addresses of people who might be of help over there, didn't it?
Kuniko	Oh, here it is. Here it is. There are two pockets and I couldn't see it, that's all.
Hajime	I think it's about time. Your flight leaves from the South Wing doesn't it?
Kuniko	Yes. Perhaps we should be getting ready.
Hajime	Was it via Moscow or via Anchorage on the northern route?
Kuniko	No, no. It's a direct flight to Frankfurt. Then I've got to change there for Cologne.
Hajime	Ah. Well, take care of yourself and work hard.
Kuniko	Yes, father.
Nobuko	You'll telephone us as soon as you arrive? We'll send the rest of the luggage as soon as we hear from you.
Kuniko	All right. Well then, I'll be off.
Hajime	Take care of yourself.
Nobuko	Take care.

Lesson 51

Tadashi talks to Marie.

正	今日は。
マリー	今日は、正さん。この間はどうも。
正	どういたしまして。マリーさん、今度の土曜日にうちでジョンの送別会をしますから是非来て下さいね。
マリー	そう言えばジョンさんの出発ももうすぐね。きっと忙しくしているでしょう。
正	昨日電話で話した時には、しなければならないことがあり過ぎて何から手をつけたらいいのか分からないって言ってました。
マリー	そうでしょうね。
正	それに荷造りをするのに思ったよりずっと時間がかかると言っていました。
マリー	そうなのよ。引っ越しをした時のことを思い出すわ。
正	あの時はマリーさん、本当に大変でしたね。
マリー	ええ。私達三人でよくいっしょに食事をしたり、映画を見に行ったりしたから、彼がいなくなるとさびしくなるわね。
正	そうなんだ。僕の場合はイギリスに留学していた時にもジョンやジョンの御両親にはずい分お世話になったし、帰国したら今度は彼の方が日本へ来ることになったのでもう長い付き合いだから。
マリー	そうね。それで送別会は何時から。
正	ジョンの友達でその日も仕事という人が何人かいるので、みんなが来られるように六時ごろからにしようと思ってるんだけど。どうかな。
マリー	私の方はその日は何も予定がないから、何時からでも。何かお手伝いすることがあるかしら。
正	母に聞いてみるけど、最後だからちゃんとした日本料理をつくるんだって張り切っていたから大丈夫だと思う。
マリー	もし私でもお役に立つようだったら言って下さいね。早目に行きますから。
正	ありがとう。母に伝えておきます。ところでこの間貸した本、

	もう読み終りましたか。
マリー	ええ、あの晩アパートにもどってすぐに読み始めたら、おもしろくておもしろくて、とうとうおしまいまで一気に読んでしまいました。
正	それはよかった。ああいう歴史小説というのはその時代のことをちょっとでも知っているとすごくおもしろいもんですね。病院の友達で一人読みたいと言っている人がいるので、土曜日にうちに来る時に持ってきてくれますか。
マリー	今日も持ってこようと思ってつくえの上に出しておいたのに忘れてきてしまいました。ごめんなさいね。手帳にちゃんとメモしておきます。このごろボンヤリしているのか、どうももの忘れをしがちで困っているんですよ。
正	そんな年寄りくさいことは言わないで下さいよ。だれだって忘れ物はしますよ。
マリー	別に、年だと思っているわけではないんですけど。もしかしたら少し仕事をつめてやり過ぎて疲れているのかもしれません。
正	そんなにつめてやっているんですか。
マリー	ええ、昼間は大学へ行っていて時間がないんです。それでほん訳の仕事にかかるのが夜うちに帰ってからだから、つい一時、二時までやってしまうことになって…。
正	それじゃあ疲れていて忘れ物もするわけだ。気をつけて下さいね。
マリー	ええ、ありがとう。土曜日には必ず持っていきますから。じゃあ、又その時に。
正	僕の方は特に急いでいるわけじゃありませんからそんなに気にしないで下さい。じゃあ、土曜の六時ごろ。お願いすることがあったら、母が直接お電話するかもしれません。
マリー	はい、分かりました。お待ちしてます。

51.1 忙しくしている

きっと忙しくしているでしょう。

At first sight this looks as though it breaks the rule that stative verbs (and descriptive verbs are normally stative) do not take 〜ている. Normally for 'he must be busy' you would say きっと忙しいでしょう. What is happening in the example in the box is that a dynamic verb has been created by adding する to the adverbial form of the stative 忙しい. This dynamic verb has then been made stative again with 〜ている. The effect is to stress the degree of activity: 'He must be in a constant state of preparation.' Study a few more examples of this transformation with する:

お酒の量を少なくしています。
I have cut down on the amount of sake.

私は熱いおふろが好きなので、もう少しお湯を熱くして下さいませんか。
I like hot baths, so would you make the water a little hotter please?

あなたがいなくて御両親は (お) さびしくしていらっしゃるでしょう。
With you away, your parents must be missing you.

However, not all descriptive verbs will lend themselves to this transformation. Neither * 悲しくしている nor * 嬉しくしている is acceptable.

51.2 Expressions of purpose with のに

> 荷造りをするのに思ったよりずっと時間がかかる。

To express the concept of 'in order to…' you can use the particle cluster のに, which normally follows verbs in the imperfective. In this construction の is acting in its role as nominaliser.

漢字を三十覚えるのに二時間もかかった。
It took me two hours to learn thirty *kanji*.

東京で生活するのに一ヶ月最低いくら必要ですか。
What do you need minimum per month to live in Tōkyō?

おすしをつくるのには新鮮な魚が要る。
To make *sushi*, you need fresh fish.

Make sure you understand the difference between this use of のに and the のに that signifies 'although' (see 38.1).

七時までに来るように言ったのに弟はまだ来ない。
Although I told my brother to come by seven, he hasn't come yet.

51.3 The difference between のに and ため

Look back to 21.7 to refresh your memory about ために. Sometimes it is possible to replace のに with ために.

疲れをとるのには睡眠が一番大切だ。
To rid oneself of fatigue, sleep is most important.

疲れをとるためには睡眠が一番大切だ。
To rid yourself of fatigue, you must sleep.

There are many occasions, however, when のに and ために are definitely not interchangeable. The general rule here is that if the verb in the main clause is stative then you should use のに; if the verb in the main clause is dynamic then you should use ために. Study the following. (a) is correct but (b) is incorrect because it violates this rule. Both (c) and (d) describe states and therefore demand のに.

(a) ピラミッドを見るためにエジプトへ行った。
I went to Egypt to see the Pyramids.

(b) * ピラミッドを見るのにエジプトへ行った。
I went to Egypt to see the Pyramids.

(c) ピラミッドを見るのに四時間もかかった。
It took me four hours to see the Pyramids.

(d) もう十時半ですから彼に電話するのにはちょっと遅過ぎますね。
It's already ten thirty so it's a bit late to ring him.

51.4 More on ように.

みんなが来られるように六時ごろからにしようと思っている。

The pattern verb (imperfective) + ように means 'so as to...'

遅れないように早目に家を出た。
So as not to be late, I left home in good time.

両親ががっかりしないようにいい成績をとりたいと思います。
I would like to get good marks so that my parents won't be disappointed.

51.5 ようだったら/ようならば

もし私でもお役に立つようだったら言って下さいね。

This means 'if it turns out that...' or 'if it looks as though...'

気になるようだったらお医者さんに診てもらったらどうですか。
If it turns out that you feel worried about it, then how about having a doctor look at you?

課長が出席出来ないようならば私が代わりに行きます。
If it looks as though the boss can't be present, then I'll go instead.

51.6 Repetition of phrases

おもしろくておもしろくて、

As you might expect, this kind of repetition is one way of stressing something. Here it means 'it was so interesting (I couldn't put it down)'.

かわいがっていた犬が死んだ時は悲しくて悲しくて一日中泣いていました。
When the dog that I had loved died, I was so dreadfully sad that I cried all day.

小学校のころ、遠足の前の晩は嬉しくて嬉しくて眠れませんでした。
At junior school the night before our school trips, we were so thrilled we couldn't sleep.

51.7 Conjunctive form of verb + ～がちだ/がちです

どうももの忘れをしがちで

This pattern means 'to tend to...' or to have a habit of...'

一度かぜをひくと長引きがちだ。
Once I catch a cold, it tends to drag on.

このごろ疲れているのかつまらないことですぐイライラしがちです。
Perhaps because I am tired these days I tend to become easily irritated by trifling matters.

Sentences with ～がち usually have neutral or negative implications. So you can say:

忙しい時には面倒な事が起こりがちだ。
It's when one is busy that difficulties are liable to occur.

but one does not say:

*嬉しい事が起こりがちだ。
Joyful things tend to happen.

51.8 わけだ

それじゃあ疲れていて忘れ物もするわけだ。

わけだ at the end of a sentence has the meaning 'It is only to be expected that…'

そんなことを言ったのなら彼がおこったわけだ。
No wonder he got angry if you said such a thing.

この事件は国内ではずいぶん騒がれたけど君は去年外国に行っていたのなら知らないわけだ。
There was a tremendous row here about that business, but if you were abroad all last year then no wonder you don't know about it.

Key to conversation

Romanisation

Tadashi　Konnichi wa
Marī　Konnichi wa Tadashi-san. Kono aida wa dōmo.

Tadashi	Dō itashimashite. Marī-san, kondo no doyōbi ni uchi de Jon no sōbetsukai o shimasu kara zehi kite kudasai ne.
Marī	Sō ieba Jon-san no shuppatsu mo mō sugu ne. Kitto isogashiku shite iru deshō.
Tadashi	Kinō denwa de hanashita toki ni wa shinakereba naranai koto ga arisugite nani kara te o tsuketara ii no ka wakaranaitte ittemashita.
Marī	Sō deshō ne.
Tadashi	Sore ni nizukuri o suru no ni omotta yori zutto jikan ga kakaru to itte imashita.
Marī	Sō na no yo. Hikkoshi o shita toki no koto o omoidasu wa.
Tadashi	Ano toki wa Marī-san hontō ni taihen deshita ne.
Marī	Ē. Watakushitachi sannin de yoku issho ni shokuji o shitari, eiga o mi ni ittari shita kara, kare ga inakunaru to sabishiku naru wa ne.
Tadashi	Sō nan da. Boku no baai wa Igirisu ni ryūgaku shite ita toki ni mo Jon ya Jon no go-ryōshin ni wa zuibun o-sewa ni natta shi, kikoku shitara kondo wa kare no hō ga Nihon e kuru koto ni natta no de mō nagai tsukiai dakara.
Marī	Sō ne. Sore de sōbetsukai wa nanji kara.
Tadashi	Jon no tomodachi de sono hi mo shigoto to iu hito ga nannin ka iru no de, minna ga korareru yō ni rokuji goro kara ni shiyō to omotterun dakedo. Dō ka na.
Marī	Watakushi no hō wa sono hi wa nani mo yotei ga nai kara, nanji kara demo. Nanika o-tetsudai suru koto ga aru kashira.
Tadashi	Haha ni kiite miru kedo, saigo da kara chanto shita Nihon ryōri o tsukurun datte harikitte ita kara daijōbu da to omou.
Marī	Moshi watakushi de mo o-yaku ni tatsu yō dattara itte kudasai ne. Hayame ni ikimasu kara.
Tadashi	Arigatō. Haha ni tsutaete okimasu. Tokoro de kono aida kashita hon, mō yomiowarimashita ka.
Marī	Ē, ano ban apāto ni modotte sugu ni yomihajimetara, omoshirokute omoshirokute, tōtō o-shimai made ikki ni yonde shimaimashita.
Tadashi	Sore wa yokatta. Ā iu rekishi shōsetsu to iu no wa sono jidai no koto o chotto de mo shitte iru to sugoku omoshiroi mon desu ne. Byōin no tomodachi de hitori yomitai to itte iru hito ga iru no de, doyōbi ni uchi ni kuru toki ni motte kite kuremasu ka.
Marī	Kyō mo motte koyō to omotte tsukue no ue ni dashite oita no ni wasurete shimaimashita. Gomen nasai ne. Techō ni chanto memo shite okimasu. Kono goro bonyari shite iru no ka, dōmo monowasure o shigachi de komatte irun desu yo.
Tadashi	Sonna toshiyori kusai koto wa iwanaide kudasai yo. Dare datte wasuremono wa

	shimasu yo.
Marī	Betsu ni toshi da to omotte iru wake de wa nain desu kedo. Moshi ka shitara sukoshi shigoto o tsumete yarisugite tsukarete iru no ka mo shiremasen.
Tadashi	Sonna ni tsumete yatte irun desu ka.
Marī	Ē, hiruma wa daigaku e itte ite jikan ga nain desu. Sore de hon'yaku no shigoto ni kakaru no ga yoru uchi ni kaette kara da kara, tsui ichiji niji made yatte shimau koto ni natte...
Tadashi	Sore jā tsukarete ite wasuremono mo suru wake da. Ki o tsukete kudasai ne.
Marī	Ē, arigatō. Doyōbi ni wa kanarazu motte ikimasu kara. Jā, mata sono toki ni.
Tadashi	Boku no hō wa toku ni isoide iru wake ja arimasen kara sonna ni ki ni shinaide kudasai. Jā, doyō no rokuji goro. O-negai suru koto ga attara haha ga chokusetsu o-denwa suru ka mo shiremasen.
Marī	Hai, wakarimashita. O-machi shitemasu.

Translation

Tadashi	Hello.
Marie	Hello Tadashi. Thanks for the other day.
Tadashi	My pleasure. Marie, do please come to my house on Saturday for John's farewell party.
Marie	Come to think of it, John's off soon isn't he? He must be terribly busy.
Tadashi	Yesterday when I talked to him on the phone, he said he had so much that had to be done, he didn't know where to start.
Marie	I'm not surprised.
Tadashi	He also said that it was taking him much longer than he had thought to pack up all his things.
Marie	Well yes. I remember what it was like when I moved.
Tadashi	Yes, you had quite a time of it then, didn't you?
Marie	Yes. The three of us have eaten together and gone to the pictures together so often that we'll miss him when he goes.
Tadashi	You're right. In my case both he and his parents were a great help to me while I was studying in England and then after I came back, it so happened that John himself came to Japan; we've known each other for a long time.
Marie	Yes. So what time is the party?
Tadashi	A number of his friends are working that day so I thought we'd make it about six

	so everyone could be there. What do you think?
Marie	I don't have any plans that day, so any time's all right for me. Is there anything I can help with?
Tadashi	I'll ask mother but I don't think so: since it's John's last time, she's getting herself ready to make him some proper Japanese food.
Marie	If I can be of any help, please say. I can come early.
Tadashi	Thanks. I'll tell her. By the way, have you finished that book I lent you the other day?
Marie	Yes. That evening I started it as soon as I got back to my flat, and I got so involved that I read it all, right to the end in one sitting.
Tadashi	Oh good. If you know even a little bit about the period concerned, those historical novels can be really interesting, can't they? One of my friends at the hospital said he would like to read it, so could you bring it with you when you come on Saturday?
Marie	I was going to bring it today and had put it ready on the desk, but I went and forgot it. Do forgive me. I'll make a note in my diary. I don't know whether it's because I'm getting absent-minded recently but I do seem to be forgetting things a lot. It's very annoying.
Tadashi	Don't go on like that! You sound like an old woman! Everyone forgets things.
Marie	I'm not saying it's got anything to do with old age! Perhaps I'm just tired out trying to do too much.
Tadashi	Are you under that much pressure?
Marie	Yes. I don't have any time during the day because I'm at the University, so I start my translation work when I get home in the evening. And I end up working through to about one or two o'clock.
Tadashi	Then it's hardly surprising you're tired and tend to forget things! Take care of yourself.
Marie	I will. Thanks. I'll make sure I bring the book on Saturday. Well, until then.
Tadashi	I'm not in that much of a hurry for it, so don't worry about it too much. OK. See you on Saturday about six. If there's anything we want you to do, mother will probably ring you herself.
Marie	Right. I'll be ready.

Lesson 52

A letter from John to Mr and Mrs Yamakawa in printed form

皆様その後お変わりありませんか。十日前に東京を発ってアメリカへ渡り、そこで大学時代の友達に会ったり、いとこを訪ねたりして一週間ほど過ごしました。イギリスへはおとといもどってきたばかりです。前々から母にはイースターまでには帰ると言ってあったので、約束通りイースターの前の日に帰ってきた私を見て両親は大喜びでした。日本はもうすっかり春らしい陽気になっていることと思います。こちらも色とりどりの花が咲き乱れています。四月の末から五月にかけてはイギリスの一番美しい季節かもしれません。朝夕はまだ冷えこみますが、日中はコートなしで歩く人のすがたも見られます。

出発前には私のためにあのように盛大な送別会を開いていただきありがとうございました。それにプレゼントまでいただいて、どのようにお礼を申し上げたらよいのか分かりません。思い起こしてみますと、私の日本到着の日からまる三年の間、何かにつけて本当にお世話になりました。下宿が見つかるまでは一ヶ月以上も泊めていただきましたし、その後もことあるごとにお宅に伺わせていただきました。まるで家族の一員のように受け入れていただけたことは、この上もなく幸せなことだったと思っております。改めて心からのお礼を申し上げます。

新しい仕事が始まるまでにはまだ五ヶ月以上もありますので、少し落ち着いて医学雑誌などを読んで暮らしたいと思っております。日本にいた間は毎日毎日が新しい経験の連続で、見たり聞いたりしたことをゆっくり消化する時間もありませんでした。これから留学中に興味を持ち始めた問題点なども整理してみたいと考えています。正君には学会その他で近いうちに会う機会が必ずあると思いますが、皆様もイギリスへおいでの節はどうぞお立ち寄り下さい。両親と共に歓迎いたします。今は両親の家におりますが、新しい住所が決まりましたらお知らせいたします。実君や国子さんにもどうぞよろしくお伝え下さい。皆様の御健康をお祈りしております。

1991年4月16日

ジョン

山川　一　様
　　　信子　様

The same letter in handwritten form

皆様　その後お変わりありませんか。十日前に東京を発ってアメリカへ渡り、そこで大学時代の友達に会ったり、いとこを訪ねたりして一週間ほど過ごしました。イギリスへはおとといもどってきたばかりです。前々から母にはイースターまでには帰ると言ってあったので、約束通りイースターの前の日に帰ってきた私を見て両親は大喜びでした。日本はもうすっかり春らしい陽気になっていることと思います。こちらも色とりどりの花が咲き乱れています。四月末から五月にかけてはイギリスの一番美しい季節かもしれません。朝夕はまだ冷えこみますが、日中はコートなしで歩く人のすがたも見られます。

出発前には私のためにあのように盛大な送別会を開いていただき、ありがとうございました。それにプレゼントまでいただいて、どのようにお礼を申し上げたらよいのか分かりません。思い起こしてみますと、私の日本到着の日からまる三年の間、何かにつけて本当にお世話になりました。下宿が見つかるまでは一ヶ月以上も泊めていただきましたし、その後もことあるごとにお宅に伺わせていただきました。まるで家族の一員のようにして受け入れていただけたことは、この上もなく幸せなことだったと思っております。改めて心からのお礼を申し上げます。

新しい仕事が始まるまでにはまだ五ヶ月以上もありますので、少し落ち着いて医学雑誌などを読んで暮らしたいと思っております。日本にいた間は毎日毎日が新しい経験の連続で、見たり聞いたりしたことをゆっくり消化する時間もありませんでした。これから留学中に興味を持ち始めた問題点なども整理してみたいと考えています。正君には学会その他で近いうちに会う機会が必ずあると思いますが、皆様もイギリスへおいでの節はどうぞお立ち寄り下さい。両親と共に歓迎いたします。今は両親の家におりますが、新しい住所が決りましたらお知らせいたします。実君や国子さんにもどうぞよろしくお伝え下さい。皆様の御健康をお祈りしております。

ジョン

一九九一年四月十六日

山川一様
　　信子様

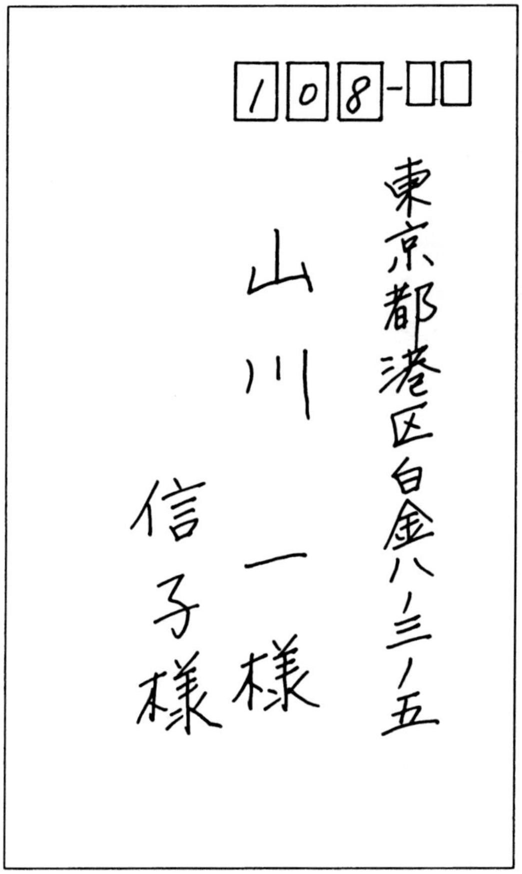

There are a few important things to note about this letter and the envelope. Although introductory formulae are common, one does not mention the addressee by name at the beginning, as in English. All the important information is listed at the end. The date comes first, near the top. Next comes your own name at the bottom, to reflect your humble stance. Then comes the name(s) of the addressee, at the top, with the polite 様 (さま) added.

The envelope is written vertically, right to left. If at all possible, the whole address is written in one line and the order is always from 'large' to 'small': Tōkyō-to, Minato-ku, Shirogane 8-3-5. The number at the top is the post code or 郵便番号. The name of the addressee should come as far as possible in the middle and should be written in larger *kanji*, as here. There will be a small space on the back at the bottom left for your own return address. The visual balance and calligraphy on an envelope is important.

A letter from John to Tadashi

正君

イギリスへもどってきてしまったら、三年も日本にいたなどということが夢のような気がします。そうかと思うと初めて君のうちへ行った時に、確かあれは一月の末だったと思うけど、干し柿をごちそうになったことなどがきのうのことのようにはっきりと思い出されます。君にはずいぶん世話になりました。本当にどうもありがとう。
帰国の途中アメリカでは何人かの古い友達に会いましたが、君も知っているスーザンには残念ながら会えませんでした。彼女は国連で働いているので、ニュー・ヨークへ行けば会えると思っていたのですが、丁度出張で中国・日本へ出かけていて留守でした。僕がわざわざ日本から出かけていった時に限って彼女は日本へ行っているというのだから余程運が悪いんですね。
出来るだけ早くアパートか小さな家を見つけて落ち着こうと思っています。君も仕事の方が忙しくてそう簡単には休暇もとれないとは思うけれど、是非近いうちに遊びに来て下さい。マリーにもそのうち手紙を書くつもりですが、よろしく伝えて下さい。新しい住所が決まり次第知らせます。体にはくれぐれも気を付けて下さい。それでは又、さようなら。

ジョン

Comment
You have reached the last lesson of this course. Whether you have completed it in one year or two, you should now be well equipped to handle most situations and you will have a solid basis in grammar, vocabulary and *kanji*. There are, of course, many more patterns and subtleties to be mastered and each style of writing and speaking has its own peculiarities, but these will now be more a matter of familiarity and practice.

We have decided to end with two letters from John, written when he is back in England. Partly because the written language can differ so much from the spoken, letter writing is an art that demands considerable practice and almost every Japanese home has at least one reference book devoted to this subject. One of the more troublesome aspects is that of tone. How formal should you be? There are many gradations: from business letters and invitations, with their rows of polite and somewhat empty formulae, to the odd postcard to a friend. The two examples here, one written to the Yamakawas and the other to Tadashi, are quite different in tone, and yet they both lie near the informal pole. The first example does contain a few set phrases that you will find useful in any letter, at the beginning and at the end for instance, which you should learn; but most people have a whole stock of these phrases that refer to the particular season and that are often used to give a letter formality and design. A few of these are given at the end of this lesson for reference.

You will note that the handwritten example to Mr and Mrs Yamakawa is written vertically. There are various conventions about how you should set out your letters. Thank you letters of this type should be handwritten in this style; business letters on the other hand are now usually word-processed and may well be written horizontally. Be on the look-out for different formats.

52.1 ことと思う

すっかり春らしい陽気になっていることと思います。

Here is our first example of a phrase that will only really occur in a letter. 'I expect' is expressed as ことと思う rather than the と思う that you might normally expect.

52.2 にかけて

四月末から五月にかけて

The phrase から…にかけて has a different nuance from the simpler から…まで. It stresses the total aspect: 'from...right through to'. Study the following:

三月上旬から四月にかけて天気のよい日が続いた。
Through early March right into April we had good weather.

東北地方は今晩から明日の朝にかけて風が強まるでしょう。
In the Tōhoku region the wind will increase in strength from this evening through to tomorrow morning.

肩から腰にかけて痛むんですが…。
I have a pain from my shoulder all the way down to my waist.

52.3 More on のように

> あのように盛大な送別会
> どのようにお礼を申し上げたらよいのか分かりません。

(a) Take note of the following phrases that use のように:

どのように	how, in what way
このように	like this
そのように	like that
あのように	like that

このような問題はアジアだけではなく世界各地で討議されているのではありませんか。
But surely questions like these are being discussed all over the world, not only in Asia.

自分の気持をどのように説明したらよいのか分かりませんでした。
I didn't know how I should have explained my own feelings.

With regard to the second sentence in the box, note that, as we explained in 41.2, reported questions tend to have a の placed before the か, as here. This must be present in a letter, but you will find it omitted occasionally in conversational Japanese.

(b) ように can also be found coming immediately after the plain verb:

おこったように出て行った。
He went out, as if he were angry.

52.4 Two written expressions

何かにつけて
ことあるごとに

Both of these will only be found in written Japanese:

何かにつけ (て)	means	'in all sorts of ways', 'no matter what'
ことあるごとに	means	'whenever the occasion allowed'

原先生には何かにつけてお世話になった。
Professor Hara was a help to me in all sorts of ways.

原先生にはことあるごとに相談にのっていただいた。
Professor Hara gave me good advice whenever I needed it.

52.5 Causatives as independent verbs

お知らせいたします。

You were introduced to the verb 知らせる 'tell', 'inform' in 27.4 and we dealt with causatives in 37.2. Note the following list of verbs, the causative forms of which have effectively become independent verbs.

知る	知らせる	inform
会う	会わせる	introduce
合う	合わせる	fit together
見る	見せる	show

みんなで調子を合わせて歌いましょう。
Let's all sing together in tune.

明日旅の写真を見せましょう。
I'll show you the pictures of our trip tomorrow.

52.6 そうかと思うと

夢のような気がします。そうかと思うと

This phrase is used here to contradict something that has just been said. 'It feels just like a dream. But then…' Literally, of course, the structure is 'when I think "is that really the case?"'. In the following sentence, however, the translation will have to be slightly different:

この赤ん坊は笑うかと思うと泣くし、泣くかと思うと笑う。
This child cries when I think it's going to laugh, and laughs when I think it's going to cry.

52.7 The verb 限る

日本から出かけていった時に限って彼女は日本へ行っている。

The verb 限る means 'limit'. It is used in various ways. Study the following examples to get some idea of how it operates:

この割り引きは六十歳以上の人に限って受けられます。
Only those who are over sixty can get this discount.

座席の数が限られていますので、どうぞ早目においで下さい。
The number of seats is limited so do please come early.

話を聞いている時はみんなうなずいていましたけれど、みんなが賛成するとは限りません。
Everybody was nodding while they were listening to the talk, but that does not necessarily mean they all agree.

52.8 Some useful phrases for letter writing

(a) Opening phrases, with some literal translations:

新緑の美しいさわやかな五月となりました。お元気でいらっしゃいますか。
Beautiful, fresh May with its new greenery has arrived. Are you well?

長いこと御無沙汰をしてしまい失礼いたしました。皆様お変わりなくお過ごしでいらっしゃいますか。
I'm sorry for not having written for so long. Is everyone as normal?

お手紙をありがとうございました。久しぶりの日本からのお便り楽しく読ませていただきました。
Thank you for your letter. It is some time since I have received news from Japan and I read it with great pleasure.

お元気ですか。この間いっしょに旅行をしてからもう一ヶ月以上になりますね。
How are you? It's already over a month since we went on holiday together.

(b) Closing remarks:

寒さに向かう折から一層の御自愛、お祈り申し上げます。
Now that we face the cold, I pray you will look after yourself all the more.

暑さの厳しい折、くれぐれもお大事に。
It being extremely hot, take great care.

また近いうちにお目にかかれることを楽しみにしています。
I look forward with great pleasure to meeting you again soon.

御家族の皆様にもどうぞよろしくお伝え下さい。
Please give my best to everyone in your family as well.

どうぞお体をお大切に。さようなら。
Please take care of yourself. Goodbye.

Key to letters

Romanisation

Mina-sama sono go o-kawari arimasen ka. Tōka mae ni Tōkyō o tatte Amerika e watari, soko de daigaku jidai no tomodachi ni attari, itoko o tazunetari shite isshūkan hodo sugoshimashita. Igirisu e wa ototoi modotte kita bakari desu. Mae mae kara haha ni wa īsutā made ni wa kaeru to itte atta no de, yakusokudōri īsutā no mae no hi ni kaette kita watakushi o mite ryōshin wa ōyorokobi deshita. Nihon wa mo sukkari harurashii yōki ni natte iru koto to omoimasu. Kochira mo iro toridori no hana ga sakimidarete imasu. Shigatsu sue kara gogatsu ni kakete wa Igirisu no ichiban utsukushii kisetsu ka mo shiremasen. Asa yū wa mada hiekomimasu ga, nitchū wa kōto nashi de aruku hito no sugata mo miraremasu.

Shuppatsu mae ni wa watakushi no tame ni ano yō ni seidai na sōbetsukai o hiraite itadaki arigatō gozaimashita. Sore ni purezento made itadaite dono yō ni o-rei o mōshiagetara yoi no ka wakarimasen. Omoiokoshite mimasu to watakushi no Nihon tōchaku no hi kara maru sannen no aida nanika ni tsukete hontō ni o-sewa ni narimashita. Geshuku ga mitsukaru made wa ikkagetsu ijō mo tomete itadakimashita shi, sono go mo koto aru tabi ni o-taku ni ukagawasete itadakimashita. Maru de kazoku no ichi'in no yō ni ukeirete itadaketa koto wa kono ue mo naku shiawase na koto datta to omotte orimasu. Aratamete kokoro kara no o-rei o mōshiagemasu.

Atarashii shigoto ga hajimaru made ni wa mada gokagetsu ijō mo arimasu no de sukoshi ochitsuite igaku zasshi nado o yonde kurashitai to omotte orimasu. Nihon ni ita aida wa mainichi mainichi ga atarashii keiken no renzoku de mitari kiitari shita koto o yukkuri shōka suru jikan mo arimasen deshita. Kore kara ryūgaku-chū ni kyōmi o mochihajimeta mondaiten nado mo seiri shite mitai to kangaete imasu. Tadashi-kun ni wa gakkai sono ta de chikai uchi ni au kikai ga kanarazu aru to omoimasu ga, mina-sama mo Igirisu e o-ide no setsu wa dōzo o-tachiyori kudasai. Ryōshin to tomo ni kangei itashimasu. Ima wa ryōshin no ie ni orimasu ga, atarashii jūsho ga kimarimashitara o-shirase itashimasu. Minoru-kun ya Kuniko-san ni mo dōzo yoroshiku o-tsutae kudasai. Mina-sama no go-kenkō o o-inori shite orimasu.

Jon

Yamakawa Hajime sama

Yamakawa Nobuko sama

Igirisu e modotte kite shimattara, sannen mo Nihon ni ita nado to iu koto ga yume no yō na ki ga shimasu. Sō ka to omou to hajime ni kimi no uchi e itta toki ni, tashika are wa ichigatsu no sue datta to omou kedo, hoshigaki o go-chisō ni natta koto nado ga kinō no koto no yō ni hakkiri to omoidasaremasu. Kimi ni wa zuibun sewa ni narimashita. Hontō ni dōmo arigatō.

Kikoku no tochū Amerika de wa nannin ka no furui tomodachi ni aimashita ga, kimi mo shitte iru Sūzan ni wa zannen-nagara aemasen deshita. Kanojo wa kokuren de hataraite iru no de Nyūyōku e ikeba aeru to omotte ita no desu ga, chōdo shutchō de Chūgoku Nihon e dekakete ite rusu deshita. Boku ga waza waza Nihon kara dekakete itta toki ni kagitte kanojo wa Nihon e itte iru to iu no dakara yohodo un ga waruin desu ne.

Dekiru dake hayaku apāto ka chiisana ie o mitsukete ochitsukō to omotte imasu. Kimi mo shigoto no hō ga isogashikute sō kantan ni wa kyūka mo torenai to wa omou keredo, zehi chikai uchi ni asobi ni kite kudasai. Marī ni mo sono uchi tegami o kaku tsumori desu ga, yoroshiku tsutaete kudasai. Atarashii jūsho ga kimari shidai shirasemasu. Karada ni wa kuregure mo ki o tsukete kudasai. Sore de wa mata sayōnara.

Jon

Translation

I hope you are all well. Ten days ago I left Tōkyō and went to America, where I spent about a week seeing friends from my university days and visiting my cousin. I have just arrived back in England the day before yesterday. I had promised my mother for some time that I would be back before Easter, so my parents were very pleased to see me when I arrived back as promised the day before Easter. I expect Japan is already having warm and springlike weather. Here too everything is blossoming in profusion. From the end of April right through to May is probably the most beautiful season in England. It is still fairly chilly in the evenings and early in the mornings, but during the day you can see people walking about without coats.

Thank you so much for arranging such a marvellous farewell party for me before my departure. You even gave me presents and I don't know how to thank you for everything. When

I cast my mind back, you have been such a great help to me for all the three years I have been in Japan. You put me up for over a month until I found lodgings, and invited me to your home on every occasion. I cannot imagine a greater pleasure that being welcomed as one of the family. Please accept my humblest thanks.

I still have about five months before my new job starts and so I intend to settle down a little and spend the time reading medical journals. While I was in Japan I had no time to digest everything I saw and heard at my leisure; a succession of new experiences every day. Now I would like to put some order into all those questions that piqued my interest during my time abroad. I am sure that I will have the chance to meet Tadashi quite soon at a conference or some such, but if you happen to come to England yourselves, do please come and see me. My parents and I would love to welcome you. I am now at my parents' home, but I will send you my new address once it's fixed. Please give my best to Minoru and Kuniko. I hope you both remain in the best of health.

John

Mr and Mrs H. Yamakawa

Now that I am back in England, the fact that I was in Japan for three years seems like a bit of a dream. But then, I can remember clearly as though it were yesterday the first time I visited your home. I think it must have been near the end of January, when you treated me to those dried persimmon. You have been such a tremendous help to me. Thank you for all you have done.

On the way home I met a number of old friends in America, but didn't manage to see Susan, whom you also know. She is working for the United Nations and so I thought I would be able to see her if I went to New York, but she had just gone to China and Japan on business and was not there. What rotten luck that she goes to Japan on the one occasion that I had left Japan to see her.

I would like to find a flat or a small house and settle down here as soon as possible. I know that you will also be very busy and will not be able to take leave that easily, but do please come for a holiday soon. I'm going to write to Marie soon, but in the meantime please give her my best. I'll send my new address as soon as it's fixed. Look after yourself. See you soon.

John

Appendix I

kinship terms	*neutral*	*respect*
family	家族 (かぞく)	御家族
father	父 (ちち)	おとうさん/おとうさま
mother	母 (はは)	おかあさん/おかあさま
parents	両親 (りょうしん)	御両親 (ごりょうしん)
elder brother	兄 (あに)	おにいさん/おにいさま
elder sister	姉 (あね)	おねえさん/おねえさま
younger brother	弟 (おとうと)	弟さん
younger sister	妹 (いもうと)	妹さん
brothers	兄弟 (きょうだい)	御兄弟
sisters	姉妹 (しまい)	御姉妹
husband	主人 (しゅじん)	御主人/だんなさま
	夫 (おっと)	
wife	家内 (かない)	奥 (おく) さん/奥さま
	妻 (つま)	
son	息子 (むすこ)	息子さん
daughter	娘 (むすめ)	お嬢 (じょう) さん
child	子 (こ)	お子さん/お子さま
relatives	親戚 (しんせき)	御親戚
	親類 (しんるい)	御親類
grandfather	祖父 (そふ)	おじいさん/おじいさま
grandmother	祖母 (そぼ)	おばあさん/おばあさま
grandchild	孫 (まご)	お孫さん
uncle	伯父 (おじ)	おじさん/おじさま
	叔父 (おじ)	
aunt	伯母 (おば)	おばさん/おばさま
	叔母 (おば)	
nephew	甥 (おい)	甥御 (おいご) さん
niece	姪 (めい)	姪御 (めいご) さん
cousin	いとこ	おいとこさん

Appendix II

The following is a list of those verbs that inflect as group I verbs, despite the fact that they appear at first glance to be group II verbs.

-*eru* verbs

帰る (かえる)	return	蹴る (ける)	kick
照る (てる)	shine	練る (ねる)	knead
喋る (しゃべる)	chat	滑べる (すべる)	slide
減る (へる)	decrease	湿る (しめる)	become damp

-*iru* verbs

限る (かぎる)	limit	切る (きる)	cut
要る (いる)	need	煎る (いる)	roast, parch
射る (いる)	shoot	知る (しる)	know
散る (ちる)	scatter	入る (はいる)	enter
走る (はしる)	run	参る (まいる)	go, come
握る (にぎる)	grasp, grip	混じる (まじる)	mix (*intrans.*)
気に入る (いる)	be pleased with	交じる (まじる)	join, take part (*intrans.*)

Appendix III

Pronunciation of number and classifier combinations. Irregular readings are marked with an asterisk.

～人 (にん) 'people'		～歳 (さい) 'years old'		～個 (こ) small things	
何人	なんにん	何歳	なんさい いくつ	何個	なんこ
一人	ひとり*	一歳	いっさい*	一個	いっこ*
二人	ふたり*	二歳	にさい	二個	にこ
三人	さんにん	三歳	さんさい	三個	さんこ
四人	よにん*	四歳	よんさい	四個	よんこ
五人	ごにん	五歳	ごさい	五個	ごこ
六人	ろくにん	六歳	ろくさい	六個	ろっこ*
七人	しちにん/ななにん	七歳	ななさい	七個	ななこ
八人	はちにん	八歳	はっさい*	八個	はっこ
九人	きゅうにん/くにん*	九歳	きゅうさい	九個	きゅうこ
十人	じゅうにん	十歳	じゅっさい*	十個	じゅっこ*

～日 (にち) 'days'		～時間 'hours'		～分 (ふん) 'minutes'	
何日	なんにち	何時間	なんじかん	何分	なんぷん
一日	いちにち	一時間	いちじかん	一分	いっぷん*
二日	ふつか*	二時間	にじかん	二分	にふん
三日	みっか*	三時間	さんじかん	三分	さんぷん*
四日	よっか*	四時間	よじかん*	四分	よんぷん*
五日	いつか*	五時間	ごじかん	五分	ごふん
六日	むいか*	六時間	ろくじかん	六分	ろっぷん*
七日	なのか*	七時間	しちじかん	七分	ななふん
八日	ようか*	八時間	はちじかん	八分	はっぷん*
九日	ここのか*	九時間	くじかん*	九分	きゅうふん
十日	とおか*	十時間	じゅうじかん	十分	じゅっぷん*

～年 (ねん) 'years'		～ヶ月 (かげつ) 'months'		～週間 (しゅうかん) 'weeks'	
何年	なんねん	何ヶ月	なんかげつ	何週間	なんしゅうかん
一年	いちねん	一ヶ月	いっかげつ*	一週間	いっしゅうかん*
二年	にねん	二ヶ月	にかげつ	二週間	にしゅうかん
三年	さんねん	三ヶ月	さんかげつ	三週間	さんしゅうかん
四年	よねん*	四ヶ月	よんかげつ	四週間	よんしゅうかん
五年	ごねん	五ヶ月	ごかげつ	五週間	ごしゅうかん
六年	ろくねん	六ヶ月	ろっかげつ*	六週間	ろくしゅうかん
七年	しち (なな) ねん	七ヶ月	なながげつ	七週間	ななしゅうかん
八年	はちねん	八ヶ月	はっかげつ*	八週間	はっしゅうかん*
九年	きゅうね	九ヶ月	きゅうかげつ	九週間	きゅうしゅうかん
十年	じゅうねん	十ヶ月	じゅっかげつ*	十週間	じゅっしゅうかん*

～匹 (ひき) small animals, fish		～頭 (とう) large mammals		～羽 (わ) birds	
何匹	なんびき*	何頭	なんとう	何羽	なんわ
一匹	いっぴき*	一頭	いっとう*	一羽	いちわ
二匹	にひき	二頭	にとう	二羽	にわ
三匹	さんびき*	三頭	さんとう	三羽	さんば*
四匹	よんひき	四頭	よんとう	四羽	よんわ
五匹	ごひき	五頭	ごとう	五羽	ごわ
六匹	ろっぴき*	六頭	ろくとう	六羽	ろくわ/ろっぱ*
七匹	ななひき	七頭	ななとう	七羽	ななわ
八匹	はっぴき*	八頭	はちとう/はっとう*	八羽	はちわ/はっぱ*
九匹	きゅうひき	九頭	きゅうとう	九羽	きゅうわ
十匹	じゅっぴき*	十頭	じゅっとう*	十羽	じゅっぱ*

～杯 (はい)
'cups'

何杯	なんばい*
一杯	いっぱい*
二杯	にはい
三杯	さんばい*
四杯	よんはい
五杯	ごはい
六杯	ろっぱい*
七杯	ななはい
八杯	はっぱい*
九杯	きゅうはい
十杯	じゅっぱい*

～本 (ほん)
long, thin objects

何本	なんぼん*
一本	いっぽん*
二本	にほん
三本	さんぼん*
四本	よんほん*
五本	ごほん
六本	ろっぽん*
七本	ななほん
八本	はっぽん*
九本	きゅうほん
十本	じゅっぽん*

～枚 (まい)
flat objects

何枚	なんまい
一枚	いちまい
二枚	にまい
三枚	さんまい
四枚	よんまい
五枚	ごまい
六枚	ろくまい
七枚	ななまい
八枚	はちまい
九枚	きゅうまい
十枚	じゅうまい

～円 (えん)
'yen'

何円	なんえん いくら
一円	いちえん
二円	にえん
三円	さんえん
四円	よえん*
五円	ごえん
六円	ろくえん
七円	ななえん
八円	はちえん
九円	きゅうえん
十円	じゅうえん

～度 (ど)
'degrees', 'times'

何度	なんど
一度	いちど
二度	にど
三度	さんど
四度	よんど
五度	ごど
六度	ろくど
七度	ななど
八度	はちど
九度	きゅうど/くど*
十度	じゅうど

～回 (かい)
'times'

何回	なんかい
一回	いっかい*
二回	にかい
三回	さんかい
四回	よんかい
五回	ごかい
六回	ろっかい*
七回	ななかい
八回	はっかい*
九回	きゅうかい
十回	じゅっかい*

～台 (だい)
cars, television sets

何台	なんだい
一台	いちだい
二台	にだい
三台	さんだい
四台	よんだい
五台	ごだい
六台	ろくだい
七台	ななだい
八台	はちだい
九台	きゅうだい
十台	じゅうだい

～軒 (けん)
'houses'

何軒	なんげん*
一軒	いっけん*
二軒	にけん
三軒	さんげん*
四軒	よんけん
五軒	ごけん
六軒	ろっけん*
七軒	ななけん
八軒	はっけん*
九軒	きゅうけん
十軒	じゅっけん*

～階 (かい)
'floors'

何階	なんかい
一階	いっかい*
二階	にかい
三階	さんがい*
四階	よんかい
五階	ごかい
六階	ろっかい*
七階	ななかい
八階	はっかい*
九階	きゅうかい
十階	じゅっかい*

～泊 (はく)
'nights'

何泊	なんぱく* いくはく
一泊	いっぱく*
二泊	にはく
三泊	さんぱく*
四泊	よんはく
五泊	ごはく
六泊	ろっぱく*
七泊	ななはく
八泊	はっぱく*
九泊	きゅうはく
十泊	じゅっぱく*

～皿 (さら)
'plateful'

何皿	なんさら いくさら
一皿	ひとさら*
二皿	ふたさら*
三皿	みさら*/さんさら
四皿	よさら*/よんさら
五皿	ごさら
六皿	ろくさら
七皿	ななさら
八皿	はっさら*
九皿	きゅうさら
十皿	じゅっさら*

～通 (つう)
'letters'

何通	なんつう
一通	いっつう*
二通	につう
三通	さんつう
四通	よんつう
五通	ごつう
六通	ろくつう
七通	ななつう
八通	はっつう*
九通	きゅうつう
十通	じゅっつう*

～冊 (さつ)
books

何冊	なんさつ
一冊	いっさつ*
二冊	にさつ
三冊	さんさつ
四冊	よんさつ
五冊	ごさつ
六冊	ろくさつ
七冊	ななさつ
八冊	はっさつ*
九冊	きゅうさつ
十冊	じゅっさつ*

～着 (ちゃく)
dresses, suits, coats

何着	なんちゃく
一着	いっちゃく*
二着	にちゃく
三着	さんちゃく
四着	よんちゃく
五着	ごちゃく
六着	ろくちゃく
七着	ななちゃく
八着	はっちゃく
九着	きゅうちゃく
十着	じゅっちゃく*

～足 (そく)
shoes, socks

何足	なんそく
一足	いっそく*
二足	にそく
三足	さんぞく*
四足	よんそく
五足	ごそく
六足	ろくそく
七足	ななそく
八足	はっそく
九足	きゅうそく
十足	じゅっそく*

Index

Lightning Source UK Ltd.
Milton Keynes UK
UKOW021034070713

213355UK00004B/133/A